The New York Times

Weekends

Macmillan • USA

MACMILLAN TRAVEL

A Simon & Schuster Macmillan Company
1633 Broadway
New York, NY 10019

Find us online at **http://www.mgr.com/travel** or
on America Online at Keyword: **Frommer's**

ISBN 0-02-861880-7

Editor: Cheryl Farr
Thanks to Tracy McNamara

Design by designLab, Seattle
Digital Cartography by *The New York Times,* except pages xii–xiii, by John Decamillis
Art on pages 1, 35, 93, 181, 209, 263, 299, and 351 courtesy of the Cousley Collections

SPECIAL SALES

CONTENTS

Other Destinations Within Easy Reach of New York City

LIST OF MAPS

❧

More Getaways in New York State

New Jersey

Pennsylvania

Connecticut

Other Regional Maps

TO THE READER

PLEASE BE ADVISED THAT TRAVEL information is subject to change at any time—and this is especially true of open hours and prices. We therefore suggest that you write or call ahead for confirmation when making your travel plans. The authors, editors, and publisher cannot be held responsible for the experiences of readers while traveling. Your safety is important to us, however, so we encourage you to stay alert and be aware of your surroundings. Keep a close eye on cameras, purses, and wallets, all favorite targets of thieves and pickpockets.

ACKNOWLEDGMENTS

THIS GUIDEBOOK REPRESENTS A lot of hard work by a host of writers and editors at *The New York Times*. Many thanks to all of the writers who gave up their Saturdays to trek up and down the New York region. Also thanks to Wendy Sclight, the deputy Weekend section editor; to Steve Hadermayer, the maps manager; to Anne Mancuso, who compiled most of the service information, and to the editors of the Culture copy desk.

A special thanks to the editors at Macmillan; to John Darnton, the cultural news editor of *The Times*, for his support of the Weekend staff, and to Mitchel Levitas, who is in charge of book development at *The Times* and who worked with Macmillan to make this book a reality.

—MYRA FORSBERG, EDITOR OF THE WEEKEND SECTION

INTRODUCTION

New York City is the world capital of everything except relaxation. But even New Yorkers, and the tourists who flock to the city, need to unwind once in a while, to come down from an emotional state that's equal parts exhilaration, irritation, and suffocation.

As luck would have it, relief is within arm's length. A mythical New Yorker living in a penthouse atop the Times Square tower can take out a compass, a pencil, and a map, draw a circle with a 250-mile radius, and come up with a very nice traveler's pie.

That's the premise behind the essays collected here, most of which appeared on the front page of the Friday Weekend section of *The New York Times*. For several years now, a happy band of correspondents have headed out, notebook in hand, with that rarest of journalistic assignments, to have fun, gather useful information, and write about it enticingly. The geographical rules are simple. The place described must be within an easy day's drive—say five hours, tops. Beyond that, anything goes, and it did.

The writers gathered in these pages have gone fly-fishing on the Farmington River in Connecticut, whale watching off Long Island, and gambling in Atlantic City. They have driven the backroads of the Brandywine Valley in Pennsylvania, explored the Ironbound District of Newark, New Jersey, and sniffed spring flowers in Westchester County, New York. In an inspired act of rebellion, one reporter left Manhattan to rusticate on a Pennsylvania farm. Canny stay-at-homes sought out corners of the city that New Yorkers themselves know little about, like City Island in the Bronx, or cast a fresh eye on familiar landmarks like the Bronx Zoo.

In their heroic pursuit of leisure, the *Times* writers traveled by car and canoe, by balloon and bicycle, while an intrepid few tied on a pair of sneakers and simply walked. No challenge was left unmet. The reporters imbibed funny-colored drinks, ordered monstrous meals and, in one case, sang "Zip-a-Dee-Doo-Dah" during an Elimination Dance and Grand March in the Poconos.

There's a common expression that harried New Yorkers use several times a day: Gimme a break. A cab cuts you off, a cop slaps a ticket on your windshield, the subway doors close in your face, the public telephone takes your quarter without producing a dial tone, the guy in front of you is walking too damn slow. Gimme a break.

Well, here are 46 of them.

—WILLIAM GRIMES

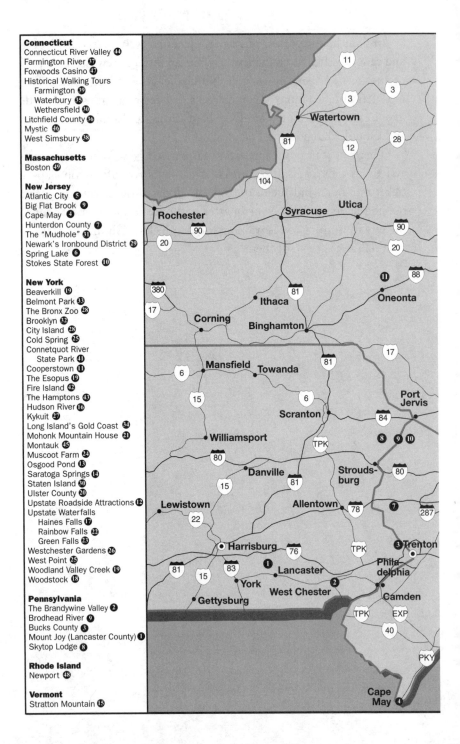

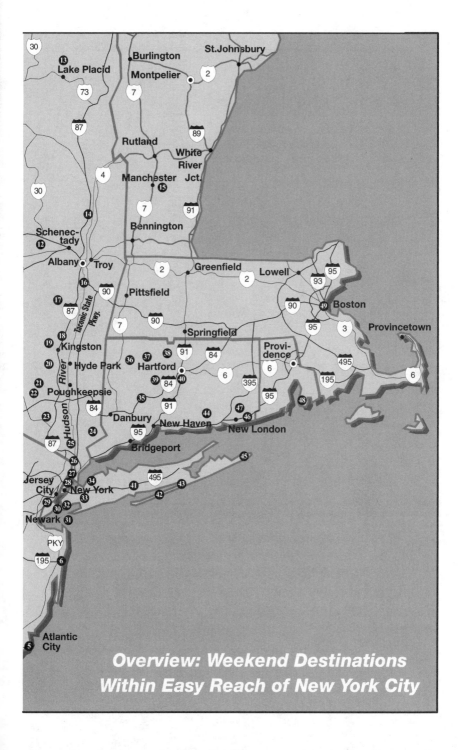

Overview: Weekend Destinations Within Easy Reach of New York City

Weekending Without Leaving the City

A French Country Inn— on City Island

by Ralph Blumenthal

W<small>E ARE IN A FRENCH COUNTRY INN.</small>
We sit on rustic chairs in a mansard room wallpapered in burgundy toile. We sip welcoming glasses of chilled chardonnay from etched goblets. We look out at the water. En famille, we inhale the musk of roasting garlic wafting up from the kitchen.

We hear: vvvvROOOOM! A motorcycle accelerating to warp speed screams past below the window, followed by a babble of radio from a passing convertible and the pounding rhythms of rap from a next-door neighbor's boombox. The water is not the Loire or the Dordogne. It is Eastchester Bay. We are abroad at home, in the Bronx.

An auberge in the backyard of the Yankees, in a borough that gave its name to a rude cheer and suffered Ogden Nash's cruel put-down, may sound like someone's idea of a joke, but just over the bridge threading Pelham Bay Park to the plump baguette of City Island, voila!: Le Refuge Inn, a 19th-century beige Victorian house that is one of New York City's few genuine inns. If it lacks some of the ambiance and *je ne sais quoi* of its cousins-cousines across the Atlantic, this one, at least, is barely 20 minutes from mid-Manhattan (not counting delays on the Bruckner Expressway).

Apart from the eight-room inn at 620 City Island Avenue, City Island itself is well worth a detour, as the *Guide Michelin* might have it. It is a quiet (except in summer) year-round virtual village of some 4,000 permanent residents, with one main drag, many boatyards and marinas, several newish condominium colonies, and some dozen and

3

a half mostly seafood restaurants. A mile and a half long and no more than a half a mile wide, the island blends the forlorn mystery of a Hopper dreamscape with a cheerful blue-collar brawn and flashes of intriguing wealth: sports cars behind gated walls; a gleaming black Mercedes convertible outside the bait shop.

A weekend's stay, one overnight, in Le Refuge is enough time to sample the land and sea offerings of City Island as well as the hospitality of the inn, particularly its classic French cuisine, its substantial wine cellar, and a special attraction: regular Sunday noon chamber music concerts and wine socials to which inn guests are admitted free. (Others pay $12.) Small children, who are welcome at the inn but might be disruptive at the recital, can spend the hour swinging and climbing on the backyard playground equipment, which our urban-bred younger daughter found endlessly entertaining.

Le Refuge Inn is the creation of a Normandy-born restaurateur and musician, Pierre Saint-Denis, who for 20 years has been running his highly rated restaurant of the same name, Le Refuge, at 166 East 82nd Street in Manhattan. Less than three years ago, en route to Connecticut "in search of a small but accessible hideaway," as he put it, he was driving up I-95 when he saw a sign for City Island, grew intrigued, and turned off to investigate. Just off the bridge, he spotted an old Victorian boardinghouse with a widow's walk and fanciful tower at 620 City Island Avenue. The rest, as they say, is *histoire*.

An athletic figure with short-cropped gray hair and the patient air of a veteran chef and proprietor resigned to the next crisis, Mr. Saint-Denis is not without a sense of humor, volunteering a parallel between his Bronx auberge and "Fawlty Towers."

Having seen a small magazine ad for the inn this spring, we drove up one Saturday to look it over and liked it immediately. We booked two $75-a-night connecting rooms and dinner for a May weekend. (The three-course dinner, prix fixe at $40 a person, is served to nonguests as well, but only by reservation.) We arrived for our stay before 1pm on Saturday and were greeted by a caretaker who swung open the white gate so we could edge the car, piled with bikes, past pink rhododendron to park in the back instead of searching for a spot on the traffic-clogged avenue.

The parlor-dining room was set with round tables and French country chairs. A grandfather clock (actually, great-grandfather clock, an heirloom that Mr. Saint-Denis's grandfather inherited from his parents) stood silent sentinel, unwound, its tolling unbearably loud, the innkeeper explained. White lace curtains screened the strong sun that was striping the walls and stout wooden beams. In the corner, a bar was set invitingly with bottles of aperitifs and liquor. The front door stood open: not just unlocked, open, testimony to the difference that 13 miles from midtown can make.

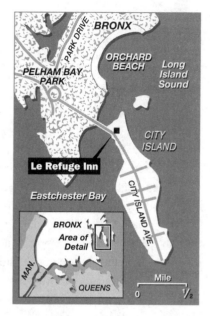

Behind the parlor sprawled a large country kitchen with cobalt blue tiles, a well-trafficked part of the inn that leads to a sunporch facing the backyard. Mr. Saint-Denis doesn't just allow walk-throughs, he encourages them.

The third-floor rooms are cozy and charming. Ours—furnished with a comfortable queen-size bed, small table and chairs, bureau, a vintage Art Deco table radio, and a very much up-to-date television— overlooked the bay, with the twin towers of the World Trade Center visible in the far distance. The girls' room had twin beds and a bureau, also an old radio and a new television, and overlooked a neighbor's yard. Ceiling fans in both rooms churned up a soothing breeze.

The first drawback, which I had somehow missed in making the booking, was that the rooms lacked a private bathroom; they shared one with two other occupied rooms on the floor. In fact, we learned, a second-floor suite with private bath is $125 a night, but it was already taken that weekend. The floor's black-and-white tile bathroom with its old-fashioned footed tub was sparkling clean, but the shower proved annoyingly fitful, with trickles of hot water and sudden gushes of cold. Between charm and plumbing, I decided, I'll take plumbing.

We spent our first few hours exploring, walking a stretch of City Island Avenue past a small private marine museum that was closed each time we looked in; Burck's Discount Boat Supplies; King Lobster; Artie's of City Island with a big sign, Mussells (yes, spelled Mussells), and a small beauty shop, Lina Petite Salon, a funky fossil from the 1950s. As it happened, it was the weekend of the island's third annual arts-and-crafts festival; past the I.G.A. market that is City Island's closest thing to a supermarket, the sidewalks were lined with vendor tables displaying inexpensive jewelry and other doodads. Not to worry: On ordinary days, much of the same merchandise is available in the stores or tag sales advertised on street poles.

We stopped for lunch in the middle of "town" at the Crab Shanty, a friendly, skylighted family restaurant where for less than $40, including tax, tip, and a beer, we were served more clam chowder, shrimp, baked clams, soft-shell crabs, linguine, salad, and garlic bread than we could ever eat.

When we returned to the room, the second drawback hove into view and earshot. The neighbors next door were setting up outdoor tables, banners, and a suitcase-size radio. Clearly a party was in store. Sure enough, over the next six hours or so, into our bedtime, we attended the celebration by proxy, hostage to the revels below.

Before dinner, my wife took our younger daughter into the backyard while our teenager and I continued our explorations on bike a mile and a quarter to the far end of City Island Avenue, where two huge eating emporiums with outdoor tables on Long Island Sound vie for visitors' dollars. To the left is Johnny's Reef Restaurant ("45 Years of Serving You") where patrons line up at fast-food counters for fried seafood platters of shrimp, scallops, squid, clams, and filet of sole, starting at $8. The scene is similar at the facing Tony's Pier Restaurant, where the menu includes oysters, soft-shell crabs, and a lobster dinner for $16. We also rode down the residential side streets that transect the spine of City Island Avenue like so many little fish bones, finding pretty vistas of bay and Sound at the dead ends. By turning right, or north, as we exited the inn, we also discovered a quieter back-water of boatyards and restaurants.

Later, reunited back in the room, we decided to feed our little one in family solitude upstairs rather than inflict her exuberance on our fellow diners. The staff, knowing what was good for them, wisely accommodated us with a room-service platter of steak and veggies. When at last sleep claimed her, despite the ruckus next door, we three felt secure (and hungry) enough to tiptoe downstairs.

We picked our way judiciously and deliciously through an appetizer selection of corn soup, salad, escargots in chablis, duck pâté, and vegetable terrine, and an entree menu of grilled tuna, soft-shell crab, pepper beef filet, duck à l'orange, pork cutlet with blueberries, and cervelle de veau. (We're not much for calf brains and we had sworn off escargots since once adopting a snail as a family pet.) For dessert there were chocolate soufflé, white chocolate mousse, strawberry cheesecake, variously prepared fruit platters, and a cheese tray. The meal was beautifully prepared and served, and it was well accompanied by a 1992 Laboure-Roi Pouilly-Fuisse at $35 and a glass of port from Mr. Saint-Denis's extensive wine cellar, encompassing some 200 varieties, many well priced. He is particularly proud of his collection of 1982 Bordeaux at $40 to $500 a bottle.

The menu changes day to day, week to week, as the whim catches Mr. Saint-Denis. For a while, for example, he was offering to pack picnic hampers for guests who spent the day away sightseeing. But he said he no longer bothered.

The party next door was winding down but still audible when we turned in. Now the night music came chiefly from hot rods and motorcycles roaring off the bridge. When we mentioned it the next morning, Mr. Saint-Denis nodded sympathetically. "Summer drives me nuts," he commiserated. "If you want to know, fall and spring are my best seasons."

Sunday breakfast was a simple but elegant affair of fresh-baked and very buttery croissants, with fresh-squeezed orange juice and good strong coffee. Then, leaving my wife to read in solitude, I took the girls on a bike ride to the island's only public school, P.S. 175, three-quarters of the way down City Island Avenue, site of a ballfield and two playgrounds, one in the yard behind the school.

By the time we returned, the musicians had arrived for the noon concert and were rehearsing, filling the house with resonant strains of Mozart and Haydn. We packed ourselves off back to town for lunch in a quirky little sandwich shop called Laura's, where colorful animal mobiles hang from the ceiling and the tables are set around the design element of an old stove.

The performance had just broken up as we returned and concertgoers holding glasses of white wine were chatting congenially on the sun porch. We took a last look around and packed up. Mr. Saint-Denis had a parting suggestion, nay command. On the way home, we must, simply must, stop at the Bartow-Pell Mansion Museum and Gardens across the bridge in Pelham Bay Park. I had to admit I had never heard of it but took his careful directions and a brochure.

Within a few minutes' drive, we reached the place, a century-and-a-half-old Greek Revival/Federal–style stone mansion in an exquisite wild setting amid (I have since learned) the largest green space in the city, nearly three times the size of Central Park. We toured the stately rooms, furnished with some especially handsome Empire pieces, and reveled in the tranquillity, blessedly free of traffic din. The Bronx? (Wise up, Ogden Nash.) Yes, thonx!

CITY ISLAND ESSENTIALS

GETTING THERE

By Car   To reach City Island from Manhattan by car, take the Triborough Bridge to the Bruckner Expressway. After I-95 joins the expressway, take I-95 to exit 8B (City Island/Orchard Beach); go to the first traffic light and make a right onto City Island Road; continue around the traffic circle to the City Island Bridge.

By Public Transportation   From Manhattan, take the Uptown no. 6 train to Pelham Bay Park (the last stop), then take the no. 29 City Island bus.

ACCOMMODATIONS

Le Refuge Inn, 620 City Island Ave. (☎ 718/885-2478). One-bedroom suite with sitting room and private bath, $125; room with shared bath, $75 (single occupancy $65). Rates are based on double occupancy and include breakfast. Children are welcome; a folding bed is available for $15. A cottage at the rear of the inn can accommodate a family of five and includes a living room and private bath; it is $125 per night for two, $15 for each additional person. Dinner, at $40 per person, is served Wednesday through Saturday starting at 6pm, and Sunday starting at 4pm.

RESTAURANTS

Crab Shanty, 361 City Island Ave. (☎ 800/640-6522 or 718/885-1810). Open Sunday through Thursday 11am to 1:30am, Friday and Saturday 11am to 2:30am. Reservations necessary on the weekend.

Johnny's Reef Restaurant, 2 City Island Ave. (☎ 718/885-2086). Open March through December, Monday through Thursday and Sunday 11am to midnight, Friday and Saturday 11am to 1am.

Laura's Cafe and Deli, 296 City Island Ave. (☎ 718/885-0947). Open May 1 through October, Monday and Tuesday 7:30am to 5pm, Wednesday through Sunday 7:30am to 10pm; November 1 through April, daily 7:30am to 5pm.

Tony's Pier Restaurant, 1 City Island Ave. (☎ 718/885-1424). Open Sunday through Thursday 11:30am to 11pm, Friday and Saturday 11:30am to 1am.

ATTRACTIONS

Bartow-Pell Mansion, Pelham Bay Park, 895 Shore Rd. (☎ 718/885-1461). Tours offered Wednesday, Saturday, and Sunday noon to 4pm. Admission $2.50 adults, $1.25 students and seniors, free for children under 12.

Focal Point Gallery, 321 City Island Ave. (☎ 718/885-1403). Open year-round with multimedia exhibitions from January to April, and all-photography shows May through December. Year-round exhibitions feature works by the co-owners of the gallery since 1974, Ron Terner, a photographer and sculptor, and Niru Terner, a painter. Open Tuesday through Thursday noon to 7pm, Friday and Saturday noon to 9pm, Sunday noon to 7pm.

North Wind Undersea Institute, 610 City Island Ave. (☎ 718/885-0701). Among the items on view, some in hands-on exhibits, are antique diving equipment and sunken treasure; a life-size model of a sperm whale;

an old tugboat; and an Atlantic diamond-back terrapin, an endangered species of turtle. In addition, field trips to the beach and other locations are available by advance reservation. Open Monday through Friday noon to 4pm, Saturday and Sunday noon to 5pm; open to school groups Monday through Friday 10am to noon. Admission $3 adults, $2 seniors and children 2 to 12.

Turtle Cove Golf and Baseball Complex, 1 City Island Rd. (☎ 718/885-2646). Golf driving range open year-round; miniature golf and baseball batting cages open March through November. December through February, daily 8am to 6pm; March through November, daily 7am to midnight. Miniature golf $4.50 adults, $4 for children under 5. Driving range: $5 for a bucket of 45 balls, $8.50 for 115 balls; 50¢ for golf club rental. Batting cages: Baseball tokens $1.75 each (17 balls); 4 tokens for $6.

MORE NEW YORK CITY INNS

The Box Tree Hotel and Restaurant, 250 E. 49th St., Manhattan (☎ 212/758-8320). Room with private bath and fireplace $190 Sunday through Thursday, $290 Friday and

Saturday; penthouse room $230 Sunday through Thursday, $330 Friday and Saturday. Daily rates are based on double occupancy and include continental breakfast; $100 of the room charge is applied to dinner in the restaurant on Fridays and Saturdays. Children welcome.

Colonial House Inn, 318 W. 22nd St., Manhattan (☎ 212/243-9669). Rooms (some with private baths) $65 to $99. Daily rates are based on double occupancy and include continental breakfast. Children welcome.

The Inn at Irving Place, 56 Irving Place (at 17th St.), Manhattan (☎ 212/533-4600).

Rooms (all with private baths) $275, suite with a sitting room $350. Daily rates are based on double occupancy and include continental breakfast. No children under 12. A five-course high tea is available Wednesday through Sunday at 3 and 4:30pm at a cost of $25 per person, excluding tax and tip.

There is a restaurant in the building, **Verbena** (☎ 212/260-5454). Lunch is served April through mid-October, Tuesday through Friday noon to 2:45pm; brunch year-round, Sunday noon to 3pm; dinner year-round, Sunday and Monday 5:30 to 9:30pm, Tuesday through Thursday 5:30 to 10:30pm, Friday and Saturday 5:30 to 11pm.

WILDLIFE IN WINTER AT THE BRONX ZOO

by Bruce Weber

For some time now, because I have a friend who travels frequently, I have lived in close proximity to animals—hers. They are a dog and a cat, Lucille and Maggie—granted, not exactly critters you find in the wild, but there is a zoolike quality that my apartment has taken on lately, a certain vibrancy and odoriferous spirit. I've been witness to (and occasionally a victim of) a lot of stalking, a participant in a lot of nonverbal communication, a monitor of mood swings. As any pet owner learns quickly, animals make you contemplate them—and yourself.

All this prepared me nicely for my recent couple of days at the International Wildlife Conservation Park, a.k.a. the Bronx Zoo, which, like many nonparents, I hadn't visited in decades. The cold-weather season is a particularly good time for adults to visit, I discovered, largely because the great herds of tiny cotton-candy eaters (a populous species of the genus children) are thinned out.

The zoo is open 365 days a year (where are the animals going to go?), but in spring and summer, it has up to 40,000 visitors on Wednesdays, when admission is free; on a winter Wednesday, the total may be only a few hundred. The local residents feel considerably less overwhelmed, and thus the possibility of encountering them closely is high. You can get near enough for long enough that, like pets, they reveal themselves.

Timmy, for example, the patriarch of the zoo's gorilla clan, doesn't care for hoopla; he tends to seek privacy when there's a crowd. Unlike a number of his showoffy relatives, "he's very, very shy," a keeper in the gorilla house told me.

But there he was sitting in full view when I wandered in, his regal belly protruding, sheltering one of his granddaughters with a protective arm. He was true to form, though, when I was followed by a chattering family of Scandinavian tourists: He stood slowly and lumbered off.

John Behler, the zoo's department of herpetology curator, acknowledged, "It's almost a daunting task to get through the reptile house in midsummer." And Pat Thomas, the assistant curator of mammals, concurred; in particular, he said, the monkey house, a relatively small enclosure (there are 16 species of tamarin, marmoset, and other primates, all from South America), can be maddeningly busy and shrill in high season. "It's not a good educational experience," he said. "You spend more time jockeying for position than watching the animals."

But on the day after Christmas, I was alone there. And I feel as though I left an impression, at least on the white-faced capuchins, many of which paused in their regular antics to regard me. One carried another on his (her?) back, both their faces turned toward me as they negotiated a horizontal vine. Another made a long leap toward the glass, clung to the vertical strip of wood between panes high above me and, looking down, mocked me with a brief screech before executing a fantastic midair backflip and landing back on a branch.

And a third waited patiently on the floor of the enclosure's foreground, until I tentatively reached out my hand and touched my fingers to the glass. A gesture of friendship, I thought. But with a yawp that sounded like "Aha!" he reacted as though I'd fallen into a trap he'd set, leaping immediately to his feet, and pounding on the glass with both hands.

"You fool!" he said, or so I thought.

Like Leaving the City

At 265 acres, the Bronx Zoo is the largest city zoo (urban wildlife conservation facility is the preferred phrase) in the country, and 90% of it is viewable in the winter. (There are two closed exhibits: the children's zoo, whose gentle barnyard animals don't do well in the cold, and Wild Asia, which is shut down because one sees it by a monorail train that is treacherous in bad weather. So tigers and rhinos, alas, are out.) With effort, you can walk it in a day, but it is nonetheless sizable enough that it almost feels as though you've left the city.

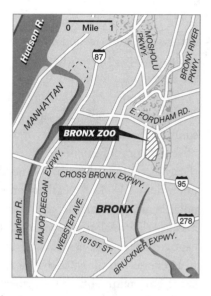

For one thing, the intermittent snorts, whinnies, yips, chortles, squawks, and growls aside, it's quiet, particularly with the attenuated winter crowds. And though the vanished greenery makes the surrounding high-rises more apparent, there's an upside to that: The outdoor animals, notably the snow leopards, have considerably less camouflage.

Indeed, the snow leopards (native to the Himalayas, the zoo's 14 examples were born in captivity), with their small, handsome heads, powerful thick tails, and muscular grace, are by themselves worth the trip to the Bronx. I spent the better part of an hour watching a pair of them nimbly roaming their steep, rocky enclosure, wrestling intermittently like the young brothers they turned out to be.

Overall, on a gray day with the wind whipping and the trees shed of leaves, the zoo isn't really a beautiful place. Like a lot of venerable, large institutions, it is in a more or less constant state of rebuilding and renovating, and for some reason in cold weather, the construction sites seem a little more glaring. The most prominent is a new indoor-outdoor exhibit, the Congo Gorilla Forest, which will not be ready until the zoo's centennial year, 1999.

But there is a kind of peace to be had, a distinct lack of clamor, and walking the footpaths in the cold, among the ponds and grassy meadows, the faux savannahs and mountainsides, you encounter the animals in fanfareless fashion, as though you were meandering the grounds of some elegant if weathered sanitarium and now and then coming across a distracted patient. The animals are just hanging out, doing what they do, and if they're not oblivious, they also aren't rude or dismayed at the gawkery as they sometimes are when the crowds are larger.

"There aren't big behavioral changes in winter," Mr. Thomas said. "Obviously, the animals can't play in the snow in summertime. In summer they seek the shade; in winter they sit in the sun. Both times of year, their movements tend to be governed by the temperature and the availability of the sun." Some animals are particularly active now, unburdened by hot-weather lethargy: the snow leopards and the polar bears, for example, and even the grizzlies, though that's partly because they're all pretty young, still playful. (They don't hibernate in captivity; hibernation, a slowing down of the metabolism, is a response to a generally diminished availability of food in the winter wild.) "For sheer entertainment, the grizzlies are tough to beat," Mr. Thomas said, watching a couple of them in athletic competition, apparently over the occupation of a rock.

You do, I discovered, bring your own biases, circumstantial and otherwise, to certain exhibits. Some of what I thought about had to do with the nature of captivity, wild creatures out of the wild, that whole bothersome issue. I found myself wondering about that at the cheetah enclosure, the two lovely animals, capable of running at the speed of a car on a highway, slinking about sleepily in view of the apartment houses on Bronx Park South. They didn't look cranky or depressed, but still and all. . . .

Not quite as profoundly, how much you enjoy the sea lions, slipping in and out of their frigid pool, probably depends on how cold you are yourself. Waiting for their daily 3pm feeding, I found them impressive at first, but then I was overcome with sympathetic chills and went inside, leaving them to dine without me.

In or Out, Depending

Much of the zoo is indoors, of course—the reptile house, the gorilla house, and the monkey house are but 3 of the 10 major enclosed exhibits—and in winter even some of its prime attractions, usually outdoors, are shut-ins.

"In the majority of cases, the outdoor animals stay out," Mr. Thomas said. "The exceptions are gorillas, elephants, giraffes—species not adapted to extreme cold." The keepers decide daily, on the basis of three factors—temperature, wind chill, and precipitation—whether to keep the animals inside, and on some days their treatment might vary.

"Elephants can be outside when it's in the 40s," Mr. Thomas said. "Giraffes are a little more sensitive to cold." When the animals are inside, he added, the keepers tend to do more of what he called "behavioral enrichment," hiding treats in their hay, for example, to encourage them to forage, so they'll still be engaged in some semblance of the activity they're accustomed to outdoors.

I've never been a big elephant guy, but watching the giraffes indoors is among the more surreal experiences to be had at the zoo. For one thing, the enclosure is the most pungent place in the zoo. ("Your nose will adjust," a zoo official told me as we walked in.) For another, the giraffe enclosure has a curved wall, painted to suggest an African savannah, and the entire time I was there, a 13-footer was stretching its neck, licking the top of it, perhaps because it was an outside wall and thus cool. In any case, I found myself humming one of the old psychedelic anthems of Jimi Hendrix: "'Scuse me, while I kiss the sky."

Weirdly rangy creatures, of course, the giraffes are startlingly close up, nearly within reach (theirs). Like cows, they stare at you with stupefaction, chewing on hay, their jaws rotating with agonizing steadiness and patience; you just know they'll never finish dinner.

Indeed, they move with a kind of underwater slowness, which is emphasized by the fact that the adjacent exhibit features a band of tiny, furiously nimble meerkats, the African rodents that are among the zoo's most popular creatures since Nathan Lane's wisecracking characterization of one in *The Lion King*. The contrast made me aware, most poignantly, of what zoos do best: illustrate by example the variety of creatures in the world. It's an obvious lesson, but for a city dweller like me to be reminded of it was one of the genuine pleasures of my visits. And the indoor exhibits of the zoo, where the animals are generally smaller and more populous, are where this particular pleasure is most intense.

Within a couple of hours, in the ingeniously luminescent World of Darkness exhibit, I found myself in the company of naked mole rats. In Jungle World, I watched an aging black leopard pacing along a branch and a family of gibbons, long-armed vine swingers, athletically making their way through the treetops. In the reptile house, I met Fidel and Maria, two Cuban crocodiles who have been at the zoo since the late 1950s, and Samantha, a 22-foot reticulated python, coiled and torpid-looking in her three or four weeks between meals, generally a 30- to 40-pound pig. "She's not bored," said Jim McDougal, a zoo herpetologist. "This is basically what she does when she's in the jungle."

Perhaps the variety is best illustrated in the World of Birds, where the names alone of the 300 species—white Bali mynah, carmine bee eater, purple lory, concave casqued hornbill, curassow, tanager, ibis, motmot—are compelling evidence. (While I was in front of his enclosure, the hornbill, a fantastically grotesque creature that suggests a Jimmy Durante caricature, sidled up to the glass and went nose to nose with a 6-year-old crouched there, eliciting an impromptu poem. "Hello, Mr. Birdie," the child intoned. "How come you're so dirty?") There is also a sobering exhibit recalling birds that are now extinct, dozens of them, many of which were still around 50 years ago. One astonishing threat to extant species, according to Donald Bruning, the curator of ornithology, is a proliferation in the wild of animals ordinarily thought of as domestic: dogs and cats. With increasing frequency, Mr. Bruning said, people are simply releasing their pets.

A cat in the wild may kill 300 birds a year, Mr. Bruning said. A recent study in Wisconsin, he said, estimated that there are 1.5 million cats in the wild in that state alone and that they are killing 36 million to 220 million birds annually.

The Lion's Message

I don't know about you. I find this amazing, and once again I found myself thinking about animals in captivity, their instincts on hold. It's a complicated issue, and I'm an amateur at it, but still: Who belongs where? I thought about Maggie and Lucille, their apparent contentment with apartment living, inanimate food, me. What do they think, really? Is this a good life?

And then I encountered the lion. It was the frigid afternoon after Christmas, and I heard him from some distance away. I'd been scrutinizing the gelada baboons, trying to figure out why a young female had apparently been banished from the family cave; she was sitting, unhappily, it seemed, her back to her relatives, shivering a bit, her tufted facial hair blowing in the nippy wind. (I was probably overpsychoanalyzing; the flat rock she was crouching on turned out to be heated.) In any case, the lion's roar, an aching bellow with the piercing resonance of the bass notes from my neighbor's stereo system, beckoned me.

I was not alone; perhaps a dozen other people also gathered round, in interesting, still silence. All, I guessed, felt isolated enough and cowed enough by the furious beastliness to contemplate themselves in awe. Unfenced in, separated from us by a wall and a moat, the lion disappeared behind a rock, then returned to view, maybe 30 feet from where I stood.

DAY-TRIPPING TO THE ZOO

The **Bronx Zoo** (☎ 718/367-1010) is at the Bronx River Parkway and Fordham Road in the Fordham section of the Bronx. To get there by subway, take the no. 2 to Pelham Parkway and walk west to the Bronxdale entrance.

If you haven't been to the zoo in awhile, you'll find a few new features awaiting you. On March 27, 1997, the zoo opened the Aitken Aviary, replacing the DeJur Aviary, which collapsed during a 1995 snowstorm. The aviary feature a South American seabird colony of Magellanic penguins, Inca terns, Guanay cormorants, and other indigenous bird species. Special penguin feedings take place daily at 11am. On May 3, 1997, the zoo unveiled a new exhibition of large birds, including ostriches, emus, and cassowaries, in an area of the park that has been redesigned for the birds.

The zoo is open daily 10am to 4:30pm. Admission is $3 for adults, $1.50 for children 2 to 12 and seniors; admission is free on Wednesday. Parking $6. The children's zoo is open from the end of March through October, weather permitting. Admission to the children's zoo is $2 for adults, $1.50 for children 2 through 12.

He shook his maned head and growled almost silently. Then he turned away; with his back to me, he began bellowing again; they were bleats of a monumental nature, and I noticed that his haunches and the muscles around his ribs clenched with each one. These were literally gut-wrenching cries, not a bellyache or any other specific complaint, but—or so I imagined—a lament of existential proportions.

Maggie and Lucille do not do this, I thought. But it hit me: I do.

FOOTLOOSE ON STATEN ISLAND

By Douglas Martin

"I AM VERY CONFIDENT," DANNY D. declared, as he loped in his trademark hop-skip style to meet me.

I was walking up the ramp from the ferry. The time was 6:50am. My confidence was less than Danny's, at least equaled by my apprehension about this strange new land. Staten Island. Our goal was to walk around the perimeter, peeling the plum, as it were. We calculated our chosen route at 47 miles.

Staten Island, for years one of New York City's five boroughs, has complained about its treatment from City Hall, not to mention all the municipal garbage. Since it hadn't been in the papers recently, my assumption was that the natives still planned to carry through on their threat to secede. Would they join New Jersey? Unlikely. I chose to believe that I was visiting an incipient independent nation.

Not to say I knew nothing about Staten Island. For one thing, I had carefully reviewed a tongue-in-cheek commercial done a few years ago for a defunct music program called "Michelob Presents Sunday Night." It was modeled after commercials for Jamaica and repeatedly used the phrase "come to the island," as it showed such highlights as people fishing, tuxedo rental shops, people fishing, the world's biggest garbage dump, and more people fishing.

It got a little publicity at the time. But one wonders if such depictions by Manhattan jokesters might not have driven anyone to thoughts of secession.

Indeed, there seems scant appreciation among the Gotham cosmopolites for the facts that Staten Island has a zoo with one of the world's best snake collections, a smashing children's museum, and absolutely stunning parks.

And there is no question that Staten Island has progressed leaps and bounds from the days its towns had names like Skunk's Misery and Linoleumville. Staten Island claims the highest point on the Eastern Seaboard, vibrant wetlands, a surprisingly extensive railroad, New York City's only house designed by Frank Lloyd Wright, and more great pizza than seems fair. It is a place where you can see magnificent blue herons and endless oil-storage tanks.

Brooklynites poured onto the island after the Verrazano-Narrows Bridge opened in 1964, and have never stopped coming. "The City" is what the other boroughs are called, and that is decidedly not a compliment.

A Two-Day Trek

But this is background research. Daniel Anthony Perasa, who works in the communications room of this newspaper, and yours truly were determined to see for ourselves. Our self-assigned mission was to view Staten Island from outside in, to walk as close to the shoreline as legal over two days of ambulation.

Just as we were convinced our own superficiality was only skin deep, so it would be for Staten Island. Not for us the beautiful 35 miles of hiking trails in those nice parks. We would glimpse the isle's soul from its skin.

Less than a year ago, we had made a similar trek around Manhattan. Then we got lost a half-dozen times, dodged bikes, cursed joggers, begged dogs for our lives. Enough time had passed—or enough brain cells perished—for us to seek a sterner challenge.

Which, truth to tell, is easier for Danny D., as he has been known since childhood. He began long-distance walking years ago to help regulate his diabetes. He has suffered a mild stroke and is in his 50's, but remains devilishly difficult to keep up with.

Where he really races, though, is on the level of his brain, which roams the lot but keeps coming back to baseball statistics. As I was getting my bearings as we began our walk by heading west on

Richmond Terrace in Livingston, Danny was already buzzing on about Staten Island's place in the global consciousness.

"I wonder if people the world over know where Staten Island is," he said. "I mean if you walked up to somebody in London." My immediate reply was that they should know. The view from Richmond Terrace was gorgeous. Manhattan rose like Oz across the shimmering water. The walkway was nice and the morning breeze cool. "This is probably the prettiest borough, because you don't have to go anywhere to see green," said Danny.

Expect the Unexpected

Soon we began seeing completely different things, then different things again. The biggest truth about Staten Island, at least its edge, is that it is a jumble of seemingly conflicting sights. You see a shack next to a multimillion-dollar home, a junkyard next to a manicured park, a topless bar next to a Colonial church. Then, randomly, of course, there are a lot of empty spaces in between. Nothing, absolutely nothing is predictable.

The sidewalk had now sprouted waist-high weeds, as we passed enormous abandoned warehouses and deserted docks. This almost moved Danny to begin his life story. He was starting to tell me about his dad, the dockworker, before I was able to divert him. But he did manage to impart his experience with Staten Island, which certainly exceeded mine. Growing up in Bay Ridge, Brooklyn, he knew Staten Island as simply "the wilds." There were summer day trips, positively idyllic ones, to Clove Lake. They would begin at 5am, when he would smell the odor of frying chicken wafting into his room as his mother prepared for the day. "For us, this was the country," Danny said.

Unlike our ever-seedier route. After passing the splendid Greek Revival buildings at the Snug Harbor Cultural Center in Livingston, we passed junkyards with guard dogs, weeds, stagnant streams, broken bottles. This patch had seen better days.

Then, suddenly, a piece of beauty would rear up. The Bayonne Bridge glistening in the sunlight. A big old house with fresh wash drying on a clothesline on a second-floor porch. The witty fantasy mural of grocery products on a deli wall. Somewhere, we must have passed the building where Alexander Hamilton expired after his fatal duel, but we somehow missed it. Just why, we wondered, was that road named Alaska Street?

But the visual complexity of a landscape devoted to low-level industrial and commercial uses was captivating enough. Walking, I realized time and again, gives one the time and mind-set to appreciate things. Particularly the seemingly mundane.

By 9am, we had reached Western Avenue, where we turned left and walked past the old Procter & Gamble plant. These fine industrial buildings are now deserted, and our words echoed as if we were in a canyon. Haunting.

Soon, though, we were in a region of utter desolation. Tall swamp grasses waved in the wind. Banks of purple wildflowers were everywhere. Danny, perhaps to get the conversation back to baseball statistics, said it reminded him of *Field of Dreams*. The sun was beating hotter, as Danny was waxing on about the illogic of naming grape-fruits grapefruits. Our pace quickened when we came to a truck car-rying gas canisters, and noticed the driver lighting a cigarette.

The absurdity of this endeavor would be clearer later but by this point it was already incontrovertible. Street signs were the only sign of civilization. Danny wondered what our wives were saying if any-body asked where their husbands were. Clearly, anything but this.

Just then, we saw our third dead rat. And within a mile, we were on the edge of the West Shore Expressway.

Here was walking at its weirdest edge, the point from which hikers of the entire Appalachian Trail would surely shrink. The expressway takes you right past the Fresh Kills landfill, which will be the highest point on the Eastern Seaboard if present disposal habits persist. On one side diesel trucks roar by, on the other is grass. I spot a live rat bigger than my bread box. "They don't make it easy for you to walk," Danny observed, though he expressed gratitude that there were no curbs.

There is a desertlike sort of beauty to the huge mounds of mauve earth being prepared for the cargo being brought by an endless stream of sanitation trucks. The odor today, unlike on some days, we were told, wasn't bad either. We were also impressed by an apparently successful effort to plant native trees and plants on hills built from garbage.

"Sit Down and Relax"

We walked from exits 7 to 4 on the freeway. We made good time, and were not lost. Danny wondered how we could have passed Yankee Stadium three times on our walk around Manhattan, underlining this year's evolving accomplishment.

We were now on Arthur Kill Road, where we spotted a newly opened deli. A Little Bit of Italy, it is called. "Sit down and relax," the proprietor said with a big smile. As we gulped sodas, he told us he has lived on Staten Island for 19 years, having moved here from Brook-lyn. He desperately wants to save enough money to move to New Jersey, he added. "I hate Staten Island," he said.

Unlike us, we were realizing. Arthur Kill Road proved delightful, again in a decidedly eclectic sort of way. We passed a nice-looking restaurant called the Old Bermuda Inn. It had a white latticework exterior and a blue canvas covering, but was unfortunately closed.

We came to the Arthur Kill Correctional Facility, a state prison whose mess hall locals like to rent for weddings, Danny's sister-in-law, a caterer, told him. Across the road was a farm run by Cornell University to teach agricultural skills to city children. At a bar named Hipps, at the intersection with Industrial Loop Road, I noticed there was both a free lunch and topless women. Danny insisted we press on.

One fascinating sight was the existence of bus stops growing out of the weeds. They were just like the ones you would see anywhere in the city, but seemed incongruous in such a rural setting. By one of them sat an abandoned velvet couch, decorated with gold paint. It looked like a refugee from a long ago theater lobby.

As Danny strode toward infinity, I stopped to check out a little cemetery. Though the graves were very old and the names had worn off most, the grass had just been mowed. Not manicured certainly, but a nice sign of respect. I made out the words on one stone and for some reason kept thinking about it. "Our Little Henrietta," it said. "Died July 17, 1853. Aged 2 years." The road meandered on past front porches with big comfortable chairs, and a sign informed us that we had passed the Black Garter Saloon. Surely such dens of licentiousness are no more numerous here than in Manhattan or Queens, but perhaps less overall density makes them more noticeable.

Again and again, Staten Island serves up the unexpected. At Kreischer Street, I suddenly glimpsed a beautiful Victorian tower peeking through luxuriant pines. It turned out to be part of an enormous Victorian house. BEWARE OF THE DOG, said a sign.

We then came to a big brick smokestack even Staten Islanders wonder about, Danny's relatives tell him. We asked a toothless man on a backhoe working out front what it was. An abandoned cable factory, of course.

Mansions and Shacks

Soon we were on tree-lined Main Street in Tottenville. Old houses, hydrangea bushes, lawn ornaments of elves and deer and ducks. We passed the South Baptist Church, where a sign said Sunday's sermon would address the topic "When Is a Sermon Over?" A Main Street bar, a dark cave from the outside, was called Two Morrows, in apparent reference to the owners. Everywhere houses were being built and roads repaired in a flurry of activity that is a fading memory in most parts of New York.

Taking a succession of pretty little streets, we found ourselves staring at mansions, some just for their grandiosity, some for their bad taste, and some for their pure beauty. "It ought to be illegal to have this much money," said Danny as he observed what looked like a Louisiana plantation mansion. Then, we would come to a shack, again proving that nothing can be assumed on Staten Island.

A gorgeous find, not least because we didn't expect anything so beautiful, was the Conference House in a park overlooking the water. It was here that Benjamin Franklin and other incipient Americans came in 1776 to talk peace with the British, shortly before the Revolutionary War. A little garden of Colonial herbs is a nice touch.

Winding It Down

We were then on Hylan Boulevard, our route for a very, very long time. This was bad walking, largely because of the construction, which considerably reduced the size of the road. Sidewalks were a rarity. But the worst thing was that we were hungry and thirsty, as Danny, experiencing a surge of energy, had not wanted to stop for lunch when food was available.

So we walked for three, maybe four hours, without so much as seeing a place to get a candy bar and a cola. Sure there were beautiful lawns, occasional views of the sea, and all manner of wildflowers. But for me, it all paled before the sign on the side of a bus. A succulent salami! I would have killed for a slice, and guess who I would most have liked to kill?

Danny's own desperateness emerged when he asked directions to the nearest restaurant from a cemetery worker who had just asked us the time and got it. He kept saying, "A long way," and laughing.

Many miles later, we came to Carmen's, a Mexican restaurant overlooking the ocean. A couple of appetizers, a dozen iced teas, and survival seemed, well, vaguely possible. What to do but hit the road?

Our day's trek was winding to a close, as the smell of barbecue wafted from the manicured yards. Staten Island lawns are the planet's most beautiful. On most, you could play tennis, a sport first played in this country on this island. We then found ourselves on what a few hours ago would have been our vision of heaven, block upon block of fast-food restaurants. At a Burger King, we each had three diet colas, watched a magician entertain the children with mediocre magic and the mothers with worse dirty jokes, and called to be picked up.

And Then to Bed

We had come 32 or 33 miles, as far as Tysens Lane and Hylan Boulevard, leaving us just a 14- or 15-mile stroll for the next day. We would overnight in Westerleigh, a little town in the interior inhabited by Danny's relatives. They live on an idyllic park with a gazebo in the middle, surrounded by proud old houses. It occurred to us that Staten Island may harbor secrets invisible from the outside, but we dismissed the notion as not self-serving.

The relatives gave us roast beef, mashed potatoes, and enough fresh vegetables to feed a buffalo or two. They also shared thoughts about the plight that just may have driven them to think about seceding. Stratospheric taxes. Used buses. All that garbage.

We awoke eager to attack the new day. We were dropped off at the Burger King, and continued northeast on Hylan. One sight to behold was Top Tomato, a fruit stand with immense and garishly wonderful pictures of veggies. WE MAKE FRIENDS . . . NOT MONEY, said a sign over the immaculate display racks.

A Friendly Place!

At Greeley Avenue, in New Dorp, we turned right to get to the boardwalk. There were some little bungalows of the type that pretty much burned down or were razed for urban renewal on Far Rockaway and Coney Island, though most houses were bigger. People seemed to think nothing of leaving toys strewn in front lawns. Mailboxes were disguised as log cabins and other clever things. We smelled fresh paint. Morning glories decorated fences. People, every one, said good morning.

The boardwalk was as beautiful and timeless as boardwalks every-where, though the first patch was cement. The elegant Verrazano-Narrows Bridge hung in the warm haze. People played softball on the diamonds. Dogs ambled with that brow-beaten certainty the day would get far hotter.

Danny was strangely subdued, for a brief interlude. Maybe it was because he had changed his shoes. "If you're thinking of something other than your feet when you're walking, you're preoccupied," he growled.

After the boardwalk, we made our way through a succession of residential and commercial streets. People stopped to let us cross the street, some waving. A man sold fresh fish from the back of a pickup.

The walking had become almost effortless. At 10:25am, Danny asked, "Is it nine yet?"

The Last Act

Bay Street was our last leg. Danny was singing a march favored by the Royal Canadian Army in World War I. Weeds grew out of the side-walks, but some had pretty flowers. We stopped at a White Castle for "the taste some people won't live without."

One of the last real wonders was a fanciful pink lighthouse tower-ing above the intersection of Bay and Hannah streets, in Tompkinsville. It belonged to Rock & Roll Motor Company, home of "Cars of the 90s at 50s prices." We took a slight detour to see the whimsically elegant Victorian cottage of Alice Austen, the pioneer documentary photographer.

Then we were back at the ferry terminal, finished at 12:55pm. We had conquered an island more than twice the size of Manhattan, which we could see rising majestically across the harbor. Danny was won-dering what challenge we should take on next year. Who knows?

In Hunter Thompson's immortal phrase in *Fear and Loathing in Las Vegas*, we were "just sick enough to feel totally confident." But let the last words be Danny's: "Just because somebody does something outrageous, doesn't mean it's wrong."

WALKING BROOKLYN'S FLATBUSH TRAIL

by Douglas Martin

LET'S BEGIN WITH THE WORST. Danny and I, old sauntering buddies, had decided to try something new, walking in a straight line. Our past perambulations had been around islands, first Manhattan, then Staten Island, attempts to glimpse truths from the outside looking in. Now we were going to walk the length of Flatbush Avenue, more than 10 miles, in search of nothing less than the soul of Brooklyn, the vast borough Thomas Wolfe said nobody could know "t'roo and t'roo."

That, without doubt, includes us, though we both live in the political subdivision taking its name from the Dutch words for broken valley. Douglas Martin, reporter, and Daniel Anthony Perasa, who takes bets over the phone for OTB, somehow turned the wrong way coming out of a diner, not realizing for almost three long blocks that we were seeing the same view we had recently passed on the other side of the street.

"If we were going to be honest about it, we'd refer to each other as Dumb and Dumber," Danny says. Then, referring to the avenues identified by letters, Dumb adds, "Before we walk next time, it might not be a bad idea to learn the alphabet."

Our only defense is that we were following a time-honored Brooklyn tradition. Douglas (Wrong Way) Corrigan had taken off from Floyd Bennett Field at the base of Flatbush Avenue on a flight to California in 1938, when this would have been quite an achievement. He misread his compass for 28 hours and ended up in Ireland. His

unforgettable first words: "Where am I?" But, hey! In no time at all, the *New York Post* printed a headline celebrating his achievement, backward of course, and in Texas, he was presented with a watch that ran the wrong way. He was featured in parades, always in cars going in reverse. And Wrong Way Corrigan is in our modern-day minds as we begin our stroll virtually where he began his flight.

At the Brooklyn side of Gil Hodges Memorial Bridge, which goes to the Rockaways, in Queens, Danny pronounces it a grand day for walking. "My mother would have said there's just enough blue in the sky for a sailor to make a pair of pants," he says.

Danny is a true Brooklynite, having lived here all his 57 years. By the time he was 12, he figures, his mother must have given him $1 about 100 times to spend an afternoon watching the Dodgers at Ebbets Field. (A nickel each way for the subway, 60 cents admission, a nickel for the scorecard, and 25 cents to apportion between hot dogs and sodas, which cost a nickel each.) Blessedly, he does not ooze nostalgia, an incurable Brooklyn disease.

So we've come to Flatbush Avenue, which bisects Brooklyn in the manner that Broadway slices and defines Manhattan. I live in a 12th-floor apartment from which all the windows look out on Flatbush, and have sat mesmerized by the endless procession of tens of thousands of vehicles, while pondering the patterns of our local migrations, the sheer magnitude of the nation's taillights.

Flatbush was first an Indian trail through the woodlands, then the site of a pretty humiliating British victory over forces led by George Washington. Later on, it became the thoroughfare for the parade honoring the one Brooklyn Dodgers World Series victory and, more recently, a favored route of protests by the Rev. Al Sharpton and of

regular streams of the Lubavitchers' recreational vehicles noisily her-
alding the imminent arrival of the Messiah. (The *Brooklyn Eagle*
reported in 1946 that the name Flatbush comes from the Dutch words
vlachte bos, which mean "plain woods.")

The meanings of the avenue, from huge to tiny, were superbly evoked
in a book published last year by Alan Abel, now a Canadian, who grew
up in the neighborhood of Flatbush, in Central Brooklyn, and went on
to practice journalism around the world. His book, *Flatbush Odyssey: A
Journey Through the Heart of Brooklyn* (McClelland & Stewart), describes
his wanderings and the lovely, evolving relationship between him and
his Brooklyn mother, united again during a three-month visit. My
favorite part was Mr. Abel's discovery while researching his book that
what he thought were the autographs of every Dodger player, in his
long-cherished team yearbook from the mid-50s, were almost surely
the work of a graphologically gifted batboy known as Charley the Brow.

Gulls and Crows

But this article is about our walk, and we're now between the bridge
and Floyd Bennett Field. It is a landscape so bleak, it reminds Danny
of the Midwest, at least *The Wizard of Oz* part. There is towering
swamp grass, scrub trees, every so often parts of cars—enough com-
ponents, Danny guesses, "to build a car that wouldn't work." Gulls
squawk, crows caw, planes descend on Kennedy Airport. It does not
seem like the city, though there is a small homeless encampment with
enough borrowed shopping carts to start a Pathmark, and we suspect
snakes lurk in the grass.

We come to the Marina at Barren Island, a parking lot for yachts.
What would you name a boat, Danny? "*Never Sink II,*" he snaps. Then
Highway Patrol Precinct No. 2, a not unhandsome brick building.
The Department of Transportation's Flatbush Yard. Then the Marine
Park Golf Course, where plaid people are waiting to tee off on a course
designed by Robert Trent Jones. A short way down, we come to some
very large fishing boats of the sort that prowl the great ocean banks.
Then Toys "R" Us and, in a little bit, Kings Plaza Shopping Center,
looking as if it had just arrived from Nowhere, U.S.A. Is this Brooklyn, root land of George Gershwin and Woody Allen?

Danny fills the emptiness with some advice to walkers: Never stop. "If you stop walking, bad things are going to happen to you," he says ominously. He is singing what I think is an old Guy Lombardo song, which was also favored by the Ebbets Field organist Gladys Goodding: "Give me the moon over Brooklyn, down Flatbush Avenue."

Just past Avenue S, we spot the New Floridian Diner and know its call is for us. We enter a palace of chrome, mirrors, and phones. Waitresses wear pink bow ties and frilly aprons. Tom Jones is on the jukebox. The cakes all have at least three layers, are a foot high, and are displayed like artworks. The menu is 14 pages. There are cocktails (the kamikaze, for $3.95), sandwiches (open-faced Romanian steak, $11.45), and acres of freshly baked muffins. They don't have pineapple knishes like the ones Danny remembers from a long time ago at Coney Island, but I think this just might be as good as it gets.

The Wrong Turn

It was here we made the wrong turn on a one-way journey. Perhaps it was the directionally challenging intersection of more than two streets. Maybe it was our genuine fascination with the menu of the Lucky Star Finest Chinese and Italian Food to Take Out. It could have been our preoccupation with the woman crossing the street against the light while reading a book. "A true New Yorker," Danny mumbles approvingly. "The lady doesn't know the meaning of fear."

Soon we are back on course, trodding back toward Manhattan with hope in our hearts and sheepish grins on our faces. At Baughman Place, we see an old-fashioned pizzeria, Lenny & John's, and bite. The excellent cheese ball is 65 cents, and on Tuesdays, you can buy a whole pie for $4.50. The photographs on the wall take you back to an older Flatbush Avenue. One was taken in 1956 and shows the view north from Flatlands Avenue. Alan Ladd was starring in *Santiago* at the old Marine Theater. A 1946 picture, showing the intersection of Flatbush and Flatlands, records the once ubiquitous trolley cars that Brooklynites used to have to dodge between. (Hence, the ball club's name.)

Most intriguing is a 1922 photo of a house built in 1800 that is said to be still standing. The address is 1587 East 53rd Street, between avenues M and N. We ask a counterman for directions. "Too far to walk," he answers.

Maybe for him. But we are now determinedly unidirectional. As the neighborhood of Flatlands oozes into that of Flatbush, we pass Four Aces Pawnbrokers, with a menagerie of stuffed game in the window, including a toothy beaver. At a bakery, we have reason to suspect we are overcharged when it becomes apparent we are both ignorant and from outside the neighborhood ($3.50 for two beef patties in cocoa bread, which would have been $1.30 each). "Pretty smooth," says Danny. "A good old-fashioned New York hustle."

An upper-floor office has signs identifying it as the Korean American Association of Brooklyn. At a fish market, shark goes for 99 cents a pound; a nearby butcher charges 59 cents a pound for cow feet. A doorway is marked, "Sexy lingerie through the travel agency," which is next door.

The silence is a distant memory. Flatbush, once a Jewish and Irish neighborhood, now teems with people from all over the world, and they race about on errands. Radios blare, and Rollerbladers, walkers' worst enemies, start to appear. A teenager passes with a carton from the ASPCA; it meows. I get my second patty, a codfish one (75 cents).

A woman who bumped Danny as she raced past, comes back when she sees him stopping to tie his shoe. "You should have told me," she says. "I would have tied it for you." Danny, who thinks his baldness is the punishment of an unjust God, does not appreciate this kindness. "I'm an athlete," he growls. "I'm a long-distance walker."

Sampling Soul Food

Knowing that lunch heals all, we find ourselves in TP's Soul Food Restaurant between Cortelyou Road and Dorchester Road. The $1.99 barbecued chicken wings with fresh corn bread had beguiled us, and does not disappoint. A long, long counter with 22 stools. Lazy ceiling fans. Free jazz on Saturday nights, a gospel choir on Sunday nights. Next time, I'm splurging $8.95 for chicken, pork chop, and beef, all smothered with country gravy. My choice of the two included vegetables will be candied yams and yellow turnips. "If this place were in Manhattan, the prices would be twice as much, the crowd would be three times the size, and it would be half as enjoyable," Danny summarizes.

Walking is slow, which is fine. We wander into African grocery stores, stop to appreciate the tinkling concerto of an ice cream truck and notice that the produce markets carry chunks of Jamaican pumpkin. A botanica offers holy water in two varieties, 99 cents and $1.59. Why? Street music changes from soca to calypso to hip-hop every few feet.

We worship at those awesome monuments to money, the corner banks. A Republic Bank branch at Caton Avenue has elegant chandeliers and words of wisdom chiseled in the walls: "The habit of saving is itself an education. It encourages every virtue. It teaches self-control." Danny shakes his head, and is walking again in no time. "That sounded like something Scrooge might have said at the beginning of the book," he puffs. "But that's all right."

We almost miss Erasmus Hall Academy, founded by Alexander Hamilton and the man who later shot him to death in a duel, Aaron Burr. Situated between Church and Snyder avenues, it grew into the adjacent high school attended by Barbra Streisand, Bobby Fischer, and Beverly Sills. Inside the gate stands the original 1786 academy building, a Georgian-Federal gem.

But we don't stop, being a bit put off by the gate. "It looks like it could be part of a penitentiary," Danny growls. We also skip the original Flatbush Town Hall, seat of Flatbush's government until it became part of Brooklyn in 1894, four years before Brooklyn itself became part of New York City. It is a half-block off Flatbush, on Snyder Avenue, and we, understandably enough, have sworn off detours.

Where we linger is the Reformed Protestant Dutch Church, with its towering steeple. It is so beautiful, we Brooklynites half forgive the fact it is made of Manhattan schist. And we find the graveyard surrounding the church a strangely peaceful retreat from the cacophonous street. The Dutch inscriptions on limestone have pretty much worn away, but some of the ones etched on brownstone remain legible. "Hier Lyt Het Lighaam."

Near the cemetery are other shells. One is Loews King Theater, once one of the most exuberant of the great movie palaces. Both Danny and Mr. Abel in his book recall fabulous ice cream places. But the way today's

Flatbush Avenue pulsates with life makes it hard to dwell on mythic yesterdays. Across the street from the dignified old church, a street preacher is just shifting into high gear, dancing as if there might be no tomorrow. "Hallelujah, Jesus, sweeter than a honeycomb!" he shouts.

Step by step, we approach the empty corner of Brooklyn's heart. Ebbets Field Houses, a housing development, loom just two blocks off Flatbush. Danny's mood turns dark. He tells of a friend who had bought an original seat from the stadium and chained it to a flagpole in his Brooklyn front yard. It was stolen in no time. He muses about the ultimate fate of the villains who stole the beloved "Bums" from their native land.

The closest we can get to a visible memory is the McDonald's on Empire Boulevard, which has taken the trouble to assemble autographed Brooklyn Dodgers pictures for its walls. Danny discusses each. Babe Ruth is a surprise to me, but he did once wear a Dodgers uniform as a coach in the late 1930s.

Danny approvingly notes that the pitcher Don Drysdale was the meanest man, definitely the meanest pitcher, ever to play. He recalls someone asking Drysdale if he would knock down his own mother. "Certainly not," he supposedly answered. "She's not that good a hitter."

We amble on, with the Brooklyn Botanic Garden on one side of Flatbush Avenue and Prospect Park on the other. You can't see into either very well, but some days you can hear the music of the exquisite Prospect Park carousel. The park's zoo has replaced its larger animals with smaller ones, more tastefully displayed. So the roars of lions that once would have accompanied our walk are no more. On the other hand, a Dutch home built in 1783, Lefferts Homestead, pulsates with new life, as it has become a focus for children's programs.

We walk through the elegant Grand Army Plaza, an expansive and tasteful urban space that is also my front yard. We walk down a long hill and come to the Brooklyn Academy of Music, a boxlike building that Caruso inaugurated in 1908 by singing the title role in *Faust*. Across the street is the Williamsburgh Savings Bank Building, Brooklyn's tallest building. Its lobby is an awesome space with pillars rising like trees. "If there were red hats hanging from the ceiling, I'd swear I was in St. Patrick's Cathedral," Danny says.

Incense and Cabs

We trudge on, somehow gaining energy as we get closer to "the City," as Brooklynites persist in calling Manhattan. The smell of peddlers' incense permeates the air, and we occasionally see yellow cabs, a sight unknown in the borough's interior. After Fulton Street, we are walking on Flatbush Avenue Extension, built as an access to the Manhattan Bridge, which opened in 1905. We pass another Toys "R" Us, reminding us that this is pretty much what we began with. We see a man wearing a Yankee cap. Good grief.

At the famous Junior's restaurant, we only window-shop the huge cheesecakes. We cross Flatbush Avenue to the former Paramount Theater—where Frankie Lymon and the Teen-Agers, Chuck Berry, and others got rock-and-roll going four decades ago—hoping to see the great Wurlitzer organ, which remains. A security guard kindly leads us to what has become a gym for Long Island University, but an archery class prevents us from entering.

We pass Steam Heat, a self-described "gentlemen's adult club," pushing the definition of gentlemen to new realms. Traffic is everywhere. Suddenly, we are at the end, the blue Manhattan Bridge with its dainty four knobs on top. Garbage surrounds us. A man slowly harvests bottles from the weeds. Clouds cover the sun.

It is 3:40pm, about seven hours after we started. We have passed seven Irish bars, six McDonald's, and more than 100 nail parlors. We look at each other and break out laughing.

"It certainly doesn't end with a glorious hurrah, does it?" Danny says.

Long Island

A DAY AT THE RACES:
BETTING AT BELMONT

by William Grimes

THE FIRST RACE AT BELMONT ON A
sizzling hot day turned out to be almost too much for one bettor.
Standing near the finish line against the chain-link fence that runs
along the home stretch, he stamped his right foot furiously, punched
the air with one hand, and, as five closely bunched horses pounded
toward the wire, screamed nonstop, a study in the more brutish emo-
tions. "Come on, move it! Get the lead out and move it! Do it!" This
ridiculous figure was none other than myself.

I had never been to a racetrack before. Except for the Triple Crown,
thoroughbred racing had seemed pointless, a small footnote to the
day's sports results on the local television news, marginally more
interesting than curling or caber tossing.

What a difference a day makes! I walked into Belmont Park in
Elmont, Long Island, a duffer, a lamb waiting to be fleeced, a low
roller with a stake of $100 and a dream: to play the ponies and win. I
left Belmont . . . well, to get the official result, read on.

Knowledge is power. I was determined to do research before placing my first bet, enough to make the afternoon something more than
an exercise in picking horses with funny names. Two books seemed
essential. The first was Tom Ainslie's *Complete Guide to Thoroughbred
Racing*. Written in a lively style, it is a sober, informed tutorial on how
to handicap a race, with an in-depth discussion of "the jockey factor,"
"the distance factor," "the speed factor," and other fundamentals, as well
as simple explanations of various types of bets and betting systems.

The second book on my self-education program was a collection of Damon Runyon stories. It seemed desirable to steep myself in the argot of the racing world, and to make the acquaintance of characters like Hot Horse Herbie and Little Alfie, the guys in yellow-checked suits whom I would undoubtedly encounter at the track.

There are few things more pleasing to the eye than Belmont Park on a fine day. The track encloses an ovoid Eden, a lush, landscaped park with two sizable ponds and topiary bushes that are cultivated in the race track's own greenhouse. High-pressure spigots spray water across the grass, swathing the infield in a romantic, shimmering mist. An intricately sculptured chamaecyparis bush stands to the left of the grave of Ruffian, a valiant filly that perished in the line of duty. Specifically, she broke a leg during a match race with Foolish Pleasure on July 6, 1975, and had to be destroyed, ending a brilliant career.

The four-story track building, which parallels the home stretch, is divided into grandstand and clubhouse areas. To enter, visitors pay $2 and walk through turnstiles to what looks like the approach to an amusement park or zoo. An additional $2 gets you into the clubhouse. At several stands, vendors sell *The Racing Form* ($3) and tip sheets compiled by handicapping experts. Also on sale is *Post Parade* ($1.50), the track program. Like *The Racing Form*, it offers past-performance stats on each horse running that day, as well as the morning line, a track expert's estimate of how the public will bet each horse.

Off to the right, just beyond the first newsstands, is the paddock, where, before each race, the horses are paraded around a small track, called the walking ring.

An Early Look

Keen-eyed bettors use the paddock parade to look for disturbing signs in their favorite horse. If you see a horse trying to kick his handler to death, for example, it might be wise to alter the betting strategy for that race. I found it immensely reassuring whenever my picks turned out to be lean, slightly high-strung animals with good posture and what seemed like a can-do attitude.

It's a short walk from the paddock to the ground-level grandstand and the real business of the park, betting. The atmosphere and the architecture are a little like a baseball stadium, with hot dog and beer stands scattered throughout. There are restaurants, too, but it's safe to say that most people do not come to the track with a fine meal uppermost on their minds. No, the 450 overhead television monitors tell the real tale of the place, flashing a constant stream of information on the changing odds, as the minutes to post time tick away.

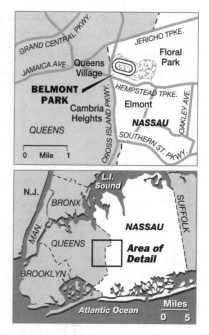

For the first time since leaving high school, I felt keen regret at not having tried harder in math. If only they had presented word problems in horse-racing terms, with actual money on the line, rather than those bland farmers plowing fields into complicated fractions, or freight trains carrying wheat. The subject takes on real urgency when you're trying to choose between two horses and can't quite figure out whether 7–2 odds are better or worse than 4–1 and by how much. My plight was even worse. Only late in the day did I discover that a $2 bet on a horse at even odds pays $4. I thought the bettor simply broke even. All around me, people who did not look like college material seemed to have no trouble performing nine-digit calculations in their heads as the odds on the board changed.

The mathematically challenged may want to request a helpful pamphlet called "Thoroughbred Racing Made Easy," which the New York Racing Association gives away at information booths on the ground floor and second floor.

Nine Little Adventures

I studied *The Racing Form*, and evolved a simple strategy. I read the capsule descriptions of each horse in the "Closer Look" section of the paper, examined the horse's recent track record and career stats, checked out the jockey's winning percentage, narrowed the field to a plausible few, and studied the odds on the board to see which way the money was flowing. For the purposes of this article, I bet every one of the day's nine races, something no real handicapper would do.

The procedure for placing a bet is simple. Walk up to a window and state, in the following order, the amount of the bet, the type of bet (for example, win, place, or show), and the number of the horse (not the name), which is indicated on all the printed guides.

There's an automated version of this procedure. At specially marked windows, bettors can buy vouchers, which they then insert into screen activated machines (called "SAM"s) that present betting options. By touching the screen, the bettor can choose the amount and type of bet.

With one exception, I stuck to win, place, and show bets, meaning that I bet that my horse would come in first (win), first or second (place), or among the top three (show).

Danger in Winning

Four great truths seemed to emerge. First, as Tom Ainslie succinctly puts it, "It is more fun to win than to lose." Too much fun, perhaps. A well-trained thoroughbred running all out is the second-most beautiful sight in nature, surpassed only by the sight of the same horse coming on strong in the home stretch and finishing in the money. In the excitement, it's all too easy to bet foolishly.

Second, it's best to study *The Racing Form* the night before the race. There's simply too much information to digest at the track, with less than 30 minutes between races.

Third, long shots are long shots for a simple reason. They are highly unlikely to win. On my race day, only one horse came in at odds much longer than 5–1, and seven of the nine races were won by favorites.

Fourth, the trickier variations on win, place, and show betting—the exactas, trifectas, pick threes, and pick sixes, intended to spice things up for the betting public—should not be tried by the novice bettor. Most bettors at the track put their money on exactas, in which they predict the first two horses to cross the finish line, in exact order, thereby getting a much larger payoff on their bet. A trifecta, as the name suggests, requires the bettor to predict the top three finishers in order. The daily double, pick three, and pick six bets require the bettor to select the winners of two, three, or six consecutive races. As Ainslie points out, it's hard enough to pick one winner in one race. The wise handicapper focuses his energies accordingly.

My first race was an emotional tuneup: $5 to win on Color Me Speed, which I thought showed potential (for reasons that are obscure in retrospect) and, as a hedge, $5 to show on Here's Noah, the odds-on favorite.

After placing my bet, I sat down on one of the green wooden benches at track level, near the finish line, by far the most exciting vantage point, I later decided. Those who wish may pay the surcharge and enter the clubhouse areas on the second, third, and fourth floors, where you get a better view of the first half of the race. But even with binoculars (rentable for $3), the action seems a little remote. At track level, you get the rawer emotions, and the unbeatable close-up view of the final drive to the finish line.

From Murmur to Roar

As the race begins, a tense quiet reigns. Most of the bettors remain seated on the benches, with scattered enthusiasts yelling out a few choice words of encouragement. "Stay up with the rat pack there, buddy boy," I heard one bettor yell. Across the infield, the horses look like mechanical models.

As the horses round the final turn, the murmur of the crowd becomes a roar. The people in the seats rise, as though gripped by a supernatural power, and advance like zombies toward the fence, eyes fixed on the race. The final flat-out stretch run unleashes pandemonium.

It's fun. I now have a better understanding of why the crowds turn out in downtown Teheran for a rousing "Death to America" rally.

Color Me Speed nearly pulled it off, but was nosed out at the finish by Here's Noah, who returned a profit of $3.50. So I was down $1.50 after one race.

In each of the next two races, I played it safe and bet one horse to place. Both finished in the top two, and I collected a profit of $31 on $20 in bets.

Over the next several races, I increased the amount of each bet, but stuck to the basic, admittedly wimpish strategy of trying to bet on one or two horses to finish in the money. I was turning a profit. Dribs and drabs, true, but while other bettors were tearing up their slips, I was returning to the windows to cash in.

The Damon Runyon color was not particularly evident, although after Julie Krone rode Great Triumph to a closely run second-place finish, one elderly fellow with no teeth repeated, "She got the old schnozzola in there, Julie, she got the old schnozzola in there!"

Off by One Place

In the eighth race, I got greedy. Ignoring Ainslie, I bet a $30 exacta. That is, I bet $30 that Splendid Buck, one of the top horses that day, and Apprentice would finish first and second, respectively. That was not a dumb bet, but it wasn't smart either. The dumb part was that I thought I was betting a quinella: that is, predicting the first two horses, but not in any particular order. It turned out to be moot, since my horses finished one-three rather than one-two.

This was a blow. My hard-won confidence was shaken. With only one race to go, I was looking at a loser of a day. Returning to basics, I applied my mind to *The Racing Form* and located two good-lookers, Out of the Realm and Incredible. A third horse, Scudbuster, looked strong on paper, but I rejected him because the name was nearly as irritating as the No. 4 horse, Homey Don't Play. I put $25 each on Out of the Realm and Incredible to place.

It was a great race, run on turf. Both horses started out at the back of the field. Out of the Realm, in fact, ran dead last through the first half of the race and for a brief moment looked as though he might stop to nibble flowers. At the three-quarter mark, he was still running eighth in a 10-horse field.

Incredible, meanwhile, was up with the leaders, in third position, just behind the detestable Scudbuster. Then, the miracle. Out of the Realm poured it on. With no more apparent effort than a driver shifting gears, he passed the field and won by a length and half.

And the second horse? It was Incredible over Scudbuster in a photo finish.

I headed to the betting window and pushed across my slip. The man behind the window pushed back a crisp $100 bill.

Memo to the boss: I'm giving three weeks' notice.

THE ARGOT TO START WITH

Here is a glossary of words commonly used at the race track:

Win: Horse bet must finish first.

Place: Horse bet must finish first or second.

Show: Horse bet must finish first, second, or third.

Daily Double: Horses bet must finish first in respective races. Available in first and second races of the day, and also in last two races.

Exacta: Horses bet must finish first and second in exact order. Available for all races.

Quinella: Horses bet must finish first or second in any order. Available for races no. 2 and no. 4.

Instant Double: Winners picked in two consecutive races. Happens when an exacta or quinella wager is canceled because of late scratches.

Trifecta: Horses bet must finish first, second, and third in exact order. Available for races no. 5, 7, and 9 and all stakes races.

Pick Three: Horses bet must finish first in races nos. 2, 3, and 4, or 6, 7, and 8.

Pick Six: Pick the winners of races no. 3 through no. 8 and you win or share in 75% of the day's pool. The consolation payoff, 25% of each day's pool (not including carry-over), is returned to bettors who have picked five winners of the six designated races. On any day that no bettor selects all six winners, 75% of the pool is held over and added to the next day's Pick Six pool and 25% of the pool (not including carry-over) will be returned to a bettor or bettors who pick the highest number of winners of the six designated races.

Parlay Wager: A way to roll over winnings from one race into a bet on subsequent races. This is a convenience only since the payoff is the same as if the bets were placed individually. Using a parlay betting slip, combine at least two races, to a maximum of six races. The slip can contain any combination of win, place or show wagers.

BELMONT ESSENTIALS

Belmont Park Race Track is located in Elmont, Long Island (☎ 718/641-4700). The season runs from May until late July, shuts down until early September, and then runs through mid-October.

Getting to the Track   By car, take the Cross Island Expressway to exit 26D. The **Long Island Rail Road** (☎ 718/217-5477) offers a round-trip rail package from Penn Station that includes $1 off the price of admission to the racetrack.

Track Hours and Admission   The track is open every day except Monday and Tuesday (on holiday weekends there is racing Monday, and Tuesday and Wednesday are dark). Doors open at 11am and the races begin at 1pm, with the last race at approximately 5pm. Admission is $4 for the clubhouse, $2 for the grandstand (seniors get a $1 discount).

Mansions of Long Island's Gold Coast

by Peter Marks

Peering out the car window at palaces protected by ornate, wrought-iron gates, pointing out homes hidden in manicured forests of linden and copper beech trees, Paul Mateyunas was in his glory. Here he was, doing what he loved best, leading a spur-of-the-moment safari into the heart of mansion country, a legendary land from the era when Long Island was still the private preserve of the very rich.

As the car criss-crossed the country lanes, the names of the wealthy families that once dominated the landscape rolled off Mr. Mateyunas's tongue: Here lived the Whitneys and Phippses; there the Vanderbilts and Du Ponts. His anecdotes were about vast fortunes and unfathomable expenses, about famous house guests and lavish parties and eccentric millionaires who built closets as big as duplexes and lay down each night on what once had been Napoleon's bed.

Mr. Mateyunas could not be described as to the manner born; his family estate is a split-level in Northport, Long Island. But he adores the great houses of Long Island's Gold Coast as if he had grown up in one, a passion stirred in him at the age of 8, when his parents took him to a concert in an amphitheater amid the ruins of a mansion in Lloyd Harbor, where he realized for the first time that not everyone on the Island grew up on a quarter-acre lot.

"It wasn't like from a purely materialistic view," said Mr. Mateyunas, a college student who during high school worked part-time as a guide in the Vanderbilt mansion in Centerport, an elegant, Spanish-style house on Long Island Sound that is now a museum run by Suffolk County. "It became an appreciation of the time period, the etiquette, the manners. It isn't the money; it's the beauty of what the money did."

During the first 40 years of this century, Long Island was not America's quintessential suburb. It was America's Monte Carlo, a place where the rich came to see, be seen, and spend exorbitant amounts of money. Mostly what they spent it on were their sprawling estates, mansions they built to impress each other and resemble the houses of the European nobility they sought to emulate. Hundreds of captains of industry and commerce, and even some from the world of entertainment, kept an estate here at one time or another, from J. P. Morgan to F. W. Woolworth, from Lewis C. Tiffany to Henri Bendel. Eddie Cantor, for a short time, maintained a small mansion in Great Neck. William Randolph Hearst had a huge one in Sands Point, but not as huge as the even grander palace, San Simeon, he built in northern California.

At its height, there were some 600 to 700 mansions on Long Island's Gold Coast, a roughly 30-mile-long stretch of the North Shore, from Great Neck to Eatons Neck. Many of them are gone, destroyed in fires, demolished by families unable to afford their upkeep, or sold off and subdivided by housing developers. Today, of the 200 to 300 still standing, about half are privately owned, and most of the others have been converted for use as schools, college buildings, religious retreat houses, and country clubs.

And then there are a handful of estates that are open to the public, a few extraordinary homes that give the ordinary wage earner of today the chance to gawk at the excesses the rich enjoyed, in the years before income taxes and the Depression made such splendor less fashionable— and less affordable. Filled with original artwork and furnishings, the treasures their owners collected on European jaunts, or commissioned from the world's leading artists and artisans, the estates are vestiges of a Long Island that has been crowded out by parkways and subdivisions. They are remnants of that Lost Island, the moneyed haven immortalized by F. Scott Fitzgerald in *The Great Gatsby*.

Robert MacKay, director of the Society for the Preservation of Long Island Antiquities, said Long Island truly was mansion central,

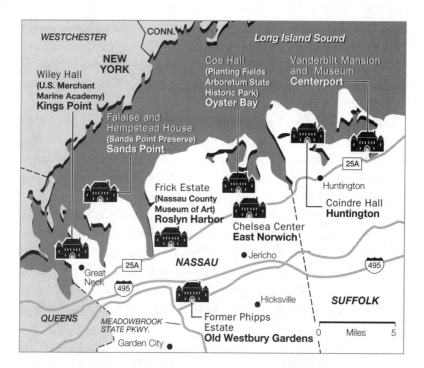

the place where the rich indulged their passion for play. "There is little question that though the Hudson Valley was important earlier, and Newport has had more visibility, more country houses were built on Long Island, and in greater concentrations, than in any other part of the country," he explained. "It was clearly their national resort."

Despite the efforts by Mr. MacKay's organization and other preservation groups, many of the old houses have not been saved, an indication, perhaps, of Long Islanders' ambivalence toward the Island's haughty roots. But even so, a few of the families managed to insure the survival of their houses by leaving them to local governments, or endowing non-profit boards to run them. Several others that remain in private hands are accessible only by special arrangement, like Oheka, the Cold Spring Harbor castle built by Otto Kahn, the German-born financier. The house, the second-largest private residence in the nation, is no longer inhabited, but it has been rented for weddings or as a movie location.

Some of the houses open to the public, like Falaise, the former estate of Harry Guggenheim, a philanthropist whose uncle Solomon built the Guggenheim Museum in Manhattan, are so meticulously preserved that they look as if the family might return in a couple of hours. In the carport of the house, which is perched on a cliff overlooking Long Island Sound, Guggenheim's purple Cadillac is parked next to a station wagon once owned by his great friend and frequent guest Charles A. Lindbergh. Meanwhile, the table in the dining room remains set with the dinner service Guggenheim used when he served as Ambassador to Cuba, and the cabinets in the trophy room remain filled with loving cups, including one from the 1953 Kentucky Derby, which was won by his thoroughbred Dark Star.

"He had an affinity for Normandy," Adele Wall said as she escorted a visitor around the house, where she has been a volunteer tour guide for more than 20 years. It was an affinity he could afford to explore, for the Norman-style mansion appears to have been spirited whole from the French countryside. Set into the walls of the lower foyer are medieval friezes taken from the wall of a municipal building, somewhere in France.

Mrs. Wall, who brought up a family just off the grounds of the estate, in Sands Point, says that when Guggenheim left the house to Nassau County upon his death in 1971, he also left precise details about how his house should be shown, right down to the placement of his favorite photographs on a table in the living room, the direction through the house that tour guides should take and the seasonal sequence of plantings around the swimming pool: blue and white lilies in the spring, followed by orange enchantment lilies, white and yellow chrysanthemums, and, in the fall, bronze and yellow chrysanthemums.

It is this kind of obsession with detail that can make the exploration of the homes so enthralling. There is always something more to see, whether it is a camouflaged doorway in the library, or a stuffed Indian tiger in the foyer.

"I just couldn't believe people lived like that," said Ruth Katz, a mortgage broker from Manhattan who grew up in Great Neck. Several years ago, she started visiting the homes that were open and got so hooked that she began to compose maps of the Gold Coast, trying to identify the precise whereabouts of houses she had read about but could not get into. Even the ruins of old homes long gone have become a source of mystery and detective work.

"We used to drive by this one place in Sands Point when we were little, and my father would say, 'A convent was here,'" Ms. Katz recalled, laughing. "He didn't know! No, a convent wasn't here; William Randolph Hearst was here!"

The wealthy came to Long Island in the early part of the century because it was convenient to New York City, where many maintained their primary homes. "For reasons of business and social discourse, America's wealth had to be in New York," said Mr. MacKay. "But it was also wound up with a new lifestyle. Whereas the Victorian wealthy had stayed in the city year-round, venturing out only to stay in hotels, by the turn of the century you had the great explosion in American recreation. It is here on Long Island that we see the development of golf, with the first country club in the country."

Once they arrived, the families, spending anywhere from several hundred thousand dollars to $5 million—fortunes at the time—created the castles of their fantasies. They hired renowned architects like Stanford White and the New York firm of Delano & Aldrich to build in the style of French chateaus and Italian villas and English country houses. They erected stables and polo fields, rose gardens and golf courses. They mounted priceless European sculptures on outside walls, and priceless Flemish tapestries on the interior. They experimented with crude forms of air-conditioning: In the home of William K. Vanderbilt, electric fans blew cool air off blocks of ice in the basement that circulated through indoor pipes.

The displays of wealth and pedigree were so ostentatious they sometimes bordered on self-parody. In 1924, for instance, *The New York Times* reported that a party for the Prince of Wales at Harbor Hill, a Roslyn Harbor estate, was attended by 1,200 guests, including people with such fanciful titles as the Duke and Duchess of Penaranda and the Marquis de Coquille.

And as if his 127-room chateau, Oheka, would not stand out enough, Kahn employed an army of laborers for two years to build a mountain on his estate: He wanted the castle to sit upon the highest point on Long Island. (Despite the Herculean effort, it doesn't.)

Many of the estates became the families' retreats during the spring and fall, part of an annual cycle of migration from one palatial abode to another. In the former home of John S. Phipps that is now called Old Westbury Gardens, visitors are provided as authentic a look at an English country house as the Guggenheims provided for the French. Phipps built the house after the turn of the century for his English wife, Margarita Grace, of the famous shipping family.

The house is grand and the gardens, grander. It is nearly impossible to believe that just beyond the walled garden of tulips and the trellises draped with wisteria and the tiny thatched English cottage—a gift from Phipps to his daughter, Peggy, on her 10th birthday—lies the Long Island Expressway. The houses, in fact, remain so peripheral to daily life on Long Island that many of its inhabitants barely know they are there. Orin Z. Finkle, an accountant who has long had an amateur's interest in architecture, has lived within a few miles of the estates since the 1950s. But it was not until about 1980, when he was given a book, *The Mansions of Long Island's Gold Coast* (Rizzoli International Publications), that he realized the scope of the legacy that had been left.

"For three months, I kept that book on my night table and looked at it every night before I went to bed," he said. The book set Mr. Finkle on a mission to catalogue the houses, and to collect old magazines and post cards from the early 1900s that mentioned the estates. Over the years, he, like Mr. Mateyunas, elevated house hunting to an art, befriending owners of many of the remaining estates, and even taking others on private tours of some of them.

"What struck me was their beauty; it was like looking at a painting or a work of art," Mr. Finkle said. "It was so different from what I knew. I had grown up in a typical development house in Carle Place. Every time I would go to one of the houses, I would feel so in awe."

It is that feeling that keeps Mr. Finkle going, the same feeling that has consumed Mr. Mateyunas. Most visitors may be able to leave the houses at the end of a tour, but these two never really do.

Mr. Mateyunas, in fact, even took a piece of one home with him: He bought a chandelier that once hung in the Mill Neck home of Alice Tully at an antiques store.

It now sits, in a box, in his den.

Gold Coast Essentials

GETTING THERE

All of the mansions listed below are accessible by car from the Long Island Expressway, or by the **Long Island Rail Road** (☎ 718/217-5477); taxis are available at the train station.

VISITING THE MANSIONS

Here is a listing of mansions open to the public on the Gold Coast of Long Island that are mentioned in the accompanying article.

Chelsea Center, Rte. 25A, East Norwich (☎ 516/571-8550). Open Wednesday through Friday noon to 4pm; closed Saturday, Sunday, and major holidays. Admission by donation.

Coe Hall (part of Planting Fields Arboretum State Historic Park), Planting Fields Rd. (at Chicken Valley Rd.), Oyster Bay (☎ 516/922-0479). Open April through September, daily 12:30 to 3:30pm; closed on major holidays. Admission and house tour $3.50, $2 for seniors, $1 for children 7 to 12, free for children under 7. Parking $4.

Coindre Hall (site of Museum of Long Island's Gold Coast), at the end of Brown's Rd., Huntington (☎ 516/423-4369 or 516/424-8230). Open Tuesday, Wednesday, and Friday 1pm to 4pm, or by appointment; closed major holidays. Admission by donation.

Falaise (the former Guggenheim estate), Sands Point Preserve, 95 Middleneck Rd., Sands Point (☎ 516/571-7900). Open May through October, Wednesday through Sunday noon to 3pm. Admission $4, $3 for seniors; children under 10 not admitted.

Frick Estate, Nassau County Museum of Art, Rte. 25A (west of Northern Blvd.), Roslyn Harbor (☎ 516/484-9337 or 516/484-9338). Open Tuesday through Sunday 11am to 5pm; closed Memorial Day. Admission $4, $3 for seniors, $2 for students, free for children 12 and under.

Old Westbury Gardens (the former Phipps Estate), 71 Old Westbury Rd., Old Westbury (☎ 516/333-0048). Open from the last weekend in April to mid-December, Wednesday through Monday 10am to 5pm; closed Tuesday and Thanksgiving Day. For the gardens alone, admission is $6, $4 for seniors, $3 for children 6 to 12; admission to the house and gardens is $10, $7 for seniors, $6 for children 6 to 12; admission is free for children under 6 and members of Old Westbury Gardens.

Vanderbilt Mansion and Museum, 180 Little Neck Rd., Centerport (☎ 516/854-5555). Open Tuesday through Friday noon to 4pm, Saturday and Sunday noon to 5pm (from June 27 through Labor Day, Tuesday through Sunday 10am to 5pm); closed most Mondays (except Memorial Day, open noon to 5pm) and Christmas, New Year's, and Thanksgiving days. Admission (including grounds and house tour) $8, $6 for students and seniors, $4 for children under 12; add $2 for sky show in the planetarium.

Wiley Hall (United States Merchant Marine Academy; former home of Walter P. Chrysler), at the foot of Steamboat Rd., Kings Point (☎ 516/773-5527). Open daily 9am to 5pm; closed July and federal holidays. Admission free.

FLY-FISHING AT CONNETQUOT RIVER STATE PARK

by Patricia Leigh Brown

EVERY ONCE IN A WHILE, WHEN THE religion and incense hawkers around Times Square become too much and the unmuffled scent of New York City shish kebob threatens to cling to the clothes forever, I do what so many other urban anglers do. I flee. I head out to a dream of a stream, to a place in Suffolk County, Long Island, that is filled with gentle forest creatures, a bewitching green refuge that feels like a scene out of *Bambi* (if you ignore the ticks).

Anglers, not unlike criminals, tend to return to the place where they've caught fish. For me, that place is (usually) the Connetquot River State Park Preserve in Oakdale, a crystalline spring-fed stream less than an hour-and-a-half drive from the city.

Well, let's be honest. I don't always catch fish. As a Mother's Day present, my husband drove me to the Connetquot recently so that I could have a few blissful hours to myself on the stream. It had been a year and a half since I'd done any fly-fishing. With raindrops pelting down, making thousands of little dimples on the water, it was difficult to see any trout rising. The temperature was numbing, the casts wobbly. The pathetic sight of a new working mother desperately flailing the water with stiff fingers in her three hours of free time resembled Lucy Ricardo in the chocolate factory, not Bambi.

But there have been other days, glorious days. Spring days, when the river's rush and the splash of a muskrat's tail were the only sounds, and the cool clear water of the Connetquot (pronounced kuh-*net*-kwat, a Wingan-Hauppaug Indian term for "wide" or "great" river) flowed into the spirit like a life force.

The experience of fishing the Connetquot (fly-fishing only, with barbless hooks please) really begins at the parking lot. It is the cement-paved gathering of the brethren, whose raised car trunks reveal waders, fishing rods, stream thermometers, and a goop known as "floatant." To do any fly-fishing at the Connetquot, which operates on the British "beat" system by reservation only, it is necessary to book one week in advance. The more fanatical anglers may be spotted the night before February 1—the official opening day here—sleeping in their cars overnight for the privilege of fishing at the crack of dawn.

In the parking lot, the latest intelligence is exchanged on stream conditions and what kind of lures the fish seem to be "taking" that day. But not too much intelligence. One reason fishing vests seem to contain so many pockets is that they are loaded with secrets, locked in Velcro.

It is about a mile's hike from the parking lot to the stream, and, despite the unwieldiness of walking in waders, it's like walking into a little bit of heaven. The welcoming committee includes wild turkeys, peacocks, and deer. The preserve contains about 200 species of birds, and a delicate ecosystem that captures some of the way Long Island used to be, before the Long Island Expressway, octoplexes, and IKEA. The water is cool and clear, perfect for trout. The spring-fed stream percolates through sand and gravel—sand being one of nature's most efficient filters, a cosmic Melitta.

Dreaming of trout, I walked past rambling old cedar-shingle club houses, their windowsills painted a deep forest green. Some of these buildings, including an old gristmill on the river, were erected by the South-Side Sportsmen's Club of Long Island, an "assembly of good fellows" who purchased the property in 1865.

What is now known simply as "the Connetquot" was the site of Snedecors Hotel, a stagecoach stop built by Eliphalat Snedecor, known as Eli, a farmer. Snedecors was the watering hole of choice for what is now the town of Islip, within shooting distance (literally) of choice hunting and fishing grounds.

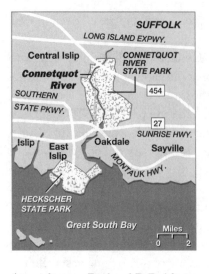

In 1865, a group of sportsmen who were having trouble booking rooms at the inn decided to purchase it and the 300-acre family farm for $42,000 from Obadiah Snedecor, known as Obie, Eli's son. The South-Side Club was a place for monied gentlemen bearing names like Bayard and Bradish to meet, fish, and shoot. Its members included many illustrious sportsmen, including Ulysses S. Grant and Charles L. Tiffany, the jeweler.

According to Richard P. Baldwin, a Patchogue historian, on November 12, 1842, John Delmonico, the famed New York City restaurateur, supposedly died of apoplexy at the edge of the stream. It was rumored he had died of "buck" or "deer" fever, an affliction of hunters overly excited by the sight of game.

I have an inkling of what buck fever was like. Standing in the water, seeing a lone shadow suddenly lurching—a trout!—I understand apoplexy. Despite X-rays, vaccinations, and other medical miracles, I know for a fact that a girl can die of trout fever.

Among anglers, the Connetquot is known to harbor some really big fish. You can see them (unfortunately, they can see you). Part of the reason there are so many big fish here is that the preserve, now 3,400 acres, which was designated in 1987 as the first state park preserve in New York, contains a fish hatchery owned and administered by the state and the Long Island State Park and Recreation Commission. Every year, says Gilbert Bergen, the park manager, about 300,000 brook trout eggs, 280,000 rainbow trout eggs, and between 280,000 and 300,000 brown trout eggs are raised, about a quarter of them to adult size, up to three pounds or more.

Like parents learning Lamaze, Mr. Bergen and his crew are unusual in their commitment to rearing the trout as "naturally" as possible, using the river's own flow to nurture them. Once or twice a week they release them, 9- to 12-inch yearlings up to 2- to 3-pound oldsters. Although there is no proof, the prevailing theory is that some of these larger trout make their way through the river to the saltwater of the Great South Bay and then return. The evidence, Mr. Bergen says, is that the fish come back bright and rich and silvery, as if they've just come back from trout Acapulco.

My favorite place to fish is a specific stretch—I won't divulge its location—a long, shallow run of water where delicate water starworts, cresslike plants, decorate the underwater landscape like a wreath.

The Connetquot does not possess the weighty history of the Beaverkill and some other fabled regional angling spots (oh, lack of storied anglers—what a liberating thing you are!). But it does possess the beat system. The beat system, in which a certain spot on the river is reserved for a certain angler, is a holdover from European feudalism, according to the angling historian Ernest Schwiebert. Fishing rights were part of property rights, the fish in private waters part of the King's game.

At Connetquot, though, the beat system is a bastion of democracy. It enables the angler to reserve his or her own spot on a first-come-first-served basis (some beats are accessible to those with physical disabilities). All access to the preserve, be it for hiking or fishing, is by reservation only. It is a means of environmental conservation, protecting the park and the trout from being overrun, otherwise known as "opening day on the Beaverkill" syndrome. For a novice, the privacy

---

GETTING YOURSELF A FISHING LICENSE

In addition to a fishing license, some parks also require anglers to have daily fishing or parking permits, which are issued at the sites themselves. For more information, call the individual site (see "Essentials," below).

In New York   New York state fishing licenses are required for freshwater fishing and can be obtained at county clerk offices and sporting-goods stores. A New York state fishing license costs $14 for state residents, $35 for nonresidents. For information, call ☎ 518/457-3521.

In New Jersey   In New Jersey, fishing licenses are $16.50 for state residents, plus $7.75 for a trout stamp; if you're a nonresident, expect to pay $25.25, plus $15.50 for a trout stamp. For information, call ☎ 609/292-2965.

In Connecticut   Connecticut fishing licenses are $15 for residents, $25 for nonresidents. For information, call ☎ 860/424-3105.

is a godsend: You can make ridiculous casts into hard-fighting bushes and nobody will see you do it.

On that woeful rainy Mother's Day, even the faint whiff of skunk after a long winter in the city was restorative. "Have you tried a woolly bugger?" said an acquaintance, taking pity on my failures and trying to be helpful.

So I tried the woolly buggers, long black feathery "streamers" meant to resemble leeches. They did yield about 10 "hits," all of which I managed to miss. The trout began to feel like errant children. "Happy Mother's Day, sucker," they bubbled. "Nyah, nyah, nyah, nyah, nyah." My acquaintance, a seasoned angler, sensed my frustration and was moved to charity. Having caught and kept two monstrous trout in his first hour of fishing, he offered to give them to me (for him there were more where that came from; the same could not be said for me). These trout were so big that when I put them in my creel, they thrashed so hard that the creel started bouncing down the trail.

I put aside my pride (it was Mother's Day, after all) and accepted his noble offer. For the next week, we dined like kings, trout on the grill, our spirits spring fed like the stream.

WHERE TO CAST YOUR LINE: FISHING ESSENTIALS

Here is a listing of some state and Federal parks in the New York metropolitan area where fresh- and saltwater fishing is permitted.

NEW YORK

QUEENS

Fort Tilden/Breezy Point, Gateway National Park, Flatbush Ave. at Marine Park Bridge, Rockaway (☎ 718/318-4300 or 718/338-3799). Twenty-four-hour saltwater fishing is allowed daily. A $25 season parking permit is needed for fishing; a driver's license, car registration, a fishing rod more than seven feet long, and a reel are required to obtain a permit. The permit can be obtained at Fort Tilden, Floyd Bennett Field, or Breezy Point.

WESTCHESTER COUNTY

Franklin Delano Roosevelt State Park, Taconic State Pkwy. at Rte. 202, Yorktown (☎ 914/245-4434). Boat fishing allowed from dawn to dusk. Boat rentals, available from 8am to 6pm, are $4 an hour or $20 per day. New York state license required; seasonal fishing permits for boat owners are $15. May 10 through September 5, daily parking fee is $4; September 6 through October 13, parking is $4 on weekend days, free on weekdays.

Rockefeller State Park Preserve, Rte. 17, Pocantico Hills, Mount Pleasant (☎ 914/631-1470). Shore fishing mid-June through the end of November with lures or worms only allowed daily from 7am to dusk. No permit required in addition to your New York state fishing license. Parking is $4 per day.

LONG ISLAND

Caleb Smith State Park, Jericho Tpk., Smithtown (☎ 516/265-1054). Season runs April 1 through October 15. Daily permits for fly-fishing are available, at $15, for 8 river and 5 pond sites. There are two daily sessions, from 7 to 11am and 11:30am to 3:30pm; Friday through Sunday there is a third session 4pm to sunset. New York state fishing license required. Reservations can be made up to two weeks in advance.

Captree State Park, Robert Moses Causeway, Babylon (☎ 516/669-0449). Surf-cast fishing daily from dawn to dusk. No permit or state license necessary. Parking $4.

Caumsett State Park, W. Neck Rd., Huntington (☎ 516/423-1770). Season runs April 1 through December 31. One-day parking permits, at $4, are issued Monday through Friday 8am to 1pm for same-day saltwater fishing from 8am to 4pm.

Connetquot River State Park Preserve, Rte. 27, Oakdale (☎ 516/581-1005). Season runs February 1 through October 15. Beginning April 1, daily permits for 32 fly-fishing sites are available at $15, for any of three daily sessions, from 7 to 11am, noon to 4pm, and 5pm to sunset. Prior to April 1, there are two daily sessions, from 8am to noon and from noon to 4pm, during which caught fish have to be returned to the water. Closed Monday during fishing season; closed Monday and Tuesday prior to April 1 and after October 15. New York state fishing license required. Reservations are required. Parking $4.

Jones Beach State Park, Meadowbrook Pkwy, Wantaugh (☎ 516/785-1600). April 1 through December 31, saltwater fishing daily from dawn to dusk. No state license required. One-day parking fee $5 is charged daily from Memorial Day through Labor Day, weekends only from May 3 through Memorial Day and Labor Day through October.

NEW JERSEY

Gateway National Recreation Area, Sandy Hook Unit, off State Hwy. 36, Sandy Hook (☎ 908/872-0115). Saltwater fishing daily at designated beach and bay areas, or from sunset to sunrise along the entire beach and bay at any time except Memorial Day through Labor Day, when fishing is not permitted on lifeguarded beaches. No permit or state license is necessary for day fishing. A $25 permit, good for the year, is required for night fishing, and can be picked up at the National Park Rangers Station. Beach parking from Memorial Day through Labor Day is $4 on weekdays, $5 on weekends and holidays; free parking at other times.

CONNECTICUT

Bigelow Hollow State Park, Rte. 171, Union (☎ 860/928-9200). From April through February, freshwater fishing daily, 24 hours; closed March. State fishing license required. Parking from Memorial Day through Labor Day, weekends and holidays $5 for Connecticut residents, $8 for nonresidents; free parking on weekdays, except holidays.

Burr Pond State Park, 385 Burr Mountain Rd. (at Winstead Rd.), Torrington (☎ 860/482-1817). Year-round freshwater fishing daily, 8am to sunset; the park is closed to fishing for a short time during the spring to allow for the stocking of trout. State fishing license required. Parking on weekends, $5 for Connecticut residents, $8 for nonresidents; weekdays, $4 for residents, $5 for nonresidents.

Day Pond State Park, Rte. 149, Westchester (☎ 860/526-2336). Year-round freshwater fishing daily, 8am to sunset. Connecticut state fishing license required. Parking on weekends and holidays, $5 for Connecticut residents, $8 for nonresidents; free parking on weekdays.

Hammanasett Beach State Park, Hammanasett Connector, exit 62 off I-95, Madison (☎ 860/245-2785). From mid-May through Labor Day, saltwater fishing from Meigs Point Jetty daily, 24 hours; free permits, issued after 5pm, are necessary for night fishing. From Labor Day through mid-May, fishing is allowed 9am to sunset. No state license or permit required for day fishing. Parking from Memorial Day through Labor Day, $5 weekdays and $7 on weekends and holidays for Connecticut residents; $8 weekdays and $12 on weekends for nonresidents. Parking from mid-April through Memorial Day and Labor Day to end of September, weekends $5 for residents and nonresidents; free parking on weekdays.

Kent Falls State Park, Rte. 7, Kent (☎ 860/927-3238). From April through December, freshwater fishing daily 8am to sunset. Connecticut state fishing license required. Parking from May through October, weekends and holidays $5 for Connecticut residents, $8 for nonresidents; free parking year-round on weekdays.

Lake Waramaug State Park, Lake Waramaug Rd., New Preston (☎ 860/868-2592). Year-round freshwater fishing daily 8am to sunset; no boat launch available. State fishing license required. Parking from Memorial Day to Labor Day, weekends and holidays $5 for Connecticut residents, $8 nonresidents; free parking year-round on weekdays.

Macedonia Brook, Macedonia Brook Rd., Kent (☎ 860/927-3238). From mid-April through December, freshwater fishing in a state-stocked brook daily, 8am to sunset. Connecticut state fishing license required. Free parking.

Mashamoquet Brook State Park, Rte. 44, Pomfret (☎ 860/928-6121). From mid-April through March, freshwater fishing daily 8am to sunset; the park is closed to fishing from March through mid-April while the water is stocked with fish. Connecticut state fishing license required. Parking from Memorial Day through Labor Day, weekends and holidays $5 for Connecticut residents, $8 for nonresidents; free parking year-round on weekdays.

FIRE ISLAND: FOR FAMILIES, TOO

by Ralph Blumenthal

I T'S A BAREFOOT SOCIETY, CAR-FREE and carefree, but as long as anyone can remember, Fire Island, the skinny sandspit stretched along the underside of Long Island, has had its distinctive hierarchy. At the top are the natives, flinty souls who live year-round on the 32-mile-long barrier island between the end of Robert Moses State Park and Moriches Inlet, where the Hamptons begin. The natives, it is said, look down on the homeowners and other summer folk who seasonally throng the roughly two dozen communities. The homeowners turn up their noses at the renters. The renters disdain the groupers who chip in for housing shares. And all feel superior to the day-trippers who sail in on the morning ferries and sail out again in the evening.

Which left us somewhere near the bottom—hotel guests on Fire Island. Yes, there are hotels on Fire Island. No, you wouldn't generally pick them over a house. But between a hotel and nothing, the choice was clear. For five days, my wife and I and our two girls sampled the many delights of New York's quasi Key West with its own rich social and cultural history. We breathed the same fresh salt air and patronized the same restaurants and shops as any third-generation islander. We splashed in the same roiling surf, hunted for the same horseshoe crabs and shells on long stretches of deserted beach, strolled and bicycled the same few blocks between the bay and beach, and took the same water taxis to the same outlying communities. And we felt entirely welcome. Indeed, there is probably only one restrictive community, Point O'Woods, where outsiders, whether natives or off-islanders, may get the cold shoulder; but even here we carried out a beach-based incursion without incident.

Yet a word of caution. To book a hotel on Fire Island on a summer weekend is to cast one's fate not to the winds but the singles. A commune of wildly celebrating youth in a Fire Island group house can be noisy, but when the party is compressed into a thin-walled hotel room, the disruption can be truly hellish, as we found out on our last night in Ocean Bay Park. Still, some hotel managements are laxer than others. And Friday and Saturday nights are definitely wilder; weekdays can be positively idyllic.

The first thing many new visitors want to know is where the name Fire Island comes from. The truth is, nobody knows. Some have linked it to the signal fires of whalers or wreckers who tried to lure ships ashore for plunder, or to the onetime fiery stands of poison ivy. Others say it grew out of a misreading on early Dutch maps of vier, or four, islands. Either way, the name, accurately enough, evokes blissful summer vistas of burning sands and blazing sun as well as the constant peril of fire.

Resort development began in the 1890s with the establishment of a Chautauqua Assembly, a movement for Christian betterment through learning and the arts, in what became Point O'Woods. In the early 1900s, just to the west, developers bought up tracts and began selling vacation lots to Brooklynites and other confined city folk for what became the village of Ocean Beach, Fire Island's de facto capital. Served by growing ferry links across Great South Bay, birds of a feather flocked to like-minded communities: boat owners to Saltaire, fishery workers to Seaview, casino lovers to Ocean Bay Park, families to Kismet. Homosexuals driven from other communities found a welcome in Cherry Grove, creating one of the earliest centers of gay life in the nation.

Stars of the Broadway stage, stalwarts of the Algonquin Round Table, artists, bohemians, and assorted hangers-on soon found their way to the quirky seasonal salons of Fire Island, where the politics were often decidedly leftist, and a Stalinist group house might well blackball an applicant rumored to be a Trotskyite. Irving Berlin, Fanny Brice, Clifford Odets, Truman Capote, Tennessee Williams, Jimmy Durante, Woody Allen, Lee Strasberg, and Marilyn Monroe all made their way there, as did Mel Brooks and Carl Reiner, who honed their

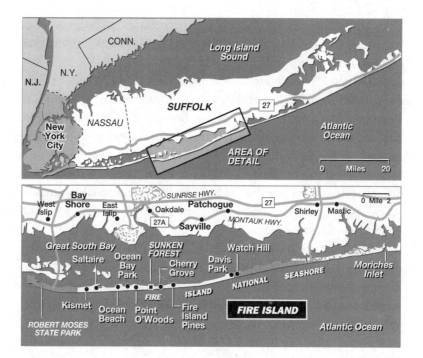

"2,000-Year-Old Man" routine on dinner audiences. And everyone mobilized in the early 1960s to thwart Robert Moses's plan to build an access road through Fire Island. (*Smile, You're on Fire Island,* a history of the island with photographs by Arthur Hawkins, published by Photo News Long Island of Bethpage, Long Island, is available for $19.95 at the Ocean Beach Historical Society on Bayview Walk.)

My own memories of Fire Island go back to the 1940s when, as a child, I stayed with friends in an Ocean Beach cottage lighted by kerosene lamps. The icebox was indeed cooled by a block of ice, hauled from the market in a red wagon. And the ferry passed a house still sunk in the water from the devastating 1938 hurricane.

Amazingly, as I found again on our most recent trip, Fire Island has changed little from those days except perhaps for the now ubiquitous deer that calmly feast on bushes and overturned trash bins as you pass. The concrete walks (rustically wooden in some communities) are still lined with old, whimsically named cedar-shingled cottages hemmed in by pines and bayberry. The shops and restaurants prettily arrayed around

Ocean Beach's mini-green may have changed names but little else. Feet, wagon, bicycle, and boat (golf carts and trucks for contractors and provisioners) are still the only means of transportation.

Reaching Fire Island from Manhattan is a kind of three- or four-corner shot requiring connections to and from the Long Island Rail Road or a jitney to the ferries at Bay Shore, Sayville, or Patchogue. You can also drive your own car, at the cost of daily charges in a parking field at the ferry dock. We reserved four seats at $15 each on a Tommy's Taxi van that left from 53rd Street and Second Avenue and delivered us an hour later to the Bay Shore ferry terminal, where $38 purchased round-trip ferry tickets (half-price for our five-year-old) to and from Ocean Beach.

I had reserved two kitchenette units for two weekday nights at a randomly selected hotel called Clegg's, which turned out to be directly across from the ferry dock (not that anything in Ocean Beach is more than a few steps from anything else). As we lugged our bags up a narrow staircase past peeling walls, I thought the place resembled an old sailor's rooming house. Indeed, we learned, it was built in the 1920s by the grandfather of the current proprietor.

Our units each came with two beds, private bathroom with shower, and a stove, sink, and refrigerator. The furnishings of table, captain chairs, chest of drawers, and makeshift closet were more Salvation Army than the Ritz, but clean if not immaculate. Apartment C faced the bay and overlooked tennis and basketball courts. A cool sea breeze from two exposures sent the blinds slapping, rendering the air conditioner superfluous. One of the bed blankets bore a cigarette burn hole. Apartment A, which our daughters shared, was even larger but with one exposure. There were four other apartments with baths, and 13 smaller rooms that shared four skylit bath and shower rooms.

Our youngish hosts, Tyler Clegg Sterck and his wife, Jeanne, threw in use of beach chairs and a sun umbrella and even two balloon-tire bicycles that could be ridden only outside Ocean Beach. (Bike riding within the village is banned in the summer season, one of many prohibitions that have earned the community a reputation as "The Land of No.") What the hotel did not provide, however, was daily room cleaning.

Still, comparing our quarters later with other accommodations in Ocean Beach, we did not do badly. The Houser Hotel, another 1920s fixture on the bay, over a popular bar and Chinese restaurant, has a dozen small rooms with sinks and toilets but shared shower rooms in the hall. The Ocean Beach Inn on Bay Walk, its name notwithstanding, has 20 motel-style rooms with private baths, also over a busy bar and restaurant.

We were taken with one little gem: the Four Seasons Bed and Breakfast on Dehnhoff Walk, a health-food–oriented lodge of eight rooms with gleaming polyurethaned wood floors, bright curtains, and plump inviting quilts on the beds. Here, too, however, the rooms are without private baths, and there are no provisions for children. Otherwise, hospitality reigned: rooms come with breakfast and a sumptuous afternoon tea, cold juice drinks for the taking, a patio stocked with magazines, and use of bicycles, fishing tackle, and a backyard gas barbecue.

Another darling guest house, Place in the Sun, on Surfview Walk halfway between bay and beach, also caught our eye. Open to nonsmokers only, it has a large skylit living room paneled in knotty pine and five rooms with two shared baths plus an outdoor shower and sauna.

Otherwise, it seemed, the pickings in Ocean Beach were slim: isolated rooms or the occasional rooming house with barrackslike accommodations and little privacy or little sanitation or neither.

When it comes to dining, Ocean Beach offers the widest selection on Fire Island. We had a pleasant alfresco lunch at Maguires on the bay, where the time waiting for your food can be whiled away with your children at the adjacent community playground and sandpit. Our younger daughter, Sophie, made the swings and climbing apparatus her favorite Fire Island destination.

We had another fine waterside seafood dinner at Matthew's on the bay, and a pleasant dinner celebrating the 17th birthday of our elder daughter, Anna, at the Island Mermaid by the ferry dock, where the setting sun reflecting blindingly in the restaurant mirrors kept us rearranging our seats like musical chairs.

We also enjoyed the Albatross, with its patio tables affording a lovely view of the passing scene in the village center, and the funky Sun and Moon Cafe across the mall. For breakfast, we favored Rachel's a few steps away, a clean, well-lighted place of knotty pine hung with photographs of Fire Island in the snow. One morning, Sophie stared toward the back and proudly read aloud, "Birthday room, parties only." I did a double take. What the sign said was: BATHROOM. PATRONS ONLY.

What you don't want to do in Ocean Beach is eat takeout with a knife and fork on the walks, another no-no, along with drinking anything at all on the walks. Because of the strict ban on consuming alcoholic beverages outside homes, bars, and restaurants, drinking from open containers, even a soda can or pop bottle, is suspect, a ticketable offense likely to land you in village court in front of a decidedly unsympathetic judge.

A sign of the times hangs at the bay bathing beach adjoining the playground: NO FACILITIES PROVIDED. NO SWIMMING BEYOND FLOATS. NO FOOD OR DRINKS. NO DOGS ALLOWED. NO DISROBING. NO RADIOS WITHOUT EARPHONES. NO BALL PLAYING OR FRISBEES. Actually, veterans like Ildiko Trien, executive editor of *The Fire Island News*, the scrappy local paper, say that things have relaxed significantly from the days when Ocean Beach was notorious for ticketing visitors so bold as to eat a chocolate chip cookie in public.

For a change of scene one afternoon, we left the girls behind and telephoned South Bay Water Taxi for a 20-minute wave-tossed ride east to Fire Island Pines, a chic community where straight and gay society intersect and Elizabeth Taylor and Richard Burton, Hedy Lamarr, Barbra Streisand, Montgomery Clift, Marlene Dietrich, and Rock Hudson have been among the many celebrity visitors. A sign by the dock advised: GROUP THERAPY 5PM. EVERYONE MUST ATTEND.

The blue-and-turquoise-balconied Botel overlooks the Italianate harbor, but except for top-floor suites that sleep four, rooms share bathrooms and offer little in the way of amenities. We meandered the wooden walkways, ogling some extraordinary mansions, and sipped banana daiquiris on the terrace of the Botel's Blue Whale, where the menu lists a "Hedda Cheddar Burger," a "Le Fifi Burger," and a "Midnight

Blue Burger." Next door, the Pines Pantry is amazingly well provisioned, stocking necessities from margarita salt to live or fresh-cooked lobsters.

We had hoped to stop at another Fire Island landmark on the way back, the Belvedere in Cherry Grove, but the water taxi was overbooked and it became too late. As it turned out, we probably would have been denied entry anyway. The "clothing optional" resort for gay men says it does not admit sightseers. I had to content myself with a description from *The Fire Island News:* a cross between "a Venetian villa overlooking the Grand Canal and the faux decoration of a Disneyland castle." Inspired by the Miami mansion Viscaya, the Belvedere is owned by John Eberhardt of the pencil dynasty, and is far and away the most luxurious hostelry on Fire Island. Clearly, though, it is not for everyone.

After several days in Ocean Beach, we were ready for the five-minute water taxi trip two communities east to Ocean Bay Park. We had booked two rooms for two nights at the Fire Island Hotel and Resort, which includes time-sharing units and boasts an island rarity, a good-size pool.

Unfortunately, our room faced it, along with loudspeakers blaring oldies. The place was also a little run-down. After a refreshing swim (and to get away from the music), we walked a block to the bay to lunch at the cavernous Flynn's, another Fire Island fixture, which becomes a raucous singles rendezvous at night. We found a place to rent bicycles for $10 each a day at the nearby Schooner Inn, another bayfront restaurant and bar next to a small pizza parlor. Debbie, my wife, settled on a three-wheeler with a rear basket that served as rumble seat for Sophie, and we rode off to explore adjacent Seaview to the west, a community of handsome homes, playground, grocery, and liquor shop.

Later, on foot we headed the other way toward Point O'Woods. A fence restricts access, but we circumvented the ban by entering on foot from the beach. Despite the vaunted exclusivity, it didn't look much different from other communities, perhaps just a little more overgrown and defiantly natural. No one challenged us, and we strolled back to the beach. We walked most of the two miles or so east along the surf to the Sunken Forest, a national park of wind-pruned 200-year-old holly and sassafras trees, but before we could make it to the raised, wooden walkway into the canopied forest, Sophie's legs wore out and we turned back.

Back in Ocean Bay Park, we had some good meals at the Inn Between, an informal restaurant on the bay walk between Flynn's and the Schooner Inn. And for future reference, we scouted the nearby Sea Shore Motel with 20 simple rooms, including six efficiency units, that might appeal, if not to the luxury-minded, then to singles, young couples, or families bent on a few economical days on Fire Island.

Our first night in the Fire Island Hotel and Resort passed quietly, at least after we prevailed on the management to turn off the loud-speakers, but on the second night the weekend brought an end to our idyll. At 2am that Saturday, we were jolted awake by a fearful shrieking from across the hall. Our neighbors, four young women, were evidently home from Flynn's with some male company. Slamming doors, hysterical laughter, and curses filled the night. Sure that the row would wake our daughters, I rapped on the opposite door and appealed for quiet, to no avail. Finally two other roused guests and I went to find the manager.

The office was locked. A handwritten sign on the door read: FOR AFTER-HOURS HELP, COME TO SECOND HOUSE ON RIGHT (BRIGHT BULB ON TOP OF ENTRANCE STEPS). KNOCK LOUDLY OR ENTER AND CALL FOR HELP. We sleepless caucused. There was no clear second house on the right with or without a bright bulb. At 3am, I went to the phone booth outside the hotel and dialed 911.

Twenty minutes later, two Suffolk County foot patrolmen and a jeep unit arrived. I led the officers to the din and went back to our room. From behind the closed door, we could hear arguing, a girl shouting for an officer to get his foot out of the door, and someone screaming that the police had no warrant. I put the pillow over my head. Slowly the fracas subsided.

Sophie and Anna, of course, slept through it. In the morning, Sophie's enthusiasm was undimmed. "After eight more grades," she asked, "can we move to Fire Island?"

FIRE ISLAND ESSENTIALS

GETTING THERE

GETTING TO THE FERRIES

By Car   To reach the Fire Island ferries in Bay Shore, Sayville, and Patchogue, Long Island, by car from Manhattan, take the Long Island Expressway to exit 53 (Bay Shore), exit 59 (Sayville), or exit 63 (Patchogue).

By Train   The **Long Island Rail Road** (☎ 718/217-5477 or 516/822-5477) provides daily service from Penn Station to the three towns; one-way fares range from $6.50 to $7.25 on off-peak trains, $9.50 to $10.75 for peak-hour trains; children 5 to 11 pay 50¢ during off-peak hours, one-half of the adult fare during peak hours; children under 5 ride free at all times. Weekdays, the trains leave Penn Station hourly beginning at 6:30am; weekends, service is also hourly from 7:30am. On Thursday and Friday afternoons during the summer, trains run every half-hour. The ferry terminal at Patchogue is within walking distance of the railroad station and the ferries at Bay Shore and Sayville are a short taxi ride away.

In summer, the railroad also offers excursions to the Watch Hill and Sunken Forest beaches and to Robert Moses State Park on Fire Island; these include a round-trip train ride and the ferry (or bus ride to Robert Moses State Park) at a cost of $12 to $18 for adults, $9 for children 5 to 11. The excursions are offered weekends from Memorial Day through the end of June and then daily through Labor Day.

FERRIES

Bay Shore Ferries, off Montauk Hwy., Main St. (☎ 516/666-3600 or 516/665-3600). Operates year-round to Ocean Beach, Fair Harbor, Dunewood, Atlantique, Kismet, Saltaire, Ocean Bay Park, and Seaview. From June 27 to September 3, ferries leave every 60 to 90 minutes for the 25-minute ride daily from 7am to 10:15pm (until 11:50pm on Friday); from September 4 to October 14, a reduced schedule (4 to 8 boats daily) begins at 7am; from mid-October to late December, 2 to 4 boats a day begin running at 7:30am; from December 24 to February 28, one boat runs Saturday at 10am and Sunday at 11am; from March 1 to mid-May, 2 to 3 boats run daily from 7am. The fare is $11 round-trip, $5.75 one way; $5 round-trip for children 2 to 12 and dogs. Reservations not necessary. Parking $10 per day Friday through Sunday, $6 per day Monday through Thursday, or $45 weekly; free parking in winter.

Patchogue Ferries (☎ 516/475-1665). Operates ferries to Davis Park and Watch Hill in the National Seashore park from two ferry terminals in Patchogue: at County Road 19 for Watch Hill (from May through November), and County Road 83 for Davis Park (from March through November). Ferries leave Patchogue Monday through Thursday 6:20am to 10:30pm, Friday from 6:20am to 11:30pm, Saturday 7:30am to 12:15am, Sunday 7:30am to 10:30pm. Fares $5.50 one-way, $10 same-day round-trip; children 2 to 11 $3.25 one-way, $5.50 same-day round-trip; $3.25 round-trip dogs. Ferries leave every 60 to 90 minutes for the 20- to 25-minute ride. Free parking at Watch Hill ferry for all; parking at the Davis Park Ferry is free for residents of Brookhaven and $10 per day for nonresidents.

Sayville Ferry Service, 41 River Rd. (☎ 516/589-0810). Operates ferries to Cherry Grove and Fire Island Pines year-round, and to

Sunken Forest and Water Island from May through October. Mid-May through mid-September, ferries leave every hour on the half-hour for the 20 to 25 minute ride on Friday 7am to 12:15am, Saturday and Sunday 8:15am to 1:30am, Monday 5:45am to 8.30pm, Tuesday and Wednesday 7am to 7:20pm, Thursday 7am to 8:30pm. October through mid-December, 3 to 5 boats run daily; mid-December through mid-March, service on weekends only; daily service starts again in mid-March, with 2 to 3 boats beginning at 10am. The fare is $10 round-trip, $5.50 one way; $5 round-trip or $2.75 one way for children under 12; $3 round-trip or $1.75 one way for dogs. Fare to Sunken Forest $8, $4.50 for children under 12. Parking $6 per day Monday through Thursday, $7 per day Friday through Sunday. Reservations not necessary.

TO FIRE ISLAND VIA LAND AND WATER TAXI

David's Taxi (☎ 516/665-4384 or 516/665-0191). Operates from May through November, weather permitting, between the Bay Shore Ferries (see "Ferries," above) and 68th St. and Third Ave. in Manhattan. Taxis depart Monday through Thursday every two hours from 9am to 8:30pm, Friday hourly from 7:45am to 10:15pm, Saturday hourly 7:30am to 9:30pm, Sunday hourly 8:15am to 7pm. One-way fare is $15 Monday through Saturday, $18 Sunday.

South Bay Water Taxi (☎ 516/665-8885). Operates year-round, weather permitting. One-way fares range from $4 to $23 per person, depending on destination; half-price for children under 12.

Tommy's Taxi, 88 Park Ave., Bay Shore (☎ 516/665-4800). Operates from April through the end of October between Manhattan and the Bay Shore Ferry. Departures from Second Ave. and 14th St., Second Ave. and 53rd St., Third Ave. and 81st St., and Central Park West at 65th and 81st Sts. in Manhattan daily from 8am to 9pm. One-way fare is $15 Monday through Saturday, $18 Sunday and holidays.

ACCOMMODATIONS

Clegg's Hotel, 478 Bayberry Walk, Ocean Beach (☎ 516/583-5399). Open May 1 through end of September. Daily rates based on double occupancy, with shared bath: Sundays, $75; Mondays through Thursdays, $60. There is a $220 weekend package for a Friday and Saturday night stay. Children welcome; those under 10 stay free. Studio apartments also available for $125 Sunday; $110 Monday through Thursday; and $320 for a two-night stay on Friday and Saturday ($350 for a bay view). Two night minimum on weekends; three night stay on holidays. Weekly rates also available.

The Belvedere, Bayview Walk, Cherry Grove (☎ 516/597-6448). Open May 1 to October 1

Fire Island Hotel and Resort, 25 Cayuga Walk, Ocean Bay Park (☎ 516/583-8000). Open mid-May to mid-October.

Fire Island Pines Botel, Harbor Walk, Fire Island Pines (☎ 516/597-6500).

Four Seasons Bed and Breakfast, 468 Dehnhoff Walk, Ocean Beach (☎ 516/583-8295). Open year-round.

Houser Hotel, Great South Bay on East Bay Walk, Ocean Beach (☎ 516/583-8900). Open May 1 through September.

Place in the Sun, 987 Surfview Walk, Ocean Beach (☎ 516/583-5716). Open May through October.

Sea Shore Motel, Bayview Walk, Ocean Bay Park (☎ 516/583-5860). Open mid-May to mid-September.

DINING

Albatross, Bay Walk, Ocean Beach (☎ 516/583-5697). Open March to early October.

Flynn's, 1 Cayuga Walk, Ocean Bay Park (☎ 516/583-5000). Open end of May to early September.

The Inn Between, at Oneida St. and Bay View Ave., Ocean Bay Park (☎ 516/583-0111). Open mid-May to mid-September.

Island Mermaid, Bay Walk, Ocean Beach (☎ 516/583-8088). Open April 15 to early October.

Maguires, Bay No. 1, Bungalow Walk, Ocean Beach (☎ 516/583-8800). Open late April to mid-October.

Matthew's Seafood House, on the bay, Ocean Beach (☎ 516/583-8016). Open mid-May to mid-September.

Rachel's, 325 Bay Walk, Ocean Beach (☎ 516/583-5953). Open May through September.

Schooner Inn, 57 Bay Walk, Ocean Bay Park (☎ 516/583-9561). Open mid-May to mid-October.

Sun and Moon Cafe, 310 Bay Walk, Ocean Beach (☎ 516/583-8300). Open March through October.

FIRE ISLAND NATIONAL SEASHORE

Sunken Forest, Sailors Haven (☎ 516/597-6183 for park information, 516/589-0810 for ferry information). A National Park Service site with beach, picnicking, nature walks, and a marina. Open mid-May through mid-October. Grounds are open daily around the clock for boaters; the visitors center, which has displays, is open Sunday through Friday 9am to 5pm, Saturday 9am to 6pm. Admission is free.

Watch Hill (☎ 516/597-6455 for park information, 516/475-1665 for ferry information). A National Park Service site, with camping, a restaurant, and a general store open May 15 through October 15. Grounds are open daily around the clock for campers and boaters; visitors center, with displays and special programs, open daily 9am to 5pm. Admission $10; reservations required.

HISTORICAL SOCIETY

Ocean Beach Historical Society, Bayview and Cottage walks, Ocean Beach (☎ 516/583-8972). "Fire Island Journal," a photography exhibition by Peter Harrison. Open Memorial Day through Labor Day, Thursday through Monday 10am to 2pm and 7 to 10pm. Donations accepted.

THE HAMPTONS
(AFTER THE CROWDS HAVE
GONE HOME)

by George Vecsey

IT'S SAFE NOW. IT'S SAFE TO GO BACK
to eastern Long Island.

I am not referring to the dangerous fire that swept through 5,500
acres of pine barrens near Westhampton in the late summer of 1995,
casting a smoky pall over the very name "Long Island." When I say
it's "safe," I am referring to the peace and quiet that falls over the land
after Labor Day. The Hollywood biggies and politicians and doctors
and writers and lawyers and junk-bond specialists who clog the narrow highways with their sports cars and four-wheel drives have now
returned to the city to make more mischief and earn more money.

That means you can hear the ocean again. Not only that, but at
this time of year you can also catch a glimpse of a few surviving acres
of cornfields, pumpkin patches, vineyards, and rolling dunes. You can
pick apples, take a walk on the beach, or sail or play golf or tennis. You
can go fishing at the peak of the striped-bass season without running
into somebody you recognize or overhearing any New York gossip.
Or you can go indoors to the museums and art galleries and occasional movies and live entertainment of the fall season.

Oh, weekends are still a bit frenzied in a few corners—most New
Yorkers wouldn't want it any other way—but in general, eastern Long
Island could almost be called bucolic.

"This is really the best time of the year out here," said George R. Eldi, the manager of the Seafood Barge in Southold, on the North (or non-Hampton) Fork of Long Island. "The weather is great for fishing and sailing right through October, and really through Christmas. Then people go to Florida or stay in Manhattan in their winter homes." The wonderful secret of eastern Long Island is that because it is surrounded by saltwater, it is often a few degrees warmer than the city is, with less snowfall.

You can even avoid the stereotypical Hamptons visit because there are two forks to Long Island. I was traumatized by the South Fork years ago when I was a correspondent on Long Island. The low point of that hitch may have been getting stuck in a hideous summer weekend traffic jam to cover a Hamptons fund-raiser for a Presidential campaign by Lloyd Bentsen.

Ever since, I have avoided eastern Long Island from Memorial Day to Labor Day. I have this recurring nightmare of being hungry and having headwaiters turn me away with the chilling words, "Sorry, pal, the Spielberg party needs the table." In the fall, however, I always love to return to the diners and the farm stands and the I.G.A. grocery stores. It's almost real country.

Recently, my wife and I needed a few hours of peace and quiet, and we braved the Long Island Expressway, with its tailgating trucks and careening vans, but somewhere around Yaphank (love that name) it all calmed down. We headed east along Sunrise Highway, noticing the burned-out acres in Westhampton, merely a blotch on the landscape now thanks to the brave people who put out the fire. We crossed the bridge over the Shinnecock Canal, a modest waterway that always gives me a tiny shiver of adventure, like crossing a frontier from France into Spain.

We took a glance at the civilized pleasures of Southampton village, near the Parrish Art Museum with its advertisements for a Roy Lichtenstein exhibition, and we made a detour through the old mansions behind thick hedges. (When I was in college in 1959, I once found myself wading next to Sen. John F. Kennedy of Massachusetts in the surf at Southampton Town Beach. I always think of that when

I drive through: a lanky young man in sunglasses, in saltwater up to his hips, the whole world in front of him.) There are plenty of trendy restaurants in Southampton, but I gravitated to the Southampton Princess Diner on Montauk Highway, for bluefish, moist and plump and not at all oily, a few hours out of the waters off Montauk. Bill Paul said his co-owner and chef, Steve Kalagoras, cooks with a dash of koutourou, which is Greek for "a little of this, a little of that."

Well fortified, I now needed closer contact with the ocean that had contributed that lovely bluefish. We drove leisurely through the main drags of Water Mill and Bridgehampton. (I once had the pleasure of visiting a military man named Powell who was staying at a summer house near here. I often wonder what became of him.) After admiring the harvested fields of Sagaponack, we kept going east past the movie theater, upscale book shops, ice cream emporiums, and art galleries of East Hampton, which were gearing up for the annual Hamptons International Film Festival.

But we were not looking for Columbus Avenue East. We wanted a beach. We kept driving until we reached Hither Hills State Park, jammed during the season with campers and day-trippers, but on a lovely fall afternoon, it was deserted. Not even a parking fee.

We parked a few feet from the beach, spotting one couple a few hundred feet away. I took off my shoes, a regular J. Alfred Prufrock, and dared to walk along the beach barefooted. There was a man with an N.Y.F.D. ball cap sitting by his surf-casting pole, smoking a Viceroy, drinking a Budweiser. He had caught a striper the night before, he said, but now the waters were roiling because of a hurricane far out at sea.

"Best time of the year for fishing," he said. He swigged his Bud. He was ahead of the game.

My wife and I found a deserted corner—in fact, a deserted mile— of beach. We lay down in the sun and fell asleep. For an hour. Worth the drive. If it gets nippy later in the fall, you'll just have to walk briskly.

Refreshed, we drove all the way to the tip of Long Island, past rolling hills and guest cottages and neat little hotels. Judging from the VACANCY signs, there is room at the inn. At Montauk Point, tourists were traipsing into the lighthouse for a $3 fee, but we made the necessary U-turn—otherwise, you get very wet—and headed for Montauk Harbor. There we saw sailboats and commercial fishing boats and ferries and cruise boats. We found out that the Riverhead Foundation for Marine Research and Preservation, formerly the Okeanos Research Foundation, would be offering seal-observation cruises in the future. We also spotted a sign for the "first annual" Oktoberfest at the Sail Inn, featuring a German menu and beer.

Back on Montauk Highway, we stopped on the hill in Napeague where you can pull off on a scenic overlook and gaze down at the ocean and Napeague Bay. In a heated car, it's probably gorgeous all winter long.

From there we drove west and cut north along Route 114, through backwoods that still look like backwoods, toward Sag Harbor, the old whaling village. We strolled along the dock, noticing signs that cultural life goes on all winter. We walked down the main street, which was sweet and quiet at the end of a working day. We half expected to see John Steinbeck and his dog, Charley. Or maybe Steve Martin and Daryl Hannah in the movie *Roxanne*. At dusk, we took an end table on the porch at the American Hotel, which would be totally impossible during the three summer months. The waiters had time to give us personal attention, touting us on the steak Fiorentine, which was so huge that a couple leaving the bar stopped and gaped at it, until my wife offered the man a bite. We were already feeling like locals.

"It's a madhouse during the season," one waiter cautioned us. "And you still need reservations on weekends in the fall." That was the end of our South Fork day trip. We didn't have time to take a ferry over to

Shelter Island, pretty but mostly private, also reachable by ferry from Greenport on the North Fork.

A few days later we returned to eastern Long Island. Our second day trip was to the North Fork, straight out to Southold, where we had a pleasant lunch by the window of the Seafood Barge, with a great view of Peconic Bay. We did not order from the handsome wine list, but Mr. Eldi, the manager, told us: "The dry summer was good for the grapes out here. If it's too rainy, they are too watery." We would inspect those grapes firsthand. After lunch, we meandered back west a few miles, toward the dozens of wineries that have been developed in the past generation. The operators of the Pellegrini Vineyards in Cutchogue brag of their 30 acres of grapevines that, "with climate and annual rainfall paralleling that of Bordeaux, we are graced with a 220-day growing season." We were attracted by the wooden cloister-style building, with a tower above the salesroom. After a dozen samples, graciously offered, we bought a number of bottles.

Next we headed to the wide-open farmland north of Riverhead, great just for light and space. We happened to drive past Briermere Farms at 4414 Sound Avenue, whose bakery sells flaky, buttery, fruity homemade pies (not inexpensively, either).

We could have gone apple and pumpkin picking at half a dozen farms on the North Fork, but I had another beach in mind: Wild-wood State Park, between Wading River and Baiting Hollow. My family used to camp there in the late 1950s. It looks exactly the same today: wooded sites in the hills, one rustic "roundhouse" (I hope they still don't have hot water in the showers; I wouldn't want to have suffered in vain) and a narrow path leading down to the beach on Long Island Sound.

The day we went, the peaceful waters were still warm enough for swimming in the 70° sun. I counted four people on the beach. We sat on the boardwalk and ate an apple turnover from Briermere Farms. The Spielberg party never showed.

HAMPTONS ESSENTIALS

GETTING THERE

By Car   Take the Long Island Expressway (I-495) to exit 70 (Rte. 111 South), then follow Rte. 27 East into the Hamptons.

By Bus   The **Hampton Jitney** (☎ 800/936-0440) provides service to the Hamptons year-round. The 2- to 3-hour trip costs $20 one-way or $36 round-trip. Most of the pick-ups and drop-offs are along the east side of Manhattan, with several on the west side.

By Train   The **Long Island Rail Road** (☎ 718/217-5477 or 516/822-5477) provides daily service from Penn Station to the Hamptons; call for timetable and fare information.

ACCOMMODATIONS

American Hotel, Main St., Sag Harbor (☎ 516/725-3535). Sunday through Thursday, $110 double; Friday through Sunday, $170 double. Two-night minimum on weekends. Dining room open for lunch Saturday and Sunday noon to 4pm, for dinner Sunday through Thursday 5 to 10pm and Friday and Saturday 5 to 11pm.

Montauk Motel, 76 S. Edison St., Montauk (☎ 516/668-2704). Most units are efficiencies with kitchenettes. September 15 through mid-May, $65 double; after Memorial Day, $100 double weekdays, $120 double weekends. Two-night minimum on weekends (three-night minimum on holiday weekends).

DINING

Also see the American Hotel under "Accommodations," above.

Sail Inn, 548 W. Lake Dr., Montauk (☎ 516/668-2800). Open year-round. December through April, open Monday through Thursday 11am to 10pm, Friday and Saturday 11am to 2am, Sunday noon to 1am; May 1 through November, open Monday through Thursday 11am to 1am, Friday and Saturday 11am to 2am (or later), Sunday noon to 2am (or later). Entrees $5.95 to $15.95.

Seafood Barge, 150 Old Main Rd., Southold (☎ 516/765-3010). Open early March through December, Friday noon to 3pm and 5 to 9pm, Saturday 1 to 10pm, and Sunday 1 to 9pm; more days may be added in summer.

Southampton Princess Diner, 32 Montauk Hwy. (☎ 516/283-4255). Open Sunday through Thursday 6am to midnight, Friday and Saturday to 1am.

ART MUSEUMS AND GALLERIES

Arlene Bujese Gallery, 66 Newtown Lane, East Hampton (☎ 516/324-2823). Open year-round. Hours change seasonally; call for exact schedule.

Guild Hall, 158 Main St., East Hampton (☎ 516/324-0806). Art exhibitions and festivals, discussions with writers, and special events offered year-round. Memorial Day through Labor Day, open daily 11am to 5pm; Labor Day through Memorial Day, open Wednesday through Saturday 11am to 5pm and Sundays noon to 5pm. Suggested admission $3 to $5 (free for members).

Lizan-Tops Gallery, 66 Newtown Lane, East Hampton (☎ 516/324-3424). Open mid-April through December, daily (except Wednesday) 10am to 5pm.

Parrish Art Museum, 25 Jobs Lane, Southampton (☎ 516/283-2118). The museum has a year-round program with exhibitions, concerts, lectures, and children's programs. Open Monday, Thursday, Friday, and Saturday 11am to 5pm, and Sunday 1 to 5pm (closed Tuesday and Wednesday, except from June through Labor Day, when the museum is closed Wednesday only). Suggested admission $3.

Vered Gallery, 68 Park Place Passage, East Hampton (☎ 516/324-3303). October through April, open Thursday through Monday 11am to 6pm; May through October, open daily 11am to 11pm.

WINERIES

Open hours at wineries change with the season; call before you go.

Bedell Cellars, Rte. 25, Cutchogue (☎ 516/734-7537).

Hargrave Vineyard, Rte. 48, Cutchogue (☎ 516/734-5158).

Lenz Winery, Rte. 25, Peconic (☎ 516/734-6010).

Palmer Vineyards, 108 Sound Ave., Aquebogue (☎ 516/722-9463).

Pellegrini Vineyards, Rte. 25, Cutchogue (☎ 516/734-4111).

Pindar Vineyards, Rte. 25, Peconic (☎ 516/734-6200).

Sagpond Vineyards, Sagg Rd., Sagaponack (☎ 516/537-5106).

OTHER ATTRACTIONS

Bay Street Theater, Bay and Main Streets, Sag Harbor (☎ 516/725-9500). Offers a weekend series of plays in April; a daily summer season of three plays from May 21 through Labor Day; and a fall weekend series Labor Day through November 18. There are also annual benefits and other events. Tickets range from $25 to $35. Call for current schedule.

Briermere Farms, 4414 Sound Ave., Riverhead (☎ 516/722-3931). Open year-round, daily 8am to 5pm (to 6pm from May through October). Pies $9 to $12.50.

East Hampton Town Marine Museum, Bluff Rd., Amagansett (☎ 516/324-6850). Operated by the East Hampton Historical Society. The museum has an ongoing exhibition, "Ray Prohaska: Painter, Photographer, Fisherman." There is also an annual mara-

thon participatory reading of Herman Melville's *Moby-Dick* in October. May 24 through June 30 and Labor Day through Columbus Day, open weekends 9am to 5pm; July 1 through Labor Day, open daily 9am to 5pm; and by appointment. Admission $2 adults, $1.50 seniors, $1 for children under 16.

Hither Hills State Park, Rte. 27, Montauk (☎ 516/668-2554; 800/456-2267 for camping reservations). Open year-round, daily from sunrise to sunset; camping allowed April 19 to November 16. Memorial Day through Columbus Day, daily parking fee $5, camping fee $16.

Manor Hill Farm, Main Rd., Cutchogue (☎ 516/298-8682). Operates from the end of May through November (weather permitting), daily 9am to 5:30pm.

Montauk Point Lighthouse Museum, Montauk State Park, 2000 Montauk Hwy., Montauk Point (☎ 516/668-2544). Hours for museum and tower: March 15 to April 27, May 3 to May 18, and November 1 to November 30, open weekends 10:30am to 4:30pm; May 19 to October 13, open daily 10:30am to 5pm (to 8pm on holiday weekends and Saturdays from June 23 to August 31); October 17 to October 31, open Friday through Monday 10:30am to 4:30pm; in winter, open holiday weekends only from 10:30am to 4:30pm. Admission $3 adults, $2.75 seniors, $1 children 6 to 12, free for children under 6. To climb the tower, you must be at least 41 inches tall.

Riverhead Foundation for Marine Research and Preservation, formerly the Okeanos Ocean Research Foundation, 431 E. Main St., Riverhead (☎ 516/369-9840). In the Aquarium Preview Center, viewers can observe the rehabilitation of seals, sea turtles, and other sea creatures. There are also salt and freshwater aquariums and a touch-tank with starfish, crabs, snails, and small fish and bone displays. January to Memorial Day and Labor Day through December, open weekends 10am to 5pm; Memorial Day through Labor Day, open daily 10am to 5pm. Suggested donation $2.

Suffolk County Farm and Education Center, part of Cornell Cooperative Extension, Yaphank Ave., Yaphank (☎ 516/852-4607). A working farm with workshops and seasonal festivals. Open April through December, daily 9am to 3pm. Donations accepted.

Wildwood State Park, Hulse Landing Rd. (off Sound Ave.), Rte. 25A, Wading River (☎ 516/929-4314; 800/456-2267 for camping reservations). Open year-round, daily from dawn to dusk; camping allowed from the first weekend in April to the first weekend in October. No parking fees mid-September through mid-May; parking $4 to $5 from Memorial Day through Labor Day.

Bicycling from Manhattan to Montauk

by Bruce Weber

A ROUTINE PLEASURE OF BICYCLING is possession of the land; you ride a mile, you feel you own it. So why would anyone want to pedal from Manhattan to Montauk? There is, after all, more accommodating and cheery real estate available to the acquisitive cyclist than Long Island, at least that portion of it between the East River and the South Fork, a stretch that many New Yorkers are familiar with only through strategy sessions aimed at devising the quickest, most painless traverses—via motorized transport, of course—on Friday and Sunday evenings.

However, as a cyclist who has made big chunks of the trip a dozen times in the last few years of renting a summer house near the beach—and now the whole thing—I can report that the journey is a worthwhile enterprise. The route has its pitfalls, yes. Long Island isn't exactly Paumonok anymore, the Indians' beach-rimmed woodland in the shape of a fish, and I don't think residents of Nassau County or even western Suffolk should be surprised or offended to learn that for the cyclist, their home terrain is no velodrome.

At more than a century (cycle-ese for a 100-mile ride), it's not a wise endeavor for the physically unprepared. But in many ways, the length of Long Island is the perfect bike ride. The path between skyline and lighthouse is a day's journey, grueling but doable, its end points compelling, even romantic demarcations, symbolically worthy as destinations. The landscape is various enough, defining a historical regression of sorts, from industry to agriculture. (Or a progression, if you're going east to west.) There are plenty of places along the way to refuel the body or repair the bike, and there are hardly any hills. As for the traffic, the malls, the unpleasant un-bucolicism of much of the trip, well, cyclists have been known to be attracted to the challenge of conquering territory as well as to the reward of possessing it.

Everyone more or less knows how to get to Montauk from Manhattan. You take the Long Island Rail Road or the Long Island Expressway. The distance, as the crow flies, is about 125 miles, according to a Rand McNally road map, three hours or so by car or rail. And, indeed, it is a function of how provincial New Yorkers are that over the years, in maybe 20 different conversations, otherwise intelligent people, learning that I'd made this trip, have said to me something like: "I didn't know they allowed bikes on the Long Island Expressway," as if it were impossible to actually get anywhere on other roads that might exist. Or else unthinkable that anyone might want to take them.

For my latest two-wheeled journey, I began in Greenwich Village and followed a not-so-straight-as-a-string route: along the northern perimeter of the island and then, instead of crossing diagonally through Riverhead, at the island's east-end crotch, to reach the South Fork, angling slightly out of the way to trace the North Fork, veering south and across Shelter Island before taking on the final eastward leg. The total distance was 137 miles, according to my odometer, and that seems about right, though truth be told it was a new one and I never did quite trust it. I left my apartment shortly after 5am (there is no better biking in America than on Third Avenue at dawn); some friends met me at the Montauk Lighthouse (thank goodness) just before 8pm.

That's slow, I grant you. But I won't apologize. I believe that when tired, you should rest.

Over the 59th Street Bridge

You probably don't think of the 59th Street Bridge as a particularly romantic spot, but as a place to experience the sun coming up, it's pretty great. Pedaling over the open-grated pedestrian path on the lower level, you get a real sense of urbanity meeting nature. There's a good view south, the East River proceeding at its stately pace, dividing Manhattan from Brooklyn and Queens almost haughtily, as if it were actually still running through the wilderness. And ahead of you, from somewhere beyond the city, the sun is coming up, setting the dense air alight and glinting off the cinders in it.

The bridge spills you into what is ordinarily one of the most traffic-congested road nests in the city. But at this hour you actually have it to yourself, more or less, and negotiating your way onto Northern Boulevard for the first lengthy leg of the ride is easy, even pleasant.

Are city streets cleaner at dawn? Probably not, but the shardlike threats to bicycle tires are not so seemingly everywhere, perhaps because everything seems a little more spread out. There's space on the street, a feeling of vacancy, room to move. The sensation is as close as I've ever had to replicating the great daydream about a New York City emptied of people. And Northern Boulevard, which at midday is as undistinguished a main thoroughfare as any in the city, seems capacious.

It's seven miles or so before you make a jog around Shea Stadium and through College Point, but after you join Northern Boulevard again you could stay on it, if you wanted to, for 100 miles (it turns into State Route 25A), all the way to Greenport. Of course, you wouldn't want to, mainly because all the way out there's the threat of congestion. It's peculiar that the most populous stretch of the boulevard's length is also the only one pleasant enough to ride, for an hour or two anyway.

Thirteen or so miles out, there's a brief but steep upward pitch, which heralds the Nassau County line. That's the good news. The bad news is that then you're in Nassau County. And by that time it's just about rush hour.

The passage through Great Neck and Roslyn is nerve-racking, with the worst stretch over the Roslyn Viaduct crossing Hempstead Harbor. There's a way to get on the pedestrian path, I assume, because there is a pedestrian path, but every time I've made the trip, hurtling downhill, I've missed it and found myself pedaling madly to get beyond the 200 or so yards of narrow roadway that has no shoulder at all but does have four lanes of rushing traffic.

Presuming you survive, the rest of the day should be considerably more relaxing.

For many New York City residents (most, I suspect), the geography of Long Island is a complete puzzle. The names of the towns are familiar from local news reports; there's even a weird music to them, like the words to a rhythmic, regional folk song: Syosset and Speonk ... Yaphank and Wyandanch ... Patchogue ... Setauket ... Ronkonkoma ... Quogue. But who really knows what these places are like or even where they are? Oyster Bay. North shore or south? How about Lindenhurst? See what I mean?

Bicycling solves this problem.

I now know, for example, that beyond Roslyn, Northern Boulevard becomes the Hempstead Turnpike, which divides Syosset from its northern neighbor (answer to quiz), Oyster Bay, before crossing the Suffolk County line and entering Huntington. I also know that Brookville, between Roslyn and Syosset (but judging from the road signs and map notations isn't so much an actual town as it is an area), is the place to veer off the main road. Muttontown Road would be worth it just for the chance to see the road sign and pronounce it out loud, but it's pleasant riding as well, shady and meandering through the woods and past a country club.

From Syosset, head for Woodbury (the road to look for is called, helpfully, Syosset-Woodbury Road) and then Huntington, where you want to get on Pulaski Road, which will take you straight through into Smithtown. Pulaski is kind of a suburban Belt Parkway, not Main Street but not the expressway; it takes you into neighborhoods, over railroad tracks, past parks, and through intermittently spaced traffic lights. It's pleasant enough, though not exactly the Natchez Trace.

Negotiating Smithtown, which on this trip is really the gateway to a better life, is a little tricky. The key is turning onto Edgewood Avenue at the top of the Main Street hill; you're suddenly away from a commercial strip and onto a more promising kind of thoroughfare, the well-traveled country road, where bikes have to coexist with cars but do so amiably. Edgewood runs into North Country Road (Route 25A again, but kind of sweet at that point), which takes you through Stony Brook.

You can follow 25A toward Long Island Sound and into the town of Port Jefferson, but you'll have to climb a nasty hill to get out of Port Jeff and back on track. You'll also miss perhaps the niftiest shortcut of the journey. A hundred yards or so beyond the Stony Brook train station, there's a right onto a semi-highway that takes you under the train tracks and past the State University campus. Just before the campus entrance, however, there's a left onto what looks like a tiny enough road to be an affluent person's driveway. Take it, and then an immediate right.

This is Lower Sheep Pasture Road, and a more agreeable, rolling ride the suburbs of New York do not offer. It ends with your being spilled across Main Street in Port Jeff, at the top of the hill you didn't have to climb, and back onto North Country Road, which has, by now, given up its designation as a state highway. Follow North Country through Miller Place (that's a town, not a street) and it will take you back to 25A. From there, through Rocky Point (where there's a Friendly's for a milkshake or, just beyond it, a pretty decent diner for lunch; I got there a little past noon), Shoreham (home of the famously ill-fated Lilco nuclear plant), and Wading River, the ride is an undistinguished but not unpleasant straight shot along a modestly traveled road with a smoothly paved, reasonably commodious shoulder. At this point, you have a decision to make.

Just east of Wading River, the road forks. Route 25A turns south, joins up with Route 25 and crosses through Riverhead on its way around Peconic Bay to the South Fork. It's not a bad journey, particularly once you hit the neck between the bay and the Atlantic Ocean. By then you're in the Hamptons. But I prefer staying north, which means turning off 25A onto Sound Avenue.

The Quest for a Second Wind

By now you're 75 miles or so into the trip and, if you're human, beginning to feel enough may be enough. Encountering at this point the best bicycling of the day is thus either a good thing or a bad thing, depending on whether you feel that a jolt of rural beauty is just what you need or that you really should be fresher to appreciate it.

Sound Avenue stretches about 17 miles to Mattituck, on the North Fork, and if you look on a map you'll see there's nothing there. It's not spectacular, just nice. It's fields and tangled woods and the kind of quaint housing with wraparound porches and big yards you associate with, say, Wisconsin. (The first time I made this trip, I sat down for a breather on somebody's front lawn, fell asleep, and was awakened when the children who lived there got off a school bus.) There are sod farms stretching to forever, like God's golf course. And as you go farther east, the vineyards and wineries begin.

There are no bike services, just a farm stand or two and maybe a gift shop and an antiques store along the way, but make sure your water bottle is full and your blood sugar plentiful: There is nowhere to get a Snapple or a Gatorade or a packet of Oreos. The little mall where the road forks toward Mattituck is welcome. It's 13 more miles to Greenport, tough miles psychologically with still about 40 to go, but the late-afternoon light is consoling (something about how the descending sun hits a spine of land with water on either side) and there's respite (albeit brief) at the Shelter Island ferry.

The Day Is Done

Shelter Island is, of course, one of the great bicycling day trips on the East Coast. There's little auto traffic; the terrain is hilly enough for a good workout but not so grueling as to discourage you from having fun. There are huge old houses along the beaches, the incredibly well groomed community of Dering Harbor, a wildly overgrown, swampy shoreline dotted with osprey nests, maybe the most civilized bicycle sightseeing available anywhere.

On this trip I was interested in none of this; it was after 4 o'clock when I got off the first ferry, and I bolted straight through along

Route 114, four miles to the other side of the island (not a bad ride, just expedient where you'd rather not have to be) and onto the south ferry, which dropped me in Sag Harbor.

If it sounds as if I'm rushing to a conclusion, well, that's realistic representation for you. Truthfully, I didn't much want to go on (I like Sag Harbor) but for the sake of completeness, I did, crossing the South Fork into East Hampton and then bolting straight east along Route 27, a.k.a. the Montauk Highway, through picturesque Amagansett and out onto the long, windswept flats. (Don't do this trip on a Friday; by this time of the evening, the highway can be bumper-to-bumper with week-enders.) At dinnertime, I passed Lunch, the diner, then climbed the cruel hills that for some reason exist out at the land's very extreme, as if Manhattan, sitting on one end, has tipped the island up like a fat man on a seesaw. Truly, the steepest climbs on the journey finish it, and as you approach the lighthouse you rise to the level of its foundation.

It was nearly dark when I finally arrived, and the lighthouse light was on. As I loaded my bike into the back of my friends' station wagon, it started to rain.

How do you feel? they asked me. Thrilled?

Pooped, I said. Hungry. I'll figure it out later.

I put Long Island in my back pocket and took it home with me.

PRACTICAL ADVICE ON PEDALING TO MONTAUK

It makes sense, if you are making the trip the way I did it this time, from west to east, to take the northern route. It's a little longer, but you get Queens and Nassau out of the way early, before the traffic problems become onerous. If you are going the other way, toward Manhattan, a route along south-ern Long Island is better.

From the Hamptons to Patchogue, it's more or less a straight shot along Route 27A (not the Sunrise Highway), with occasional ventures off the beaten path. Once into Nassau, if you take Merrick Road—a passable, if busy suburban main drag—through Massapequa, Seaford, Freeport,

and Valley Stream, there's reasonably easy access to the subway at Jamaica Station, where I recommend you hop on the train instead of negotiating, in the late afternoon, an increasingly difficult web of streets the rest of the way.

Those who want to modify their trip by shortening it might consider going part way on the **Long Island Rail Road** (☎ 718/217-5477 for schedule and fare information). Along the north shore, you can skip Queens and Nassau County entirely, for instance, and take a train from Penn Station to Cold Spring Harbor or Huntington, skipping over about 35 rather unscenic miles. Or, along the south shore, you can go to Patchogue, about half-way out.

The Long Island Rail Road requires a permit, for children as well as adults, to take a bike on board. Available by mail, it costs $5 and takes about 10 days to process, but once you've got it, it's good until you lose it. (I'm on my third.) Applications are available at train stations and terminals. There are some restrictions—bikes aren't allowed on most rush-hour trains, for instance. For bike permit information, call ☎ 718/558-8228.

Another option is to take your bike part of the way on the Hampton Jitney, a bus line serving the South Fork of Long Island, with stops from Westhampton to Montauk. It costs an additional $10 to board the **Hampton Jitney** (☎ 800/936-0440 for information and reservations) with a bicycle, and reservations are suggested; there are no restrictions on time or day of travel.

ON THE LOOKOUT
FOR WHALES

by Michael T. Kaufman

C ALL ME A SCHLEMIEL.

But there I was, some dollars in my purse and not much to interest me on shore as summer was wearing down on the island of the Manhattoes. I felt the call of the sea and thought I would sail about a little in search of whales and adventure.

I could have signed on with any of a number of companies offering whale-watching expeditions from ports stretching up the coast from Mystic, Connecticut, to Bar Harbor, Maine, but the closest was one offered out of Montauk Harbor on Long Island.

In response to a call, I was told that whale-watching excursions departed every weekend until the end of September, when both whales and watchers petered out. The voyages, the voice on the telephone explained, take four to seven hours. There are no guarantees of seeing whales or anything interesting. It could be cold, so passengers should bring layers of clothing. It could be very choppy, so they should dose themselves with Dramamine. The sun might be very strong, so they should bring sunblock.

Listening to this remarkably soft sell, I envisioned myself spending the full seven hours queasy with *mal de mer*, skin scorched yet chilled to the bone, and nary a whale in sight. But if mankind allowed its will to bend and break under such premonitions, Columbus would have hugged European shores and the world would still be flat. Boldly I reserved two places for a Sunday voyage for myself and my wife, committing $32 a seat.

Following instructions, we were at the pier next to the Block Island ferry slip by 10am. Along with 212 other prospective watchers, we boarded the *Viking Starship*, a sturdy vessel of 140 feet. There are hard metal seats running the length of the ship on both port side and starboard. Inside there are upholstered seats, but these offer poor views of the water. There is a canteen selling candy, potato chips, hot dogs, hats, sunblock, and whale-watch T-shirts. As the motor turned over, the woman behind the counter was talking with a volunteer crew member about a recent voyage. "It was really a great trip," she said. "Nobody threw up."

At that moment the water was calm, the sky was blue and cloudless, and a strong sun was made more tolerable by pleasant breezes. The only tension involved the prospect of whales. Would there be any whales? How many whales? What would we have to see for the outing to be successful? What was the minimum basic experience we should expect for our $32? A whale's back arching as it disappeared? A spewing whale and excited cries of "thar she blows"? A breaching whale flying out of the water? Or maybe even a spectacular literary metaphor?

Soon we left Peconic Bay for the swells of the ocean. Montauk Lighthouse lay off to port, and straightaway in the distance was the silhouette of Block Island. Suddenly the captain cut the engines. The watchers stopped chattering. Could we have whales already?

"One o'clock, right next to the ship," said Annie Gorgone, a naturalist speaking over a loudspeaker. The passengers all rushed to the starboard side to look. "It's not a whale, but it's pretty weird," said Ms. Gorgone, describing what she identified as an ocean sunfish.

About five feet from the ship and about a foot below the surface was a four-foot-long fish that looked as if whoever designed it had stopped in the middle of the job leaving its torso to end abruptly without a tail. It kept flipping its dorsal fin through the air

from one side to the other, but it stayed stationary, looking at the people who were looking at it. "These fish can move pretty fast," Ms. Gorgone said. "But this one doesn't seem to be in any hurry. They eat jellyfish."

Whale Bonding

In the stare-down between fish and passengers, the fish won and we were again under way. It was good to see the sunfish, but what of whales? Would there be whales? It was easy to see how someone might obsess over whales.

Then, after a little more than an hour at sea, there was a whale, "Eleven o'clock," Ms. Gorgone shouted as the captain slowed the ship. Now people ran to port, watching as the whale broke the surface some 150 feet ahead of the *Viking Star*, only to dive down with a wave of its splendid eight-foot-wide flukes.

"That's a humpback whale," the naturalist explained. "He is not fully grown yet. He seems to be two or three years old, and he measures about 35 or 40 feet long. Actually, we don't know if he's a he or a she, but I've been calling him a he. If that bothers anyone, I apologize." Ms. Gorgone went on to explain that this same whale had been spotted in this patch of ocean on every voyage for the previous four weeks. In fact, she said, the whale was the only whale spotted in that time. The ship maintains regular contact with fishing boats in the region seeking information about whale sightings, but for some time no one had reported seeing anything more than the adolescent humpback that was submerged somewhere around us.

"Nine o'clock, right next to the boat," Ms. Gorgone shouted, and sure enough up came the whale about 10 feet from the middle of the ship, close enough so that some passengers could feel the spray of its spout and smell its breath, which by human standards was foul. "What it blows out through the blow hole is not water," Ms. Gorgone said. "It is mucus, similar to what happens when we sneeze." I was not lucky enough to get sneezed on, but I was pretty close. I definitely felt that, however briefly, the whale and I shared private if not intimate space. I can't speak for the whale, of course, but from my vantage point, something like bonding had taken place. It had become my whale.

Ms. Gorgone explained that the whale had moved away from its pod to graze on its own on large quantities of bait. On each deep dive it descended to a depth of 40 feet and stayed down for about three minutes before coming up for breath. As she spoke, the captain steered the ship, positioning it in anticipation of where my whale would next surface.

And so for the next hour and a half, passengers with cameras at the ready rushed from 9 o'clock to 3 o'clock and back again to catch glimpses of the whale—my whale—coming up and going down. Sometimes the creature would be off our side by a city block, sometimes much closer, though never again just a spit and a sneeze away.

In all I counted 37 deep dives, a number confirmed by the Okeanos volunteers who were keeping records on how long it stayed down, how far it went, and what the sonar revealed about fish stocks below. The nonprofit foundation, which runs a telephone hotline service to spot and rescue beached whales, also studies whale behavior and movements.

At one point, my whale vigorously slapped its tail as it descended. "He does that sometimes, but we don't know what that maneuver means," said Ms. Gorgone. She said that a week earlier the whale kept breaching, hurling his entire body out of the water. "He did it 36 times," she said. "We don't really know why they do that either."

As the whale kept diving, not all the passengers kept watching. A bearded man approached Ms. Gorgone and asked, "Are we going to try to find other whales or are we going to stay around here?" You could see he wanted to move. Patiently, she explained that if we left we would probably not find any other whales, and if we were lucky enough to spot some minke whales, they would quickly descend and vanish. "This guy here is pretty wonderful, and he keeps coming back," she said.

Another passenger approached to ask if the whale would do any "other tricks." With even more patience, Ms. Gorgone explained that it was a wild animal and that no one could tell what it would do.

Each new surfacing now brought fewer oohs and ahs, and no longer did quite so many people rush from one side of the ship to the other. Aware of ripples of antsiness among the passengers, Ms. Gorgone and the captain decided to head back for Montauk after less than four hours at sea.

For one last time I watched my whale break through the plane where water and air met and then arc down. I imagined it was singing.

WHAR SHE BLOWS: WHALE-WATCHING ESSENTIALS

Here is a sampling of whale-watching trips departing from harbors in the Northeast:

A. C. Cruise Line, 290 Northern Ave., Boston, MA 02210 (☎ 800/422-8419 or 617/261-6633). Trips lasting about 6½ hours. Mid-April to mid-October, Tuesday through Sunday at 10:30am. Tickets, $19; $13 for seniors; $10 for children 12 and younger.

Cape Ann Whale Watch, Post Office Box 345, Rose's Wharf, Gloucester, MA (☎ 800/877-5110 or 508/283-5110). Four-hour trips. May through October, weekends at 8:30am and 1:30pm, weekdays at 10am Labor Day through September 30, weekends at 8:30am and 1:30pm, weekdays at 1:30pm. October 1 through October 20, daily at 10am. Tickets $23; $18 for seniors; $14 for children under 16.

Cape May Whale Watch and Research Center, 1286 Wilson Dr., Cape May, NJ (☎ 609/898-0055). Three-hour trips depart at 1pm (weather permitting) Saturday and Sunday from April through May 15 and October through December, and daily from May 15 through September. Tickets $26; $20 for seniors; $10 for children 7 to 14; free for children 6 and under.

Captain John Boats, 117 Standish Ave., Plymouth, MA 02360 (☎ 508/746-2643). Trips of 4 to 4½ hours from early April to early November. April 5 to May 4 and October 11 to November 1, weekends only at 11am. May 14 to June 6, daily at 2pm. June 7 to September 1, daily at 8:30am and 1:30pm. September 1 to October 17, weekdays at

11am and weekends at 9am and 2pm. Tickets $24; $19 for seniors; $15 for children 12 and younger.

Dolphin Fleet Whale Watch, MacMillan Wharf, off Commercial Street, Provincetown, MA (☎ 800/826-9300 or 508/349-1900). Daily trips, lasting 3½ to 4 hours, from mid-April to the end of October. The number of daily trips depend upon the season with two in the early spring and late fall and as many as nine during the summer; departure times are at 9am in the spring and fall and 8:30am in the summer. Tickets, in spring and fall, $17; $15 for seniors; $14 for children 7 to 12; free for those 6 and younger. In the summer, each fare is an additional $1. Reservations recommended.

Fisherman's Wharf, off Rte. 1 (at the drawbridge), Lewes, DE (☎ 302/645-8862). Four-hour trips depart Saturday and Sunday at 2pm in May and from Labor Day through September, daily at 2pm from Memorial Day to Labor Day. Tickets $19; $10 for children under 13.

Hyannis Whale Watcher Cruises, 269 Mill Way Barnstable Harbor, Barnstable, MA 02630 (☎ 800/287-0374 or 508/362-6088). Three-and-one-half-to-four-hour trips daily April through October. Two trips, at 9am and 1:30pm, April through mid-June and mid-September through October; three trips, at 8am, noon and 5pm, mid-June through mid-September. Tickets $3; $19 for seniors; $15 for children 4 to 12; free for those under 4. Reservations suggested.

New England Aquarium Whale Watch, Central Wharf, off Atlantic Ave. and Milk St. Boston, MA (☎ 617/973-5281). Five-hour trips, from early April through the end of October. Weekends only at 10am in April and the last two weeks in October; weekdays at 10am and weekends at 9:30am and 3:30pm, May 1 through June 30; daily at 10am and 4pm, July 1 through September 1; weekdays at 1pm and weekends at 9am and 3pm from September 2 to October 13. Tickets $24; $19 for seniors; $17.50 for children 12 to 16; $16.50 for children 3 to 11. Reservations recommended.

Portuguese Princess, 70 Shankpainter Rd., Provincetown, MA (☎ 800/442-3188 or 508/487-2651). MacMillan Wharf. Season runs May through October. Daily three-and-a-half-to-four-hour trips, weather permitting, at 9am and 1pm from May through mid-June; three trips daily, at 9am, and 1 and 5pm from mid-June through Labor Day, a second boat offers three trips starting a bit later. From Labor Day through October, it returns to a schedule of one or two trips daily. Tickets $18 in summer; $16 in spring and fall; $16 in summer; $14 in spring and fall for seniors and children 7 to 16; free for children 6 and younger.

Riverhead Foundation for Marine Research and Preservation, formerly the Okeanos Ocean Research Foundation, 431 E. Main St., Riverhead, LI (☎ 516/369-9840). Plans are not in place for whale-watching excursions this season. The foundation does offer educational displays and various aquariums that demonstrate sea life on Long Island. Open 10am to 5pm weekends January to Memorial Day and Labor Day through the end of December; daily from Memorial Day through Labor Day. Suggested donation $2.

Viking Fishing Fleet, Edgemere Road, off Rte. 27 East, Montauk, LI (☎ 516/668-5700). Whale-watching weekends only in June, then daily from July 4 through Labor Day; boarding is at 10am and sail is at 11am; the boat returns between 2 to 6pm. Tickets $32; $29 for seniors; $15 for children 5 to 12.

Whale Watcher, 1 West St., near Town Pier, Bar Harbor, ME (☎ 800/508-1499 or 207/288-3322). Three-and-one-half-hour daily trips from May 17 to Nov. 1. Boats leave at 11:30am, May 17 to June 16 and September 26 to November 1; at 9am and 2pm, June 17 to July 14 and August 2 to September 25; at 8:15am and 12:30 and 5pm. July 15 to August 21. Tickets $28; $25 for seniors; $18 for children 5 to 15; free for those under five. Also, sightseeing, sailing, and fishing excursions.

The Hudson Valley

GARDEN-HOPPING IN WESTCHESTER

by William Grimes

Iɴ ᴛʜᴇ ʀᴇsᴛ ᴏғ ᴛʜᴇ ᴡᴏʀʟᴅ, sᴘʀɪɴɢ arrives in a riot of color and a burst of warmth. Birds chirp and hearts gladden. In New York, the schedule is a little different. After winter slams down on the city like a frozen, cast-iron lid, imposing a color regime of gray and black, spring works a cruel hoax. It lingers just offstage in the seasonal drama and, with the audience primed for an appearance—it lingers some more.

The calendar pages flip from mid-April to mid-May. The city is lashed by a cold, stinging rain; the ground is held captive in a binding frost. Then, it happens. The long-awaited star steps out onto center stage, executes some frantic dance steps, sings three songs, and then races off. If you blink, you miss it. That was spring. Now it's summer.

For the color-deprived, mid-May is the time. Throughout the region, gardens come into their glory, working double time to make up for a punishing winter. In Manhattan, of course, the grand seasonal shift is purely a matter of temperature and foot-level visibility. (In winter, you can't see the sidewalk; in spring, you can.) Farther afield, though, nature puts on a show.

Here's the drill. Take a map, trace a circle with a radius of about 100 miles, and divide the circle into bite-size sectors. The belt that begins about 40 miles out from Times Square includes prime horticultural territory and therefore is the ideal destination for a quick day trip to take in a handful of public and private gardens.

The Garden Conservancy, a nonprofit group that helps preserve fine gardens, has made life easier for anyone who wants to smell the roses in New York and Connecticut. The group, which was founded in 1989 and has its headquarters in Cold Spring, New York, took its lead from a highly popular British program run by the National Gardens Scheme, in which gifted amateurs open their gardens to the public for browsing.

In its *Open Days Directory*, the Conservancy put together a list of 110 private gardens in the New York area that the public could visit on certain days. The admission fee for each garden was $4, with the proceeds going to the conservancy's preservation programs. The directory, sold for $8, included a guide to public gardens in the areas, making it a one-stop-shopping guide for the garden-happy. The first year's print run was 5,000 copies, which sold out almost immediately. In 1997, the program expanded to 258 private gardens in 17 states, with Long Island and New Jersey added to the list. The gardens are open on selected Saturdays and Sundays from late April to late September.

Showoffs and Foliage

Pick a weekend, a nice destination, and some gardens. My wife and I settled on a doable chunk of northern Westchester that included Bedford and Katonah, rich and rolling country with imposing Colonial houses and some very serious gardens.

Stop no. 1 was the Katonah home of Roxana Robinson, a gardener better known as the author of *Georgia O'Keeffe: A Life* and the short-story collection *Asking for Love*. The *Open Days Directory* gives precise driving directions to each garden, and participants put out a helpful sign with the conservancy's symbol, a blazing sun with a human face. Ms. Robinson's husband, Tony, collected admission fees at the garage, and visitors simply walked into the family's backyard through a white wood gate flanked by two enormous hostas.

The Robinson garden lies somewhere in the middle range of gardens in the conservancy's list. It's not too big, not too small; it's not too structured, but not haphazard either. It provokes envy, but it's possible to believe that two hardworking enthusiasts created it, rather than a team of specialists.

When the Robinsons bought their house in 1978, the garden consisted of foolproof plants like hostas, peonies, and daylilies. Ms. Robinson went to work. "I began making beds, and gradually it took me over," Ms. Robinson said. "It's the reason my novel isn't finished."

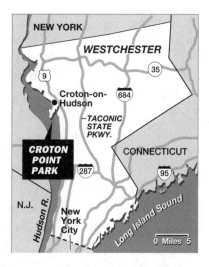

Her method was simple. "It was trial and error and survival of the fittest," she said. Antique roses did not make it. Rugosas did. Other survivors, deployed in modest-size beds, include bleeding hearts, their bunched, cup-shaped petals dangling like cluster earrings, and brunnera, an almost absurdly tiny flower with a blue so deep it pierces. Intermingled with the showoff flowers are foliage plants, like lamb's ears (named for their droopy, fuzzy leaves), which serve as foils. Clusters of phlox spill over a stone wall, and extensive, neat beds of lavender-colored veronica lead to a large dogwood tree.

There was trouble in paradise on the fine May day we visited. In broad daylight, unembarrassed at being perceived as a total cliché, a large king snake slithered across a path and into a tight cluster of lamb's ear, whose trembling marked the fiend's progress. Ms. Robinson was nonchalant. "They're good for the garden," she said. Not good for birds, however. Ms. Robinson, investigating cries of distress from a nearby tree, found out that the snake had snatched a baby cardinal from its nest.

Garden stop no. 2 was a bust, a rather feeble string of borders that looked anemic against a Colonial house of grand proportions set on multiple hilltop acres. Gardens nos. 3 and 4, however, were showstoppers.

In Bedford Hills, Phillis Warden has planted perennial beds punctuated by weird, desert-type shrubs that move along the perimeter of the backyard, leading to a water garden and a carp-filled pool. Outside the backyard fence, the plantings follow shelflike outcroppings of rock in a waterfall that leads to a woodland area.

Planting Xanadu

Not far away, in Bedford, Penelope and John Maynard have created a kind of Xanadu around their house, on a commanding height over-looking Indian Hill in Bedford. A winding stone walkway leads from one pocket-size garden to the next, each with its own color scheme and subtle variations on major themes.

In a formal garden, surrounded by a stone wall, dramatic purple-black Queen of Night tulips dominated the central bed. Nearby, taxicab-yellow lily tulips with racily pointed petals played into a color scheme of burgundy, white, and yellow. Ms. Maynard, a garden designer who helped create the open-days program, makes the most of foliage plants like a variegated euonymus, which droops over the stone wall near the lily tulips in a pompadour of green-and-gold leaves. "Flowers come and go, fleetingly, but the leaves remain," said Ms. Maynard. "Variegation is very important," she added. "It draws a plant forward."

Another bed contains Actinidia kolomitka, the male kiwi plant, whose leaf ends look as if they have been dipped in white paint. As the season progresses, the tips turn pink, producing a tricolor effect—again, variegation. Stalking the grounds are two caramel-colored ocicats. A short-haired breed with brown dots, ocicats are a cross between a Siamese and Abyssinian.

The John Jay Homestead, in Katonah, has three gardens that are tended by three volunteer groups, and the site is worth a flying visit, especially if you are packing a picnic lunch. Roam the Federal-style house and its immediate grounds, by all means, and admire the rose arch that protects the grave of one of the family horses. The standouts, though, can be found well below the house, near the drive.

The sunken formal garden, shaded by enormous red cedars, strikes a romantic note, and lilacs perfume the air. At the center of the garden is a sundial, surrounded by beds of lady's mantle, bleeding hearts, ferns, and thistle. Next to the formal garden is an extensive herb garden maintained by the Herb Society of America. Its brick-lined beds enclose the usual suspects, like chives, sage, and tarragon, along with more exotic citizens like hyssop, rue, and tansy.

Music and Color

The extensive and varied gardens at the Caramoor Center for Music and the Arts, also in Katonah, demand a long, leisurely look. Caramoor, a Mediterranean-style estate built in 1912 by a very rich lawyer, is best known for its summer music festival, but the horticultural program is outstanding. In 1989, the Caramoor Garden Guild took on the responsibility of restoring the gardens, which had languished.

"The gardens had fallen into disrepair, if you can use the word to describe a garden," said Eileen Burton, Caramoor's horticultural director. "There was poison ivy in the beds." There's no poison ivy now. The formal sunken garden was replanted in roses, lilies, and daisies, in a color scheme of pink, white, and silver, the better to be seen at night during the music festival. In the center of each of the four main beds stands a huge terra-cotta amphora, and at the corners, there are urns filled with heliotrope, giving off a seductive licorice-vanilla perfume.

Near the Italian pavilion, a roofed picnic area with an antique tile floor, the Guild recently created a butterfly garden. As luck would have it, butterflies are attracted to violet, gold, and orange, the colors in the tiles, so the color scheme dovetailed perfectly with the existing decor.

Another innovation was the Sense Circle, a garden and moatlike fountain surrounding an old dovecote. The garden, with trees, hedges, grass, and flowers arranged in concentric circles, has been designed to appeal to the visually impaired and handicapped, with bright colors, strong perfumes, and the pleasing sounds of splashing water and rustling trees.

The entire estate is a kind of folly, and maybe even a little foolish. What sense does it make to create an Italo-Spanish estate in suburban New York? None at all. At Caramoor, Venice meets Tuscany by way of Byzantium, yet in an American melting-pot kind of way, this seemingly preposterous mix works. For the city-bound, it offers space, light, color, and fragrance, all the things that spring is supposed to be about.

ESSENTIALS FOR GARDEN-HOPPING IN THE TRI-STATE AREA

The **Garden Conservancy** publishes a tour guide of private and public gardens in New York, Connecticut, New Jersey, and 14 other states. The 1997 *Open Days Directory,* which costs $10 ($8 for conservancy members), plus $2.95 shipping and handling, can be ordered by telephone (☎ 888/842-2442) or by mail from the Garden Conservancy, P.O. Box 219, Cold Spring, NY 10516. Mastercard and Visa are accepted.

Admission is $4 to each private garden in the directory, or $20 for six tours ($16 for conservancy members). Reservations are not necessary. A sampling of public gardens in the metropolitan region follows. Days, hours, and admission prices vary, so you should call ahead to the specific gardens before you visit.

NEW YORK CITY

Brooklyn Botanic Garden, 1000 Washington Ave. (at Prospect Park) (☎ 718/622-4433). A 52-acre site that includes a rose garden featuring 5,000 bushes and 1,200 to 1,500 varieties, as well as a Japanese garden and a children's discovery garden.

New York Botanical Garden, Southern Blvd. and 200th St., Bedford Park, the Bronx (☎ 718/817-8700). A 250-acre site where more than 230 varieties of roses bloom.

Queens Botanical Garden, 43-50 Main St., Flushing (☎ 718/886-3800). Thirty-nine acres with a Victorian wedding garden, demonstration garden, a rose garden with 20 varieties, an herb garden, a pinetum, a woodland garden, and workshops.

Wave Hill, Independence Ave. and 249th St., Riverdale, the Bronx (☎ 718/549-3200). A 28-acre site with several gardens, greenhouses, historic buildings, woodlands, and

lawns. Hours and admission prices are seasonal. From mid-October to mid-May, open Tuesday through Sunday 9am to 4:30pm; from mid-May to mid-October, open Tuesday through Sunday 9am to 4:30pm. From March 15 to November 14, $4 general admission, $2 seniors and students, free for members and children under 6; free admission for all visitors all day Tuesday and Saturday from 9am to noon. Admission free for all visitors from November 15 to March 14.

Family Art Projects, a series of free workshops, is offered year-round on Saturday and Sunday from 1 to 4pm. There are free dance performances on Wednesdays and Sundays in July. From September through April, the park stages classical and jazz concerts; $12 general admission, $10 for seniors and students, $8 for members.

HUDSON VALLEY

Caramoor Gardens, Girdle Ridge Rd. (off Rte. 22), Katonah (☎ 914/232-5035). One hundred acres with woodlands, meadows, perennial, medieval, and butterfly gardens; art exhibitions, workshops, and a performance series.

Hammond Museum and Japanese Stroll Garden, June Rd. (off Rte. 684), North Salem (☎ 914/669-5033). A three-acre Japanese garden.

John Jay Homestead State Historic Site, Jay St. (off Rte. 22), Bedford (☎ 914/232-5651).

Local garden clubs maintain three garden areas, including a herb garden and planting designs from 1800 through the 1930s. Nature activities for children; walking tours every Sunday.

Kykuit, North Tarrytown (☎ 914/631-9491). The Rockefeller estate, with woodlands, a rose garden, and sculpture. Guided tours of the estate are offered from April through early November. Guided tours of the gardens begin in early May and end Columbus Day weekend. The tours, which begin at Philipsburg Manor in North Tarrytown (recently renamed Sleepy Hollow), take two hours. Reservations are required. Each tour is $18, $16 for senior citizens. Not recommended for children.

Montgomery Place, River Rd., Annandale-on-Hudson (☎ 914/758-5461). A 435-acre, 200-year-old estate with a 19th-century picturesque landscape, including thematic gardens, perennial rose borders, a lily pond, an herb garden, orchards, forests, and waterfalls. Open daily (except Tuesday) 10am to 5pm from April 1 through October, and on Saturday and Sunday 10am to 5pm in November and the first two weeks of December.

LONG ISLAND

Longhouse Foundation, 133 Hands Creek Rd., East Hampton (☎ 516/329-3568). Sixteen acres divided into areas of hedges, grasses, and flowering plants. Irises bloom in summer.

Madoo Conservancy, 618 Sagg Main St., Sagaponack (☎ 516/537-8200). Two acres with a hooped rose walk, an Oriental bridge, sculptures, fountains, and gazebo. Among the varieties are roses, poppies, and rhododendron.

Old Westbury Gardens, 71 Old Westbury Rd. (☎ 516/333-0048). About 88 acres of gardens, with a walled perennial garden, formal rose garden, cottage garden, Japanese and vegetable gardens, demonstration garden, meadow, nature walks, and cafe. Concerts held every Wednesday in July.

NEW JERSEY

Cross Estate Garden, Morristown National Historic Park, Ledell Rd. (off Rte. 287), near Mendham (☎ 201/539-2016). A six-acre site with a walled formal garden, pergola, rhododendron and woodland garden, shrubbery; walks and lectures.

Frelinghuysen Arboretum, 53 East Hanover Ave., Morristown (☎ 201/326-7600). Two hundred acres with a rose garden, antique rose collection, fern garden, 11 demonstration gardens, and shade gardens.

Leonard J. Buck Gardens, part of the Somerset County Park Commission, 11 Layton Rd., Far Hills (☎ 908/234-2677). Thirty-five acres with woodlands, forests, wildflowers, a lake and stream, azalea meadow, fern collection, and rhododendrons. There is also the Rudolf van Dergoot Rose Garden in East Millstone with a perennial garden, arboretum, and shrubs.

New Jersey State Botanical Garden at Skylands, Morris Rd. (Rte. 511, Sloatsburg Rd. exit), Ringwood (☎ 201/962-9534 or 201/962-7527). Ninety-six acres with gardens of lilacs, azaleas, peonies, evergreens, wildflowers, and woodlands; lectures, workshops, and other activities.

CONNECTICUT

Gertrude Jekyll Garden at the Glebe House Museum, Hollow Rd., Woodbury (☎ 203/263-2855). One-half-acre English-style mixed border and foundation planting, stone terrace, and rose allée.

Hillside Gardens, 515 Litchfield Rd., Norfolk (☎ 860/542-5345). Five acres with blooming peonies, irises, azaleas, honeysuckles, geraniums, and woodlands.

University of Connecticut Bartlett Arboretum, 151 Brookdale Rd., Stamford (☎ 203/322-6971). A 63-acre garden with woodlands, annual and wildflower gardens, a perennial border, workshops, and a greenhouse.

A Rockefeller's Aerie: Kykuit

by Paul Goldberger

FORGET BILL GATES, NEVER MIND Leslie Wexner; no name in American history connotes money like Rockefeller. Public enough to have a consistently high profile, private enough to have an aura of mystery that never entirely disappears, this family has symbolized American wealth for most of the 20th century.

So it should not be at all surprising that the public opening of Kykuit, the Rockefeller family estate at Pocantico Hills, New York, was greeted with an interest more or less akin to that surrounding the start of public tours of Buckingham Palace. Historic Hudson Valley, the nonprofit organization (and Rockefeller creation) that is managing the tours of Kykuit (rhymes with "high cut"), reports that the first few months of tours in 1994 were virtually sold out, and that demand remains high, three years after the first tour group passed through Kykuit's iron gates.

The Rockefeller property is like nothing else in the United States. Kykuit (the name comes from a Dutch word meaning "lookout") is not by any means the largest villa built by an American fortune, and it is far from the most distinguished one architecturally. As a house, it is, in fact, oddly restrained, almost hesitant, and rather tight in its proportions. But it stands at the crown of a hill overlooking the Hudson River, commanding a stunning 300-acre site in the midst of several thousand more acres of Rockefeller land, all in the middle of the Westchester suburbs. Barely more than 20 miles from Manhattan, and within view of the Tappan Zee Bridge, the site contains the expanse of a vast estate in the Adirondacks, and confers upon the visitor every bit as much of a sense of distance from the city.

This is the true test of great wealth: not the mere possession of land, but the possession of a huge expanse of land close to the city, where others are content with half an acre. Is it an accident that John Hay Whitney and William S. Paley had huge estates in Nassau County just a few miles east of the Queens line? Huge private holdings have all but disappeared within 50 miles of New York City, and the Rockefeller property today is larger than almost any of them ever were, even in the heyday of American fortunes. It's notable that when John D. Rockefeller began acquiring land in the Tarrytown area in 1893, the first 400-acre parcel he purchased had already been earmarked for a real estate subdivision. He bought all the lots and took it off the market, then kept expanding.

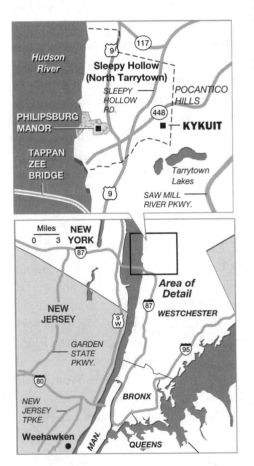

Some years ago, 800 of the Rockefeller acres were given to the State of New York as a park preserve. The heart of the Rockefeller holdings, however, is not the public park but a 300-acre fenced site including Kykuit, not to mention a nine-hole golf course, numerous formal gardens, a huge stone garage structure called the Coach House, an indoor athletic building called the Play House, and a greenhouse pavilion called the Orangerie. (The last two are not part of the public tour, but the Coach House, which holds the family's collection of antique coaches and automobiles, is.)

Eighty-seven of these 300 acres are now owned by the National Trust for Historic Preservation, which acquired them under Nelson Rockefeller's will. Rockefeller, the former Vice President and Governor of New York who died in 1979, was the most public and flamboyant Rockefeller, and he envisioned the estate—which he owned jointly with his brothers, Laurence and David—less as a private retreat than as a monument to the family. Several family members were more than a little surprised when, after Rockefeller's death, it turned out that he had left his one-third interest in the property entirely to the National Trust.

Nelson Rockefeller's gesture set in motion the process that led ultimately to the opening of the estate to the public. It took 15 years, however; in part because his brothers, preferring not to share owner-ship of the whole property with the National Trust, made a deal to swap their interest in Kykuit and its immediate surroundings for the trust's share of the whole property. The trust ended up owning 87 acres and the house outright; the family kept the rest and, since the trust has no funds of its own, agreed to maintain the property through the Rockefeller Brothers Fund. The fund assigned Historic Hudson Valley, operators of Westchester County properties like Sunnyside and Philipsburg Manor, to run the public tours.

Cartesian Order on Top

Visitors who book tours (admission is by reservation only) drive not to the Rockefeller property but to the visitors center of Philipsburg Manor, a mile or so away on Route 9 in the village of Sleepy Hollow (formerly North Tarrytown). Vans carry each tour group of 18 up to the estate, through the main gate and up a winding road to the forecourt of Kykuit at the hilltop.

The landscaping is relaxed and easy in the lower reaches of the hill-side, with wide expanses of rolling lawn, carefully tended trees, and pieces from Nelson Rockefeller's impressive collection of 20th-century sculpture, placed with precision by Rockefeller himself. But the mood changes at the hilltop, where the Beaux-Arts sensibility of William Welles Bosworth, the architect who more than any other gave Kykuit its form, takes over. Suddenly the natural lushness gives way to formal geometries, and the rural ease to a rigid Cartesian order.

Is Kykuit a French chateau sitting atop an English landscape, then, a kind of Versailles in the sky? It's actually even more of a hybrid than that, both as a building and as a total work of architecture and landscape. The history of Kykuit's design, not unlike the negotiations over its ownership that consumed much of the 1980s, is a complex tale. Suffice it to say that the original house on the property was relatively modest, fitting the preferences of the senior John D. Rockefeller. When it burned in 1902, Rockefeller first asked Dunham A. Wheeler to design a simple house to go at the highest point of the site, but eventually gave in to the view of his son, John D. Rockefeller, Jr., who had more ambitious notions of what sort of country seat the Rockefeller family should have. The Rockefellers hired Delano & Aldrich, who later became one of the most celebrated purveyors of traditional architecture to the rich, to produce a Georgian house, but the senior Rockefeller insisted that the design follow the outline of the relatively modest T-shaped floor plan of Wheeler's unbuilt design.

Eventually John D. Rockefeller, Jr., managed to bring in two other players: Ogden Codman, to design the interiors and furnishings, and Bosworth, to lay out the gardens, which soon became grander and more elaborate than the house itself. When the senior Rockefellers decided they were less than happy with the house, which was completed in 1908, the younger Rockefeller had it almost completely reconstructed, expanding it from three to four stories and giving it a new classical facade of rough stone by Bosworth.

Five Different Visions

Kykuit as it stands today, then, is a collaboration of three architects and two clients, none of whom had precisely the same vision of what it should be. (There is actually even a fourth architect: Herbert Newman, who was brought in by the Rockefeller Brothers Fund to make some behind-the-scenes improvements to ready the house for public visitation. Mr. Newman also renovated the basement of the old carriage barn into a handsome private conference center for the fund.) Considering the complexity of its authorship, the place is not nearly as much of an architectural camel as it could have been; there is a certain graciousness to Bosworth's classical facade, and the house's mix of idiosyncrasy and restraint stands in welcome contrast to the self-important hauteur of the average pile of stone in Newport.

And it turned out, perhaps in spite of itself, to be a perfect expression of the Rockefeller ethos. This is not a modest house, as the Rockefellers were not modest, but neither is it a house that seems designed to project any sense of extravagance. A great deal of money was spent here, but every stone proclaims money spent out of a sense of duty, not out of a sense of hedonism. There is nothing vulgar here, and that alone separates Kykuit from almost every great house produced in the golden age of American wealth.

You might say that Kykuit is what you get when you merge John D. Rockefeller's Baptist restraint with American extravagance: something slightly at odds with itself, a house that seems to want to be grand and to disappear at the same time. The shape of the house is itself tight, almost urban, disproportionately tall and narrow in the manner of a great town house. It is a country house in a corset.

An Urban Feel Inside

It feels even more urban when you go inside, to a narrow, vaulted vestibule that seems like the ground-floor entrance to a town house. A small paneled sitting room, once John D. Rockefeller's office, is to the left; another small sitting room, with delicate, Adamesque detailing, is to the right. It is only the view straight ahead through the house to the extraordinary vista of the Hudson beyond that reminds you where you are.

The main tour takes visitors through the main rooms of the first floor, moving in and out of the building to encompass portions of the surrounding gardens. (A separate tour, called the Garden and Sculpture Tour, offers a more in-depth view of the gardens.) It is the gardens, mostly laid out by Bosworth, that are the truly spectacular thing here. In many ways, the land has it all over the architecture, since the site is so full of grand gestures, and the house, whatever its virtues, is so empty of them. The one room that tries to do something spectacular, the so-called music room at the heart of the structure, which has an elliptical opening to the floor above, sums up the problem of this house: it is too tall, too tight, too unwilling to let itself go.

Yet how like the generation of Rockefellers who built Kykuit! John D. Rockefeller disapproved of drinking, dancing, and other pleasures; the music room was designed to hold a pipe organ, and Sunday afternoon organ music was the elder Rockefeller's favored entertainment. His son, John D. Rockefeller, Jr., was more comfortable with grand architectural gestures, but even for him, a sense of duty always came first. He envisioned Kykuit not as a palace of pleasure but as the serious expression of the stature of a great family. If this freed Kykuit from the vulgar excesses of Newport and Fifth Avenue, it also gave the estate more than a whiff of dry formality.

It's no accident, then, that Kykuit lacks such showy symbols as a grand staircase; the second floor (which is not included in the public tour) is reached by a stair that is not much larger than the one you would find in a suburban house, tucked behind the partition that once contained the pipe organ. The main public rooms are hardly small, but neither do they approach the institutional scale of the ballrooms and reception rooms of so many American palaces of this period; indeed, these rooms always feel domestic, which was presumably the intention. They are furnished conservatively, with a mix of antiques and plain upholstered pieces, and have a number of paintings of note, including a Gilbert Stuart portrait of George Washington in the library and John Singer Sargent's portrait of the senior Rockfeller in the dining room, as well as numerous examples of Chinese ceramics.

Paintings and Sculpture

The real energy in both the house and grounds, however, comes from those portions of Nelson Rockefeller's collection of 20th-century painting and sculpture that remain here. Rockefeller, who occupied the house from 1960 on, removed the old pipe organ and put a large Miro in its place (the original has since gone to the Museum of Modern Art in Manhattan, with a copy now hanging in the Kykuit music room). He put Giacometti lamps in the alcove overlooking the river, and Picasso etchings in the stairwell, starting a dialogue between the generations that enlivens the house considerably.

Rockefeller also converted portions of the basement and underground tunnel system into contemporary art galleries, which remain
more or less as he left them, period ensembles from the early 1960s.
The first two rooms, jammed tight with smaller works by Fritz Glarner,
Larry Bell, Robert Motherwell, Ernest Trova, Ibram Lassaw, and Mary
Callery—not to mention Picasso, Braque, and Calder—provide splendid insight into the catholicity of Rockefeller's modernist taste. These
rooms were a marvelous, highly personal indulgence, not just in the
quantity of art they contain—there are more than 100 works—but also
in the way in which Rockefeller intended them to make up a complete
and discrete modernist world within the historical fabric of Kykuit.

Visitors walk through most of the galleries, passing some larger
portraits of Nelson and Happy Rockefeller by Andy Warhol, as well
as two George Segals and two Leger rugs, with glimpses of several
Picasso tapestries, before moving outdoors again to the gardens. The
tour includes most, but not all, of Bosworth's formal gardens, which is
where the architect's Beaux-Arts instincts took full reign: There are
planted terraces, reflecting pools, an allee of linden trees, a semicircular rose garden, and numerous distinct gardens, each a kind of outdoor room in itself. (A Japanese garden, a stone grotto, and a putting
green can all be viewed from a distance, but are not included on the
tour.)

The landscape has a clear order to it: rigid and formal at the hilltop close to the house, gradually opening up to wide, rolling vistas as
the space tumbles down toward the river. The high site creates the
marvelous illusion that the property runs all the way to the Hudson
River (in fact, the whole village of Sleepy Hollow exists between Kykuit
and the river, utterly invisible from the house); and with the Palisades
largely protected from development on the river's west side, the sense
of being in a distant wilderness is nearly total.

Most spectacular, however, is Nelson Rockefeller's sculpture, which
was placed sensitively, and at times brilliantly, around the property.
Some pieces, like Max Bill's granite *Triangular Surface in Space*, at the
end of a formal pergola, are on a formal axis, very much part of
Bosworth's Beaux-Arts organization. Others, like Calder's metal sta-
bile *Large Spiny* and Maillol's *Night*, are set more in nature; some

pieces, like an unusually strong Henry Moore, *Knife Edge—Two Piece,* have been sited both to tie into the axis of the house and to be out on the open landscape. Rockefeller is said to have moved his favorite pieces frequently, and to have chosen many of the sculpture sites by hovering over the property in a helicopter.

The 20th-century sculpture remaining at Kykuit is, on balance, the best art at the estate, and its relationship to the architecture, the gardens, and the natural landscape is the most powerful esthetic experience to be had here—at least, the most powerful manmade one. Few things can equal the drama of Kykuit's site, a drama enhanced by the sense that it is almost illicit to have a piece of landscape like this in the midst of suburbia. Rockefeller's sculpture, placed with precision and with total respect for the order of the house, nonetheless manages to break the place wide open, celebrating Kykuit's natural glories and at the same time filling the property with a sense of fresh air.

KYKUIT ESSENTIALS

Kykuit, the Rockefeller family estate in Pocantico Hills, New York, can be visited only on a two-hour escorted tour. Visits to the 300-acre estate leave daily (except Tuesdays) from the visitors center at nearby Philipsburg Manor, on Route 9 in Sleepy Hollow (formerly North Tarrytown).

GETTING THERE

By Car   Philipsburg Manor can be reached by the Gov. Thomas E. Dewey Thruway to Tarrytown (exit 9); take Rte. 119 to Rte. 9. Or take the Sawmill River Pkwy. to Rte. 287, then follow Rte. 119 to Rte. 9.

By Train   There is also a Tarrytown stop on the Hudson line of **Metro-North** (☎ 212/ 532-4900); weekend round-trip fare from Grand Central Terminal is $10. Taxis are available at the train station for the short ride to Philipsburg Manor; one-way fare is about $2.75.

By Bus   The no. 13 **Beeline Bus** (☎ 914/ 682-2020) makes a stop at the Tarrytown train station and runs north along Rte. 9; the southbound bus is the no. 13B; one-way fare is $1.15.

TOURING THE ESTATE

There are two separate tours, both of which take approximately the same length of time: the House and Galleries Tour and the Garden and Sculpture Tour. The first tour includes some minor glimpses of the gardens, and the second includes a few minutes inside the house, so either can serve as a basic introduction to Kykuit. Both tours, administered by Historic Hudson Valley, begin at Philipsburg Manor with a short film about Kykuit and the Rockefeller family; visitors are then taken by shuttle van to the estate.

Tickets for either tour are $18; $16 for seniors, students, and children. Tours begin daily at 10am and run every 20 minutes; the last tour departs Philipsburg Manor at 4pm on Saturdays and Sundays and 3pm on weekdays. For reservations, call ☎ 914/631-9491.

CRUISING TO KYKUIT

In addition, there is a special seven-hour Hudson River cruise and guided Kykuit estate tour offered by **New York Waterway** (☎ 800/533-3779). Boats leave Thursday through Sunday from Port Imperial in Weehawken, New Jersey, and the Manhattan terminal at 12th Avenue and 38th Street, for a one-and-a-half-hour cruise up the Hudson River to Tarrytown; buses will then transport passengers to Phillipsburg Manor. Round-trip cruise and tour tickets are $60. Reservations are necessary.

FARM LIFE OF THE TWENTIES FOR CHILDREN OF THE NINETIES

by Jo Thomas

🍁

I TOOK MY TWO CHILDREN TO Muscoot Farm on a dreary Sunday in November, when the bored quarreling that begins on a day to be spent indoors sent me running for a map and extra sweatshirts and dry socks to stuff in a shopping bag. The farm, in the Westchester County town of Katonah, was a long drive from our house in New Jersey, and there were moments, as we approached the Tappan Zee Bridge, when I had my doubts as the rain and the unseasonably warm temperature wrapped the car in a white haze. My daughters ate the Halloween candy they had brought and submerged themselves in headsets and the silence that usually means the Offspring and Pink Floyd. But it was raining, and I was on the run from a Sunday indoors.

"A farm?" Susan, 12, had asked in disbelief. In an instant, she remembered a major school project on Ulysses S. Grant that was due the next day. She didn't need a trip to a farm. She had to do her homework.

"Do it later," I told her.

Kathleen, seven, was eager to go. In five minutes, she packed a raincoat, two soft drinks, candy, a large stack of story tapes, a camera, two books, crayons, and a notebook. By the time we had turned north on Interstate 684, just outside White Plains, she was hungry. We stopped at the Friendly's in Mount Kisco, New York, for cheese sandwiches, pizza, and ice cream cones, which turned out to be a good idea because the snack bar at the farm was closed. (There were picnic tables.) The restaurant was full of children and parents getting out of the house, and as we left, the rain was still beating down.

It wasn't until we had turned off the interstate and were driving south on Route 100 that the world flying past the windows caught my daughters' eyes, and we all saw it at the same time: a vast black lake and, in the distance, a white swan, like a vision from a fairy tale, swimming alone under a leaden sky. In a moment, we were past it and into the trees. "Did you see that?" asked Kathleen. "Did you see that?"

The lake is Muscoot Reservoir, part of the New York City system. It was on land owned by the Hopkins family for three generations, starting in 1880. When New York City bought the land, the main farmhouse was moved several hundred yards to save it. In 1965, the family sold Muscoot Farm, 777 acres of farmland and forest, to Westchester County, and the farm's operation was taken over by the Department of Parks, Recreation, and Conservation.

From the 1880s to the 1950s, Muscoot Farm was a country gentleman's farm. It is now an "interpretive farm," the brochures explain. You can't feed or touch the animals. It is not, a multitude of signs repeat, a petting zoo. When my daughters were small, we visited a few commercial petting zoos. The animals were usually goats or deer, and the children loved touching them. But the sale of feed paid the bills in these places, and the animals always looked stuffed and torpid. After a few visits, we avoided petting zoos.

The Muscoot Farm brochure promised farm life "as it would have been lived in the 1920s." I wondered how. I didn't want animation or characters from costume shops. We passed a large white Colonial Revival house with white columns, as beautiful as anything in a movie, and turned into the parking lot. The rain was now a fine mist, but there were only a few cars. No out-of-state license plates. No visitors in sight. There was a World War I exhibition in the main house, but the girls had already spotted the animals, so we walked toward a cluster of outbuildings, some dark red and some white. A long-haired farm cat, gray with touches of marmalade, was curled up in a bed of red geraniums. My daughters made a dash for a pen of geese and

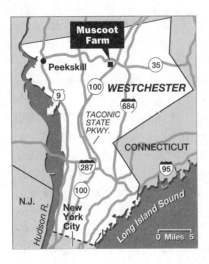

ducks, but I stopped to look at the colors of the cat and the geraniums, realizing for the first time that we hadn't yet seen a frost this season.

The ducks were asleep, their heads tucked back under their feathers. Kathleen tried twisting her own head back, then gave up. "It'd be hard to sleep like this," she said.

"Look!" Susan said. "The geese are standing on one foot." The geese ignored us. But the turkeys didn't. They were in a shed beyond the barn. They showed off, fluffing out their black feathers like dancers. It was the first time we'd seen turkeys that weren't in a frozen-food case, and they didn't go "Gobble, gobble" as they do in books. They made a whistling sound, a kind of begging noise that made us sad.

"Their faces look all warty," said Susan.

"Why are they so ugly?" asked Kathleen.

We looked at the obvious things: the cows in the pasture, the sheep and pigs in the barns. A long white grape arbor led from the main house to an outhouse, a four-and-a-half holer, the brochure explained. We skipped the trip inside. I asked Kathleen what she would do if she had to make her way through such an arbor in the middle of the night.

"I'd ask my parents to build a bathroom," she said.

There was a horse barn, with two large box stalls and an array of harnesses. The girls, who love horses, rushed in, then backpedaled in terror as a flock of small birds whizzed out of the dark loft above their heads. The horses, as brown as the muddy paddock, were outside, along with an elegant pair of mules, both dapple gray. In good weather, the mules pull hayrides. But the farm roads were full of puddles, and the mules kept a good distance from the visitors, wagging their ears but refusing my daughters' entreaties to come closer.

Muscoot Farm is surrounded by stone walls, supplemented now with white board and wire fences. In the 1920s, although the Hopkins family used cars for transportation, draft horses were still used for plowing. The tractors couldn't fit through the openings in the stone walls.

"They were hand-laid, in my mother's time," said Charlie Bassett, whose grandfather was the superintendent of the farm for 40 years. Mr. Bassett, in his 60s, worked on the farm as a young man and was paying a visit to the blacksmith shop when Kathleen picked up a black fistful from the cold furnace and asked him, "Is this real coal?" Mr. Bassett seemed happy to explain that it was.

A sign outside said Jasper Booth, a blacksmith, had lived and worked at Muscoot Farm for most of his life, shoeing horses and making tools. "He made the hinges," Mr. Bassett said. "He made the shovels."

Clearly, he was a good source. Susan and Kathleen asked if he could get them into the modern milk house. They had visited the old milk house. A sign there explained that in the days before electrification, cans of milk were cooled in cement troughs of ice water until they could be taken by draft horses to the depot at Whitehall Corners, a mile and a half away. The girls had been too short to look in the windows of the old milk house, but when they tried the latch, the door opened. Inside, the room was bare and a little dusty, but they could see the old troughs. They'd had no such luck at the modern milk house. It was locked.

No, Mr. Bassett couldn't let them in, but he could show them the pond where blocks of ice were cut in winter, then taken to the ice house and covered with sawdust and straw to keep it well into the summer. Susan wasn't so keen to see the pond; she asked for the car keys to get her Walkman. She could catch up with us later.

We walked through the barns and out toward the fields, with Kathleen skidding through the mud, her battered tennis shoes turning black. We passed giant trees, leafless but labeled so we wouldn't mistake them even in winter: a majestic white oak, a red maple, a shagbark hickory tree. I was beginning to realize, with relief, that no one was selling anything here. There was nothing to buy.

"When the farmer is through, the developer comes in," Mr. Bassett said, waving his arm at the hills, the pastures, and the old apple orchard. "If the county didn't get it, this'd be all houses."

"There's coyotes here," he told Kathleen. "And a wolf, too. Last year I saw that wolf three or four times."

"What does he look like?" she asked.

"Like a big, heavy dog. He's in good shape."

The pond was silver, surrounded by woods, silent, empty, shimmering beyond a wooden dock that had a single bench. Not a bird. Not a sound. The afternoon was fading: It was 2:30, and we hadn't seen the main house yet. The exhibition there closed at three. We walked back. Susan met us at the entrance to the barnyard.

The World War I exhibition had been set up in the drawing room. It was an old-fashioned display, without Plexiglas or glass cases. The uniforms and medals and letters were laid on tables, and a small crowd stood talking quietly. Kathleen picked up one of the pistols lying next to a hand grenade.

"Put that down!" I hissed, grabbing it from her. It was heavy and old. Nobody seemed to mind that we had touched it. Kathleen fingered an old medal hanging from a uniform. "It's very pretty," she said.

Only the first floor of the house is open to the public, and only on summer weekends these days, from May to October, but the house alone is worth the trip. It is furnished with antiques that would crowd a lesser house, with fireplaces, lace curtains, and glassed-in bookcases. The girls quickly lost interest in the furnishings, but Susan stopped to watch a weaver work at a loom in one of the halls, and Kathleen sat down at the big kitchen table to color in a drawing of a trumpeter of the Hussars in the French Army of 1914. She went out to look at the uniforms again, hoping to get the color right.

There was a wood stove in the kitchen, and in the adjacent laundry, three great washtubs and some washboards, hanging on a nearby wall. There were no smells of a farm kitchen, only the pale light falling through blue gingham curtains and a group of children trading drawings, but it was not hard to imagine the tremendous labor it had taken to keep such a farm going.

The tools were in a building out back: crosscut saws, a potato planter, a bucksaw, a cider press, a bone grater, a treadmill, a work sled, a festive red sleigh. I told Susan she had to see the lake. The three of us walked back, past the corn crib, past a crowd of toddlers looking at the goats, past a showy black pony, finding a large rabbit hole on the way.

It was beginning to get dark. We sat on the pier and looked at the gray sky and the black water. "Do you know fish like ice cream?" Susan asked. "I went fishing once, and I dropped my cone." The farm would close at 4pm. No one wanted to leave.

We promised we would come back. There are trails through the farm. On weekends, there is always some activity: a nature walk, a blacksmithing class, lessons in making bread-dough vegetables and fruits for a Thanksgiving cornucopia, or a demonstration of how to make a gingerbread house. A few require preregistration or a small fee. Admission to the farm is free, so we left a donation for animal food.

MUSCOOT FARM

Muscoot Farm is on Route 100 in Katonah, NY (☎ 914/232-7118). From Memorial Day and through Labor Day, the farm is open daily 10am to 6pm; the rest of the year, it is open daily 10am to 4pm.

To reach the farm from Manhattan, take the Hutchinson River Parkway to Interstate 684 North; follow I-684 to Route 35 (exit 6) and turn left onto Route 35 West. Continue to Route 100. Turn left onto Route 100 South, and continue for a little more than a mile. The entrance to the farm is on the right.

In addition to buildings dating from the 1880s (some filled with antiques), the trails on the farm's 777 acres, a display of tools and machinery, and the animals that roam the property, there are free activities for families on Sunday afternoons; these may be demonstrations of traditional crafts like smocking, or activities such as cooking in which children can participate. At various times, there are also classes in crafts like blacksmithing, which require payment and preregistration.

Admission to the farm is free for individuals and families; larger groups pay a fee and need to preregister for special activities. Information and a quarterly calendar are available by calling the number above.

On festival days, Mr. Bassett told us, there are huge crowds. We hope to go back for one of those. But on Muscoot Farm it will be hard to beat a Sunday in late autumn when little more than the rain is going on.

HAPPY TRAILS
ALONG THE RIVER

by William Grimes

For most of this century, the Hudson has been the John Barrymore of rivers, noble in profile but a sorry wreck. Decades of binging on toxic chemicals gradually took its toll, and although the river's grandeur could not be denied, most people, looking at the Hudson, could only shake their heads in sorrow. The mighty river, once home to porpoises and even one reported whale, had entered the final stages of decline, fit habitat only for a few funky fish.

Then, the impossible happened. In an awesome display of will-power, the Hudson took the pledge. Thanks to the good efforts of environmental and education groups like Scenic Hudson, the Open Space Institute, and the Hudson River Valley Greenway, along with large infusions of cash from the Lila Acheson and DeWitt Wallace Fund for the Hudson Highlands and the political push behind the Federal Clean Water Acts and other environmental laws, the river came back from the brink and is on the way to sound health, with two pleasing results.

First, a cleaner river has meant a return of fish and other wildlife. Second, heightened river consciousness has led many riverside towns and counties, as well as the above-mentioned organizations, to reclaim land along the riverfront and open it up to hikers, bikers, and picnickers. In the last few years, acres of land that had been languishing in government hands, as well as new parcels acquired by environmental groups, have reconfigured the Hudson's banks.

For day-trippers, fishermen, history buffs, boaters, hikers, bikers, and, yes, even swimmers, the Hudson River Valley has taken on a new allure. A decade ago, travelers had to search long and hard for a decent bed and a good meal. In recent years, dozens of new restaurants, inns, and bed-and-breakfasts have filled the gap.

The grand estates along the banks of the Hudson have always drawn a big audience, but these box-office stars now have a strong supporting cast. Visitors can round out a trip to the Vanderbilt Mansion, for example, by hiking downriver along a new trail to the Franklin D. Roosevelt estate. Up and down the river, parks and boat launches have been opened and new hiking trails have been marked. Beginning in the summer of 1996, swimmers were able to bathe in the Hudson for the first time in nearly a decade, when the river beach at Croton Point Park reopened.

"In the last 10 years, the area has really come together in a way it never had," said Tim Mulligan, the author of *The Traveler's Guide to the Hudson River Valley*. "In the next edition of my book, I'm going to have to redo the whole thing."

In June 1996, Scenic Hudson, a nonprofit preservation group that has acquired many sites along the river, opened Poets' Walk, a 120-acre park in Red Hook, New York, just north of the Kingston-Rhinecliff bridge in Dutchess County. In an area dominated by grand robber-baron estates, Poets' Walk competes by appealing to the more lofty human faculties. Billing itself as a "romantic landscape park," it offers a seductive blend of meadow, glade, and woodland, with sinuous trails descending to the banks of the Hudson.

Meadows and Flowers

The only manmade real estate comes in the form of rough-hewn bridges that cross streamlets, a gazebolike viewing pavilion overlooking the river from a commanding height, and a shelter with benches at the end of a woodland trail.

But who needs real estate? Visitors follow a mowed path across bright meadows scattered with wildflowers: bachelor's buttons, Queen Anne's lace, black-eyed Susans, and daisies. The silence is thick enough to slice.

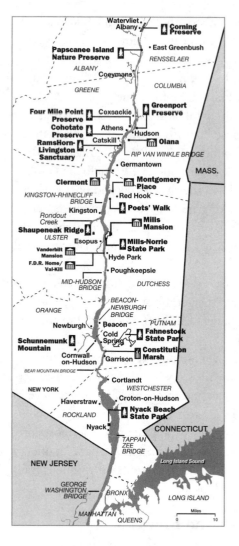

The viewing pavilion makes a convenient halfway stop. A half-mile downhill, the Hudson rolls along between shapely hills, its placid surface lightly supporting small sailboats and enduring with mild patience the torment of type A jet skiers.

The prospect is indeed romantic, with the Catskills floating bluely to the northwest. More pleasure lies ahead, as the path turns rightward and winds through a cool forest downward to the "summer house" shelter, overlooking a small pond, railroad tracks, and the river. After a poetic, romantic pause, visitors can pick up the trail and follow it as it loops back toward meadowland with views of the river and back uphill to the starting point.

Anyone with a hankering to see a house can follow River Road north to Montgomery Place, in Annandale-on-Hudson, a 19th-century country estate set on more than 400 acres of rolling woodland, lawns, gardens, and waterfalls. The house itself is a gem. The original house, a somewhat austere Federal-style structure built in 1802, was transformed by the architect Alexander Jackson Davis and the landscape architect Andrew Jackson Downing into an elegant country estate, with porticos, pavilions, verandas, and a spacious north portico with a stunning view of the river.

Poets' Walk created a park where none existed. In other projects along the river, parcels of land have been stitched together by trails, a less dramatic approach that has opened up long stretches of riverfront. Visitors to the Mills Mansion in Staatsburg can now walk down to the riverside, turn just below an old logging trail, and follow a challenging trail along the river as far as Norrie Point Park. In its first couple of hundred yards, the trail takes you up and over mini-precipices with rather fearsome sheer drops to the river below. Immediately, the trail heads downhill, and hikers can gaze across the glassy waters of a broad inlet, a scene straight out of a Fitz Hugh Lane painting.

"This is all owned by the state and all cohesively managed," said Dave Sampson, the executive director of the Hudson River Greenway Communities Council, a branch of the Greenway. "You couldn't put that together now for all the money in the Environmental Trust Fund."

Similarly, the Vanderbilt Mansion in Hyde Park has been linked by a trail system to the Franklin D. Roosevelt Home and Val-Kill cottage, the Eleanor Roosevelt National Historic Site. The river path, separated from the riverbank by railroad tracks, affords only intermittent glimpses of the Hudson, but the path is cool and soft underfoot, and at Bard Rock, hikers can turn left, cross the tracks, and arrive at a breezy outcropping with picnic tables.

For years, conservation groups have reached into their arsenal for a sobering statistic: More than 70% of the population that lives along the Hudson does not have access to the river. "I grew up on the river, and you didn't have a problem with access," said Rene Van Schaack, the executive director of the Greene County Soil and Water Conservation District. "As time passed, it became tougher and tougher to get access, as parcels were bought up, especially with the boom in second-home ownership during the 80s. As the river has gotten cleaner, though, more people want to get to it." Esopus, which has more shoreline along the river than any town between New York City and Albany, had no public access to the river until 1990, when Scenic

Hudson acquired land and created a pocket-size park of about three-quarters of an acre, which it has added to more recently.

A Different Landscape

There's a finite amount of riverfront. Rather than sit still as more and more of it fell into private hands, state and local officials, along with environmental groups, have moved quickly in recent years to acquire land and open it up. The landscape along the river looks quite different now than it did even five years ago.

"In a way, it all has to do with the decline of IBM, which dominated the valley for so long," said Mr. Mulligan. "People were thrown back on their own resources. Local papers now talk about their communities as tourist destinations, and towns up and down the river, which used to be highly competitive and jealous of each other, are now working with each other." In East Greenbush, near Albany, the Open Space Institute and Scenic Hudson opened Papscanee Island Nature Preserve, a string of three parcels of land near the fringe of an industrial area. The 150 acres include woodland, wetlands, and a small farm.

In Greenport, the Columbia Land Conservancy now runs a 450-acre park called the Greenport Preserve, with hiking trails that lead to bluffs overlooking an extensive wetland complex along the Hudson. New York State has added 2,000 acres to Fahnestock State Park in Cold Spring that include ridge trails with breathtaking views of Storm King Mountain. At the same time, the New York–New Jersey Trail Conference cleared and marked 22 miles of trails in the park.

On Schunnemunk Mountain, in Cornwall-on-Hudson, the Open Space Institute has acquired a 2,100-acre tract, with ridge trails maintained by the New York–New Jersey Trail Conference, that permits hikers to look out over 50 miles of the Hudson Valley and long stretches of the river. Since May 1996, hikers have been able to walk the Shaupeneak Ridge, west of Kingston, for a commanding view of the river.

In Greene County, the Soil and Water Conservation District manages a 52-acre parcel just south of Athens. Called the Cohotate Preserve, it includes 3,500 feet of river frontage. The preserve has self-guided interpretive trails. The county has also created, with Scenic Hudson, a small seven-acre preserve at Four Mile Point, near Coxsackie.

Paddling in the Marshes

For years, the Audubon Society has offered guided canoe trips through Constitution Marsh, midway between Garrison and Cold Spring, in the Hudson Highlands. In cooperation with Scenic Hudson, it added another expanse of wetlands to its portfolio, the RamsHorn-Livingston Sanctuary, situated along RamsHorn Creek, south of Catskill and across the river from Olana, the estate of Frederic Edwin Church. At nearly 800 acres, RamsHorn is the largest tidal swamp forest on the Hudson, a kind of northern bayou that visitors can explore by foot or canoe (bring your own), paddling along the creek to its confluence with the Hudson. The preserve encompasses nearly 500 acres.

Several towns along the river, including Cortlandt, Coeymans, Beacon, and Haverstraw, have cleaned up existing river parks or opened new ones. Kingston, in particular, has energetically restored its historic waterfront area, Rondout Landing, and visitors can take ferries and cruise ships from the old port.

For bicycle riders, as well, the picture is becoming brighter. "The Palisades Interstate Park Commission and the Taconic Region are getting more biker-friendly," said Peter Kick, the author of *Twenty-Five Mountain Bike Tours in the Hudson Valley*. "At Norrie Point, for example, they opened their trails to mountain bikers." Mr. Kick singled out the 14-mile stretch of the Mohawk-Hudson Bikeway between Watervliet and Albany for special praise, as well as the bike trail at Nyack Beach State Park, a 10-mile round-trip between the park and Haverstraw.

Whales and porpoises have not yet returned. Modern-day Americans can only wonder at Walt Whitman's description of the bald eagle he saw soaring over the river as he rode a northbound train. But the river itself flows on, cleaner than it has been in living memory, imposing and lovely, what one 19th-century guidebook called "a noble threshold to a great Continent."

ESSENTIALS FOR HUDSON-HOPPING

GETTING THERE

By Car   There are so many destinations that there are no one-size-fits-all travel directions. In general, to reach the towns along the eastern Hudson by car, take the Saw Mill River Parkway or the Thomas E. Dewey Thruway to Tarrytown; pick up Rte. 9 and follow it north along the river. For towns on the west side of the river, cross the Tappan Zee Bridge and take the Palisades Parkway north to Rte. 9W.

By Train   The Hudson line of Metro-North (☎ 212/532-4900; outside New York City, 800/638-7646) provides train service as far north as Poughkeepsie, originating at Grand Central Terminal. Metro-North also offers travel and tour packages to West Point, Hyde Park, and the Hudson River estates operated by Historic Hudson Valley; special day trips are also offered to various fairs throughout, including the Croton Point Park River Fair in early August and the Hudson River Arts Festival in late September. Call Metro-North at the number above for train schedules and other information.

HUDSON RIVER CRUISES

The *Rip Van Winkle*, Rondout Waterfront, Rondout Creek (at the foot of Broadway), Kingston (exit 19 of the Gov. Thomas E. Dewey Thruway; ☎ 914/255-6515). Two-hour cruises south to Hyde Park, past lighthouses and mansions, and back to Kingston. May through October, Saturday and Sunday at 2pm; July 4 through Labor Day, also Tuesday through Sunday at 11:30am and 2pm. Tickets (available one hour before cruise time) are $12.50, $11.50 fir seniors, $5.50 for children 4 to 11, free for children under 4.

Great Hudson Sailing Center (☎ 800/237-1557 or 914/429-1557) operates 43-foot sailing vessels from the Rondout Waterfront in Kingston, and from the Haverstraw Marina, Beach Road, Haverstraw. From April through October, two-hour sunset cruises are offered at 6pm. Tickets are $35 per person in Kingston, $40 in Haverstraw. Wine and cheese are included.

North River Cruises, Rondout Waterfront, Kingston (☎ 914/679-8205). You can take a 90-minute trip on the Hudson River aboard the motor yacht *Teal*. May 1 through October 31, cruises are offered Saturday and Sunday at 1pm and 3pm; sunset trips are also offered Friday, Saturday, and Sunday at 7:30pm from July 4 through Labor Day. Tickets $10, $5 for children under 12. Call a week in advance to check schedule, since the boat is not available if chartered.

A MUSEUM

Hudson River Maritime Museum, Rondout Waterfront (at the foot of Broadway), Kingston (☎ 914/338-0071). Open May through October, daily (except Tuesday) 11am to 5pm. Admission $2, $1.50 seniors, $1 children 5 to 12; free for children 4 and under and museum members.

Boat trips to the lighthouse are offered weekends from May to June, daily (except Tuesday) in July and August, and weekends in September and October. Boat trips depart from the museum beginning at 12:30pm. Tickets, which include admission to the museum, are $6, $5 for seniors and children 4 to 11, children under 4 free.

HISTORIC HOUSES

Clermont State Historic Site, Rte. 9G, 15 miles south of Hudson in Clermont (☎ 518/537-4240). A 485-acre estate with the mansion of Robert R. Livingston, a drafter of the Declaration of Independence; there is also a formal garden, hiking trails, and the exhibition "Robert R. Livingston and the Age of Enlightenment," a collection of 90 objects including furniture, paintings, and decorative arts. Open Tuesday through Sunday 11am to 4pm, and Monday holidays 10am to 4pm. Admission $3, $2 seniors, $1 children 5 to 12; free for children under 5.

Mills Mansion, Mills-Norrie State Park, Rte. 9, between Hyde Park and Rhinebeck in Staatsburg (☎ 914/889-4100). The 900-acre Beaux-Arts estate of Ogden and Ruth Livingston Mills is a New York State Historic Site with hiking trails, river views, and guided tours. Open mid-April through October and December, Wednesday through Saturday 10am to 5pm and Sunday noon to 5pm (last tour at 4:30pm). Admission and house tour $3, $1 for children 12 and under. Free admission to grounds.

Montgomery Place, River Rd., Annandale-on-Hudson (☎ 914/758-5461). The early 19th-century, 434-acre estate of Janet Livingston Montgomery, widow of Gen. Richard Montgomery, who was killed during the Revolutionary War. The estate features gardens, hiking trails, picnicking, a waterfall, and pick-your-own raspberries. Open daily (except Tuesday) 10am to 5pm; guided tours begin every 45 minutes.

Admission to house and tour $6, $5 for seniors, $3 for students and children over 6; free for children 6 and under. Admission to the grounds is free.

Olana, Rte. 9G (one mile south of the Rip Van Winkle Bridge), Hudson (☎ 518/828-0135). The 250-acre estate of the 19th-century artist Frederic Edwin Church is now operated by the New York State Office of Parks, Recreation, and Historic Preservation. Open April through October, Wednesday through Sunday 10am to 4pm; 50-minute guided tours begin every 20 to 30 minutes. Last tour starts at 4pm; tours limited to 12 people, so reservations are recommended. Admission $3, $1 for children 5 to 11; free for children four and under. Student and group rates available.

Roosevelt-Vanderbilt National Historic Site, Hyde Park. Includes the **Vanderbilt Mansion** (☎ 914/229-7770), a 211-acre estate with a formal Italian garden, and the 300-acre estate composed of the **Franklin D. Roosevelt Home** (☎ 914/229-2501) and **Val-Kill** (☎ 914/229-9115), the Eleanor Roosevelt cottage. All of the sites, which are operated by the **National Park Service** (☎ 914/229-9115), have walking trails and are part of the Hyde Park Trail. Open May through October, daily 9am to 5pm; November through April, Thursday to Monday 9am to 5pm. Admission to Vanderbilt Mansion $2, free for children under 17; to the Roosevelt Home $5, free for children under 17. Admission to Val-Kill is free.

PARKS AND PRESERVES

Cohotate Preserve, Greene County Environmental Education Center, Rte. 385 (north of the Rip Van Winkle Bridge), near Athens (☎ 518/622-3620).

Croton Point Park, Croton Point Ave. (off Rte. 9), Croton-on-Hudson (☎ 914/271-3293).

Clarence Fahnestock State Park, Rte. 301 (off Taconic State Pkwy.), Cold Spring (☎ 914/225-7207). 22 miles of trails newly added. Open daily, dawn to dusk. Free admission. Beach parking for Canopus Lake $5.

Four Mile Point Preserve, Four Mile Point Rd. (Rte. 385), near Coxsackie (☎ 518/622-3620).

Greenport Preserve, Joslen Blvd., Greenport (☎ 212/505-7480). A 450-acre park with trails and extensive views across the river to the Catskill mountains. Open daily from dawn to dusk. Free admission.

Nyack Beach State Park, Rte. 9W at Broadway, Nyack (☎ 914/358-1316 or 914/786-2701). Hiking, biking, fishing, picnic tables.

Papscanee Island Nature Preserve, State Rte. 9J, East Greenbush, Albany (☎ 212/505-7480). About 150 acres with woodland, wetlands, and a farm. Open daily from dawn to dusk. Free admission.

Poets' Walk, County Rd. 103 (River Rd.), north of the Rhinecliff-Kingston Bridge, Red Hook (☎ 914/473-4440). A 120-acre park with trails for hiking and benches for contemplation. Open daily 9am to dusk. Free admission.

RamsHorn-Livingston Sanctuary, Grandview Ave. (off Rte. 9W), Catskill (☎ 518/943-6895 or 914/473-4400). A tidal swamp forest with 480 acres operated by Scenic Hudson and the North Catskills Audubon Society. Open daily from dawn to dusk. Free admission.

Schunnemunk Mountain, Otterkill Rd. (off Rte. 32), Cornwall-on-Hudson (☎ 212/505-7480). A preserve of several miles along a mountain ridge, with hiking trails. Open daily from dawn to dusk. Free admission.

FURTHER READING

The Traveler's Guide to the Hudson River Valley, third edition, by Tim Mulligan (Random House; $14).

The Hudson Valley and Catskill Mountains: An Explorer's Guide, second edition, by Joanne Michaels and Mary-Margaret Barile (The Countryman Press, Woodstock, Vt.; $16).

Fifty Hikes in the Hudson Valley, by Barbara McMartin and Peter Kick (Backcountry Publications, Woodstock, Vt.; $12.95).

Twenty-Five Mountain Bike Tours in the Hudson Valley, by Peter Kick (Backcountry Publications, Woodstock, Vt.; $15).

Walks and Rambles in the Western Hudson Valley, by Peggy Turco (Backcountry Publications, Woodstock, Vt.; $15).

Twenty-Five Bicycle Tours in the Hudson Valley, by Howard Stone (Backcountry Publications, Woodstock, Vt.; $15).

WEST POINT: PITCHING CAMP WHERE THE OLD SOLDIERS LIVE ON

by Ralph Blumenthal

Here TOWERED PATTON, BINOCU-lars in hand, vigilant against an unseen enemy. Or perhaps, as West Point lore has it, looking for the library. There stood bronzed MacArthur, defiant, campaign jacket flung over an arm. And the five-star Ike, businesslike, hands on his hips, gazing over the Plain.

We had come to the granite Army citadel some 60 miles up the Hudson from Manhattan to rub shoulders with history and perhaps a future President and set up base to reconnoiter the mid–Hudson Valley. Our contingent numbered four: two generals and two recruits, gender female.

We found no shortage of attractions, martial or pacific. Perched on a bluff on the west bank of the Hudson estuary where plunging hills squeeze the water into placid pools, the United States Military Academy occupies one of the more spectacular pieces of real estate in the East, as George Washington recognized when he ordered its fortification during the Revolution as "the Gibraltar of America." All around lie reminders of the republic's embattled past: statues to heroes and martyrs, captured trophies of war, and, in the bristling museum, weapons of every murderous variety from caveman spears and medieval maces to models of a tactical atomic cannon and the "Fat Man" nuclear bomb dropped on Nagasaki, Japan.

Beyond, the Hudson Valley beckoned with more side trips than we could ever hope to make in a weekend: manor houses and historic mansions and restorations, antique villages, Colonial churchyards, old inns, and waterfront restaurants. Although West Point can be reached from midtown Manhattan in an hour-and-a-half, for historical interest I mapped a midway stop at the Old Dutch Church in Sleepy Hollow on Route 9 in Sleepy Hollow (formerly North Tarrytown). Over the years, I had driven past it countless times, always vowing someday to, well, tarry, just as I promised that someday I would stop to read all historic markers I whiz by. Alas, the little stone church built in 1697 was locked. I learned later that it was closed to public tours until June.

But the graveyard yawned open, ancient tombstones pitched at grotesque angles. We picked our way among them as I told the girls the story of Ichabod Crane and the Headless Horseman, who in Washington Irving's picaresque tale carried his severed head in his hands and began his nightly ride in the burying ground.

It got my younger daughter's attention. "Headless Horseman?" Sophie repeated.

"It's just a story, honey," my wife said reassuringly.

"I smelled the gravy," Sophie said.

We looked at each other. Gravy? "From the graves," Sophie said.

At Peekskill, routes 6 and 202 veer west, hugging the cliffs over the Hudson for a roller coaster ride to the Bear Mountain Bridge. (Stop at the scenic overlook before the bridge for a panoramic view.) From the bridge, it was only a few minutes' ride north on 9W to Highland Falls, the one-street village of small restaurants and souvenir shops that abuts the academy. At Thayer Gate, one of the three access points to the reservation, an M.P. sized us up and waved us through to the Hotel Thayer, its Neo-Gothic turrets and crenellated roofline looming just above us on the right.

The 194-room hotel, built in 1926 and named for Superintendent Sylvanus Thayer, who arrived in 1817 to set the academy's rigorous standards, exuded baronial grandeur. The lobby of pitted black and white marble and unit escutcheons featured a large stone fireplace, rustic chandeliers, and massive beams hung with flags.

We had booked the $185-a-night "A" suite, the best regularly available unit, comparable in layout if not decor to the Presidential Suite, which is not ordinarily open to the public. (Smaller rooms start at $75.) Our fifth-floor suite, with three exposures overlooking the shimmering Hudson, comprised a bedroom with a queen-size bed and adjoining bath, a large living room with a pullout couch, a formal dining room and kitchenette, and two televisions. It took repeated calls to obtain the rollaway bed we needed.

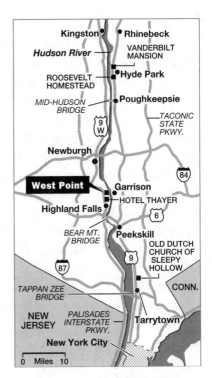

There were other annoyances. When our teenager, Anna, unfolded her convertible couch for the night, a dozen Cheerios tumbled out. Whether they had been in the bedding (an unappetizing thought, that) or (only slightly better) in the cracks of the couch, it didn't speak of fastidious housecleaning. And Sophie pulled something old and dried from under a bookcase. We didn't try to examine it too closely.

A corner of the living room ceiling was peeling and spongy, apparently from a leak. The bathroom badly needed updating. I've had stronger showers from buckets in Vietnam. The walls were so thin that Sophie awoke to someone else's wake-up call, and Anna overheard a couple conspiring to enter a room next door. "Is it safe to come in?" whispered a female voice. The waitress who brought up our continental breakfast (the only kind delivered to the rooms) forgot the hot water for cocoa. When she came back, she put the boiling hot metal pot in my unsuspecting hand. Then we found we were missing the milk for the coffee.

Learning that the Thayer in its time had housed Presidents Dwight D. Eisenhower, Richard M. Nixon, and Gerald R. Ford, the American hostages freed from Iran, Bob Hope, Bill Cosby, Brooke Shields, Phyllis Diller, and the Smothers Brothers, among other luminaries, I wondered how this could be. And then the answer presented itself: this was a Government hotel, the only such enterprise, apparently, open to the public. Now under the privatization program, the Thayer faces sale to commercial interests, along with renovation and, presumably, a more competitive standard of service.

But the mystique of West Point soon overpowers such trivialities. At dusk, while the rest of the squad bivouacked in the room, I drove down Thayer Road marveling at the granite-hewn administration buildings and barracks. Continuing on foot to the main parade field, called the Plain, I stopped at the stations of American military piety: the larger-than-life statues of Washington, who had first laid out the site and now sat stiffly on horseback outside his eponymous dining hall; Eisenhower (class of 1915); Gen. Douglas MacArthur (1903), whose mother moved into the since-demolished West Point Hotel while he was a cadet; and Gen. George S. Patton, Jr. (1909), whose borderline grades were only later traced to undiagnosed dyslexia. Far from needing binoculars to find the library, authorities now say, Patton in fact may have been one of West Point's brightest graduates.

I was crossing the Plain when a distant bugler sounded "Retreat" and the Stars and Stripes at Trophy Point began to inch down the pole. Two cadets heading home for the weekend stopped midfield hand over heart and so, reflexively, did I. Then came a puff of smoke and a beat later, a thunderous report from a blank charge in a cannon by the flagpole.

At Trophy Point, where a soaring granite cylinder memorializes the Regular Army dead in the "War of the Rebellion" and a ring of 150-pound links recalls the immense chain the Colonists stretched across the river to stymie the British navy, I watched a pink sunset glow settle over the fjordlike vista of snaking river and mirrored mountains.

In case we didn't realize that the buffet dinner in the mullion-windowed dining room was a good deal at $19 a person, our waitress was glad to tell us, poking my shoulder for emphasis. "You can"—poke—"go back as many times"—poke—"as you like," she said cheerily. And so we did, repeatedly filling our plates with salad and shrimp, raw vegetables, seafood salad, chicken breast in cream sauce, carved roast beef, lamb chops, and breaded fish. Across the candlelit chamber, several couples slow-danced to a pianist's repertory of Chopin and Tchaikovsky.

We began the next day at the visitors center and museum in Highland Falls on the former site of Ladycliff College, which the military academy absorbed in 1984. The museum has a grisly enough collection of armaments to satisfy the blood thirstiest little Power Ranger. Of particular interest are the early firearms and this quote, which I thought had a lot to say about the direction of civilization: "A man with a gun was capable of defeating a mounted knight who had spent his whole life training for combat and whose weapons had cost a fortune." Both the museum and visitors center have gift shops well stocked with Army sweatshirts, caps, books, tchotchkes, and the like.

A commercial tour bus leaves from the visitors center for an hour's excellent tour of the military academy, at a cost of $5 for adults and $2.50 for children under 12.

We learned, for example, that women, first admitted to the academy in 1976, now account for 10% of the enrollment. That 13,000 applicants compete for the 1,100 plebe openings. That West Point boasts five Presidents: Eisenhower, Ulysses S. Grant, Jefferson Davis of the Confederacy, Fidel V. Ramos of the Philippines, and Gen. Anastasio Somoza Debayle, who graduated in 1946 and became the dictator of Nicaragua; he was assassinated in Paraguay in 1980. That all 4,000 cadets dine together and that if they perform their jobs properly they can all be served in three minutes and finish eating in twenty. That it's considered unlucky to catch your own hat after you fling it into the air at graduation. And that if a cadet escorts his date to Kissing Rock overlooking the Hudson, said date must kiss said cadet or said rock will crash into the water, killing all of West Point.

We didn't do much mingling with the cadets we saw walking around in their traditional gray tunics. Most were off for the weekend and others went about their business in areas of the academy off limits to visitors.

To explore more of the Hudson Valley, we drove through the reservation, north on 9W, over the Mid-Hudson Bridge and north on Route 9 to the village of Rhinebeck, a nascent Hampton on the Hudson. I had made reservations for the restaurateur Larry Forgione's storied Sunday brunch at the 1766 Tavern of the Beekman Arms, which calls itself the oldest continuously operated inn in America.

Although the drive took well over an hour and we arrived after the ostensible 1:30pm buffet cutoff, we were nonetheless graciously seated and loosed on the tables groaning with Belgian waffles, cheese blintzes, salmon, pâté, bagels, bacon, sausages, salads, eggs of all kinds including omelettes to order, fruit, and fancy desserts, all for $19.95 each for the grown-ups, $10.95 each for the kids. "Look," said Sophie, spearing melon on a swizzle stick, "fruit-fa-bob."

Waddling out two hours later, we explored the stores and boutiques set along the village's crossroads. Summer Moon had an ecological special, 20% off jeans made with hemp. At the Antique Market and Gallery I bought a flaking issue of *The New-York Times*, as it was then hyphenated, from 1868 for $7.

We were hoping to see some of the mansions we had passed south along Route 9, so we pushed off. At Hyde Park, we drove into the Vanderbilt estate, just missing the last tour, which had filled up at 3:30pm. But we were rewarded by views of the colossal 1890s mansion, rearing up through the trees like Manderley. The visitors center afforded some exhibits of the yachts and other accouterments of the family called the richest in America in their time.

Next we tried the Franklin Delano Roosevelt homestead just to the south and here we were in luck. There was still time to visit the house, grounds, and museum. After the palace of the Vanderbilts, the little 35-room granite house with green shutters seemed almost quaint, but, as at West Point, history supplied the drama.

We gazed at the simple bed where the future President first greeted the world on January 30, 1882, his wheelchair made of a kitchen chair with the legs sawed off, the leash and blanket of his beloved Scottie, Fala, the encoded black phone for wartime calls to the White House, the strange sequence of bedrooms: Eleanor's sandwiched between her husband's and her mother-in-law's.

Crossing the grounds past the garden where he and Eleanor now lie together under a simple block of marble, we entered the museum, exclaiming at the girlish frocks young Franklin wore, the accomplished letter he wrote his mother at the age of five, the drama of his 1932 acceptance speech: "I pledge you, I pledge myself, to a new deal for the American people. . . ." My favorite exhibit was Roosevelt's 1936 Ford Phaeton, a blue-green convertible with brown leather seats and hand controls and an ingenious metal box on the steering column that dispensed lighted cigarettes.

On the way home the next day we crossed the Bear Mountain Bridge and detoured north to Garrison's Landing for a last view of West Point, perched on the ramparts, glinting like gunpowder in the morning light.

WEST POINT ESSENTIALS

GETTING THERE

By Car   To drive to the United States Military Academy, near Highland Falls, New York, use the George Washington Bridge or the Tappan Zee Bridge to reach the Palisades Pkwy. Continue to the end of the parkway and there, at the Bear Mountain traffic circle, take Rte. 9W north to Rte. 218, and continue to West Point.

By Bus   Bus service to West Point is provided by **Short Line** (☎ 212/736-4700) from the Port Authority Bus Terminal, Eighth Ave. and 41st St., Manhattan. Weekend buses run four times a day, beginning at 8:45am. One-way fare $12.20, round-trip $23.20; half-fare for children 5 to 11.

VISITING WEST POINT

Visitors Center at West Point and **West Point Museum** (☎ 914/938-2638). The visitors center operates daily from 9am to 4:45pm (closed Thanksgiving, Christmas, and New Year's days). Academy grounds are open daily 9:30am to dusk, and the museum is open daily 10:30am to 4:15pm. Admission is free.

Daily one-hour bus tours of the Academy are offered by **West Point Tours** (☎ 914/446-4724). From November 1 to March 31, tours leave from the Visitors Center daily at 11:15am and 1:15pm. From April 1 to October 31, tours leave every half-hour from 10am to 3:30pm from Monday through Saturday, and from 11am to 3:30pm on Sundays. The fare is $5 ($2.50 for children under 12 and free for those under 2). From May to October, two-hour tours that include more walking are also offered at 11:15am and 1:15pm; the fare is $7, $5 for children.

ACCOMMODATIONS AND DINING

Hotel Thayer, on the grounds of the Academy (☎ 800/247-5047 or 914/446-4731). Weekend rates $75 to $100 double or single, $110 to $185 for suites accommodating 2 to 8; children 17 and younger stay free with accompanying adult. Dinner buffets $18.50, half-price for children under 12. Sunday brunch (9:30am to 2pm) $17.75 per person, $8.50 for children under 12. "Murder Mystery Weekends" are offered during the winter; "Murder Mystery Dinners" run through the spring and summer. Each "Murder Mystery Weekend" is $245 per person, including accommodations and meals.

Beekman 1766 Tavern, Beekman Arms, Rte. 9, Rhinebeck (☎ 914/871-1766). Sunday brunch 10am to 2pm (last seating at 1:30pm), $19.95 per person, $10.95 for children 10 and under. Sunday dinner 3:30 to 8:30pm, entrees $14.95 to $23.95. Other dining hours: Lunch Monday through Saturday 11:30am to 3pm (last seating at 2:30pm); entrees $7.75 to $10.95. Dinner Monday through Thursday 5:30 to 9pm (last seating 8:30pm), Friday and Saturday 5:30 to 10pm (last seating 9:30pm); entrees $14.95 to $23.95. Reservations suggested.

OTHER AREA ATTRACTIONS

Vanderbilt Mansion, Rte. 9, Hyde Park (☎ 914/229-7770). November through April, open Thursday through Monday 9am to 5pm (closed Tuesdays and Wednesdays). May through October, open daily 9am to 5pm. Admission $2 adults, free for children under 17.

Franklin Delano Roosevelt Home, Library, and Museum, Rte. 9, Hyde Park (☎ 914/229-2501; library 914/229-8114). The home and museum are open November through April, Thursday through Monday 9am to 5pm (closed Tuesday and Wednesday); May through October, daily 9am to 5pm. The library is open daily year-round from 9am to 5pm. Admission to all three

sites is $5, $4 for seniors, free for children under 17. On Tuesday and Wednesday from November through April (when the home and museum are closed) admission to the library is $3, $2 for seniors.

Old Dutch Church of Sleepy Hollow, Rte. 9, Sleepy Hollow (☎ 914/631-1123). The church, a branch of the Reformed Church in America, is open for tours Memorial Day weekend through Labor Day on Monday, Wednesday, and Thursday from 1 to 5pm and by appointment. The graveyard is open all the time; graveyard tours are offered Sunday at 2pm from Memorial Day weekend through October 31. Admission is free.

WOODSTOCK'S OLD-TIME NEW AGE KARMA

by Jon Pareles

BACK IN THE 1980S, I WAS WALK-
ing down a street in Woodstock when a Volkswagen microbus pulled
over and the scraggly haired driver asked, "Can you tell me where the
rock festival was?"

At the time, I was in Woodstock, England.

The Woodstock festival of 1969, and its 25th anniversary sequel
in 1994, didn't happen in Woodstock, New York, either. The first one
was in White Lake, New York, 60 miles away in Sullivan County; the
second one was closer to Woodstock, in the neighboring Ulster County
town of Saugerties. Yet a hippie mythos still clings to Woodstock
itself, where my wife and I recently spent a long weekend.

Tucked among bucolic and sometimes spectacular Catskill scenery, with a full-time population of 6,290 (as of the 1990 census),
Woodstock is the counterculture's country retreat, where the upstate
woodlands meet the New Age. It's a haven of hearth-baked bread,
folk-rock on the local radio station (WDST, at 100.1 and 96.9 FM),
art galleries, artisans, and spiritual seekers. Under houses of worship,
a Chamber of Commerce brochure lists not only the Dutch Reformed
Church but also a Tibetan Buddhist monastery. Among the various
"Welcome to Woodstock" stickers at local stores, one reads, "If you
lived here, you'd be Om now."

Yet despite its legendary name and a century of experience as a
tourist magnet, Woodstock remains a friendly, close-knit small town.
There is no traffic light at Woodstock's main intersection, where Tinker

Street meets Rock City Road, and the cluster of stores stretches just a few blocks.

On a recent Friday afternoon, before the weekend influx from New York City, Tinker Street was populated by women without makeup and men with ponytails. People in their 20s and people in their 50s all wore the ponchos and fringed buckskin, patched jeans, and embroidered shirts of the international peasant-wear economy. Running shoes were the only sign of the 1990s. Still, the shoe store in the center of town featured Birkenstocks.

Woodstock drew utopian free thinkers long before the 1960s. During the 19th century, according to Alf Evers's comprehensive *Woodstock: History of an American Town* (Overlook Press, 1987; $39.50), it was an industrious (and none too environmentally conscious) hamlet, logging hemlock trees from the Catskill mountainsides and using the bark to tan leather.

In 1902, a wealthy Englishman, Ralph Radcliffe Whitehead, started an arts colony, Byrdcliffe. To realize the ideals of the Arts and Crafts movement, it would produce old-fashioned handmade goods and run a summer arts school. Handicrafts couldn't support Byrdcliffe, but painters, potters, musicians, weavers, and actors had discovered Woodstock.

The Art Students League, based in Manhattan, opened a Woodstock summer school in 1906, and other groups of artists soon followed. The Maverick colony, just across the town line, drew social reformers, visual artists, and performers, and presented summer festivals from 1915 to 1931, the real Woodstock festivals. In 1921, factions of the Communist Party convened at the Overlook Mountain House hotel and united as the Communist Party of America. Through the 1920s, artists, theater people, and the tourists who arrived to gawk at them kept Woodstock thriving.

Rockers arrived later, when Bob Dylan and the Band settled upstate in the late 1960s and recorded *Music From Big Pink* (a big pink house in West Saugerties) and *The Basement Tapes*. Other musicians, including a jazz contingent, are still in the hills, descending to play rock at the Tinker Street Cafe or the Joyous Lake, the town's two rock clubs, or jazz at the intimate auditorium of the Kleinert/James Arts Center.

Well-known bands like Phish record albums in the wooded privacy of Bearsville Studios.

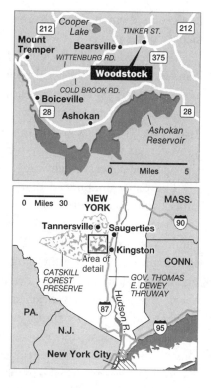

We visited the Woodstock Historical Society, which displayed a newspaper clipping from 1929, headlined "Nude Bathing Parties Offend"; the town was divided over whether to restrict such shenanigans at risk of losing tourists. An exhibition of paintings by Woodstock artists included a striking self-portrait from the early 1930s by Petra Cabot: a young woman with a modish black hat and a confident gaze. A woman with long white hair walked in and told the caretaker, "I must have that painting, so I can photograph it." It was Ms. Cabot, who smiled as she looked at her self-assured 21-year-old self. "Oh, we had some great times," she said. Woodstock, we kept realizing, is a place unto itself. It is a town where the biggest, pushiest crowd we saw was the one that mobbed the biweekly Saturday-morning used-book sale at the library. We had been told about it by the proprietor of Readers' Quarry, a small, well-organized used bookstore. "If I see you there," she said, "I won't be able to talk. I'll be too busy."

Peace and Apples

One attraction during our weekend visit was the town's "harvest festival." Like other town fairs, it had a local apple farmer demonstrating an antique cider press. But being Woodstock, it also started with a "peace ceremony," a parade of school children with assorted national flags. A man walked by wearing a crystal the size of a dill pickle around his neck; a teenager had a saucepan for a hat. On the outdoor stage,

the group Women Who Drum followed a Hebrew blessing with a
Seneca peace prayer.

We picked up *The Woodstock Journal,* a weekly paper run by Ed
Sanders that prints the local police blotter (with regular marijuana
possession arrests) and poetry along with muckraking. Mr. Sanders,
now an author and historian, was a prime mover in the zoning laws
that keep Woodstock green; in the 1960s, he founded the folk-rock
provocateurs the Fugs, whose song title "Refuse to Be Burnt Out"
provides the paper's watchwords.

The paper announced that it would celebrate a move to new
offices with an exhibition of paintings by Alf Evers, whose book we
had been consulting. The paintings were Depression-era scenes of a
rural Woodstock and of Mr. Evers's travels; a label on a Bermuda
landscape read, "Notice the pink sand." Mr. Evers, now in his 90s,
and Mr. Sanders were surrounded by well-wishers at the opening. On
the doorstep a woman was exclaiming: "He's not just a writer! Everyone has multiple personalities!"

At Bread Alone, the Woodstock outlet for a bakery in nearby
Boiceville, we could easily distinguish unhurried Woodstockers from
the jostling weekenders who mobbed the place on Saturday morning.
We tried the organic breakfast tea and substantial currant scones; on a
return visit, we picked up a flourless chocolate torte, rich but not overly
sweet. A sign in the bathroom read: THIS NOTE IS SINCERELY ADDRESSED
TO THE PERSON STEALING THE POSTERS OFF THE BATHROOM WALLS.
PLEASE STOP! IF YOU HAVE ANY REGRETS, YOU'RE FORGIVEN. ENJOY THE
ART AND PLEASE DON'T TAKE ANY MORE POSTERS.

Down the block is Pieces of Mine, which sells stones and crystals;
its advertisement promised consultations. "What are you drawn to?"
asked the woman at the counter. "What you are drawn to is what you
need." We picked red tiger eye, jade, amethyst, and turquoise. The
woman smiled. "You've covered almost all seven chakras," she said.
"You just need something yellow."

"I was just looking at the amber," my wife said.

"It looks like a higher power has directed you," the woman said.
Quickly, she added: "I don't mean to say that you're not responsible

for your decisions. It's your own higher power from within that has guided you."

All for the Spirit

Mirabai Books, one of the five bookstores in town, concentrates on spiritual and New Age books. One bookcase covers a full cycle: "Death and Dying," "Reincarnation," and "Channeling." We looked into Dharmaware, which sells Buddhist items. An employee with his dreadlocks looped into a topknot was busy moving merchandise between storefronts. "We're in a state of transformation," he said. Nearby was the Tibetan Emporium; as we walked in, the proprietor was chanting along with a CD of Buddhist monks. The emporium is run by the director of Karma Triyana Dharmachakra monastery, a traditional Tibetan Buddhist temple built in the 1980s. We drove up Meads Mountain Road to see the impressive white-and-red temple, with its multicolored floral ornaments, and happened onto the daily tour.

"Nothing here is for decorative purposes," the guide said, taking us through the main temple, with its golden statues, bright banners, and embroidered pictures of saints, all of them sewn by the temple's abbot. "Everything here has a spiritual meaning behind it."

We wished we had worn thick socks; we took off our shoes before entering the temple, and the floors grew cold during the tour. The guide invited people to come back for the regular prayers at 5am and 5 and 7pm. Forgoing materialism, she didn't mention the center's bookstore and gift shop.

Across the street was the path up Overlook Mountain, renowned for the view from 3,140 feet. The trail ascends about two miles on a steady upward grade to the hulk of the Overlook Mountain House, the third hotel on the same site. Affixed to the concrete walls, eroding photographs and documents (all biodegradable, a sign said) describe the three attempts to maintain a luxury hotel on the slope, all commercial failures; all three burned down.

Past the hotel site, the main trail leads to a former fire observatory tower. The stairway to the second story has been removed, but intrepid types still climb the scaffolding for the view above the trees.

A narrower path, to the right after the hotel ruins, heads along a ridge and offers a less perilous unobstructed view, with a silvery ribbon of the Hudson River, forested hillsides, and the gleaming Ashokan Reservoir below. James Fenimore Cooper, writing before the reservoir was created, declared, "It is a spot to make a man solemnize."

Up Meads Mountain Road from the monastery is the Magic Meadow, a Woodstock landmark that was mired in small-town controversy. Some Woodstockers had made a ritual of going to the meadow to greet the full moon. But the meadow is on private property, and to discourage moonstruck trespassers, the town put up NO PARKING signs. Claiming an infringement of religious freedom, people who received parking tickets took the case to court, where it was pending during our visit. We looked at the meadow by daylight; it is a neatly mowed clearing with a peaceful pond.

There was more mountain scenery to explore. Cold Brook Road, from Woodstock to Boiceville, snaked through a valley with fields and mountains on one side. And when we picked up *Hiking the Catskills* (New York–New Jersey Trail Conference, 1989; $14.95) at the Bookmart, the thoughtful owner was ready to suggest her favorite walks. After we admitted we were tired from our Overlook climb, she suggested a spectacular drive, climbing Platte Clove Road through Saugerties to Tannersville, and back via Main Street in Tannersville and Route 214 to Route 28. The road's hairpin curves keep it closed from November to April.

We spent nights at two different bed-and-breakfasts. The Woodstock Country Inn—on a secluded road in Bearsville, part of Woodstock Township—is in a house built by an artist, Jo Cantine, whose luminous portraits and tropical landscapes still decorate the walls. Our room was whitewashed and uncluttered, with wicker furniture and a firm, comfortable bed; it had a view of the surrounding hills.

The innkeeper, Carol Wandrey, has lived in Woodstock for 27 years, and she was a fount of information on everything from visiting rockers to good places to stroll. She also introduced us to the web of small-town connections. Jo Cantine's grandson owns the Bear Cafe, generally considered the best restaurant in town.

Like so much else in Woodstock, the Bear mingles the home-grown and the internationalist. It's a high-ceilinged place with one windowed wall looking out over the Sawkill Brook. Its bread, baked by someone named Heather, is like a model grandmother: crusty on the outside, tender within. The mixed green salad was organic and very fresh, and we followed it with noodle dishes from disparate cultures: udon noodles with shredded vegetables in a complex, spicy broth, and penne with grilled vegetables in a portobello broth. Dinner for two was about $55. The Bear eclipsed the other local restaurants we visited.

For our last night in Ulster County, we moved to the Onteora Mountain House in Boiceville. Richard Hellmann, the mayonnaise mogul, retired to the mountainside lodge at the age of 50 on a doctor's advice and lived for 44 more years. Built on Mount Ticetonyk, it faces a spectacular panorama of mountains stretching into the distance, with the sunset framed by distant hills.

Its owners have filled its high-ceilinged Arts and Crafts interior with Korean antiques, making it more formal than the Woodstock Country Inn; at the head of our bed was a painting of the Buddha and his disciples. The lodge's original pool table, with Mission-style legs, is in a downstairs game room. Breakfast was eggs Hellmann, a high-cholesterol construction of an English muffin, spinach, poached eggs, and, of course, mayonnaise. "Our founder," the innkeeper said.

For dinner, we tried a place where it seemed as if the 1960s had never happened. La Duchesse Anne, a French restaurant in the former Mount Tremper Inn, has a player piano by the bar, stocked with James P. Johnson and Fats Waller classics. For dinner, we enjoyed a *cotriade,* a Breton fish soup with tomato and a hint of cream, and a grilled trout in sorrel sauce, neither in the least multicultural and both satisfying. We declined the foot-high napoleons on the pastry cart. Dinner for two was about $50.

On the way home, we made two stops. One was the Sunfrost Farms in Woodstock for local apples (at $2.99 a peck) and Bosc pears (99 cents a pound). It also runs a juice bar and stocks foods like olive spread (black and green) and the rare maitake (hen of the woods) mushrooms.

Sampling Ice Cream

And in Kingston, we visited the headquarters of Jane's Homemade Ice Cream. We had sampled Jane's at Bread Alone and concluded that her Killer Chocolate surpassed any other chocolate ice cream in our experience. At the main store, we asked if it was sold anywhere in New York City; only, we were told, at the restaurant at Saks Fifth Avenue.

Our disappointment was tempered by the availability of two dozen other flavors. At $2.55 for two hefty scoops, we chose pralines and cream and pumpkin, both worthwhile, and the remarkable cappuccino Kahlúa calypso, with deep espresso flavor and a crunch. The ice cream would speed us back to Manhattan, while the apples and pears, over the days to come, would continue to remind us of pastoral surroundings and small-town hospitality.

Woodstock Essentials

GETTING THERE

By Car   From Manhattan, take Thomas E. Dewey Thruway to the Kingston exit (exit 19) and pick up Rte. 28 West; follow Rte. 28 West to Rte. 375 North and take Rte. 375 North to Rte. 212 West; continue on Rte. 212 West, which turns into Tinker Street, the main street in Woodstock.

By Bus   Adirondack Trailways (☎ 800/225-6815 or 212/967-2900) provides daily bus service to Woodstock from the Port Authority Bus Terminal, Eighth Ave. and 42nd St., Manhattan. Buses depart for the 2½-hour ride daily at 10am and 12:30, 3:30, and 5pm. Fare $20 one way, $38 round-trip ($10 and $19 for children 11 and under; free for those 4 and under who sit on a parent's lap).

ACCOMMODATIONS

Onetora, the Mountain House, 96 Piney Point Rd., Boiceville (☎ 914/657-6233). Friday through Sunday, $95 room with shared bath, $135 with private bath; Monday through Thursday, $85 and $125. Rates are based on double occupancy and include full breakfast; two-night minimum stay on weekends. Children over 12 welcome.

Woodstock Country Inn, Bearsville (☎ 914/679-9380). Summer weekend rates (through November 1) range from $95 with shared bath to $145 with private bath; after November 1, weekend rates range from $70 to $115. Rates are based on double occupancy and include breakfast; two-night minimum stay on weekends. No smoking; not recommended for children.

DINING

The Bear Cafe, Bearsville Theater Complex, Rte. 212, Bearsville (☎ 914/679-5555).
Bread Alone Woodstock, 22 Mill Hill Rd., Woodstock (☎ 914/679-2108).

Jane's Homemade Ice Cream and Restaurant, 305 Wall St., Kingston (☎ 914/338-8315).
La Duchesse Anne, Rte. 212 and Wittenberg Rd., Mount Tremper (☎ 914/688-5260).

LOCAL LANDMARKS

Dutch Reformed Church, 18 Tinker St., Woodstock (☎ 914/679-6610).
Karma Triyana Dharmachakra, 352 Meads Mountain Rd., Woodstock (☎ 914/679-5906).

Woodstock Historical Society Museum, Comeau Rd. (off Tinker St.), Woodstock (☎ 914/679-2256).
The Woodstock Journal, 12 Tannery Brook Rd., Woodstock (☎ 914/679-2969).

HIKING

Overlook Mountain, off Meads Mountain Rd., Woodstock (☎ 914/256-3000). Open daily from dawn to dusk.

SHOPPING

BOOKSTORES

The Bookmarket, 40 Mill Hill Rd., Woodstock (☎ 914/679-4646).
Mirabai Books/Sacred Space, 23 Mill Hill Rd., Woodstock (☎ 914/679-7819).
Reader's Quarry, 70 Tinker St., Woodstock (☎ 914/679-9572).
Woodstock Library, 5 Library Lane (at Tinker St.) (☎ 914/679-2213).

A FARMERS' MARKET

Sunfrost Farms, 217 Tinker St., Woodstock (☎ 914/679-6690).

OTHER SHOPPING

Dharmaware, 54 Tinker St., Woodstock (☎ 914/679-3270).
Pieces of Mine: A Metaphysical Gateway, 7 Maple Lane, Woodstock (☎ 914/679-4289).
Tibetan Emporium, Rock City Rd., Woodstock (☎ 914/679-3808).

LIVE MUSIC

ROCK

The Joyous Lake, 42 Mill Hill Rd., Woodstock (☎ 914/679-1234).
Tinker Street Cafe, 59 Tinker St., Woodstock (☎ 914/679-2487).

JAZZ

Kleinert/James Art Center, 34 Tinker St., Woodstock (☎ 914/679-2079).

WHERE HISTORY MEETS NATURE

by Lisa W. Foderaro

Cold Spring, N.Y.

THIS HUDSON RIVER VILLAGE, ITS Main Street lined with antiques stores under ornate cornices, appears caught in a time warp, a faded Victorian postcard sprung to life.

In recent years, people have streamed in from all over just to admire the architecture or browse in Salmagundi Books or sup at the Vintage Cafe. Most end up at the river's edge, awed by the ancient Hudson Highlands, which loom from the opposite bank: enormous mounds of granite and dense green forest.

There is, in fact, not a whole lot to do right in the village, except soak up the atmosphere. But that seems to be exactly the point.

Fifty miles north of Manhattan on the river's eastern shore, Cold Spring is too far away to be a suburb and yet too close to be a farm community. It has thus escaped the bland shopping center culture of the one and the hardworking pragmatism of the other. Instead, it seems to have found its calling by tapping into an odd but distinct pastime: the search for small-town America.

People want intimacy, charm, a whiff of history. Cold Spring seems to be the answer, if at times self-consciously so: Under a shingled gazebo, a quartet in red-and-white-striped vests can be found on weekends belting out songs by Duke Ellington and Hoagy Carmichael.

Modern facts of life like the dry cleaners and the supermarket moved, conveniently, from the heart of the village to a retail strip out on Route 9D years ago. That left the Main Street, which slopes toward the river, poised to become a National Historic District in 1982. And that, in turn, led to the germination of antiques stores, boutiques, restaurants, and inns.

What makes Cold Spring a weekend retreat rather than merely a stopover during a Sunday drive is its proximity to some of the historic and natural highlights of the region. There is, for instance, Boscobel, a lavishly restored Federal mansion, and Constitution Marsh, a small private wildlife sanctuary managed by the National Audubon Society whose watery labyrinth is home to many species of birds and fish.

Cold Spring's 19th-century streetscape isn't entirely museum quality. There are some forgettable dwellings from the 1950s and 60s included in the mix of antique two- and three-story houses and buildings. But there are enough of the latter to make up for the former. Two that stand out are 73 Main Street, a faded brick building dating from 1820 that houses the Pig Hill Inn, and 49 Main Street, an 1898 ecru structure whose facade is decorated with cast-iron Corinthian columns. It is occupied by the Irish Imports gift shop.

Guided walking tours, led by the Putnam County Historical Society, depart from the building at 72 Main Street on Sundays from May through mid-November. The tour provides a satisfactory overview of Cold Spring's beginnings, but be prepared for the possibility of a long-winded narration of sometimes dubious veracity. One guide punctuated several accounts by saying, "Again, I'm taking liberty, but I think I might be right on that." A more focused examination of the region's past can be found in Frances F. Dunwell's *Hudson River Highlands* (Columbia University Press, 1991). The book, available at Salmagundi, at 66 Main Street, includes a chapter on Cold Spring and is generously illustrated with maps, color plates, and photographs.

Cold Spring grew up almost overnight with the creation of a federally subsidized iron foundry in 1817. From then until the end of the Civil War, it cranked out cannonballs and artillery, as well as cotton presses, steam engines, and other cogs in the accelerating Industrial

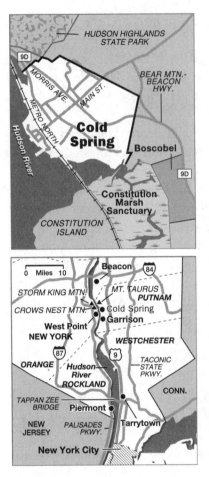

Revolution. At the same time, the Hudson Highlands were gaining international attention for their staggering beauty: 15 miles where the river narrows and deepens, slicing through the Appalachian Mountain range. The founding of the popular new military academy at West Point, across the river, in 1802, and the invention of the steamboat five years later, drew travelers from the United States and Europe. Gliding up the river in style, they took in the voluptuous mountains on either side and learned of America's military heroism during the Revolutionary War.

In the early 1830s, Fanny Kemble, a visiting British actress overcome by the scenery, wailed in her diary: "Where are the poets of this land! Have these glorious scenes poured no inspiration into hearts worthy to behold and praise their beauty?" Actually, painters like Thomas Cole, Asher B. Durand, and Frederic E. Church had already arrived, and an art movement, the Hudson River School, was born.

Today, the best place in Cold Spring for viewing the Highlands is from a plaza with Victorian-style benches that juts into the river at the foot of Main Street. (To get there, you must cross under the Metro-North train tracks.) Directly opposite is Crows Nest Mountain, whose timeworn, rounded peaks rise to 1,400 feet. To the north is Storm King Mountain; to the south, the fortresslike campus of West Point.

The Hudson Highlands and surrounding countryside also offer dramatic views of fall foliage. Two especially scenic drives are along the Taconic Parkway from Putnam County through Columbia County, and on Route 9D between the Bear Mountain Bridge and the city of Beacon.

Pig Hill Inn

Right at the river's edge in Cold Spring is Hudson House, an 1832 inn with two tiers of verandas offering water and mountain views that keep guests happily anchored. Its rooms are comfortable and, as the inn's brochure attests, "quaintly decorated." But the Pig Hill Inn's eight rooms, each filled with antiques and each done in a different style, are notable in the village for charm and originality.

One bizarre twist: All of the furniture and accessories at the Pig Hill Inn are for sale, from four-poster beds to hatboxes. The prices are tucked discreetly under chair cushions or inside armoire doors. At times, amid the cherry wood and chintz, you feel as if you're staying overnight in an antiques store, but it can be educational. Two intricately carved Italian ballroom chairs? They are $450 for the pair.

Comforts are sprinkled throughout the inn. All rooms come with queen-size beds and air-conditioning, and most have either woodstoves or fireplaces. The bathrooms are equipped with fluffy white towels and bars of Neutrogena, in addition to bath soap. And newspapers are left outside guests' doors in the morning. Televisions and telephones are nowhere to be found, or heard, adding to the inn's serenity.

Breakfast is served until the civilized hour of 10am, either in the dining room or out back in a quiet garden. An egg soufflé roll stuffed with spinach, mushrooms, and cream cheese was as light as a cloud. It was sufficiently weighed down, however, by a basket of buttery biscuits and a parfait dish of berries and heavy cream. In the afternoons, a plate of homemade chocolate chip cookies is put out for guests in the lobby, on an antique American farm table, $1,750.

Antiquing

If you are still in the market for old furniture and collectibles, there are several stores to choose from just outside the inn's door. They range from the flea market flavor of Downtown Gallery, at 40 Main Street, to the hushed drawing-room atmosphere at Ann Stromberg, at 167 Main Street, which seems to purr, "You can't afford it." At Downtown Gallery, you could discover a 1920s Silvertone record player ($75), a shapely black rotary phone from the 1930s ($22), and a Lady Remington electric shaver ($15). At Ann Stromberg, you might find a coin silver tea set made in New York City in 1825 ($3,600) or a massive mahogany sideboard from 1820 Philadelphia ($6,500).

One antiques shop that strives for eclecticism is the Tinman, at 93 Main Street. The owner, Liza Sherman, scouts around for anything that is "offbeat and interesting," including chunks of bygone buildings and businesses. Recently, there were some elaborately painted shutters from 17th-century Persia ($2,200 each) and a pair of red wicker bar stools from the 1930s ($450).

Boscobel

In neighboring Garrison, Boscobel, which loosely translated from the Italian means beautiful woods, offers a window onto the tastes and manners of the aristocracy during the region's infancy. Begun in 1804 by States Morris Dyckman, a Loyalist in the American Revolution, and completed by his widow, Elizabeth, the mansion is a striking example of New York Federal domestic architecture. Its exterior, painted a muted gold, is festooned with cream-colored, carved wood swags linking columns that support a unifying pediment. Its interior, filled with the works of the 19th-century New York cabinetmaker Duncan Phyfe, is accented with needlepoint rugs, crystal chandeliers, clocks, and spyglasses.

The house was originally situated 15 miles to the south. But threatened with demolition in the 1950s (to make way for new construction), the structure was saved by the philanthropist Lila Acheson Wallace, who had it dismantled and moved, piece by piece, to its current site on a bluff overlooking the Hudson.

When the house first opened in 1961, it had been restored with all things English. But then the inventory lists were found. Mrs. Dyckman, it turned out, was a patriot after all, at least in terms of design. All her furniture had been American, and the interiors had to be completely redone by the private group, Boscobel Restoration Inc., which owns and operates the site.

The tours are packed with interesting facts about the challenges of a life of luxury predating electricity and plumbing. The grounds, with their formal gardens and river views, are as special as the house itself, which is set back from Route 9D.

Xaviar's

After experiencing such refinement, dinner anywhere other than Xaviar's would seem an anticlimax. The 1997 *Zagat Tri-State Survey* gives the two Xaviar's restaurants—one on Route 9D in Garrison and the other farther south, in Piermont, New York—the top two ratings for food in the three-state region outside Manhattan.

But it's not the intoxicating flavors of the cannelloni of quail or the salmon with coriander and caviar that linger longest. It is the grandeur of the setting: the ballroom of the Highlands Country Club, where 20-foot ceilings and oceans of space between tables create a palatial atmosphere.

The decor is elegant but spare. The walls, painted a pale blue-gray, are lined with portraits. At either end of the room are fireplaces whose mantels hold great sprays of fresh flowers, illuminated by recessed spotlights. The tables are awash in linen, crystal, candles, and flowers, and in one corner of the room, a harpist performs.

Through the arched windows, the golf course appears as a throbbing emerald sea in the fading light. As the Tahitian vanilla bean soufflé with chocolate sorbet arrives, you realize you're having one of Spalding Gray's perfect moments.

The Xaviar's in Garrison serves dinner Friday and Saturday nights only. Diners choose between two tasting menus, each with six courses and six different wines. There is also a Sunday brunch. The dinner prix fixe is $72, but the blow is softened when the check comes on a bed of rose petals, inside a silver-plated chest.

Constitution Marsh Sanctuary

The Hudson River has a way of making you want to get closer to its rhythms, and Constitution Marsh Sanctuary, off Indian Brook Road in Garrison, puts you right on its surface. The small number of visitors that can be accommodated will find a 270-acre tidal marsh that is a rich environment for all kinds of birds, as well as freshwater and saltwater fish, from brown trout to needlefish.

The trail from the eight-car parking lot passes by the visitor's center and reaches a short boardwalk leading into the marsh's pale green forest of narrow-leaf cattails and pickerelweed, waving in the breeze. The visitor's center focuses more on the river's ecology than on birdwatching. But the sanctuary is still a birder's paradise. Recently, an osprey hunting for fish flew directly overhead, its gigantic wings flapping as if in slow motion.

From the sanctuary, colors turn electric as the sun deepens the blue of the river and brightens the green of the marsh. Dimensions expand, too. Without trees or buildings for scale, the Hudson, Highlands and sky seem to merge, rising and widening before your eyes. Back toward Cold Spring, Mount Taurus—or Bull Hill, as locals prefer—reveals itself for the first time, hovering over the village like a giant protector.

TOURING, EATING, SLEEPING: COLD SPRING ESSENTIALS

GETTING THERE

By Car   To drive to Cold Spring from New York City, take the Henry Hudson Pkwy. to the Saw Mill River Pkwy.; continue on the Saw Mill to the Taconic State Pkwy.; take the Taconic to Rte. 301, which becomes Main Street in Cold Spring.

By Train   Cold Spring can also be reached by train on the Hudson Line of **Metro-North**

(☎ 212/532-4900). Trains from Grand Central Terminal run about every hour, beginning at 7:58am on weekends, and the ride takes about an hour and 20 minutes. Round-trip fare on Saturdays and Sundays is $15.50, $1 for children 5 to 12, free for children under 5. Some taxi service is available from the train station in Cold Spring.

ACCOMMODATIONS

The Hudson House, 2 Main St., Cold Spring (☎ 914/265-9355). May through November, $125 to $150 double; December through April, $105 to $125 double. Rates are based on double occupancy and include full breakfast. Closed January. Children over 12 are welcome.

Pig Hill Inn, 73 Main St., Cold Spring (☎ 914/265-9247). $100 to $150 double, depending on the day (weekend or weekday) and the amenities (private or shared bath). Rates are based on double occupancy and include full breakfast. Children are welcome; an additional cot in the room is $25 per day.

DINING

Xaviar's, Rte. 9D, Garrison (☎ 914/424-4228). Open for dinner Friday and Saturday 6 to 9pm and for Sunday brunch (sittings at 11:30am and 2pm). $72 for prix fixe six-course dinner; $32 for prix fixe brunch. No credit cards accepted.

ATTRACTIONS

Boscobel, Rte. 9D, Garrison (☎ 914/265-3638). March, open weekends only 9:30am to 4pm; last tour at 3:15pm. April through October, open daily (except Tuesday) 9:30am to 5pm; last tour at 4:15pm. November and December, open daily (except Tuesday) 9:30am to 4pm; last tour at 3:15pm. Closed January and February. Tour $7 adults, $6 seniors, $4 children ages 6 to 14, free for children under 6. Admission to grounds only $4 adults, $2 children.

Constitution Marsh Sanctuary, Indian Brook Rd. (off Rte. 9D), Garrison (no phone). The visitors center and trails are open daily 9am to 5pm; closed from November to May. Admission to the grounds and visitor's center is free. When the parking area is full, visitors are asked to return at another time.

Paddling Downstream, Slowly

by Bruce Weber

We launched at Catskill, New York, from a public park just below the Rip Van Winkle Bridge, in the dense, warm air of a fog lifting at dawn. There, about 30 miles south of Albany, the Hudson River, its sleepy girth about 1,000 yards across, moved lazily southward, and we were grateful for its laziness, neither of us (I had solicited the aid of a friend for the occasion) having been in a canoe in some years. The water was bath warm, and we were grateful for that, too.

Our first few strokes were awkward, and the nose of our borrowed canoe wandered back and forth across the longitudinal center for a while as I, in the stern, steered us uncertainly around the mouth of Catskill Creek and into the main current, toward New York City.

How did this happen to a couple of landlubbers like us?

It was my fault.

When a river runs by the house, I want to hitch a ride on it. I can't help it. All that movement, from somewhere, to somewhere: It's piquing.

So what is it about the Hudson, the huge beckoning thing that most New Yorkers ignore? Like the purloined letter hidden in plain sight, it has been flowing within view of my windows (well, some of my windows; I've moved a lot) for 20 years now, but until I decided to solve the situation recently, I'd never been out in it. Not on my own steam, anyway; the Circle Line ferry doesn't count.

Besides, the imagery in my head was irresistible: me in a tiny canoe, paddling home from the far north, finally riding the lethargic current under the George Washington Bridge and down the west side of Manhattan; to the west, the Palisades, with the late afternoon shadows being cast over the water by the sun fading over New Jersey; to the east, the rush-hour traffic heading up along the West Side Highway toward the Bronx. As I pull ashore at Battery Park, the Statue of Liberty waves at my back. In this fantasy, I'm wearing fringed buckskin, a primitive discovering the city.

It is possible to do this, I learned, buckskin or no, but for me it didn't work out quite that way, there being problems in reconciling the imagery with my ambition of a mere weekend's worth of paddling and the logistics of undertaking such a journey with rusty skills and, crucially, no canoe.

It was John Cronin, the executive director of the Hudson Riverkeeper Fund, an environmental watchdog group, who pointed out that though the Hudson is a fine and underused venue for paddlers, the closer you get to the city the less accommodating the riverbanks become. Places to dock safely are few; leaving the canoe becomes a problem, and motels aren't particularly easy to find or get to. (As it turns out I'm not much of a primitive when it comes to sleeping out at night.) "It's adventurous, but in lower Westchester and New York City you've kind of stranded yourself," Mr. Cronin said.

Nowhere, in fact, Mr. Cronin added, does the Hudson have a terribly booming riverside culture that would encourage precisely the kind of endeavor I'd proposed. In the end, he recommended the Catskill region, where the river is peaceful and wide and scenic, generally crossable in a canoe without overt danger from wind-whipped whitecaps or ships churning up a threatening wake, and with reasonably accessible amenities on shore.

The lower Hudson, Mr. Cronin reiterated, is great for canoeing, but canoeists don't use it much. Perhaps, he said, this is because it is dominated by motorcraft, from jet skis to pleasure yachts to the occasional tour boat and barge. He didn't, in any case, know where I could rent a canoe, and neither did anyone else I spoke with.

You can rent canoes on the upper Hudson, way to the northwest above Albany in the Adirondacks, where whitewater enthusiasts are challenged by a 14-mile sluice between the Indian and Boreas rivers known as the Hudson Gorge. You can rent canoes on the Delaware, to the southwest, but none of the outfitters I called were willing to cart a canoe several hours to the Catskills for me, and I didn't even ask if they'd let me do it myself. The tourist board for Greene County, where Catskill is, couldn't help me, either.

"Why don't you come up here and go golfing?" the woman at the tourist board suggested on the phone. "We have plenty of that." A marine yard in Catskill was willing to sell me a new aluminum canoe for $700 and then buy it back from me after the trip for $500. But for a trip such as mine, I was advised, an aluminum boat would be about as comfortable and sleek as a bathtub. (As it happens, I missed a place, Loric Sports in Staatsburg, near Rhinebeck, that rents canoes and kayaks for use on the Hudson.)

In the end, happily, I was able to borrow a canoe, and it was a beauty. Made by We-no-nah, it was a two-seat, 17-foot boat made of lightweight Kevlar. And it was painted a nifty, woodsy color I came to think of as Hiawatha green.

We outfitted ourselves—life jackets, paddles, waterproof baggage toters, and map covers—at Cold Brook Canoes, a garage-based business in Boiceville, New

York, some 16 miles off the Thruway, where the proprietor, Ernie Gardner, wouldn't let us go without being assured we knew what we were doing (we lied a little), and without suggesting that we pay $25 to join the Hudson River Waterway Association, a group of boaters and environmentalists who promote the river as a recreational site. It wasn't the association Mr. Gardner was touting; with the membership comes the *Hudson River Waterway Guide*, a mile-by-mile description of sights on the river between Troy and the Battery, along with suggestions of places to rest, swim, camp, or store your canoe for the night while you're off in search of a motel. It was invaluable.

Waters in Motion

In 1990, an adventurer named Peter Lourie canoed the entire 315-mile source-to-mouth length of the Hudson, from Lake Tear of the Clouds on the slope of Mount Marcy in the Adirondacks to the Battery, and wrote a book about it, *River of Mountains* (Syracuse University Press, 1995).

"The northern half is a true river with a strong current," Mr. Lourie wrote of the Hudson, "but the lower half is tidal, a leviathan's arm of the sea, an estuary, a sunken river from the days of the glaciers, not a normal river at all. In the first 165 miles from Lake Tear to Albany, the Hudson drops nearly 4,300 feet. But from Albany to Manhattan, for another 150 miles, the Hudson drops a mere one foot." This explains why Mr. Lourie had a guide with him in the northern waters and why he was able to paddle the lower Hudson alone. The water is wide, essentially calm, imminently negotiable. Still and all, it must have been quite a haul, mainly because of the tides from the Atlantic Ocean, which run all the way up river beyond Albany. These fight the generally slow-moving current to the degree, Craig Poole, president of the waterway association, wrote in the guide, that "a log dropped in the water at Troy would take months to reach Manhattan." For every eight miles the log was carried down river on the current and the ebb tide, he continued, "the flood tide might shove it back up as much as 7½ miles."

The Indian name for the river—Muhheakunnuk—is translated by Mr. Poole as "great waters constantly in motion." Mr. Lourie's translation is "water that flows both ways." Either way, for canoeists the message is clear: You're better off traveling with the ebb tide.

It is the shifting tides, by the way, stirring up the river bottom sediment that are responsible for the river's characteristic mud brown color. In fact, the river is reasonably clean these days, especially compared with the way it was before the Federal Clean Water Act of 1972.

The tides shift in cycles lasting about six hours, so each day there are two optimal canoeing intervals, though one of them is in the middle of the night. (A tide table, available at most marinas, as well as in the waterway guide, is essential.) Our first day, high tide at Catskill was about 6am, and by my amateurish calculations that meant the tides would shift and be moving in the proper direction about an hour later. We pushed off about 7:30am, and I must have been more or less correct; the water was slow but we didn't seem to be fighting it. There was no wind, the surface of the river was glassy, and the sense of steady movement was encouraging if not exhilarating. We were moving; it was apparent we could get somewhere.

For a time, I stayed close to the reedy western shore, working on my J-stroke, trying to stay in sync with my partner, who was working out a rhythm of her own, paddling first on one side of the canoe, then the other, flexing her shoulder muscles. The river was ours at that hour, and it was marvelously quiet, the boat almost imperceptibly shushing through the water. There were wooden duck blinds like gaping faces waiting empty in the marshes, but no ducks. The only wildlife were gulls preening on the river buoys.

An inlet to the west—Inbocht Bay, the map called it—left us in open water for the first time, and it was emboldening, a look-ma-no-hands sensation. We began to wonder how fast we were traveling, how to read the map and the river for distance (no odometer on the canoe, after all), how far we could get in a day. We didn't have a plan, really, for our two-day journey, or a solid destination. Figuring this was New York State and not the wilderness, we just trusted we'd be somewhere we could stop comfortably when we needed to, and we'd see where we were when we got there.

We passed a few small villages on the banks—Cementon on the west (with its gargoyle-ish cement factory), the more benign-looking

Germantown on the east, a more benign and bucolic shore in general—and by midmorning we'd gone 10 miles or so and reached Esopus Creek, the entrance marked by an old and creakily elegant lighthouse. Up the creek is the pleasant town of Saugerties, reviving as a weekend retreat after a bout of hard times, where we had thought we might stop for lunch after the tide shifted, but we were ahead of our estimated schedule and so we pushed on. We snacked in the boat, doffed our sweatshirts, and paddled in earnest, sweating.

I suspect, in our enthusiasm to get someplace, to put some distance behind us, we missed some things—some silent, overgrown, and twisty creeks, wildlife in the marshes, the exploration of some islands (the waterway guide says Magdalen Island, just below Saugerties, contains Indian ruins and middens)—but by midday the trip had become travel, the pleasure of it the pleasure of traveling on one's own power, not unlike that of hiking or bicycling. The river was a road.

Battling the Flood Tide

We took a break about noon, hauling the canoe up on a gravelly beach just north of the Kingston-Rhinecliff Bridge, where we promptly fell asleep and were wakened, I would say an hour later, by some roughhouse waves lapping the beach as the tide shifted. The water climbed the shore and nearly carried the canoe away; our towels got soaked.

For the rest of the day we battled the flood tide, which was a weird sensation because it doesn't feel as though the river is backing up on you. What it feels like is that your paddling has gone ineffectual; you're working harder for less reward. In addition, other boats were now in evidence, and avoiding the larger ones, the yachts, so as not to wobble in their wakes, became part of the strategy.

Many people had told me before the trip that the river would be so crowded on a weekend, particularly on Labor Day weekend (which was when we traveled), that it could get dangerous for a canoe. But it never became so, though there was ample river traffic, and the sheer size of the two barges that passed us was intimidating. I was surprised at the general courtesy of the yacht captains, who frequently would slow to a crawl as they passed us. (A notable exception to this were the police boats, which blew by us without a look, so quickly we could barely read the word "sheriff" emblazoned on their hulls.)

For all of those reasons, it was late afternoon by the time we pulled onto the sand at Kingston Beach; there, a local man advised us not to stay there. It was a hangout for teenagers at night—"a bad element," he said—and the canoe would be gone by morning. He directed us around the point (another lighthouse) and into Rondout Creek, where we'd find restaurants, a marina to leave our boat, and easy access to town. I missed the turn, though, and we ended up a little bit south, in Port Ewen.

There we paddled into the Hidden Harbor Yacht Club, a private marina, and had to do some fast talking before the commodore, Spencer Rohrlick, allowed us to be the first canoeists ever to leave a canoe there. He lightened up after a bit, though, and even offered to let us sleep on his boat, the *Edelweiss*. We declined. Instead, another club member drove us to a motel in town. Nice folks.

"I have an affinity for people who like the water," the club member explained.

At the motel, where the accompanying restaurant had a wedding room, we had the option of taking the honeymoon suite. We declined that, too.

On Esopus Island

The next morning, we called a cab for the ride back to the yacht club, and the cabbie, who bragged he'd been on the job for 15 years, promptly got lost and drove us into Kingston before we managed to correct him. On the water, things immediately went better, the morning once again tranquil and the river, for a while, beatifically serene.

We had the boon of a following breeze and the confidence brought by a day's experience, and we traveled briskly around a river bend marked by the Esopus Lighthouse, which, built in 1837, rebuilt in 1872, is now being restored, for which a sign on the side makes a plaintive request for donations. A man in the nearby marsh was readying a duck blind for duck season, which begins in October, and before the sun rose above the trees on the eastern shore, it felt like autumn.

By late morning, however, it was hot, and we pulled to shore on Esopus Island, at the top of another bend in the river, known as Crum

Elbow. We swam in a cove in the island lee, the water warm and shallow, and the river bottom so mucky that I lost a boat shoe in it. It is a lovely spot (marred only by the graffiti on the island rocks), the moored boats of the Poughkeepsie Yacht Club visible, swaying like cradles in the water on the eastern shore.

The rest of the morning was a bit more exciting, as the wind gained momentum and the first real waves arose in the river. Happily, for an hour they pushed us along, a mild surf that angled toward the east and downstream. Just north of Poughkeepsie, however, where two bridges span the water, the tide began to shift and the waves that had been working in our favor began to rollick in place. We had to fight through them. We stuck close to shore; the wind was strong and we bobbed with increasing ferociousness.

The bridges stayed in front of us, it seemed, forever, a sort of mockery of our lack of progress. We crawled past the boathouses for Marist and Vassar colleges and finally crossed under the first of the bridges, a disused railroad trestle, and docked for a rest in a town park where the jet ski rental concession was doing a great business. It was noisy, the first city feeling I'd had on the trip. And so we didn't rest as long as we wished, plunging off again into the flood tide and an afternoon of hard paddling.

Below Poughkeepsie, the eastern shore of the Hudson gets rather un-scenic—a highway runs along it part of the way, and several industrial sites also mar the view—so, with a hubristic push, we crossed the river and sought the opposite shore, which was indeed more pleasant. By late in the afternoon, with the sun on the downward slope and heading behind the trees on the small hills, we were able to trail through the shade on the western bank. By that time, my legs were good and sunburned, and my partner had need to soak a T-shirt in the water and wrap it around her head to fend off a swoon.

By 5 o'clock, we were ready to quit for the day, but there was nowhere to quit; the shore was green but uninhabited. A freight railroad track followed the riverbank and above it was nothing but woods. The waterway guide suggested that a town called Milton might provide a stop—there's a winery on the shore, it said—but the winery was closed down and all that was there was a dilapidated dock and some propane tanks. It took us another hour to find welcoming civilization, another private club, alas—the Marlboro Yacht Club, just north of Newburgh—but the same sense of welcome. Another invitation to leave our canoe. Another ride to a motel.

And so we were back on land for good.

Roots in the Watery Soil

Perhaps this sounds like an anticlimactic or even melancholy finish, but in fact weariness at the end of a journey is a good thing, begetting reflection and satisfying sleep. Besides, our shoulders were well exercised and our sea legs sturdy.

The next morning my partner had a business appointment in Manhattan and took the train from Beacon, and it was left to me to reclaim the car in Catskill, drive back down Route 9W to pick up the canoe, and return it. This is a whole other story, involving some fruitless hitchhiking and eventually a long cab ride with, coincidentally, the same hapless cab driver in Kingston who had lost himself on his own home turf. Once he drove me to my car, he insisted on following me back. In the future, I'll plan better, borrow a second car, plant it down river, and aim for it as a destination.

Or maybe I'll just stay on the river.

It took a whole day of riding in one car or another to get the canoe back to its rightful owner and to get myself back to the city, long enough for me to begin missing my brief life on the Hudson, which no longer seemed like such an evanescent thing. I'd been in it, grown to know it, left my modest mark: a wake that in a way felt a little like roots in soil.

And if I'd been a little more patient it would have brought me all the way home.

CANOEING ESSENTIALS

CANOE RENTALS AND GUIDED CANOE TRIPS

Appalachian Mountain Club, New York–North Jersey Chapter, 5 Tudor City Place, Manhattan (☎ 212/986-1430). Offers guided day canoe trips on the lower Hudson River that circumnavigate Manhattan and New York Harbor, and weekend trips on the northern Hudson, above Warrensburg. Season runs from late May to early September.

Beaver Brook Outfitters, Rtes. 8 and 28, Wevertown (☎ 518/251-3394). Canoe rentals $25 a day, $20 for each additional day; rates include life vests (child-size vests available), paddles, and padding for transporting canoes. A credit card is necessary for rentals. Open Monday through Thursday 8am to 6pm, Friday and Saturday 8am to 7pm, Sunday 9am to 5pm. Single and multiple-day canoe trips on the Hudson River are offered; $75 per person for day trips, $180 to $300 for multiple days, depending on the number of participants.

The Boat House, 2855 Aqueduct Rd., Schenectady (☎ 518/393-5711). Canoes to be used on the nearby Mohawk River are rented hourly, with all necessary equipment; $10 for two people for up to two hours, $3 an hour thereafter. The daily rate is $30 if you want to take a canoe to another destination; $20 for the second day, $10 for each additional day. A credit card is required. Open year-round. April 1 through Labor Day open Monday through Friday 10am to 8pm, Saturday 10am to 4pm, closed Sunday. Labor Day through March open Tuesday through Friday 10am to 6pm, Saturday 10am to 4pm; closed Sunday and Monday.

Champaign Canoeing, Brayton Park, Beach Rd., Ossining (☎ 914/762-5121). Offers weekend whitewater canoeing trips on the Croton River and weeklong trips in Canada from mid-May through the end of September. Weekend trips $100 per person; weeklong trips $400 per person. Pickup from Croton-Harmon station of Metro-North is available.

Cold Brook Canoes, Rte. 28, Boiceville (☎ 914/657-2189). Canoes, kayaks, and related water equipment are for sale, along with books and videotapes. Open Thursday through Monday 10am to 5pm.

Loric Sports, 912 Rte. 9, Staatsburg (near Rhinebeck; ☎ 914/889-4320). Daily canoe rental $39.95, including all necessary equipment and transporting of canoes to the Hudson River. March through November, open daily Wednesday through Saturday 7am to 7pm (until 6pm after Labor Day), Sunday 10am to 5pm, Monday 8am to 6pm (closed Tuesday). Bed-and-breakfast accommodations available.

Mountainaire Adventures, Rte. 28, Wevertown (☎ 800/950-2194 or 518/251-2194). Guided canoe trips on the Hudson River, from Warrensburg to Lake Luzerne. Day trips $80 per person, $60 each additional person (includes all equipment and lunch). Overnight trips $100 per person, $80 each additional person (includes equipment and meals).

Northern Pathfinders, Lake Clear (☎ 800/882-7284). Daily canoe rental $25, including life jackets and equipment (padding for transporting canoe on car is additional). Credit card or $300 deposit is necessary. Guided daily and overnight canoe trips on the Hudson River are also offered. Day trips $125 per person, $90 each for two people, $75 each for three, and $65 each for four or more. Open year-round.

Recreational Equipment, 500 Main St., New Rochelle (☎ 914/632-9222). An outdoor retailer cooperative that offers canoe rentals. Daily rates for nonmembers $40 per day ($50 maximum for two or more days), which includes two life vests, two paddles, and padding to transport canoe on car; for members, $30 ($40 maximum for two or more days). Lifetime membership fee is $15. A $150 deposit and a credit card are required for canoe rental. Instructional books and videos about canoeing are available. Open Monday through Friday 10am to 9pm, Saturday 10am to 6pm, Sunday 11am to 5pm.

ORGANIZATIONS

American Canoe Association, 7432 Alban Station Blvd., Suite B-226, Springfield, VA 22150 (☎ 703/451-0141).

American Red Cross, Westchester County chapter, 106 N. Broadway, White Plains, NY (☎ 914/946-6500, ext. 250). Offers pamphlets, films, and videotapes on water safety. Classes are held depending upon enrollment.

Professional Paddlesports Association, P.O. Box 248, Butler, KY 41006 (☎ 606/ 472-2205).

FURTHER READING

Quiet Water Canoe Guide: New York State, by John Hayes and Alex Wilson (Appalachian Mountain Club Books; $15.95). Can be ordered by calling (☎ 800/243-0495).

Hudson River Waterway Guide, available to members of the Hudson River Waterway As-sociation (☎ 201/333-5857). Membership fee $25.

River of Mountains: A Canoe Journey Down the Hudson, by Peter Lourie (Syracuse University Press, 1995; $29.95).

Horse Racing and More at Saratoga Springs

by William Grimes

THE WORLD OF HORSE RACING CAN be harsh, even seamy, sometimes. Aqueduct on a freezing winter day, for example, is not a sight to gladden the heart, and the sound of grown men banging on trash cans and cursing when their longshot falters does not please the ear. The horses still look noble, but there's not much else to prop up the image of thoroughbred racing as the sport of kings. When the wind off Jamaica Bay howls down the back stretch, there's only one thing to do: dream of Saratoga.

The annual summer meeting at Saratoga Springs, New York, now more than a century and a quarter old, is horse racing's Garden of Eden: five weeks of top-quality racing presented in ideal surroundings, and wrapped in the festive atmosphere of a county fair. Money is wagered, of course. But for a brief, idyllic interlude, finer feelings come to the fore.

Love would not be too strong a word to introduce here. Horseplayers really do love their sport, and the horses that compete in it. It says everything about Saratoga that one year a fan organized Fourstardave Day, in honor of the old-timer who trotted out onto the main track and won a turf race eight years in a row. For his special day, Fourstardave was walked over to Siro's restaurant, a Saratoga institution situated just through the trees near the clubhouse entrance. There he was presented with the keys to Saratoga Springs.

Come on, now. Admit it. That's nice.

If racing fans go a little crazy at Saratoga, it's not their fault. The atmosphere intoxicates them. The race track itself, laid out in 1863 and remodeled in 1902, has the charm of Fenway Park multiplied by Wrigley Field. In the all-wooden grandstand (a Victorian master-piece with cupolas), old-fashioned ceiling fans stimulate the air. To signal the scratches for the next race, a worker hoists wooden plaques up a pole. It's one of the few racecourses anywhere in the world with a gazebo in the infield.

Most unusually, the track is of a piece with the town, a genteel mineral springs spa with gambling and racing tacked on. It was a Victorian Las Vegas, a town for high rollers, swells, and nabobs riding the big-money wave of the Gilded Age. Henry James found the place disgusting. But time has worked a transformation. A bit of the raffish feeling lives on. There is excitement in the air. But the summer homes that James dismissed as vulgar eyesores now count as masterpieces, high-Victorian jewels set in spacious lawns, radiating a sense of am-plitude and the platinum-plated confidence that comes with multiple millions of dollars.

A century ago, big-money people lived more publicly, on a broader stage. The noble obligation to make a spectacle of oneself lives on in the fabled theme parties given by Marylou Whitney, now well on in years but still game. One summer, Mrs. Whitney, dressed as the Good Witch Glenda, set out arm in arm with the Cowardly Lion, the Tin Man, the Scarecrow, and Dorothy, skipping her way to Canfield Casino for the Over the Rainbow Ball as a crowd of 300 commoners gaped. Score one for the good old days.

Somewhat more seriously, Saratoga Springs attracts thousands of visitors who have no intention of placing so much as a $2 show bet. Throughout the summer the Saratoga Performing Arts Center offers a schedule of rock concerts, concerts by the Philadelphia Orchestra, and performances by the New York City Ballet. The town is also the site of the National Museum of Dance. There is more to the place than horses. But no horses, no Saratoga.

For the horseplayer, Saratoga is summer camp, a place to watch horses, think horses, and talk horses from dawn to dusk. For some time now, my wife and I have nourished the theory that we could be winning horseplayers if only we had the time to focus on the game full time, undistracted by the annoying intrusion of things like jobs. We gave it a good try one year, using Saratoga as our proving ground. For four days, we watched the early-morning workouts at the main track and the nearby Oklahoma training track (the origin of the name is a mystery). We attended handicapping seminars. We paid homage to the great names of racing, past and present, human and equine, at the National Museum of Racing. We watched the two-year-old horse auctions. To get in

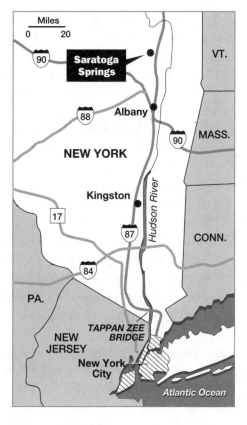

the spirit, my wife read *Saratoga Backtalk,* the latest in Stephen Dobyns's excellent series of Saratoga mysteries, and we both consulted a volume on the secret language of horse behavior. We studied *The Daily Racing Form* with the devotion of yeshiva students, bet our way through the day's card, and, on leaving the track at the end of the day, picked up the next day's Racing Form and prepared to do it all over again. It was heaven on earth.

Morning's Clarity

The morning workouts, and breakfast at the main track, are a Saratoga institution. Check out both tracks. Workouts at the Oklahoma training track are quieter and less public. Trainers use the track as a stamina-builder, because its deep surface (it looks like chocolate cake mix) makes the horses work harder. In the morning, you can hear the sounds that get obliterated by the crowd: the snorting and snuffling as the horses shift into high gear, the back and forth between riders, the one-way conversation between rider and horse.

At the main track, breakfast is served in the Clubhouse Porch from 7 to 9:30am on race days. As trainers, jockeys, and big-name horses turn up, Mary Ryan delivers running commentary, more or less in the manner of a Hollywood reporter covering the entrance of the stars on Oscar night. For the benefit of the crowds, she will coerce trainers and jockeys into raising their hands for easier identification. This is all highly entertaining.

"Now, here's a trainer we don't see that often on the track, Christophe Clement," said Ms. Ryan one bright morning. "Bon-JOUR, Christophe." Mr. Clement, a Frenchman who specializes in turf runners, smiled indulgently. Ms. Ryan followed up with a bit of expert commentary, pointing out that Mr. Christophe likes to have his horses begin their workout by standing stock still for several minutes, observing the action but not moving.

The horses, of course, get the star buildup. Who's this? Why, it's Fourstardave himself, out for a morning constitutional. He gets a nice hand from the crowd.

Tips From Insiders

Several times a week, *The Daily Racing Form* presents hourlong free seminars at Siro's, which begin at 10:30am. This is the best deal in town. Racing Forms in hand, my wife and I sat down under a tent next to the restaurant, ordered coffee and coffeecake, and settled in for a highly educational session. Each seminar starts off with a guest, usually a jockey or a trainer. Then a Racing Form editor and a handicapper go over the day's card, debating the pros and cons of various horses.

Tony Heyes, at that time a handicapper for *The Daily News,* talked about his approach to analyzing races and betting. Mr. Heyes, who is British, also offered some useful tips on how to size up European horses and recalled, wistfully, the day that he managed to collect five win bets on the same race, thanks to the peculiarities of the British betting system.

At another seminar, Mike Luzzi, a New York jockey, carefully avoided giving any inside tips, but he did reminisce on his early days racing horses at the Timonium Fair in Maryland, whose tiny race track presents unusual challenges. For one thing, horses that can't negotiate the tight turn into the home stretch often crash right through the rail and wind up next to the Ferris wheel.

As one day blended into the next, the world of the racetrack seemed to unfurl slowly, revealing itself in brief flashes: an insight here, a choice bit of language there, a pungent anecdote. Hanging over the rail one morning, I struck up a conversation with a part-time horse owner from Virginia who gave his theory as to why horses shipping in from Laurel and Pimlico in Maryland do well at Saratoga. He affection-ately referred to his own steeds as "a bunch of bums."

This sort of trackside talk is as old as the sport, whose history in America is the subject of the National Museum of Racing, situated directly across from the track. Its permanent exhibition describes the earliest days of racing in Colonial America, when horses sped along irregular paths through the woods. Visitors can read about Sir Archy and Diomed, the fathers of all-American race horses, and about the rise of New York in the 19th century as the power center of American racing. In the Hall of Fame room, visitors can call up pictures of the great horses and jockeys on computer terminals. In many cases, the computer file includes scenes of winning stretch drives, so you can see the likes of Ruffian and Secretariat in action.

Go with a Plan

Watching the races at Saratoga requires a game plan. Weekends, es-pecially, can be an unholy crush, and even the weekday crowds are no joke. A reserved seat is a must, and repeat visitors often order theirs as early as January every year. The sections run from B to Y (excluding I), with B halfway between the finish line and the sixteenth pole and Y overlooking the turn into the stretch. Each day, tickets for that day's grandstand sections W, X, and Y go on sale at 8am at a booth near the grandstand entrance. Limited number of clubhouse seats (sec-tions B through L) are available as well, except on the days of the three biggest stakes races, the Travers, Alabama, and Whitney. The price is $4. About 500 clubhouse seats for the next day's races go on sale in the evening at the Holiday Inn downtown. Starting at 10am, the booth also sells advance tickets for sections R through V at $4. Advance ticket holders often have extras that they need to unload, usually at face value. Look for a cluster of people holding tickets aloft.

Learn to use the screen-activated machines, known as SAMs, which allow you to place a bet using a voucher. This beats standing at the end of a long line with a sure thing and only two minutes left before the race starts. Go to any window, ask for a voucher in the amount of money you intend to spend that day, and use the slip as cash. After the voucher is inserted into the machine, the screen presents a menu of options that are easily deciphered. Simply press the option you want. Bet as little or as much as you like, up to the amount of the voucher. After placing your bets, don't forget to remove not just the betting slips, but the voucher with your remaining cash on it.

If you want to check out the horses in the paddock parade, get out there early. Places along the rail fill up quickly. Also, remember that it is a long, long walk back to the grandstand seats.

My wife and I did not become winning horseplayers, but we did become more scientific losers. There is some satisfaction in knowing that your losing bet was not a stupid bet. There's a difference.

Besides, we collected other, richer dividends. One afternoon, on the way back to the Six Sisters bed-and-breakfast, a Victorian guest house just up the street from the race track, we saw a strangely familiar figure on the porch of the house next door. It was Mike Smith, one of the nation's top jockeys and the rider of Sovereign Kitty, a disappointing second in that day's seventh race. We went up to our room, sat down on the balcony, and discreetly listened in as Mr. Smith replayed the race. It was the next-best thing to riding the horse ourselves. Sure, we had a win bet on the horse. But we didn't hold a grudge. We didn't even want to bang a trash can and curse.

At and Around the Track: Saratoga Essentials

GETTING THERE

By Car   If you are driving, take the Gov. Thomas E. Dewey Thruway to exit 24 and pick up the Northway (Rte. 87 North) and take it to exit 14 (Union Ave.); the entrance to Saratoga Raceway is on Union Avenue.

By Train   Amtrak (☎ 800/872-7245) offers a special round-trip package every Saturday and Sunday during racing season. Trains leave Manhattan's Penn Station early in the morning, arrive in Saratoga Springs in time for the first race, and return in the early evening. The round-trip fare includes a free beverage each way, free bus transportation to and from the racetrack, grandstand admission, and a racing program.

ACCOMMODATIONS

Saratoga Springs positively bristles with bed-and-breakfast establishments in eye-catching Victorian houses. The four cited below represent a small sampling; the rates quoted are for double occupancy. Rooms are extremely difficult to reserve and cost much more in August, as well as during Skidmore College's parents weekend (first week in October) and graduation weekend (last week in May) and the Newport Jazz Festival (late June or early July).

The **Saratoga Springs Chamber of Commerce** (☎ 518/584-3255) offers help in finding a room, but in racing season it can give only one or two listings to each caller. **The Adelphi Hotel,** 365 Broadway (☎ 518/587-4688). Built in 1877, the Adelphi offers old-time Saratoga atmosphere in spades. The hotel shows its age, but the public rooms reflect the Victorian era in full flower. Open mid-May to late October. Rooms are $90 to $320, based on double occupancy. Closed November through mid-May. Cafe Adelphi, with garden tables in the back, serves dinner in July and August, Wednesday through Sunday nights, 5:30 to 10:30pm. **The Batcheller Mansion Inn,** 20 Circular St. (☎ 518/584-7012). Racing season, $200 to $360; May 1 until racing season and September and October, $115 to $230; November to April 30, $80 to $155.

Chestnut Tree Inn, 9 Whitney Pl. (☎ 518/587-8681). Racing season, $125 to $235; off-season, $65 to $125 (higher on special event weekends).

The Six Sisters, 149 Union Ave. (☎ 518/583-1173). Racing season, $225 to $265; September, October, and April through mid-July, $95 to $140; November through March, $70 to $115. Except in July and August, the Six Sisters offers a two-night spa package with Crystal Spa for $250 to $350. No smoking allowed.

Union Gables, 55 Union Ave. (☎ 800/398-1558 or 518/584-1558). Racing season, $215 to $240; May through mid-July, September, and October, $95 to $105; November through April, $95.

Eartha's Kitchen, 60 Court St. (☎ 518/583-0602). Nouvelle American. Open Wednesday through Sunday 5:30pm to 10pm. Entrees $13 to $19.

43 Phila Bistro, 43 Phila St. (☎ 518/584-2720). Nouvelle American. Open Monday through Thursday and Sunday 5pm to 9pm, Friday and Saturday 5pm to 10pm. Entrees $15 to $25 (less in off-season).

Hattie's Chicken Shack, 45 Phila St.(☎ 518/584-4790). Old standby serving Southern home cooking. Open Wednesday through Saturday 5pm to 10pm, Sunday 4pm to 8:30pm. Entrees $6.25 to $13.50.

Siro's, 168 Lincoln Ave. (☎ 518/584-4030). Contemporary continental. Open daily starting mid-July 6pm to 10pm. Entrees $20 to $38.

The Wheat Fields, 440 Broadway (☎ 518/587-0534). Pasta. Open Monday through Thursday and Sunday 11:30am to 9pm, Friday and Saturday 11:30am to 10pm. Entrees $7.95 to $16.95, specials $11.95 to $17.95.

SARATOGA RACEWAY

Schedule and Tickets   Starting in late July and ending around Labor Day (July 23 to September 1 in 1997), there is racing daily except Tuesdays, beginning at 1pm. Tickets are $2 for general admission and $4 for the clubhouse; admission is free for children 12 and under. Parking gates open at 7am; $2 for general parking, $5 for preferred parking.

For information, ☎ 518/584-6200, ext. 4306 or 4686.

Racing Seminars   Free hourlong seminars on the day's races are sponsored by **The Daily Racing Form** at 10:30am Wednesday and Friday through Sunday at Siro's restaurant, 168 Lincoln Ave. (☎ 518/584-4030).

MUSEUMS

National Museum of Dance, just down the road from the Saratoga Performing Arts Center on Rte. 9 (☎ 518/584-2225). Photographs and video displays about George Balanchine and Bronislava Nijinska, sister of Vaslav Nijinsky, can be seen at this museum. Memorial Day to mid-December, open Tuesday through Sunday 10am to 5pm. Admission $3, $2 for students and seniors, $1 for children 12 and under.

National Museum of Racing, 191 Union Ave. (☎ 518/584-0400). Paintings, historical photographs, videos, and life-size re-creations of paddock areas and jockey rooms are included in the exhibitions here. During the racing season, the museum is open daily 9am to 5pm; at other times of the year, it is open Monday through Saturday 10am to 4:30pm and Sunday noon to 4:30pm. Admission $3, $2 for students and seniors, free for children 5 and under; admission free on Sunday.

The museum also offers walking tours of Saratoga Raceway during racing season; see "Walking Tours," below.

WALKING TOURS

Congress Park Walks   In July and August, the **Urban Cultural Park** (☎ 518/587-3241) offers one-hour walking tours of Congress Park that focuses on Saratoga's mineral springs and its social history. The tour leaves from the Saratoga Springs Urban Cultural Park Visitors Center across from Congress Park, Tuesday through Thursday at 10:30am. $2 per person. Call the number above to reserve.

Self-Guided House Tours   The Saratoga Springs Preservation Foundation's brochure *A Stroll Up North Broadway* allows visitors to take a self-guided tour of the North Broadway neighborhood, featuring houses from the 1880s to a contemporary solar home. Brochures can be obtained from the **Saratoga Springs Preservation Foundation,** 6 Lake Ave. (☎ 518/587-5030; open

Monday to Friday 9am to 5pm), or at any of the visitors centers in town.

Track Tours   The **National Museum of Racing** (☎ 518/584-0400) offers a two-hour walking tour of the training track during the racing season at the Saratoga Raceway that focuses on the early history of racing at Saratoga. Tours leave rain or shine from the museum, 191 Union Ave., daily (except Tuesday) at 8am during racing season. The cost is $10 for nonmembers. Reservations recommended.

PERFORMING ARTS

Saratoga Performing Arts Center, off Rte. 9 (☎ 518/587-3330; or visit the center's website at http://www.spac.org). The center holds an annual arts festival that begins in June and continues through Labor Day. The New York City Ballet performs here for three weeks in July, Tuesday through Saturday. The Philadelphia Orchestra performs for three weeks in August, Wednesday through Saturday. The center also has a six-series chamber music festival that complements the orchestra's season, and it offers about 30 special-event concerts featuring leading pop, country folk, and rock artists. In late June or early July, it hosts the two-day Newport Jazz Festival. Call for this year's schedule.

In the past, the New York City Opera has been in residence in June giving five performances, but 1997 will be its last year of residency. Plans remains uncertain after that.

To reach the center, take the Thomas E. Dewey Thruway to exit 13N to Rte. 9; the entrance to the center is on Rte. 9.

RAMBLING THROUGH ULSTER COUNTY

by William Grimes

LONG BEFORE ULSTER COUNTY, New York, came into being, Indians of the Mingua nation planted maize in the fields around present-day Kingston. They fished and hunted. They lived the good life. They called their domain "the pleasant land."

Well, fair enough. The no-frills appellation suggests that the Mingua (the Mingos of James Fenimore Cooper's *Leatherstocking Tales*) were a judicious people, not inclined to boosterism, ill-adapted to practice the dark arts of public relations and advertising. In short, reliable.

The pleasant land of Ulster County lies along the west bank of the Hudson River, about 100 miles north of Manhattan. It is neither spectacular nor chic. If its principal towns—Kingston, Woodstock, Saugerties, and New Paltz—could qualify as jewels, they would be small carat. The scenery delights and soothes rather than overwhelms. It is a land of small pleasures.

Ulster County has a little of this, a little of that. It has vineyards and rolling hills. It has large forests, lakes, and reservoirs. It has ice caves. It has not one but two mountain ranges, the Shawangunks and the Catskills, and two splendid parks. It has decent restaurants, a microbrewery, and its very own wine trail. It has an annual garlic festival. It is, in the words of a turn-of-the-century guidebook, "a land flowing with milk and honey, a land of corn and wine." Thumbs up to all of the above.

Manhattan's Dutch heritage survives only in the city's place-names. But in Ulster County, the Dutch influence pops up at every turn in the form of stone houses, many of them built in the late 17th and early 18th centuries. Built of Shawangunk (that's pronounced *shon-gum*, locally) grit, with sloping, high-pitched wooden roofs, the houses have distinctive jambless fireplaces that date back to medieval Flanders.

Ulster County takes great pride in these little houses. Huguenot Street in New Paltz has six, making it the oldest street in the United States with its original houses. One, the Jean Hasbrouck Memorial House, was named by the *Architectural Record* of March 1926, a monthly trade publication, as the finest example of medieval Flemish stone architecture in North America—a rather arcane honorific, but the house is indeed eye-catching. The local Huguenot Society operates tours of the houses on Huguenot Street and of Locust Lawn, a nearby 1814 Federal mansion once occupied by Josiah Hasbrouck, the local grandee. The little town of Hurley has 10 stone houses and 15 others are nearby.

Many of the stone houses carry on as private homes and inns. One is Baker's Bed and Breakfast, outside Stone Ridge, a farmhouse built in 1780. Baker's sits on high ground overlooking a few nearby farms, a gaggle of geese, and, off in the distance, the tower at Mohonk Mountain House, the county's most renowned resort. The farmhouse is a gem, a tight-knit package of stone, thick beams, and foot-wide floor planks. Upstairs, it still has the original wall paint, made with buttermilk and blueberries. The smell of wood smoke permeates the place, and in cool weather, a cast-iron stove in the communal living room radiates warmth, slowly sending the resident cat, curled underneath, into a narcotic daze.

My wife and I took a room with private bath for $98 a night (a third-floor loft with sitting room and fireplace is $128). It had a solid old four-poster bed, a rusticated armoire, and a dresser. They built solid in the old days, but they didn't build big. The bathroom and the closet occupied mere niches. Nevertheless, the room was cozy and pleasing to the eye.

There's something important to know about geese. They rise early, and they celebrate the morn with a "Hallelujah" chorus of honks that

continues for a very long time. You'd think that a toot or two would do it, but no. Geese go at it with the gusto of a barroom drunk into the third verse of "My Way."

There was no problem, therefore, in rising for breakfast, which is huge. One morning it was smoked trout, eggs Benedict with sautéed Jerusalem artichokes, and scones with raspberry jam. The next it was homemade granola and yogurt, ham, and something called a Dutch baby, sort of a glorified popover with a thick, almost custardy base. It comes out of the oven in a crock; it's eaten with maple syrup and it is very, very good.

The inn owner later informed me that the geese were in the midst of mating season, hence the high volume, but that nevertheless, as a concession to guests, he had slimmed down the flock to just a few geese.

Heading Out

Stone Ridge turned out to be a good base of operations. It is attractive but not twee, little more than a few stone houses strung along a state road, along with the imposing Inn at Stone Ridge (known locally as Hasbrouck House). The inn, a Dutch Colonial mansion, has a highly inviting little tavern just inside the entryway with seasonal beers on tap from the Woodstock Brewery in Kingston. The inn's restaurant, Milliways, specializes in regional American cuisine. The extensive wine list is all-American.

Another advantage to Stone Ridge is its proximity to High Falls, a tiny hamlet with much historical interest. Like many other towns in

Ulster County, High Falls is witness to an economy that came and went. It flourished in the heyday of the Delaware & Hudson Canal, built in 1828 to carry household coal from northeastern Pennsylvania to Kingston, where it was transferred to large barges that floated down river to New York City. High Falls had the highest concentration of locks on the canal, five of them, which raised or lowered barges 70 feet. The railroad made the canal obsolete by the late 19th century, and High Falls settled into a doze. The Delaware & Hudson Canal Museum in High Falls tells the tale, and it offers self-guided walking tours to the canal, the locks, an old ice house, a telegraph office, and the remains of sawmills that predate the canal.

A Tavern from 1797

High Falls is also home to the county's most celebrated restaurant, the Depuy Canal House, a comfortable tavern from 1797 that serves dinner Thursday through Sunday and lunch on Sunday. The bill of fare is ambitious and, if you take advantage of the set menus, a bargain. The three-course menu for $30 consists of soup or salad, entree, and dessert. The restaurant also offers a four-course menu for $42 and a seven-course menu for $55. A la carte prices are $8 to $11 for soups and appetizers and $20 to $28 for entrees.

We started with a half-bottle of Veuve Clicquot and nibbled on free hors d'oeuvres: chickpea puree on endive and a mock black caviar in a phyllo pastry cup. The caviar was made of amaranth, a grain, which had been soaked in brine and then cooked in squid ink and a little Vietnamese fish sauce. Although it didn't taste all that much like caviar, it was at least cruising in the neighborhood.

Things got rolling with the appetizers: morels and cottage goat cheese in an essence of mushroom sauce and a smoked-salmon quesadilla with smoked Gruyere and capers on a sesame sake sauce.

At the Canal House, the food gets a real makeover. Do not look on its text-heavy menu for a simple turbot in beurre blanc. Think in terms of rare duck breast and polenta served with hot dandelion and green olive salad with a red wine, shallot, and roasted garlic brown sauce or red snapper poached with red bell pepper miso sauce served with mushrooms, peas, tomatoes, black salted beans, and a potato croquette. Fortunately, the waiters do not announce specials. It would make a long evening.

All-American Main Street

Ulster County has no mandatory tourist destination. Therefore, it is perfectly O.K. to browse, guilt-free. An hour here, a couple of hours there should do it. Saugerties gets my vote as having the main street most likely to restore faith in traditional American values. Around one corner lies the heartwarming sight of a real, live small-town movie theater, the kind that has to be described as "the local bijou." At the same time, Saugerties has more than its share of spiffy restaurants, including Cafe Tamayo (nouvelle-ish) and Featherstone's (English).

Woodstock no doubt has abundant charms, but for purely personal reasons, I made a wide detour around it. Any town boasting of its artists' colony earns my instant suspicion. The term conjures up images of bad, overpriced jewelry and unspeakable objects labeled "sculptures." I prefer to visit a good reptile farm, and Woodstock doesn't have one.

Although Kingston shows every sign of having fallen on irreversible hard times circa 1920, it should have historical interest for New Yorkers. It was once the state's third-leading metropolis, after New York City and Albany, and for a time was the state's capital. The river made it. The fortunate confluence of Rondout Creek and the Hudson transformed a small Dutch settlement into a thriving center for the warehousing and distribution of flagstones, bluestone, cement, gravel, coal, and agricultural produce. After the Revolution, New Yorkers voted to make Kingston the capital of the United States.

A whiff of the glory days can be felt at Rondout Landing, on the river, and along the West Strand, a block of 19th-century Italianate commercial buildings that have been restored. The chief feature of the waterfront is the Rondout II Lighthouse, built in 1913.

Along the Wine Trail

Enough history. On to the wine trail, Ulster's highway of pleasure. Actually, there are two trails. The Shawangunk Wine Trail, marked by signs decorated with a cluster of grapes, starts south of New Paltz at Modena. Follow Route 44-55 west to Route 7. Turn south, then west again on Route 52. The white-streaked Shawangunks loom off to the west. A second string of wineries is off Route 9W between West Park and Marlboro. Most wineries offer tastings and sell their wares. (Some impose a small tasting fee, which is deducted from the price of the bottle if you buy.)

The Hudson Valley is not the Côte d'Or, but there are some decent Chardonnays to be found. West Park Wine Cellars is probably the best known. The bold few may wish to sample a Hudson Valley red. The standout wine on my visit was a grape variety new to me, a weirdo French hybrid called Ravat, after its inventor. Walker Valley Vineyards in Walker Valley produces a sterling specimen, off-dry or off-sweet, depending on where it hits the taste buds. It's a fairly hefty, fruity white that makes a terrific aperitif. It's a good souvenir and a good symbol for Ulster County. It's not a great wine, but a good wine, a little off the beaten track and worth the search. It's the wine you'd expect from a pleasant land.

TOURING, EATING, SLEEPING: ULSTER COUNTY ESSENTIALS

GETTING THERE

To reach Ulster County from the metropolitan area, take the George Washington Bridge to the Palisades Interstate Pkwy. North to Gov. Thomas E. Dewey Thruway.

BEDS AND MEALS

Baker's Bed and Breakfast, 24 Old Kings Hwy., Stone Ridge (☎ 914/687-9795).
Cafe Tamayo, 89 Partition St., Saugerties (☎ 914/246-9371).
Depuy Canal House, Rte. 213, High Falls (☎ 914/687-7700). Closed January 1 to February 14.

Featherstone's English Tea Room And Restaurant, 97 Partition St., Saugerties (☎ 914/246-6898).
Inn At Stone Ridge (Hasbrouck House), Rte. 209 North, Stone Ridge (☎ 914/687-0736).

ATTRACTIONS

Delaware and Hudson Canal Museum, Mohonk Rd., High Falls (☎ 914/687-9311). Memorial Day to Labor Day, open Thursday through Monday 11am to 5pm and Sunday 1 to 5pm; May, September, and October, open Saturday 11am to 5pm and Sunday 1pm to 5pm. Suggested admission $2 adults, $1 for children, $5 for families.

Hudson River Maritime Museum and Rondout Lighthouse, 1 Rondout Landing, Kingston (☎ 914/338-0071). May through October, open daily (except Tuesday) 11am to 5pm. Admission $2 adults, $1.50 seniors, $1 children 5 to 12, free for children 4 and under and museum members.

Boat trips to the lighthouse are offered weekends from May to June, daily (except Tuesday) in July and August, and weekends in September and October. Boat trips depart from the museum beginning at 12:30pm. Tickets, which include admission to the museum, are $6 adults, $5 seniors and children 4 to 11, free for children under 4.

Hudson Valley Garlic Festival, Cantine Field (exit 20 off the Gov. Thomas E. Dewey Thruway) Saugerties. Food, lectures, cooking demonstrations, crafts, and entertainment sponsored by the Kiwanis Club of Saugerties. Held on the last weekend in September (September 27 and 28 in 1997), 10am to 5pm. Admission (good for both days) $3 in advance, $5 at the door. For information, send a stamped self-addressed envelope to the **Garlic Festival Committee,** P.O. Box 443, Saugerties, NY 12477, or call ☎ 914/246-3090 for a recorded message.

Hugenot Street Stone Houses, New Paltz. The Jean Hasbrouck, Abraham Hasbrouck, Bevier-Elting, Lefevre, Deyo, and Freer-Lowe houses, as well as the French Church and the Grimm Gallery and Museum, line Huguenot Street. From the Thomas E. Dewey Thruway, take exit 18 and turn left onto Main Street (Rte. 299); continue to Huguenot Street and turn right. The interiors of the houses may be seen only on guided tours (see Hugenot Historical Society, below).

Huguenot Historical Society, New Paltz (☎ 914/255-1660 or 914/255-1889). The group sponsors tours of the stone houses along Huguenot Street. Tours are offered Wednesday through Sunday from 9am to 4pm; the can also be arranged by appointment. The 2½-hour Hugenot Street tour includes stops at all the stone structures; the fee Is $7, $6 for seniors, $3.50 for children under 12, free for children under 7. The 1½-hour tour includes two houses and the stone French Church; the fee is $4 per person, including children. A tour of one house is $2.75 per person.

A tour of the Terwilliger House and Locust Lawn, also in New Paltz, is available by appointment through the Hugenot Historical Society; $5 adults, $4 seniors, $2.50 children under 12.

Old Dutch Church, 272 Wall St., Kingston (☎ 914/338-6759). Self-guided tours Monday through Friday 9am to 4pm; guided tours by appointment. Admission and tours are free.

Senate House State Historic Site, 296 Fair St., Kingston (☎ 914/338-2786). Mid-April through October, open Wednesday through Saturday 10am to 5pm and Sunday 1 to 5pm; open to groups by appointment in winter. Admission $3 adults, $2 for groups, $1 for children under 12 and school groups.

Trolley Museum of New York, 89 E. Strand, Kingston (☎ 914/331-3399. Open Saturday, Sunday, and holidays noon to 5pm.

Volunteer Firemen's Hall and Museum of Kingston, 265 Fair St., Kingston (☎ 914/331-0866). April and May, open Friday 11am to 3pm and Saturday 10am to 3pm; June through August, open Thursday and Friday 11am to 3pm and Saturday 10am to 4pm; September and October, open Friday 11am to 3pm and Saturday 10am to 3pm.

VINEYARDS

Here is a sampling of vineyards in the Shawangunk region and along Rte. 9W. Many of them close or cut back their hours from December to June.

Adair Vineyards, 75 Allhusen Rd., New Paltz (☎ 914/255-1377).

Baldwin Vineyards, 1786 Hardenburgh Rd., Pine Bush (☎ 914/744-2226).

Benmarl Winery, Highland Ave. (off Rte. 9W), Marlboro (☎ 914/236-4265). A music and art festival with concerts, art displays, and crafts demonstrations is planned on July 6 from noon to 5pm; admission is $5 for adults, free for children.

Brimstone Hill Vineyards, 61 Brimstone Hill Rd., Pine Bush (☎ 914/744-2231).

Royal Kedem Wineries, Rte. 9W, Marlboro (☎ 914/236-4281); also at Dock Rd., Milton (☎ 914/795-2240).

Walker Valley Vineyards, Rte. 52 and Oregon Trail Rd., Walker Valley (☎ 914/744-3449).

West Park Wine Cellars, Rte. 9W, West Park (☎ 914/384-6709).

More Getaways in
New York State

In Search of Waterfalls

by William Grimes

E<small>VER SINCE</small> M<small>OSES STRUCK THE</small> rock, and it gushed forth, bringing cooling water to the blistered desert landscape, the waterfall has been a powerful symbol of all things good. It stands for creativity, abundance, and life, for relief from drought and the burning of the sun, for the cessation of thirst, both physical and spiritual.

It also stands for nature's raw power. The makers of the Tarzan movies understood this. Every Tarzan movie builds toward the eye-popping moment when the arrogant white hunter, at the head of a long line of native bearers, breaks out of the sweltering jungle and, deafened by a mighty roar, beholds stock footage of Victoria Falls. This is the moment when the audience realizes that there are some things even bigger than bwana's greed and ambition. It is the moment when nature reclaims its due and humbles the puny fellow in the ridiculous pith helmet.

Waterfalls chasten and refresh, providing an extraordinary combination of moral instruction and physical pleasure. As a consequence, they make ideal summer destinations. In one compact package tour, you can worship at the shrine of nature and get a cool, uplifting payoff at the same time. Try these three waterfalls, which are presented in order of difficulty and which move from the picturesque to the sublime. All are well within three hours of New York City.

Green Falls

Closest to the city are the Green Falls in the Hudson Highlands, near Cornwall-on-Hudson, New York, within Black Rock Forest. Local residents know them, if they are aware of them at all, as the Old Mineral Springs Falls, a name that comes from the nearest road (presumably named after some nearby mineral springs, although none are in evidence). It's an easy quarter-mile hike to the falls, which, like all cataracts, reach peak volume in spring with the melting of snow. In summer, the rushing torrent that feeds it quiets down to a gurgle, and the falls subside to a gentle, decorous cascade.

The Green Falls may take their name from the five-o 'clock shadow of moss that decorates most of the boulders in their path, and deepens the hush of the dark hemlock grove that forms their setting. The scene is romantic. There are enough blasted trees and rotting stumps for several paintings by Ruisdael. The stream that feeds the falls spills over rocks arranged in layers with a marked diagonal tilt, as though a giant fist had slammed down and bent them beyond repair.

The water descends, rather feebly in dry weather, in a triple cascade past hemlock trees that grip the edges of the stream bank with fanatic tenacity. Just below the first cascade is a large, off-balance boulder, improbably supported by three small rocks. Even nature, it seems, suffers from bad public sculpture.

For the most part, however, the falls exhibit good taste. The sunlight filters attractively through the forest canopy. The ascent to the top of the falls is brief, untaxing, and pleasant. And the town of Cornwall has a restaurant, Painter's, with brightly colored outdoor tables and a stunning range of imported beers.

Rainbow Falls

Day-trippers fortified by a cold one can press on to Minnewaska State Park, on the Shawangunk Mountain ridge near New Paltz, New York. For most pleasure seekers, the big draw here is Lake Minnewaska and its shimmering twin, Lake Awosting. Both lie in serene repose beneath dry white limestone cliffs. Away from the crowd and off the main path, Rainbow Falls await, about a mile and a half along the Upper Awosting Carriageway, which is clearly marked.

The walk begins at high altitude, perhaps 2,000 feet, so the ascent is minimal, with memorable sights along the way. A few hundred yards into the carriageway, the dense curtain of mountain laurel pine and shockingly white birch parts briefly to reveal the Catskills in the distance. Seen across a flat expanse, they look brownish green and curiously soft, like the mossy mountain ranges on model railroads. The day I hiked the trail, three hawks circled overhead, idly flexing their pinion feathers—clearly up to no good.

Shortly after the lookout point, an abandoned orchard looms on the left, now a grassy meadow, with the old apple trees still standing in file. Soon after crossing a small wooden footbridge, hikers will see a tree on the right with a double daub of blue paint, which signals the turn to Rainbow Falls. Here the forest floor is springy and soft with pine needles, and teeming with intertwining, crazily patterned tree roots that struggle to gain a foothold in the shallow earth.

The waterfall makes its presence felt by a sudden drop in temperature, as if someone had flipped the switch on the air-conditioning. A moment later, the splatter of falling water can be heard. Four streams descend from a broad lip of rock, past a sheer cliff face and onto a jumble of broken rocks below. In spring, the water forms a solid sheet, and you can stand behind it. In summer, the flow resembles four running showers, giving off a chilly spray as they hit the ground. On a hot summer day, when the world is woozy from humidity, pollution, and bad news, this is a blessed sanctuary, a cool, dark secret that even the blinding light of day cannot penetrate.

For the stout of heart, the long way back (three and a half miles) offers riches. Briefly retrace your steps and turn right at the double daub of blue on a tree at the right side of the trail. This is the exit for Blueberry Run, a sinuous trail that climbs across a startling landscape of broad, flat rocks, blueberry bushes, and stunted pitch pine, with uninterrupted views of the Catskills behind.

Eventually, the trail hooks up with the Castle Point Carriageway. Named for a breathtaking overlook that opens onto views of the Hudson Valley and the Taconic range, the carriageway follows a route that keeps the vista in sight almost without interruption.

After seven miles of hiking, the sight of a parked refreshment truck near the lake looks better than the Catskills.

Kaaterskill Falls

The Catskills abound in waterfalls, all of them attractive—there is no such thing as an ugly waterfall. But none compare with the Kaaterskill Falls, near Haines Falls. At 280 feet, this is the highest waterfall in New York, a thrillingly slim, speedy bolt of water that immediately triggers thoughts of suicide and mortal danger.

The name comes from the Dutch word kaater ("lynx"), recalling the frontier days when the woods teemed with bear, panthers, wolves, and deer. "The best piece of work I've met with in the woods," Natty Bumppo called the falls in James Fenimore Cooper's *The Pioneers*. He went on to describe its wonders in detail to a slack-jawed listener: "The first pitch is nigh 200 feet, and the water looks like flakes of driven snow afore it touches the bottom; and then the stream gathers itself together again for a new start, and maybe flutters over 50 feet of flat rock, before it falls for another hundred, when it jumps about from shelf to shelf, first turning this-a-way and then turning that-a-way, striving to get out of the hollow, til it finally comes to the plain."

Thomas Cole, Frederic Church, and Asher Durand painted it. In the 19th century, romantic couples visited it in all seasons, even the dead of winter, when the column of water froze into a white cone, expanding as the cold weather bit harder and harder.

For the daring, the easiest way to see the falls is from the top, a few dozen feet from a parking area at the end of Laurel House Road in Haines Falls. Like a doomed innocent, Kaaterskill creek races along, collecting in enticing blue-green pools from time to time, and then takes the wild, sickening leap to glory. On the day I visited the falls, two teenage girls, showing no fear, advanced to the precipice and lay prone on a flat rock to look over the edge. The very sight turned this reporter's knees to jelly.

The more traditional (and surely much safer) observation post is below, a short walk from the parking area at the horseshoe bend of Route 23A. The initial climb off the highway is steep and rugged, but for the rest of the half-mile trail, the going is manageable, with crooked roots and small boulders offering footholds.

My wife and I made decent progress, although at one point we were passed by two men and a woman, probably of college age, who effortlessly and heedlessly strode past at twice our pace. It was an allegory of life's progress—youth overtaking middle age—and it provided me with a moment of sullen reflection.

The trail follows Kaaterskill Creek, which is small, "yet a thing of life and motion," Thomas Cole wrote in 1843, "sufficient at all times to give expression to the scene, which is one of savage and silent grandeur." The creek ends at the cathedral-like rock face that encloses the falls. It's fairly easy to pick your way past the enormous boulders that fan out from the base of the falls and reach the falls themselves. Some climbers press onward and upward to the massive shelf overhead.

It is here that the saddest story ever told has its origins. On August 11, 1862, a trusting dog watched as his master, in jest, threw a stone over the edge of the falls for him to fetch. Consulting only his noble heart, the dog gave chase and was dashed to death on the rocks below. For years, a stone tablet commemorated the tragedy, dedicated to "the memory of the Bayard of dogs, 'sans peur et sans reproche,' who precipitated himself over these falls."

There's a lesson for comedians here: Always size up your audience before telling a joke.

HOW TO FIND THE FALLS: ESSENTIALS

GETTING THERE

GREEN FALLS

From New York City, take the Palisades Pkwy. to Rte. 9W North. Exit at Angola Rd. and follow it south toward Mountainville. After about 2 miles, the road forks. Follow the left fork (Mineral Springs Rd.) for about 1 1/4 miles and turn left on Old Mineral Springs Rd., which is dirt. You will see the trail, marked with white blazes, almost immediately on the left. Its official name is Scenic Trail, and it runs for 7.2 miles from Rte. 32 to Mount Misery.

RAINBOW FALLS

From New York City, take the New York Thruway (Interstate 87) north to exit 18 (New Paltz). Drive west on Rte. 299 for 10 miles to Rte. 44/55 and follow signs to Minnewaska State Park.

In spring and fall, admission to the park is $4 per vehicle weekends, free on weekdays; admission is $5 per vehicle every day in summer. In winter, if there is snow, the park opens for cross-country skiing, with a per-person ski fee on weekends of $6 for adults and $5 for juniors (under 17); on weekdays the fee is $5 for adults, $4 for juniors, and $2 for senior citizens.

In October 1996 the park opened the Peterskill Area for hiking and technical rock climbing (a $5 permit is required for rock climbing). A trail map is provided with admission, upon request.

There are two other waterfalls in the park: Awosting Falls, which is near the park entrance, and Stoney Kill Falls, which is a five-mile hike. For more information, contact **Minnewaska State Park,** P.O. Box 893, New Paltz, NY 12561 (☎ 914/255-0752).

Opened Oct. Open April 1 through December 15.

KAATERSKILL FALLS

From New York City, take the New York State Thruway (Interstate 87) to exit 20 (Saugerties). Follow Rte. 32 west to Rte. 32A northwest to Rte. 23A west. The trail to the falls begins at the small cascade off to the right, where the road has a horseshoe bend. There is a parking lot on the left, a few hundred yards past the trail.

FURTHER READING

The New York–New Jersey Trails Conference publishes detailed guides to the areas discussed in the article, notably *Hiking the Catskills* ($14.95), which includes a chapter on the Kaaterskill Falls area. Highly detailed trail maps for Minnewaska State Park are included in the conference's *Southern Shawangunk Trails Package* ($7.95). Maps for Black Rock Forest, home to the Green Falls, are included in the *West Hudson Trails Package* ($6.95). The conference's books and maps are available in bookstores and outdoor equipment stores. They can also be purchased through the conference, which offers discounts to members. For a flier of maps and other publications offered by the conference, write the **New York–New Jersey Trails Conference,** 232 Madison Ave., Room 401, New York, NY 10016, or call weekdays between 11am and 5:30pm (☎ 212/685-9699).

A *BELLA* WEEKEND AT
MOHONK MOUNTAIN HOUSE

by Michael T. Kaufman

L'ALBERGO DI MONTE MOHONK E bello e romantico—molto bello, molto romantico.

I probably could not have said that before I recently spent a Tower of Babble weekend learning Italian at Mohonk Mountain House, a remarkable hotel magnificently situated within a 7,000-acre wilderness in the Shawangunk Mountains, just 90 miles from New York City. But the resort, which has been a moderately well kept secret since it was founded in 1869, does encourage flights of rhapsody, in whatever language.

Still owned and managed by the descendants of Alfred and Albert Smiley, the Quaker twin brothers who first stumbled on the site and set about developing it, Mohonk Mountain House has acquired its very own atmosphere, a blend of splendor and comfort with a bracing touch of ennobling asceticism.

The awesome views of glacial lakes, mountain crests, and sloping valleys are all the more impressive for lying so close to the city. There are 85 miles of private paths that can be used for walking, cross-country skiing, or carriage rides. There are cliffs to climb and well-tended gardens to look at and sniff, and more than 100 gazebos in which to rest, read, or scan the horizon in solitude. There is a golf course. There is a library. And many of the 261 rooms have working fireplaces.

Not one of them, however, has a television set. Nor is there a bar in the hotel, though liquor is available with meals, a departure from tradition. Of the many public rooms in the sprawling main building, there are only two where smoking is permitted. And despite the many sports and activities available, there is no indoor swimming pool. No stars entertain in the evening, though there are often talks by naturalists and it is not uncommon for guests to organize their own concerts around the piano. Pets are forbidden. Children, on the other hand, are very much welcome and much in evidence. There is an old-fashioned soda shop and, in what seems to be a concession to those who think croquet too tame an after-dinner activity, there is a small room of pinball machines and electronic games.

"All of this has been thought out over decades," said Helen Dorsey, the hotel's promotion manager, in a conversation that took place after I had checked out. "Mohonk is not for everyone. It is not and never has been restrictive, but the kind of people who find their way here do not need to be entertained. From the beginning, our greatest attraction has been this setting." Indeed, for the first century of its existence Mohonk never needed to advertise. Friends of the Smileys were the first guests and they carried the word, first, through Quaker communities, and then to the well-to-do of all religions who were fascinated by nature and interested in its conservation.

By the late 1960s, when a portion of the old, largely patrician clientele was flying to more distant holidays, Mohonk, which was designated a National Historic Landmark in 1986, began to change a little. Liquor was made available. Cars were admitted onto the grounds instead of being confined to lots a mile or so away, from which guests and baggage had been transferred to the hotel by horse-drawn carriages. Special day programs were established, so that visitors could book ahead to eat a single meal and visit the grounds, or just hike or ski. And programs organized around different themes were expanded, particularly for the off-season months.

It was just such a program—the Tower of Babble Weekend—that drew my wife and me to the hotel on an early April weekend. We had reserved our places a month earlier, sending off tuition checks of $250 each to the Language Immersion Institute at the State University College at New Paltz, which had developed this particular program and which conducts similar workshops at a number of different locations. I picked beginning Italian; my wife registered for intermediate

Spanish. We could have picked almost anything, from Arabic to Yiddish, provided that a minimum of four others did the same.

We drove from the city on Friday evening, arriving within two hours at the hotel's lower gate off Mountain Rest Road, some four miles past New Paltz. After checking for our names, a staff member waved us through to start up the magic mountain. We emerged from heavy forest to a plateau and lake, over which the hotel loomed, a massive stone and wood building that is an eighth of a mile long with towers standing six stories high. Built in sections over the years, it stands as an integral whole, combining the outdoorsy utility of Adirondack camps with an imposing, castlelike grandeur.

Valets, part of the year-round staff of 250, parked our car and we were led to our fifth-floor room in the tower, overlooking the frozen lake and the labyrinth, a jumble of rock formations on the far shore. The room, about 30 feet square with large windows, had a balcony with three rocking chairs, but the freezing temperatures made the fireplace much more appealing. The wood was already stacked, and with the help of a packet of some kind of incendiary gel that was provided, it took only a single match to start a happy fire.

On the Arts and Crafts-style desk, which coexisted nicely with Victorian and Adirondack pieces of furniture, a booklet of guest information included a greeting from the Smiley Family that said in part: "We invite you to follow in the footsteps of our predecessors; waken to the sounds of nature; view a panorama virtually unchanged

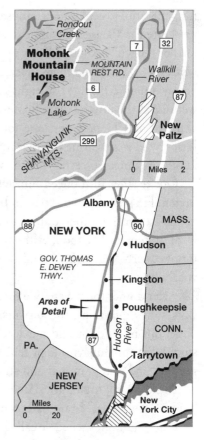

for generations; explore our House, a building of immense architectural interest. Please allow time to sit quietly in a comfortable nook to read or reflect." It sounded very appealing but there was no time. My wife and I had arrived there to learn, and the instruction started with Friday dinner. My table had eight students of beginning Italian. There were 12 at the intermediate Spanish table. There were also tables for German and French, and one for five teachers from Tenafly, New Jersey, who were setting out to learn Korean because there were many pupils of Korean ancestry in their school.

Our teacher introduced himself as Francisco Bonavito from Isla Staten. He kept speaking to us in Italian, explaining one Italian word or phrase with another Italian word or phrase. Remarkably, things were sinking in. The food, by the way, was varied; hearty and plentiful if not superb. We tended to talk about it a lot, but mostly to acquire vocabulary.

After dinner there were two more hours of Italian, these involving skits, songs, questions, and answers. The theory seemed to be to break down our inhibitions and our fear of making mistakes or sounding stupid. Signor Bonavito kept telling us that speaking was most important, and that grammar and structure would come later.

At 10:30pm, tired but excited, I joined my wife for some tea in a lounge. "Cara mia," I said. "Mi corazon," she answered.

Since Saturday's schedule called for virtually uninterrupted instruction until 11 at night, I decided to get up at dawn and scout the grounds. It was snowing and the footing was icy as I started out around the lake. At the far side there were trails leading up through the rocks and boulders that looked enticing, but signs barred the way because of ice. A broader path led up toward Paltz Point, rising above the hotel to a height of 1,500 feet. On clearer days, the tower at the top offers views stretching up the Rondout Valley of the Catskills and down the Hudson River toward New York City.

Braced by the jaunt, I was ready for breakfast and Italian at 8 o'clock. I am not bad at languages but I am terrible at school: I have trouble sitting. And yet I not only endured the proceedings, I thoroughly enjoyed them, all through Saturday and half of Sunday. (It might have been worse if the weather had been better.) Among the things I learned from Signor Bonavito was what to say when I visit a farm in Umbria, how to argue for a hotel room in Rome, and how to chat with an old high school instructor when I meet him at a bus stop in Bologna.

Thanks to the teacher and his energetic, enthusiastic approach, my classmates and I were able to play charades, sing "Old MacDonald," read magazines, and argue politics, albeit primitively, all in Italian. I also learned the etymology of the Italian word *ciao*, which derives from the word *schiavo*, meaning slave. People would greet each other by saying, "Sono vostro schiavo," ("I am your slave"), and after a while that was shortened to the now cheery and democratic ciao.

As for the efficacy of the method, my wife and other students seemed very pleased. Some spoke of returning for more when the next Tower of Babble Weekend was held.

As for me, all I can say is that 37 years ago as a Columbia University graduate student, I spent a full academic year learning Finnish. Now, after just one weekend at Mohonk, there is absolutely no question that my Italian is much, much better than my Finnish.

MOHONK MOUNTAIN HOUSE

Mohonk Mountain House is on Mohonk Lake near New Paltz, NY (☎ 800/772-6646 or 914/255-4500), and can be reached via exit 18 of the Gov. Thomas E. Dewey Thruway. The hotel's 261 rooms range from $175 for the least expensive single to $445 for the most expensive double. Suites range from $410 to $490. Rates include three meals and afternoon tea daily.

The resort offers a variety of special programs, among them the Writer's Workshop; Holistic Way: Dreams, The Forgotten Language; the Photographer's Holiday; A Laurel Walking Weekend; Birding and Spring Nature; Hiker's Holiday; Joy of Singing; Summer Nature Week; and Music Week. All involve prior registration; some require a fee in addition to the hotel's charges for room and board. Call for the current schedule and further information.

EXCESS AND ODDITIES: UPSTATE'S ROADSIDE ATTRACTIONS

by Michael T. Kaufman

I AM A SUCKER FOR ROADSIDE attractions. My idea of glorious slumming is to drive through stretches of country new to me and stop along the way to look at the biggest chair in the world or performances by diving pigs.

So there I was happily driving west through the Green Mountain National Forest in Vermont, twisting through stands of proud old trees and catching glimpses of valleys offering themselves in the distance. On the radio, a highbrow disk jockey was introducing Renaissance lute music.

Then as I crossed into New York the physical and emotional terrain leveled prosaically. I passed a miniature golf course and I knew I was getting close to ground zero, which in this case was Lake George, the first stop of a two-day excursion into schlock, kitsch, and excess that I had charted with the help of *Roadside America* (Simon & Schuster), a book I keep on my bedside table.

It was a weekday just before the summer season began, and while the resort was far from thronged, you could see why the place could upset naturalists and purists. A lovely lake that in Europe might have been rimmed by pathways for walkers, sitters, and sighers was surrounded by water slides, fun parks, arcades, parlors, and store after store that sold things on which "Lake George" was inscribed. These included cups, belts, plates, pens, nail clippers, combs, cutlery, wind chimes, and T-shirts. It seemed that faux Southwestern pottery and stained-glass tchotchkes were gaining on the more traditional cedar souvenirs.

Several Olde Time photography shops offered portraits in period dress, and on the lake front Olde Time paddle boats offered cruises to some ersatz past, reflecting what Umberto Eco, the Italian philosopher and novelist, describes as the "hyperreality" concocted from the fact and fiction of various epochs for the benefit of fun seekers in America.

Since hyperreality was essentially what I was looking for, after a hamburger at the shore front I headed straight for the Movieworld Wax Museum, the first of two wax museums on my list. It proved a disappointment. The displays, dioramas showing scenes of well-known movies, were static. There was a bit of hyperreal dissonance in not exactly knowing whether the three-dimensional figures you were looking at represented Dorothy or Judy Garland, Rhett or Clark Gable, Quasimodo or Lon Chaney.

Much more exciting was the House of Frankenstein Wax Museum. Here, for 50 cents more, were movement and nonstop recorded screams. Though the scenes of horror blurred history and literature, most portrayed horrors that had in fact occurred. A medieval torture chamber showed moving figures being whipped, flayed, roasted, and stretched.

In a display about the guillotine, the viewer was invited to push the button that activated the blade. Farther along there was another button that set off a simulated execution of a woman bound to an electric chair. I pushed the buttons and felt something like shame. I wondered whether this was a universal or general response and, if so, thought it might be a good thing to have young people do to heighten empathy. Then I stood back to watch a young teenage couple come through. They laughed as they pushed the buttons. I wondered if they thought the torture and the executions were as unreal as the displays of Dorothy and Rhett at the other museum.

Another display showed a kneeling woman knifing a man in the tub. The man had a towel around his head, and despite the modern plumbing, the scene was obviously inspired by the killing of Marat by Charlotte Corday, which I assume has been a wax museum perennial since shortly after Thermidor. But these days it was titled merely "The Bathroom Murder," presumably not to overburden or intimidate anyone.

I had come to laugh and take in the folly, but I ended up queasy and troubled. Most of what was represented had actually happened, but except for the electric chair, the deeds were all remote and distant. The message seemed to be that horror was a thing of the past. Where were the more contemporary examples? Why no scenes of war, slave auctions, concentration camps, famine, Khmer Rouge killing fields, Bosnian villages? Would people pay to see such things? Would I?

From Bats to Caves

In this frame of mind, it was comforting to look at the purely fictional panoramas, like the one in which a bat turns into Dracula with the aid of mirrors. Stepping out of the kitschy stew of cheap thrills into unsynthetic daylight, I had to admit I had been more stimulated than I usually was by museums.

But enough was enough. I got out of town, visited friends, and the next morning set off for my second stop, Secret Caverns, near Cobleskill. To get to Secret Caverns you have to pass Howe Caverns, then drive three miles more. Years ago when my children were young, we went to Howe Caverns. I remember riding down in an elevator and following a name-tagged and uniformed guide into boats for the quarter-mile ride on an underground pool. I was assured by *Roadside America* that Secret Caverns would be different.

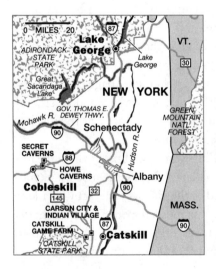

It was. In contrast to the three tourist buses and the 50 or so cars I could see parked at Howe Caverns, my car was the only one at Secret Caverns. I got out to admire the advertising of ghosts and dinosaurs drawn in a very free hand. Inside the ramshackle ticket house I was welcomed by Todd Del Marter, who was sweeping up. "I'll take you down in a few minutes," said the long-haired, un-uniformed guide. "Why don't you look around. We've got some old buildings in the back, a nature trail, a pond, a gift shop with a lot of cedar boxes, and fairly clean restrooms." I liked Todd's style.

Nobody showed up by the time he finished sweeping so just the two of us descended the 103 steps. To someone like myself who does not know the difference between a cavern and a hole in the ground, Todd's geological explanations sounded honest. His commentary on other things was pleasantly nondogmatic. "That formation we call the Crocodile's Teeth; there are some others we call Niagara Falls, the City of the Future, the Golden Domes. But talk is cheap and you can call them anything you want to."

We walked along slowly for about 10 minutes before we came to the end of the paved and illuminated pathway. There before us was Secret Caverns' major feature, an underground waterfall in which water cascaded in a thick silvery column a hundred feet down to where we were standing. "It's a good cavern and it's a darn good waterfall," said Todd.

On the way back he explained that Secret Caverns was opened

SEEING THE SIGHTS

Clyde Peeling's Reptiland, Rte. 32, Catskill (☎ 518/678-3557). Hours and admission prices vary; call ahead before you go.

House of Frankenstein Wax Museum, 213 Canada St., Lake George (☎ 518/668-3377). Open April 15 through October 31. April through June and Labor Day through October, open daily 10am to 6pm; July through Labor Day, open daily 9am to 11pm. Admission $5 adults, $2.75 children 6 to 12, free for children under 6.

Howe Caverns, Caverns Rd., off Rte. 7 (exit 22 off I-88), Howes Cave (☎ 518/296-8990). Open year-round, daily 9am to 6pm. Admission $11.50 adults, $6 for children 7 to 12, free for children 6 and younger.

Movieworld Wax Museum, 109 Canada St., Lake George Village (☎ 518/668-3077). Open mid-May through early October. Mid-May through June, daily 9am to 6pm; July through Labor Day, daily 9am to 11pm; Labor Day through October 31, daily 9am to 6pm. Admission $4.50 adults, $2.50 for children 6 to 12, free for children under 6.

Secret Caverns, Rte. 7 (exit 22 off I-88), Cobleskill (☎ 518/296-8558). Open May 1 to October 31. May, June, September, and October, open daily 10am to 5pm; July and August, open daily 9am to 7pm. Admission $8.50 adults, $5 for children 6 to 11, free for children under 6.

41 years ago when a member of the Mallory family, which owns it, had an argument with the management of Howe Caverns, where he had been working as an electrician. Over the years competition between the two caverns has at times led to the disappearance of their advertising signs. Todd, who once worked as a guide at Howe Caverns, was quite respectful to the neighboring hole, but anyone could see where his heart was. "They are like Howard Johnson," he said. "They are run by a corporation. We're more like a mom-and-pop cavern. We're the underdog. We're Brand X. Maybe we're no frills but we have a 100-foot waterfall." The cost of admission to Secret Caverns was $8.50, or $3 cheaper than at Howe Caverns.

"What's the secret?" I asked as I prepared to get going.

"It's so deep that none of us have been able to figure it out," said Todd.

Limits of Education

I headed south for the last stop on my schlock itinerary, Clyde Peeling's Reptiland on Route 32 at Catskill. The uniformed attendant explained that since the shows in which people could hold the snakes and listen to lectures would not begin until the next day, he could let me in for less than the full adult price.

I was sorry not to be able to hold a python, but I happily inspected several dozen healthy-looking snakes and lizards behind glass, among them deadly African mambas, rattlesnakes, cobras, and venomous gila monsters. The posted signs were informative, maybe a little too educational, but Reptiland was a worthwhile stop.

I headed for home. But just down the road I saw a roadside booth with a big sign that said MYSTERY SPOT. I slowed down, but just for a second. Save it for next time, I thought.

In Pursuit of the National Pastime: Cooperstown

by Bruce Weber

❧

THIS MAY NOT BE YOUR RECRE-
ational fantasy, but it is mine: You wake up in a small village on a
pristine morning, a midnight storm having cleared the air and left it
clean and aromatic. You climb on a bicycle and cruise around the
corner and down Main Street, around the traffic circle, past the
National Baseball Hall of Fame and Museum, and before you know
it, you are out of town, on the quiet, gently sloping road heading north
along Lake Otsego.

The east side of the lake, which James Fenimore Cooper called
Glimmerglass, remains almost entirely, and remarkably, undeveloped.
The sensation is of passing through an underused wooded park, the
still water (almost no boats) on your left, a hill rising to the right on
which a semi-groomed cemetery is cut into the trees.

About 10 miles out of town, the woods give way to fields, a farmhouse here and there. And then, the first commercial establishment: a
batting range! It's 10am, and the proprietor is just opening for the
day. Nothing like swatting a few majestic home runs against the back-
drop of a blue mountain. A Sunday dream.

This actually occurred (O.K., except for the home runs), the highlight of the recent weekend I spent in Cooperstown, New York, wor-
shiping at the shrine of the national pastime and marveling at the
authentic aura of small-town America the place gives off in spite of
the tourists who are drawn there like runners being waved home by
the third-base coach.

It's not an ersatz thing; this is an old-timey-feeling place, maybe the most nostalgia-inducing locale in America. And though there's more to Cooperstown than baseball, baseball is in the air, and if not right in front of you, then around every curve.

Baseball, in fact, serves Cooperstown like a talisman, fending off the cheapening effects of commerce even as it attracts them. Historically, this is baseball's established trick; it has itself, after all, survived artificial turf, the designated hitter, domed stadiums, expansion, and players' strikes with its fundamental integrity if not entirely intact, then having sustained only superficial injury. It says something, I think, that though the outskirts of town are getting crowded with motels, in the village itself the bed-and-breakfast rules, often in 19th-century homes.

"Ninety-five percent of our guests are here for the Hall of Fame," said Pam Miller. In 1988, she and her husband, John, turned their home into the Chestnut Street Guest House, the pleasant bed-and-breakfast where I stayed. "Baseball fans are interesting, nice people," she said. "We might not feel as comfortable if it was the Wrestling Hall of Fame."

It's true that Cooperstown has sprouted the unsightly whiskers of opportunism. Just south of town, for instance, there's an undistinguished roadhouse called the Hamburger Hall of Fame; next to a miniature golf

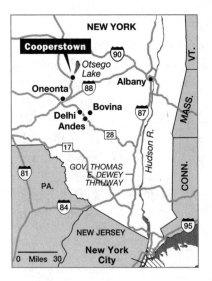

course, it attracts the kind of person who would fill out a scorecard (as the guy sitting next to me did) with the headings "Me" and "Her." A little farther down the road is the Corvette Americana Hall of Fame, an auto exhibition of high, unintended camp, with a $9.50 admission fee, housed in a prefab warehouse that the proprietor has inexplicably dedicated to Woody Guthrie.

So, yeah, there's some tacky stuff. Think of it as Cooperstown's Marge Schott.

Built on a Fiction

There is something to be said for Cooperstown as a place that feels genuine but isn't, entirely, and that is lent its sheen of bucolic Americana by baseball. Spawned by the American spirit of enterprise in the wake of the Revolution, Cooperstown, after all, was founded by a man who was something of a pretender.

William Cooper, who established the village on the south shore of Otsego in 1786, grew up poor but married above his station and tried his whole life to achieve a gentleman's bearing and reputation. As portrayed by Alan Taylor in his book *William Cooper's Town*, which won the Pulitzer Prize for history, Cooper was a Quaker-born, badly educated wheelwright who parlayed a hifalutin ambition and a gift for real estate speculation into a judgeship and a stint as a United States Congressman.

His youngest son, James Fenimore, became a novelist, according to Professor Taylor, only when his inheritance began to dwindle under the burden of his father's bad debts. In *The Pioneers*, the son's third novel, set in the fictional village of Templeton (read Cooperstown), he drew on his father for the character of Judge Marmaduke Temple, "a man of good intentions but loose scruples, of expansive vision but flawed manners," Professor Taylor writes, "of benevolent paternalism but blundering execution."

It was in June 1816, seven years after the founder's death, that the town trustees, led by Isaac Cooper, James's older brother, enacted a fine of $1 for anyone playing "at ball" in village streets; the ordinance was directed at town ball, a game played with a ball and bat that did not originate in Cooperstown and that would later evolve into baseball.

By now, historians have discredited the legend that Abner Doubleday invented baseball in Cooperstown in 1839. (Its development is more rightly associated with Alexander Cartwright, whose Knickerbocker Baseball Club played in and around New York City in the 1840s.) But as Professor Taylor writes, "Because of its 1816 ban on ballplaying in the village center, Cooperstown can better claim to have tried to prevent the invention of baseball."

Still, for a fan, a trip to Cooperstown feels like traveling to the beating heart of something. But it's not just the famous shrine. It's also that baseball is a pastoral game, transplanted to our urban centers; part of its nostalgic appeal for the urban population has undoubtedly to do with its being played on greenswards in the middle of cities. So even if the Abner Doubleday story is a fiction, the surroundings nonetheless honor the nature of the game.

Verdant Territory

For a city dweller, particularly a New York City dweller, the sense of visiting the idyllic womb of baseball begins before you get there. The whole area—Delaware and Otsego counties, which lie underpublicized north and west of the Catskills and east of the Finger Lakes—is surprisingly and consistently verdant and charming. It is characterized by the kind of landscape—rolling farmland, wildernessy foothills, lush valleys—that is featured in "I Love New York" ads, but that I always envision as having been borrowed from the state tourist bureau of Virginia or somewhere. The two-lane roads, winding and bucolic, that separate the well-spaced towns—Andes, Delhi, Bovina—bespeak the kind of territory that is just out of convenient reach of the city; from Manhattan, it's about a four-hour drive to Cooperstown.

O.K., in a baseball mood, maybe I had an inclination to romanticize it all. From my downtown perspective, this was real country, though I said as much out loud to a local hitchhiker I picked up—"Real country here, huh?"—and he rolled his eyes. In Andes, attracted by a thickly crusted and juicy-looking blueberry pie in the window of a cafe, I stopped for a lunch that promised to be countrified.

As it turned out, though, the real find in town was the import shop next door, Paisley's Country Gallery, whose owner, John Gregg, said he transplanted himself there nine years ago from New York City after driving through town, just as I was doing, and falling in love with the two-story building in which he now had his shop. His place smelled of wood chips and pine needles, and most of the merchandise was good country stuff offered inexpensively (I bought wind chimes and woven baskets to hold flowerpots), even though it turned out that most of the inventory was from places like the Philippines and Sierra Leone.

Far less exotic and not even authentic, unfortunately, was the blueberry pie, which had a canned filling that I might have bought at my neighborhood Sloan's.

Replete with History

In the village itself, baseball sits like Kellogg's in Battle Creek, the proud raison d'être but an ordinary part of things. Most days, Doubleday Field, the bandbox semipro ballpark that witnesses a major league exhibition game once every summer, is quiet. The Hall of Fame is at the end of the block, looking more like a small, noble high school than a mecca for nostalgia buffs and hero worshipers.

"Full of baseball vacationers, Main Street has the soullessly equable, bustly air of a better-than-average small college town the week the kids come back for fall," wrote Richard Ford in his novel, *Independence Day,* whose climactic scenes take place in Cooperstown. (Nineteen ninety-six was a good literary year for Cooperstown: *Independence Day* also won a Pulitzer.) "Shops on both sides are selling baseball everything: uniforms, cards, posters, bumper stickers, no doubt hubcaps and condoms; and these share the street with just ordinary villagey business entities—a drugstore, a dad 'n lad, two flower shops, a tavern, a German bakery, and several realty offices."

On my Cooperstown weekend, there was a baseball day and there was a nonbaseball day, which inevitably had some baseball in it. (That batting cage out at the other end of the lake, for one thing.) It isn't the Metropolitan Museum of Art or anything, but you could—and I did—spend hours at the National Baseball Hall of Fame.

It was founded by Stephen C. Clark, whose grandfather was the business partner of Isaac Merritt Singer, the man who popularized the sewing machine; the ensuing fortune made the Clark family a dominant influence in Cooperstown for generations. Sometime in the 1930s, Clark acquired a weathered ball reputed to have been owned by Abner Doubleday, and recognizing a marketing opportunity when he saw one, he used it to establish a museum, which he opened in 1939, exactly a century after Doubleday was supposed to have had the brainstorm that spawned the game.

Today, the National Baseball Hall of Fame and Museum is replete with stuff that, if you are the kind of person who watches the "Baseball Tonight" recaps of the day's major league action on ESPN (I am such a person), will make you gasp with a child's pleasure. There's the Babe Ruth room, with his bat and his locker, and the Hank Aaron room, ditto. There are Rickey Henderson's shoes from the season he set the stolen-base record. And there's the newer, techno stuff: the interactive video screen where you can choose which presentations to watch, film clips of Clemente or Koufax.

Even if you are just along for the ride with someone whose obsession is as thorough as mine, there is interesting history to be witnessed. The evolution of the catcher's mask and the first baseman's mitt. A collection of original scores of popular songs about baseball. A room devoted to baseball movies, from *The Pride of the Yankees* (a goofy, sentimental biography of Lou Gehrig, starring Gary Cooper, which I loved) to *A League of Their Own* (Penny Marshall's much more artful look at the women's professional teams of the 1940s, which bored me).

I'd actually been here before, but it pleased me that the place holds up after multiple viewings. I felt validated in my interest; baseball has depth. The museum proves it. (It was also satisfying to me that discount admissions are available to the Hall of Fame and the nearby Farmers' Museum and Fenimore House, if you buy tickets to all three at once.)

One thing that is a little strange is the Hall of Fame itself, the paneled vestibule in which the plaques honoring the greats of the game are somberly displayed. The plaques are boring, with little information beyond dry statistics. The room is uninspiring. And the faces of the enshrined, beaming gold and in relief from each of the plaques, look nothing like the men themselves actually did (or do). I don't get why this has to be; it isn't comforting.

A Cap for Every Head

There are better likenesses up the street in a delightfully weird commercial establishment called the American Baseball Experience, which, among other things, features a wax museum in which Casey Stengel sits grumpily in a corner hunched over a crystal ball and Pete Rose is depicted in a head first slide, though he's suspended overhead, as if Superman were wearing a Cincinnati Reds uniform instead of his blue pajamas.

The rest of the day I spent happily consuming—books, a key chain, T-shirts, postcards, and, nearly, a Thurman Munson rookie card. (I decided against it; I'm not a collector of any kind. It's just cheap souvenirs that appeal to me.) Cooperstown is not just the baseball capital of America, it's the capital of baseball stuff. Main Street, for its three-block length (this is a remarkably small town), is lined with memorabilia shops of particularly inelegant design.

And though the real antiques are far too expensive, the browsing is fun, and there is no place in the world where there is a better selection of high-quality baseball caps. Many are the good wool kind, with an actual size that doesn't depend on an adjustable plastic strap on the back, and nowhere did they cost more than $20, which helps explain why everyone walking on Main Street is wearing at least one. (It's not unusual to see a boy with a couple of them stacked on his head.) Having not been paying attention a couple of years ago when Spike Lee's *Malcolm X* inspired the wearing of caps with Xs, I managed to fill a gap in my alphabet collection, with a white cap emblazoned with an orange X, for the 1936 Cuban X Giants, a Negro League team.

As it turns out, Cooperstown is not a great eating town. They say the Otesaga Resort Hotel, a gigantic place on the lake that is far too grandiose for its surroundings, serves equally grandiose fare, but I didn't go there. Too formidable. I had a nice bowl of chowder and a Caesar salad at T. J.'s Place, which also displayed and sold memorabilia, and, more pertinently, had a big-screen television. The Yanks were on.

Cultured Neighborhood

In season, I probably would have gone to the opera. That's no joke. The Glimmerglass Opera opened its season recently with Jack Beeson's 1965 opus, *Lizzie Borden*, and Donizetti's *Don Pasquale*. I stopped there on my bicycle circumscription of the lake after my pause at the batting cage—the whole bike route is about 27 miles, a truly exemplary recreational ride—and found the place well groomed bordering on elegant. The grounds of the 900-seat Alice Busch Opera Theater, on the west shore of the lake, are, in the manner of Tanglewood, a place for picnicking on the lawn and strolling in the summer sunset before the music begins.

The whole southwestern corner of the lake turned out to be what I ended up thinking of as the cultured neighborhood, though it had elements of the upper-caste pretension I imagine was in the character of William Cooper. The Otesaga is here, with the Leatherstocking Golf Course and its prerequisite men in plaid pants, pastel sweaters, and tam-o'-shanters.

Just a half-mile or so north of the village, on opposite sides of the shore road, are two fine museums, both run under auspices of the New York State Historical Association. One, the spacious and pristine Fenimore House Museum, built on the site of the novelist's home, has a superb collection of American Indian art and craft—clothing, pottery, beadwork, utensils made by artisans—as well as examples of American folk art, local paintings, and historical artifacts (including the desk at which DeWitt Clinton, once Governor of New York, was sitting when he died).

Perhaps the most striking exhibit features the life masks done by the 19th-century sculptor John H. I. Browere: 22 bronze heads of American statesmen and celebrities made between 1823 and 1833. Men like John Quincy Adams, Martin Van Buren, and Thomas Jefferson are arranged in an eerie circle, their lines of vision crossing, their visages far more persuasively real than any of the more recent stars totemized at the Baseball Hall of Fame. Then, too, the Fenimore House sits on a great lawn above the lake, and the view over it from the back terrace garden is more regal and deliciously high-handed than most baseball fans are used to.

If the Fenimore House has a delicacy to it, an intellectual bent, the Farmers' Museum across the road celebrates more earthy qualities. Once a working farm owned by James Fenimore Cooper, the site replicates an entire 19th-century village; original buildings, from as early as 1795—including a tavern, a schoolhouse, and a blacksmith shop—have been moved to Cooperstown from as far as 100 miles away. It's quaint, impressive in an almost-but-not-quite European sort of way. (Americans don't often get a chance to appreciate many such homegrown collections of century-old structures.) And on a warm morning, with Historical Association employees demonstrating broom- and cabinetmaking, or reenacting a game of town ball on the lawn, you can almost regret progress.

The Farmers' Museum was my last stop, and just before I left, I ducked into one of the transplanted buildings, the general store (circa 1828), for a last bout of shopping. There, among the rock candy, beeswax candles, freshly made brooms, and cast-iron candleholders, was a hand-sewn baseball. Wound yarn wrapped in graying leather, it was soft, a little misshapen, more on the order of what a cat, rather than a Little Leaguer, would play with today. I picked it up, had a catch with myself, then put it back, solid in the knowledge that some things do, in fact, improve with age.

COOPERSTOWN ESSENTIALS

GETTING THERE

From New York City, the quickest, if least amusing, route to Cooperstown is north on the Thomas E. Dewey Thruway (Interstate 87) to Albany; then west on Interstate 88 to Rte. 20, continuing west on Rte. 20 to Rte. 80 South; continue on Rte. 80 South along the west shore of Otsego Lake to Cooperstown.

Alternatively, there are several scenic roads through the Catskills that are accessible from I-87. For example, at Kingston, take New York State Rte. 28 West, which winds through the mountains and turns north at Oneonta. At Colliersville, take Rte. 28 North to Cooperstown. Drive time is about four hours, a little less perhaps by the first route, a little more by the second.

ACCOMMODATIONS AND DINING

Chestnut Street Guest House, 79 Chestnut St. (☎ 607/547-5624). Open mid-April through November. Rooms (all with private bath) $75 to $90; $125 suite. Rates are based on double occupancy and include continental breakfast. Two-night minimum on weekends. Children are welcome.

Otesaga Resort Hotel, Rte. 80 (Lake Rd.; ☎ 800/348-6222 or 607/547-9931). Open

late April through October. Rooms range from $260 double to $370 suite. Rates, based on double occupancy and include breakfast and dinner. Children staying with parents are charged only for meals.

T. J.'s Place/The Home Plate, 124 Main St. (☎ 607/547-4040). Open daily 8am to 8pm.

THE BASEBALL HALL OF FAME AND OTHER ATTRACTIONS

Combination Tickets   Combination tickets are available for admission to the Baseball Hall of Fame, the Farmers' Museum, and the Fenimore House Museum for $22, $9.50 for children 7 to 12.

The American Baseball Experience, 99 Main St. (☎ 607/547-1273). Includes a tribute to Mickey Mantle, with more than 1,000 autographed, items, and a wax museum. Open daily 9am to 9pm; closed January and February. Admission $5.95 adults, $2.95 for children 8 and over, free for children under 8.

Corvette Americana Hall of Fame, Rte. 28 (☎ 607/547-4135). More than 35 cars dating from 1953, each displayed with memorabilia from the time period, plus music and videos. March through November, daily 9:30am to 5pm. Admission $9.95 adults, $8.95 seniors, $6.95 for children 5 and over, free for children under 5.

Farmers' Museum, operated by the New York State Historical Association, Rte. 80 (Lake Rd.; ☎ 607/547-1450 or 607/547-1500). Ten historic buildings, including a tavern and a general store, re-create an 1840s village. Also, the Lippitt Farmstead, a working farm that features demonstrations of crafts of the period, with exhibitions of tools, stoneware, and folk art. Open April through December;

in April and Labor Day through December, open Tuesday through Sunday 10am to 4pm; from May through Labor Day, open daily 9am to 5pm. Admission $9 adults, $4 children 7 to 12, free for children under 6.

Fenimore House Museum, Rte. 80 (Lake Rd.; ☎ 607/547-1400). The house, which dates from 1932, has exhibitions of North American Indian art, paintings, photographs, and other items. Open April through December, daily 9am to 6pm. Admission $9 adults, $4 for children 7 to 12.

Glimmerglass Opera, Rte. 80 (☎ 607/547-2255). Call for current schedule. Tickets $19 to $70.

Hamburger Hall of Fame, Rte. 28 (☎ 607/547-4113). Through Labor Day, open daily 6am to 10pm; after Labor Day, open daily 7am to 8pm.

National Baseball Hall of Fame and Museum, 25 Main St. (☎ 607/547-7200). May 1 through September 30, open daily 9am to 9pm; October 1 through April 30, open daily 9am to 5pm. Admission $9.50 adults, $8 seniors, $4 for children 7 to 12, free for children under 7.

Paisley's Country Gallery, Main St. (Rte. 28), Andes (☎ 914/676-3533). Open Thursday through Sunday 10am to 5pm.

New Jersey

A Piece of Portugal: Newark's Ironbound District

by Clifford J. Levy

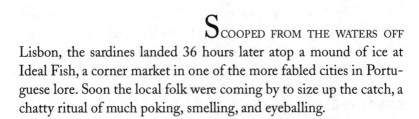

S COOPED FROM THE WATERS OFF Lisbon, the sardines landed 36 hours later atop a mound of ice at Ideal Fish, a corner market in one of the more fabled cities in Portuguese lore. Soon the local folk were coming by to size up the catch, a chatty ritual of much poking, smelling, and eyeballing.

"These sardines, they look like life," declared Julio Pereira, who owns the market and is, like many of his Portuguese compatriots, a connoisseur of things from the sea. (The Portuguese know fish the way the Americans know the difference between a Big Mac and a Whopper with cheese.)

Many customers bought sardines, a few did not, but almost everyone lingered amid the tidal odors. They were a nice reminder of home, for though the neighborhood seemed as if it were in Portugal, it was in fact a replica. The Portuguese have been fanning out across the globe since the days of Magellan. In the late 20th century, many have headed straight for Newark.

With nearly 30,000 Portuguese, Newark may be better known in Portugal than it is in the United States. Clustered in a neighborhood called the Ironbound, the immigrants have laid down a latticework of ties between the old country and new, from the many seafood restaurants and Portuguese bakeries to cultural clubs that each represent an area of Portugal. The Portuguese Government even maintains a consulate here.

You can often tell whether an ethnic enclave is thriving by counting the number of blank stares you receive when you speak English. In the Ironbound, where the Lisbon newspapers are delivered to the Tucha gift shop even before they reach some parts of Portugal, where the bars are packed on Sunday afternoons with people watching the satellite feed of their beloved Benfica soccer team, it is easy to get by with only Portuguese. Some residents have lived here for 20 years understanding just enough English to navigate the Division of Motor Vehicles.

"This is Portugal," said Isabel Fernandes, who runs Socafe, which caters to the local taste for espresso, selling Portuguese coffees and espresso machines at its shop on Ferry Street, the neighborhood's main thoroughfare. "You can walk into any store and find a little bit of Portugal. Most Americans find themselves in a foreign land down here."

The Ironbound, which is about 20 to 30 minutes by train or car from Manhattan, got its name because it is enclosed by railroad tracks and major roadways. Those barriers have tended to isolate the area from the rest of Newark, which is predominantly black and Hispanic and has struggled to revitalize itself since the riots of the late 1960s. There are few overt tensions between the Ironbound and the rest of the city, yet there is also little amity. Coutinho's bakery, an institution in the Ironbound, sells ornaments for the top of its wedding cakes that have black brides and grooms as well as white ones, but on a typical afternoon there are not many black people on the streets or in the stores.

Autumn is a time of renewal here. The many residents who have gone to Portugal during the summer to see family have returned. The aisles are clogged again at Seabra's, the sprawling Portuguese supermarket on Lafayette Street where the butchers often buff their sausages with cloth and one of the best sellers is Luso mineral water from Lisbon. The local councilman, Henry Martinez, begins to receive more complaints about double parking, a chronic problem now in an area that has not experienced such commercial bustle in decades.

On Sundays, after mass at Our Lady of Fatima Church on Congress Street, the sidewalks resound with greetings—"Tudo bem?" ("Everything good?")—and the neighborhood feels like a village. "You

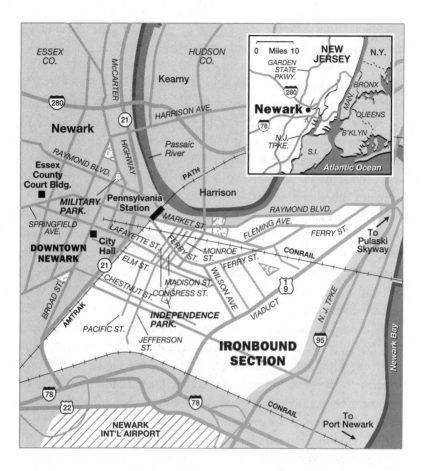

must know what it is like, to walk down the street and feel good?" said Helen Enes, who organizes exhibitions in the neighborhood of the works of local Portuguese artists.

The most maddening way to explore the Ironbound is on a full stomach, for a walk down Ferry Street provides an enticing survey of the Portuguese culinary landscape, even if the food has at times been doctored for American tastes. There are so many bakeries and cafes that you can buy espresso and *pastel de nata,* the small custard cups that are something of a Portuguese addiction, on practically every other block.

And it is not only Portuguese specialties. There is a small but venerable Spanish population, represented in the Spanish restaurants. And

Brazilians, drawn by the language they share with the Portuguese, have also settled here in recent years, opening restaurants, bakeries, and bars.

The dominant notes, though, are Portuguese. That was clear late one Thursday afternoon, when cafes and bars like the Riviera and La Moda on Ferry Street were filling with construction workers and women were stopping by the stores for the weekly shipment of Portuguese fish. (Fresh sardines and horse mackerel, a kind of tuna, always arrive on Thursdays so fish can be served on Fridays, following Roman Catholic custom.)

At Ideal Fish, which is on Pacific Street, a few blocks off Ferry Street, Mr. Pereira said his right-hand man, Bertino Rocha, had gone to Kennedy International Airport on Wednesday afternoon to pick up the fish. To comply with airline rules, the sardines and horse mackerel had to be transported in ice in Styrofoam boxes—393 in all—that were sealed in plastic.

It is easy to spot the immigrants at the market. Upon entering, they typically march right past the American seafood—the red snapper from Florida, the lobster from Maine, the clams from Long Island—to the sardines, which at six inches long tend to be larger than sardines canned in oil (though the Portuguese gobble those up, too). Fresh sardines are cooked simply, fried, barbecued, or broiled with little more than a dash of salt.

The other Portuguese staple is cod from Norway, which is salted, dried, and stacked in the stores like plywood. A customer selects a piece, which is then sliced with an apparatus that looks like a paper cutter. The cod must be soaked in water for two or three days before it can be cooked; it is often broiled with potatoes and garlic.

The sardines are $2.50 a pound and the horse mackerel is $3.25 a pound. That is more than the canned variety, though the customers, who inspect and place the fish in plastic bags with their own hands, don't care. "Every week," Maria da Cruz, who left Portugal in 1972, said of her trips to Ideal Fish. "Some weeks, I spend $100 or more."

The influx to the Ironbound from Portugal, one of the poorest countries in Western Europe, is relatively recent. Before the 1970s, the neighborhood was largely populated by Italian, Irish, Polish, and other European immigrants, many of whom referred to the area as Down Neck. The Portuguese began settling in the 1950s and 60s, many of them drawn by opportunities at the newly expanded Port of Newark. But unlike the other large Portuguese community in the United States, in New Bedford, Massachusetts, the Portuguese of Newark did not concentrate on fishing or other maritime ventures. They moved into other fields, particularly construction, carpentry, restaurants, and bakeries.

"In Portugal, everybody knows about Newark," said Tony Oliveira, whose family came from Portugal in 1967 when he was 11. Mr. Oliveira is a local officer at the Heavy and General Construction Laborers' Union, whose chapter in northern New Jersey has about 7,000 members, about a third of them Portuguese.

Immigration, both legal and illegal, peaked in the mid-1980s. Then Portugal was admitted to the European Community, now the European Union, which allowed its citizens to find jobs in other member countries, and the number of arrivals dropped. Even so, the Portuguese remain the largest group of illegal immigrants in New Jersey.

"The value of labor and wages travels very fast," said Albert Coutinho, whose immigrant parents own Coutinho's bakery. "People all over Portugal know how much a carpenter is making in Lisbon, how much he is making in Newark, how much he is making in New Bedford or Paris or Bonn or London."

The immigrant success stories here often run through the kitchen. Joao Loureiro and Jorge Fernandes, who left Portugal with little money more than 20 years ago, worked as waiters here before buying the Iberia restaurant (82 Ferry Street) and later opening the Iberia Peninsula (67 Ferry Street). They are now hoping to open the city's largest catering hall nearby.

The food at those two restaurants, as well as at some other stops in the area, including Fornos of Spain (47 Ferry Street), is often more Iberian, a hybrid that appeals to Americans, than distinctly Portuguese or Spanish. Portuguese basics like sardines or salt cod are not prominent on the Iberian menus. Instead there are the familiar seafood stews like *paelha* (*paella* in Spanish), a mix of shellfish and rice that may include chicken or chorizo, a spicy sausage. The prices are

HOW TO VISIT THE IRONBOUND

By Subway   PATH (☎ 800/234-7284) has 24-hour service to the Penn Station stop in Newark. Weekend trains leave every 20 minutes from the World Trade Center, Tower 1, for the 22-minute ride. The one-way fare is $1.

By Train   Amtrak (☎ 800/872-7245 for information and reservations) trains to Newark's Penn Station–Raymond Plaza West leave approximately hourly from Penn Station in Manhattan for the 15-minute ride. Trains generally begin running around 9am. The one-way fare is $9, $7.75 for seniors, $4.50 for children 2 to 15.

New Jersey Transit (☎ 201/762-5100) trains to Penn Station in Newark leave twice an hour on weekends from Penn Station in Manhattan beginning about 5am. The one-way fare is $2.50.

By Bus   New Jersey Transit's (☎ 201/762-5100) no. 108 bus to Newark's Penn Station leaves daily every half-hour beginning at 6am from the Port Authority Bus Terminal, Eighth Ave. and 42nd St. The one-way fare is $3.25.

By Car   Take the Lincoln Tunnel to the New Jersey Turnpike, to exit 15E; look for Raymond Boulevard sign and follow the boulevard into the Ironbound district.

cheaper than in Manhattan: The paelha in the Ironbound is often about $12 to $14, for portions that can serve two. Salad, thinly sliced fried potatoes, and fluffy Portuguese bread are usually included. There are also plenty of lobster and shrimp dishes.

In restaurants like Iberia, Seabra's Marisqueira (87 Madison Street) or Jack's Place (99 Monroe Street), the lunch trade on weekdays is mostly Americans who work in offices in downtown Newark. At other times, there are more Portuguese, and in the early evening construction workers sit at the bar, shoveling down broiled shrimp or pork and clams while sipping Borba wine.

On weekend nights, some places, like Mediterranean Manor (225 Jefferson Street), may feature live fado, the Portuguese blues music. One of the most popular local fado singers is Jorge Quaresma, who during the day sells Portuguese suits at Pappillon Boutique on Ferry Street.

Brazilian restaurants, many specializing in *churrasco,* or barbecue, have sprung up in recent years. At Brasilia (132 Ferry Street), for $14 you can order rodizio de churrasco, an all-you-can-eat barbecue binge of beef, sausage, chicken, and pork, brought to the table on skewers.

After dinner, the bakeries beckon. Three of the largest in the state—Coutinho's, Teixeira's (whose owners are related to the Coutinho family), and Vieira's—were founded by Portuguese immigrants. At the Coutinho's shop at 121 Ferry Street, there are rows of *pastel de coco* (coconut cups) and *bolo de arroz* (rice pudding cakes) for 60 cents each. At Padaria Brasileira (44 Ferry Street), *queijadinha*, a Brazilian concoction of cheese, milk, coconut, eggs, and flour, is $1. Portuguese bakeries like Coutinho's also make an array of breads, from *broa*, a dense corn bread ($1.50), to the ubiquitous *papo seco*, the basic dry roll (35 cents), and *padinha*, the rye roll (40 cents). At Coutinho's headquarters (417 Chestnut Street), many products are still made by hand, though it would be cheaper to use machines.

Mr. Coutinho is part of the second generation, fluent in Portuguese but rooted in America. Freed of the financial pressures that his parents faced, he heads the family charity, the Bernardino Coutinho Foundation, which sponsors the annual Portuguese festival in the Ironbound in June and supports other cultural activities. He is also trying to raise political awareness: nearly 20,000 Portuguese were counted in Newark in the 1990 Census, but there are only a few thousand registered voters.

Others, too, are grappling with how the community can mature. Ms. Enes, the sponsor of the art exhibitions, said it was sometimes difficult to interest the neighborhood in art. People are so focused on immigrant priorities—making enough money, learning English, supporting relatives—that culture may seem a luxury. But art, she said, can help the Ironbound find its identity.

"You have to understand that once you're uprooted, you come to America and the Americans think of you as a foreigner, but then when you go back to Portugal, the Portuguese think of you as American," she said. "So you are nothing. Where do you belong? Somewhere in the middle of the Atlantic?"

WILDERNESS ADVENTURES IN STOKES FOREST

by Ralph Blumenthal

"ARE WE OUTSIDE?" WE MOST AS-
suredly were outside, on a trail deep in the piney woods of Stokes
State Forest in northwesternmost New Jersey, but my city-bred daughter looked unconvinced. Where was the sky? Why was it so spooky?
Where was everybody?

We were alone. Outdoors. That was the point. This, after all, was
what we had come for: a weekend of camping while the elements still
posed a challenge and the wilds were largely free from interlopers like us.

Well, semi-camping. In a concession to the unpredictabilities of
the season and a mom's skepticism ("You're taking her where?"), I had
given up the idea of tenting and instead reserved one of the state
forest's 15 lean-tos, an enclosed 12-by-14-foot shelter equipped with
a woodstove. We would have use of communal restrooms with flush
toilets and sinks. Otherwise, we'd rough it, cooking our meals on an
open fire and relying on flashlights and candles for light at night.

It seemed, in particular, a perfect formula for a jaded, animal-loving
5¹/₂-year-old, and it was, not counting the maddening swarms of gnats
and some anxious moments over a snake.

In fact, as we were to learn, Stokes State Forest, an unlikely wilderness in an easily accessible nook of one of the more industrialized
states, abounds in wildlife, noxious and benign. The census of species
includes the venomous northern copperhead and timber rattlesnake,
snapping turtle, bear, bobcat, coyote, gray and red fox, weasel, porcu-
pine, skunk, otter, mink, and deer, as well as 209 species of birds, from

rarely spotted golden and bald eagles to wild turkeys, egrets, herons, hawks, hummingbirds, and woodpeckers.

The preserve, which dates from 1907 and is named for a former governor, covers 15,000 acres of highland forest, land that less than 10,000 years ago lay under several thousand feet of glacial ice. It was an area of thriving American Indian communities with gardens of pumpkins, maize, and tobacco before the first English and Dutch settlers arrived, and the early pioneers built sawmills and dug silver, zinc, and manganese mines, remains of which are still visible today. The park office displays cases of Indian arrowheads and bones of a mastodon dug up in the area in 1939.

Our original plan was more adventurous: winter camping. One frigid weekend, we actually scouted potential sites on Ward Pound Ridge Reservation in Westchester County, where three-sided rustic lean-tos are available year-round. But we decided they were too exposed to severe cold, even with a tarpaulin covering the open side. Stokes's enclosed lean-tos, too, are available year-round, but almost every other campground in the region closes for the season, which, I realized after calling around fruitlessly for weeks, might be something of a message. As it was, I had to postpone our spring camping expedition several times because of unseasonable snowstorms and plunging temperatures.

But the winter that would not die finally did, yielding to a tentative spring. Early on a recent Saturday, I loaded the car with the sleeping bags, food, and gadgetry that camping gives guys an excuse to play with—ax and knives, folding saw, kerosene lantern, tarpaulin, grills, stringy light hammock—and set off.

The trip from mid-Manhattan to Stokes State Forest, near Branchville, New Jersey, is an easy one, a straight 1¹/₂-hour shot across the George Washington Bridge, west on Interstate 80, and then north on routes 15 and 206. From the backseat, Sophie kept up a diverting barrage of conversation.

"Benjamin has an ant farm. Can we have an ant farm?"

"I don't think so."

"Guess how many cough drops I had?"

"I don't know. Twenty?"

"I'm having my second one now. Know what I think eyelashes are made of? Daddy longlegs' legs."

In Sparta, New Jersey, we stopped for last-minute provisions at a market where Sophie grabbed a *Pocahontas* video. Was she expecting a VCR in the lean-to? We had a tug of war and compromised on a 50¢ container of slime from a vending machine. Back in the car, Sophie said, "I don't want to go camping."

A Welcoming Swarm

Finally, we pulled into the lot outside the rustic park office. As soon as we got out of the car, clouds of gnats and blackflies swarmed around our heads. A bad omen. Sophie started flailing and whimpering.

We made a dash for the office, stopping to read a posted leaflet: "You are in bear country," it began rather ominously. "Black bears are part of the forest environment. People are visitors. Think of yourself as a guest of the forest wildlife." It warned against feeding bears or leaving garbage around and urged that food be locked up in car trunks and never, never, left in lean-tos or tents. The details began to sound a little alarming: "If a bear approaches you, blow a whistle, bang pots and pans together, make noise!" At the service window, where I picked up our lean-to key and a park map, a young park worker said she hadn't seen any bears lately, but others in the office said they were around, especially by the garbage dumpsters. As for the flies, the woman said we might try some bug spray, which I had forgotten to bring. But, she added cheerfully, it probably wouldn't help anyway.

"Did she get hurt by the bear?" Sophie asked gravely as we left. "How did she see one?" But then she was on to bug spray. "Would I like the smell? I'm a strange smeller, so maybe I would like it. I like oily smells." Checking the map, I followed a paved and winding road through the forest for about three miles to the lean-to, passing substantial-looking comfort stations.

The one-room lean-to, painted chocolate brown, was small and boxy but, I couldn't help reflecting, still somewhat larger than the 10-by-12-foot Montana shack where the man suspected of being the Unabomber had lived for years. It had a steeply pitched roof and three steps up to the door. It was, strictly speaking, not a cabin, that term reserved for far more sophisticated—and eagerly sought-after—units with electricity, kitchens, bathrooms, and furniture in another area of the forest.

The inside of the lean-to was bare, with only a wood-burning stove, still stocked with split logs from a previous occupant. The park does not sell or provide wood, but plenty was lying around in the woods for the taking. The interior walls were painted gray. They were clean except for a few marks of graffiti. The floor, also cleanly swept, was a dull red. Outside there was a picnic table and a fire ring with an adjustable cooking grill.

We spread out our sleeping bags and foam pads, laid out the flashlights, candles, and kerosene lantern, and hooked open the two large screened windows. The space accommodated the two of us amply. Four could also have fit, albeit a little snugly.

We collected wood for the fireplace and kindling for the stove and reconnoitered, keeping an eye out for bears and swatting at flies.

"Is it the year of the rat?" Sophie asked.

I said it might be. Why?

"Because there's so many bugs out," Sophie said, not bothering to explain.

We walked back to the car and drove out of the park to a nearby fish and game store, the Stokes Forest Sport Shop. While Sophie looked agog at the tubs of live minnows and walls of glittering lures, I bought some insect repellent. We slapped some on and headed back to the forest.

Just past the office, we parked the car and headed down one of the many park trails, Lackner, marked with black circles. The trail paralleled Stony Brook, where some trout fishermen were trying their luck. Sophie stepped to the mushy shore and reached out her hands. "Here fishy, fishy, fishy," she called. "Know why I'm saying that? Because in

Sesame Street Ernie had a call, and fish jumped in the boat and a shark jumped in the boat. If we don't capture an animal by tomorrow, I'm going to be so angry." She went on, but I had stopped listening. Maybe 10 feet away was something that looked like a gnarled black branch. Or maybe it was a snake. I decided it couldn't be a snake because it was completely motionless. Then I thought: yes, it was a snake. But it was probably dead.

I pointed it out to Sophie and her eyes grew wide. Impulsively, I picked up a long branch and gave it a poke. It was a snake! It shot about a foot in the air and then resettled, once again completely motionless. Sophie was aghast. I was a little shaken myself. "Daddy," she pleaded, "let's go back to the ranger." I was still watching to see if it would move again. "Mommy would say: 'Go back! Don't you dare go so close,'" Sophie said. "Mommy would be terrified."

We walked back to the park office, where parties of other campers were checking in. "We saw a snake! We saw a snake!" Sophie announced, gaining everyone's immediate attention. I described it to the park superintendent sitting behind the window. "Black snake," he said, "a small one." They are harmless, he said confidently. But he said we should keep an eye out for the timber rattlesnake, with its triangular head, elliptical eyes, hourglass markings, and, of course, telltale rattle. Mostly, he said, they were up on Sunrise Mountain.

Looking for a less stressful diversion, we drove a few miles to a playground and recreation area, Kittle Field, where Sophie cavorted on swings and climbing equipment with other children and then joined one of them in a hunt along the brook for water spiders. We filled our water bottles at a hand pump that gushed deliciously cool well water and drove a little farther, to Stony Lake, where we walked along a wide sandy beach and found another playground.

On the drive back to the lean-to, a car ahead of us abruptly pulled over and I could see why. There was something strange by the side of the road. I pulled over, too, and we ran out to look. It was a large snapping turtle, its green-mottled shell perhaps 18 inches in diameter. It had a sharp pointy snout, legs swathed in armorlike plate, and vicious-looking claws with long sharp talons. It sat there unmoving, looking very old. I decided not to poke it.

Sophie wanted me to move it off the road, or at least tell the office, but I figured that it had survived this long without our help and could continue to.

We headed back for dinner. I started a fire, pleased that the smoke seemed to be keeping the gnats at bay. I boiled water in an open pot, which took a long time, and dropped in a bag of frozen mixed vegetables. Then I started grilling franks and hamburgers, some carefully wrapped in aluminum foil; Sophie objects to food with a burn mark. Afterward, we toasted marshmallows, but as each of hers caught fire and blackened, she threw them away.

We cleaned up extra carefully—the prospect of bears will do that—walked down the road to the comfort station to wash up, and prepared to turn in. By 8:30pm, there was still enough fading light to crawl into our sleeping bags and gaze out at the treetops. There was no need to make a fire in the stove; the evening was even warm enough to keep the windows open. Sophie made sure I latched the door with the eyelet hook. We chatted sleepily and then I heard Sophie's measured breathing.

The foam pad notwithstanding, I found the floor uncomfortably hard. Was it worse on my back or my side? I couldn't decide. But I must have dozed off because the next thing I felt was a finger poking my face. It was pitch black. "I have to go," Sophie whispered.

My watch showed a little past 1am. I flicked on the flashlight, we slipped on our sneakers, unlatched the door, and stepped outside. As we walked down the road, Sophie said she was afraid of seeing bears. "I want to call Mama," she whimpered. Trying to keep my voice level, I said the pay phones at the office were probably shut off for the night and belittled the idea of bears out at that hour. In truth, I was far from confident. To make matters worse, as I played the flashlight along the sides of the road, large rocks threw humped shadows that looked exactly like bears. And I wasn't carrying any pots and pans.

We did what we had to do and nervously retraced our steps to the lean-to. I barred the door and we crawled gratefully back into our sleeping bags. "Dad," Sophie said in the dark, "for some reason I think there are snakes here." I said, no, they didn't get into lean-tos. And then my stomach gave a mighty growl. Sophie flinched. "What was that?" she asked, alarmed. I said I was getting hungry again. "I know how flies protect themselves," she said. "Move fast." I told her to go back to sleep. And she did.

She woke me at 5:45am, as dawn was lightening the lean-to. We made another trip down the road, this time more relaxed, and started the fire for breakfast. There was a tree trunk that someone had started to saw into logs and with Sophie's help I finished the job, happy that I got to use my folding saw after all. Then—oh happiness!—I got to use my ax to split the logs and gave Sophie a few carefully supervised swings. I boiled water for instant hot cereal and cooked scrambled eggs in a pan. Then we hung the hammock outside and Sophie lazed while I cleaned up. We emptied and padlocked the lean-to, packed up the car, and left to explore other parts of the forest, stopping at the park office to return the key.

A nature trail called Tillman Ravine in the southwest corner of the park looked inviting from a brochure and we headed there, leaving the car in a parking area and following what the map and signs said was a half-mile trail loop down to Tillman Brook and back. The path was steep and dark, the sky obliterated by a canopy of pine and hemlock. We saw the gushing brook with its crossings of rustic bridges and paralleled it, following what I thought was the trail.

It wasn't. I had lost my bearings. We couldn't get too lost because the road and parking lot were clearly up the hill from the brook, but exactly what was the trail and what wasn't? Then something else occurred to me. I couldn't remember packing up the hammock. Had we left it on the trees at the lean-to? I asked Sophie. She didn't remember taking it down either. "The hammock," she wailed. "The hammock." I promised to go back for the $10 hammock. But first I had to get us out of there. I was looking for the laid logs that were supposed to mark the trail when something by a fallen tree caught my eye.

It was a dark form, partly covered by underbrush. I froze and caught Sophie's hand. She saw it, too. I thought it was a dead black dog, maybe a dog that had drowned in the brook. I could see a bit of tail and what I thought was a muzzle. But what if it was a bear, dead or otherwise?

Sophie wanted a closer look. Maybe the dog was sick, she said. We had to help it. We had to bury it. I pulled her away. What if it—whatever it was—wasn't dead, like the snake? Trail, or no trail, I hightailed it up the hill pulling a protesting child along. The trail suddenly materialized, and we followed it quickly to the road.

We drove back to the lean-to. There were the two trees that had suspended the hammock. But the hammock was gone! Sadly, we drove to the office to report the loss. The park superintendent listened to the story and unclipped a walkie-talkie from his belt. In minutes he had good news. Maintenance men had recovered it from our spot. We raced to meet them and made the retrieval. We'll need it for our next expedition.

ESSENTIALS: CAMPING IN STOKES FOREST AND AROUND THE TRI-STATE AREA

Reservations are recommended for most campgrounds in the three-state region Memorial Day through Labor Day. Listings of state and private campgrounds and what they offer are available from the **New York State Tourism Information Center** (☎ 800/225-5697 or 800/456-2267); the **New Jersey Department of Environmental Protection,** Division of Parks and Forestry (☎ 800/843-6420 or 609/984-0370); the **Connecticut Vacation Center** (☎ 800/282-6863); and the **Connecticut Campground Owners Association** (☎ 860/521-4704).

Stokes State Forest, the campground mentioned in the accompanying article, is off Route 206, Branchville, NJ (☎ 201/948-3820). Open year-round, its daily rates range from $10 for a campsite with flush toilet within walking distance to $28 for a furnished cabin.

A sampling of other campgrounds in the New York metropolitan area follows. Reservations at state parks can be made up to 11 months in advance by calling ☎ 800/456-2267.

LONG ISLAND

Cedar Point County Park, Alewive Brook Rd., East Hampton (☎ 516/852-7620).
Eastern Long Island Campground, 690 Queen St., Greenport (☎ 516/477-0022).
Indian Island County Park, County Rd. 105, Riverhead (☎ 516/852-3232).

Hither Hills, Rte. 27, Montauk (☎ 800/456-2267 or 516/668-2461).
Wildwood State Park, Hulse Landing Rd., Wading River (☎ 516/929-4314).

HUDSON VALLEY

Croton Point Park, Croton Point Ave. (off Rte. 9), Croton (☎ 914/271-3293 or 914/271-6858).

Harriman State Park, Beaver Pond, Bear Mountain (☎ 914/947-2792 or 914/786-2761).

Interlake Farm, 45 Lake Dr., Clinton (☎ 914/266-5387).

Oleana Campground, Rte. 7 (off Rte. 22), West Copake (☎ 518/329-2811).

UPSTATE NEW YORK

Clarence Fahnestock Memorial State Park, Rte. 301 (off Taconic State Pkwy.), Carmel (☎ 914/225-7207).

Margaret Lewis Norrie State Park, Rte. 9, Staatsburg (☎ 914/889-4646).

NEW JERSEY

Allaire State Park, Rte. 524, Wall Township, Farmingdale (☎ 908/938-2371).

Belleplain State Forest, Rte. 550, Woodbine (☎ 609/861-2404).

Bull's Island, Rte. 29 (8 miles north of Lambertville; ☎ 609/397-2949).

Wharton Forest, Atsion Recreation Center, Rte. 206, Shamong Township (☎ 609/268-0444 or 609/561-0024).

CONNECTICUT

Camp Niantic by the Atlantic, 271 W. Main St., Niantic (☎ 860/739-9308 or 860/647-9806).

Hammonasset Beach, Rte. 9 (off I-91), Madison (☎ 203/245-1817).

Lake Waramaug, 30 Lake Waramaug Rd., New Preston (☎ 860/424-3200).

Looking Glass Hill Campground, Rte. 202, Bantam (☎ 860/567-2050).

STROLLING BUCOLIC HUNTERDON COUNTY

by Lisa W. Foderaro

NEW JERSEY IS KNOWN FOR MANY
good things, from beefsteak tomatoes to Bruce Springsteen. But as a
place to head for a quiet country weekend in late fall, the state usually
falls off the radar of urbanites who drive north to Litchfield County
in Connecticut or to the Hudson Valley in New York.

Well, commit this name to memory: Hunterdon County.

Little known beyond New Jersey, Hunterdon is extraordinary for its
rural beauty and urbane sensibility. In the last 10 to 15 years, it has
sprouted enough restaurants, inns, and interesting boutiques to become
a natural extension of Bucks County, its better-known neighbor across
the Delaware River in Pennsylvania. "What a wonderful place this is,"
wrote an unsuspecting visitor in the guest book of Hunterdon House,
an Italianate Victorian bed-and-breakfast in the borough of Frenchtown.
"With all the bad rap you hear about New Jersey, it's hard to believe
that's where we are." Indeed. With undulating farmland studded with
wineries, and the Delaware flowing past such historic villages as
Frenchtown and Stockton, Hunterdon entices comparisons not to
Litchfield but to the Dordogne region in southwest France.

More than half the land is still actively farmed, and although
Hunterdon is the second fastest growing county in the state, it is the
third least densely populated. A government-sponsored farmland preservation program has kept more than two dozen working farms working, while gentlemen farmers and horsewomen like Gov. Christine Todd
Whitman have made Hunterdon synonymous with hunt country.

Missing from much of the landscape is the background static of suburban sprawl—strip malls, billboards, and the like. Instead there are long country roads flanked by woods, streams, and, at this time of year, pale fields of withered cornstalks. The only surviving covered bridge in the state is here, too.

Plenty of Charm

The municipalities dotting the banks of the Delaware, from Milford in the north to Lambertville in the south, were once rough-and-tumble mill towns. But over the years most of the factories closed, and so far no new industry has swept through. This leaves the streetscapes—neat but motley rows of Queen Anne, Georgian, Neo-Gothic, and Federal architecture—relatively untouched, like bees preserved in amber. Now tourism is a major industry. But it's an understated sort of tourism that doesn't feel stagy. A better name for it might simply be pleasure.

Fall is an especially pretty time of year to see Hunterdon. The chill in the air inspires walks by day and wood fires by night. And root vegetables, roast meats, and mysteriously rich stocks have taken the front burner at local restaurants, among them two highly praised kitchens.

Staying for a weekend makes it possible to squeeze in all there is to do, from taking a quiet walk on the old canal towpath running along the river, now preserved as the Delaware and Raritan Canal State Park, to stopping by a winery, to visiting tiny villages like Sergeantsville or larger towns like Lambertville, crammed with antiques stores, atmospheric gift shops, and restaurants. A weekend trip will also do justice to the transporting experience that is the Ryland Inn, a white clapboard restaurant in Whitehouse whose chef, Craig C. Shelton, has worked with both Joel Robuchon in Paris and David Bouley in Manhattan.

There are a number of charming places to stay in the county. One popular lodging, and certainly the most whimsical building in Frenchtown, is Hunterdon House, a three-story olive stucco mansion with burgundy gingerbread trim and arched windows, set back from Bridge Street, the main thoroughfare. The inn, built in 1864, has seven

rooms; the most spectacular is the William Apgar Room on the ground floor, with a working fireplace and a hand-carved headboard that soars seven feet above the bed.

Some of the decor strokes are slightly off, like the shade of powder blue chosen for the walls in the parlor and the vase of faded silk flowers on the stair landing. In general, though, the rooms are tastefully decorated in restrained Victoriana and carried by a few significant furnishings and Oriental rugs. The sort of personal kindness offered by a small inn was evident on a recent Saturday evening when the innkeeper, V. Eugene Refalvy, offered one of his dress shirts and a tie to a desperate guest who had forgotten his own.

Arts, Crafts, and Pastries

The towns of Hunterdon County beckon to be walked through, their old buildings looked at, their occasionally eccentric shops browsed in. Frenchtown made a fine place to start on a recent visit. At the western end of Bridge Street is the Delaware River. Its swirling, mocha-colored waters, churned by a recent rain, moved swiftly south under a steel truss bridge whose heavy stone piers and abutments date back to 1843.

Along Bridge Street are a number of places worth discovering. The Bridge Cafe, housed in a former train station overlooking the river, has excellent baked goods. Arcadia, next door, offers a colorful selection of fine crafts: playfully conceived ceramics, glass objects, jewelry, clocks, mirrors, and lamps. Across the street stands the Frenchtown Inn, a cozy brick restaurant built in 1805. (Its $18.95 brunch, for the hearty of appetite, includes a basket of warm pastries, fruit cup, a choice of entrees ranging from eggs Benedict to leg of lamb, and dessert.)

A few storefronts down is the Delaware River Trading Company, a purveyor of rural-chic garden and home furnishings, as well as a few peculiar antiques. Here you'll find everything from silver-plated mint julep cups to hammocks, four-poster cherry beds to antique pitch-forks. There was even a photo album from the 1920s displaying dozens of police mug shots of jewelry thieves.

The next stop is Stockton, reached by driving south on lovely Route 29, or River Road. (The Delaware can be glimpsed through the trees on the right.) Slightly smaller than Frenchtown, Stockton is home to the Stockton Inn, made famous by the Rodgers and Hart song "There's a Small Hotel," from the Broadway musical *On Your Toes*. The inn's fieldstone structure, dating from 1710, has 10 rooms, most with fireplaces and canopy beds, and a restaurant with murals depicting 18th-century farming villages. The stone wishing well of the song is still there, its pool carpeted with coins.

One remarkable store is the half-century-old Phillips' Fine Wines, a veritable museum of the viniculture art and considered by many to be the state's best wine store. There are eight rooms on two floors displaying roughly 5,000 labels, including 200 different Australian wines, 175 California Chardonnays, and 150 Burgundies. There's even a room devoted just to port.

An example of how Hunterdon's image has recently been polished is the transformation of the low-slung building at the corner of Main and Bridge streets from a gas station to a restaurant called Meil's. At once homey and hip, Meil's has stenciled walls hung with quilts and a menu offering chicken pot pie with buttermilk biscuits, warm sesame duck salad, and a grilled sandwich of brie, tomato, and onion on seven-grain bread.

Lambertville, the southernmost river town in Hunterdon, is also the largest. It could be seen as the rapidly growing kid sister of New Hope, Pa., right across the Delaware. Eighty percent of Lambertville's handsome brick buildings and row houses were built before 1900. One of the most notable is the James Wilson Marshall House at 60 Bridge Street, an 1816 Federal house with pale green shutters that was the boyhood home of its namesake, the discoverer of gold at Sutter's Mill in California in 1848.

But perhaps more than anything, Lambertville is a shopper's paradise. Whereas Flemington, the county seat, is prized for its outlet shopping, Lambertville does not possess a single chain store. It is known instead for dozens of one-of-a-kind shops reflecting the tastes and personalities of their owners.

Reinboth & Company, at 121 North Union Street, offers things to make life a little more ethereal, from mineral bath salts and German linens to overstuffed leather sofas. Meld, at 53 North Union Street, sells "20th-century antiques," like campy bar ware from the 1950s, including a "Trav-L-Bar" briefcase complete with tumblers for $65, and an oscillating fan from the 1940s for $75.

The Five and Dime, at 40 North Union Street, is an emporium of toys and games from the last several decades: an Osmond metal lunch box ($65), a 1960s blond G.I. Joe Action Soldier ($200), a Snoopy humidifier ($75), and a 1982 Brooke Shields doll ($45). And the People's Store Antiques Center, three floors at 28 North Union Street, represents the goods of 40 dealers, everything from a mounted elk's head ($975) and an 1860 jam cupboard ($1,150) to an elaborately carved oak icebox ($1,595).

A Diversity of Tables

There is no paucity of fine restaurants in Lambertville. Siam, at 61 North Main Street, features fresh and inexpensive Thai food, while Anton's at the Swan, 43 South Main Street, is the archetypal romantic restaurant. Baroque music fills the dining rooms, where huge gilt-framed mirrors and old engravings surround tables laden with hurricane lamps and china in a pleasing hodgepodge of patterns.

Away from the river, Hunterdon becomes slightly more hilly, and while driving along back roads through the countryside is the main attraction, there are a handful of villages deserving of a quick stop. Sergeantsville in Delaware Township is a mere intersection marked by a blinking light, but on one corner is the Sergeantsville Inn, a beguiling restaurant in a fieldstone house with a wood-burning fireplace. Crossing a swollen creek a mile west of Sergeantsville on Route 604 is a white covered bridge, the last public one in the state.

Also in Delaware Township is Rosemont, another one-horse town that is perhaps best known for Cane Farm Furniture, a 30-year-old maker of Early American and Shaker reproductions, displayed in a series of renovated chicken coops.

Farther north is the village of Oldwick in Tewksbury Township, its Main Street a seeming New England tableau, with two dazzling white churches and an antiquarian bookstore. The Main Street is also home to the deceptively low-key Tewksbury Inn, where in 1994 chef Patrick Robertson (formerly of Le Cirque in Manhattan) catapulted what was essentially a local burger hangout to culinary high ground. The new chef, James Mignola, has apparently kept the standards high.

Dining at an Inn

But the most special dining experience in Hunterdon, possibly in the state, some restaurant critics say, can be found at the Ryland Inn on Route 22 in Whitehouse. The reputation of Mr. Shelton, the chef and owner, clearly reverberates beyond the state's borders, as the helipad on the 50-acre property, where he grows his own herbs and vegetables, attests. His résumé lists several culinary stations of the cross in Manhattan, from Bouley to Le Bernardin to La Côte Basque.

The center section of the inn was built before 1800 as a private home, and indeed, the feeling here is one of dining in the house of a very congenial and very wealthy friend. But the food manages to steal the show from the impeccable service staff and the gracious decor. A recent tasting menu, for $80, was a dizzying survey of Mr. Shelton's talents. Among the eight dishes were grouse and mallard consommé with spaghetti squash, zucchini, and thyme; sautéed wild mushrooms between disks of dried root vegetables; a ragout of salmon and crabmeat, fava beans, peas, and mint; and grilled foie gras with peasant-style lentils and celery-root puree. Dessert was a creamy confection described as pineapple-coconut layers between pina colada mousse and coconut sorbet.

The weighty wine list includes a $3,000 bottle of 1945 Château Latour as well as two pages of bottles at $25 and under. A snifter of cognac—there are 28 to choose from—is best savored in the cigar room on the ground floor, an appropriately masculine sanctum with black walls, formal drapes, and a painting of two golden retrievers. Cigars are available from $5 to $16; thankfully, an effective ventilation system makes a pilgrimage by the nonsmoker bearable.

Post-Prandial Strolling

After such a rich feast, some low-impact exercise (walking, for example) is in order. The Delaware and Raritan Canal State Park, a 72-mile corridor with 19th-century bridges and stone culverts, runs most of the length of Hunterdon County and continues south to Trenton, where it veers inland toward the Raritan River. The towpath is mostly flat and makes for easy walking and biking. Naturally, it borders the canal, which was one of the country's busiest navigation routes in the 1860s and 70s, when Pennsylvania coal was brought to New York City to fuel the industrial boom.

Today, the canal is a lazy finger of water that reflects the tall trees overhead, while just beyond is the Delaware River, moving at twice the canal's pace. The section of the path behind Prallsville Mills in Stockton is especially scenic. The mills, a collection of eight historic buildings, are open occasionally for special events, but reservations may be made for a tour. The public is welcome on the grounds, however. Before embarking along the towpath, visitors might walk around the outside of Prallsville Mills. Two of the most striking structures are the grist mill, a four-story building of stone and stucco that dates, in part, from 1711, and the linseed oil mill, a tiny 1790 building made of rich brown stones held together by white mortar.

After a stroll along the canal, a visit to one of the state's most notable wineries, Unionville Vineyards at 9 Rocktown Road in Ringoes, might be a nice finish for the weekend. When you think of the wine-growing centers of the New York region, the North Fork of Long Island probably comes to mind, or even the Finger Lakes in upstate New York. But New Jersey, which counts 15 wineries in the north and south, has a long history of wine making, and in the last few years has finally gained some recognition. It could be called a renaissance, for London's Royal Society of Arts recognized two New Jersey vintners back in 1767 for their success in making the first decent wine from Colonial grapes. Today, the wineries produce 180,000 gallons a year, placing New Jersey among the top 15 wine-producing states in the country.

Unionville Vineyards was opened in 1993 by Kris Nielsen and Patricia Galloway, although the first vines were planted five years earlier. There are now 32 acres of vines, 12 of them in full production. Hunter's White, a refreshing table wine produced from a blend of Vidal Blanc and Cayuga grapes, sells for $7.99 a bottle. The Hunter's White Reserve, made from Vidal Blanc grapes and aged in new oak barrels, sells for $9.99. Unionville's most popular label is Fields of Fire, a fruity rosé wine at $6.99 a bottle.

Free tastings are offered Thursdays through Sundays from 11am to 4pm. The tastings are held on the second floor of a former dairy barn whose 1848 post-and-beam construction was preserved during a recent renovation. The barn is set amid folds of muted green meadows and farms that stretch to the horizon, forming a bucolic idyll.

Suddenly, you realize why they call it the Garden State.

HUNTERDON COUNTY ESSENTIALS

GETTING THERE

To reach New Jersey's Hunterdon County from Manhattan, take the Holland or Lincoln Tunnel to the New Jersey Turnpike to Interstate 78 West; continue on I-78 West to exit 15 (Clinton and Pittstown) and pick up Rte. 513 South; continue on Rte. 513 South into Frenchtown.

ACCOMMODATIONS

FRENCHTOWN

Hunterdon House, 12 Bridge St. (☎ 800/382-0375 or 908/996-3632). Friday and Saturday, $110 to $145; Sunday through Thursday, $85 to $100. Rates are based on double occupancy and include full breakfast.

STOCKTON

Stockton Inn, 1 Main St. (Rte. 29; ☎ 609/397-1250). Monday through Thursday, rooms $60 to $125; Friday through Sunday and holidays, rooms $85 to $165. Continental breakfast included; children welcome. Restaurant open Monday through Thursday 11:30am to 2:30pm and 4:30 to 9:30pm, Friday and Saturday 11:30am to 2:30pm and 4:30 to 10pm, Sunday 11 to 2:30pm (for brunch) and 3:30 to 9pm. Entrees $6.95 to $15.95 at lunch, $14.95 to $28 at dinner.

RESTAURANTS

FRENCHTOWN

Bridge Cafe, 8 Bridge St. (☎ 908/996-6040). Open daily 7am to 5pm. Dinner seasonally; call for hours. Entrees average $6 at lunch.

Frenchtown Inn, 7 Bridge St. (☎ 908/996-3300). Open Tuesday through Friday noon to 2pm and 6 to 9pm, Saturday noon to 2pm and 5:30 to 9:30pm, Sunday noon to 2:30pm (for brunch) and 5:30 to 8:30pm. Entrees $7.75 to $14.95 at lunch, $19.50 to $26.95 at dinner; Saturday prix-fixe dinner, $48 per person.

STOCKTON

Also see Stockton Inn under "Accommodations," above.

Meil's, Bridge and Main sts. (☎ 609/397-8033). Open Monday through Thursday 9am to 9pm, Friday and Saturday 8am to 10pm, Sunday 8am to 9pm. Entrees $3 to $12 at breakfast, $6 to $14 at lunch, $9 to $20 at dinner.

LAMBERTVILLE

Anton's at the Swan, 43 S. Main St. (☎ 609/397-1960). Open Wednesday through Saturday 6 to 10pm. Entrees $22 to $30.

Siam, 61 N. Main St. (☎ 609/397-8128). Open Tuesday 6 to 9pm, Wednesday and Thursday 11am to 2pm and 6pm and 9pm, Friday to Saturday 11am to 2pm and 6 to 10pm, Sunday 11am to 2pm and 4 to 9pm. Entrees $8 to $13.

SERGEANTSVILLE

Sergeantsville Inn, rtes. 523 and 604 (☎ 609/397-3700). Open Wednesday and Thursday 5 to 9pm, Friday and Saturday 5 to 10pm, Sunday noon to 2:30pm (for brunch) and 5 to 8pm. Entrees $18.75 to $28.50 at dinner; brunch and grill menu, $8.95 to $15.95.

OLDWICK

Tewksbury Inn, Main St. (Rte. 517; ☎ 908/439-2641). Open Tuesday through Thursday 11:30am to 3pm and 5:30 to 10pm, Friday 11:30am to 3pm and 5:30 to 10:30pm, Saturday 11:30am to 3:30pm and 5:30 and 10:30pm, Sunday noon to 3:30pm and 5:30 to 9pm. Entrees $6 to $13 at lunch, $14 to $24 at dinner.

WHITEHOUSE

Ryland Inn, Rte. 22 West (☎ 908/534-4011). Open Monday through Friday 11:30am to 2pm and 5:30 and 11pm, Saturday 5:30 to 11pm, Sunday 4 to 9pm. Entrees $9.95 to $15 at lunch, $26 to $34 at dinner; Friday and Saturday nights, prix fixe menu $60 per person. There are also daily 8-course tasting menus, $80 a person ($75 for vegetarians).

ATTRACTIONS

STOCKTON

Prallsville Mills, Rte. 29 (☎ 609/397-3586). Eight historic buildings maintained by the Delaware River Mills Society. They are open occasionally for special events, but reservations can be made for a tour. The public is welcome on the grounds.

LAMBERTVILLE

James Wilson Marshall House, operated by the Lambertville Historical Society, 60 Bridge St. (☎ 609/397-0770). Closed November through March; call for open hours from April through October.

DELAWARE RIVER

Delaware and Raritan Canal State Park (☎ 609/397-2949), a corridor along the Delaware River, from Frenchtown to Trenton to New Brunswick; accessible from Rte. 29. There are parking lots at each crossing of the canal. Open year-round; free admission.

RINGOES

Unionville Vineyards, 9 Rocktown Rd. (☎ 908/788-0400). Free wine tastings Thursday through Sunday 11am to 4pm.

SHOPPING

FRENCHTOWN

Arcadia, 10 Bridge St. (☎ 908/996-7570). Open Tuesday through Thursday and Sunday 11am to 5pm, Friday and Saturday 11am to 6pm.

Delaware River Trading Company, 47 Bridge St. (☎ 800/732-4791 or 908/996-3447). Open Monday through Saturday 9am to 6pm, Sunday 11am to 5pm.

STOCKTON

Phillips' Fine Wines, 17 Bridge St. (☎ 609/397-0587). Open Monday through Thursday 9am to 9pm, Friday and Saturday 9am to 10pm, Sunday noon to 6pm.

LAMBERTVILLE

Five and Dime, 40 N. Union St. (☎ 609/397-4957). Open Monday through Friday

11am to 5pm, Saturday 10am to 6pm, Sunday 10am to 5pm.

Meld, 53 N. Union St. (☎ 609/397-8487). Open Thursday through Monday 11am to 6pm.

People's Store Antiques Center, 28 N. Union St. (☎ 609/397-9808). Open daily 10am to 6pm.

Reinboth & Company, 121 N. Union St. (☎ 609/397-2216). Open Monday through Saturday 10am to 6pm, Sunday 11am to 5pm.

ROSEMONT

Cane Farm Furniture, Rte. 519 (☎ 609/397-0606). Open Friday and Saturday 10am to 5pm, Sunday 1pm to 5pm, or by appointment.

BY THE SEA IN SPRING LAKE

by William Grimes

THE STRING OF BEACH TOWNS THAT extends from Long Branch to Atlantic City can seem like an endless radio dial of heavy-metal stations, cranked up and blasting at full volume. Spring Lake is the weak classical signal offering an instant of blessed repose. More than any other town in the northern half of New Jersey, it has preserved the special appeal that made the Jersey Shore a magnet for 19th-century city folk keen to try out a thrilling new experience: summer vacation at the beach.

The pleasures of Spring Lake are small but satisfying. The town's name comes from a large spring-fed lake in its center. The beach is clean and uncrowded, and the boardwalk is noncommercial, anchored at either end by a huge municipal swimming pool and bathhouse pavilion. The white heat of the beach gives way to deep shade and lush green lawns on the town's residential streets, where the sprawling Victorian houses come fitted out with long verandas and canvas awnings.

Twentieth-century lawn culture has achieved a high level of development in Spring Lake. As the town drowses in the daytime heat, the rhythmic ticking of a thousand automatic sprinkler guns, turning back and forth, punctuates the humid silence. The grass seems to be a deeper and springier species than normal. A hefty percentage of bushes and hedges are shaped into impeccable topiary balls and squares.

At the corner of Lake and Mercer avenues, behold what may well be the finest lawn in America. The owner maintains the lawn precisely like a putting green, clipped to a quarter of an inch with special mowers, watered by a system of automatic sprinklers sunk into the ground, their perfectly round burrows adding to the putting green effect.

Passing cyclists, stunned, stop and reach out their hands to caress the green expanse. The house, a pristine white with grass green shutters, makes the ensemble a set waiting for the next David Lynch movie.

Spring Lake has another surprise.

Croquet, Anyone?

The Green Gables Croquet Club is at 1401 Ocean Avenue, just south of the Breakers Hotel. The club was founded on a whim in 1956 by Mrs. Carvel Cabell Linden, who had set up a large tent on her lawn for her daughter's wedding reception and the next day invited a few friends over for a game of croquet.

The Green Gables, a private club with 50 members, later became a charter member of the United States Croquet Association. It has three championship croquet courts (also known as greenswards), highly unusual for a private residence, and becomes the center of the croquet world in mid-July, when it is the site of an invitational tournament. Mrs. Linden died in 1996 but the croquet club and the tournament live on.

The day I visited, Ted Prentis, a touring pro of substantial girth, was giving a croquet clinic to aspiring players in regulation whites. The game looks only slightly more strenuous than lifting a gin and tonic, but devotees insist that the mental aspect is quite challenging, a combination of billiards and chess, in which the player has to think "three moves ahead."

Location, Location

Spring Lake attracted its first tourist in 1874, when Alfonso A. Willits, a Philadelphia clergyman and surf fisherman visiting Ocean Grove, heard of a nearby farm with a large spring-fed lake. He paid the farm a visit, saw the potential of the site and decided to develop the area as a resort for Philadelphians. The timing was correct, since the railroad was beginning to reach the area. Two years later, a grand hotel, the Monmouth House, opened its doors. Two more hotels followed in the next two years. Soon, prosperous burghers were building private residences, and guest cottages began popping up; in 1892, Spring Lake was incorporated as a borough.

The grand hotels no longer exist. But Spring Lake offers an extensive menu of bed-and-breakfast establishments. Two of the best, the Normandy Inn and Sea Crest by the Sea, sit side by side on a residential street a block from the ocean. Both date from the 1880s and come equipped with breezy verandas for creative loafing. The Normandy, which fills up quickly, is decorated in serious Victorian antiques and offers a locally renowned mega-breakfast with plate-size pancakes and English bangers.

Sea Crest by the Sea, where my wife and I stayed, has themed bedrooms. We drew the George Washington room, with a massive French walnut featherbed, an ocean view, and tiny portraits of George and Martha over the toilet tank, a winning touch. A fleet of bicycles is available for guests to use, and the room price includes metal tags for admission to the town beach. If you're quick off the mark, you can reach one of the few small tables in the dining room and thereby avoid the dread communal table. For reasons that defy explanation, all bed-and-breakfast owners entertain the fantasy that their guests are dying to mingle and converse first thing in the morning.

Rooms with Views

Those in search of more modern conveniences can check into the Breakers, a newly renovated hotel right on the ocean, with the best views in town: out front, the Atlantic Ocean; to the north, the visual delights of Lake Como, and onward to the teenage Sodom and Gomorrah of Belmar; to the south, the manicured courts of the Green Gables Croquet Club. The hotel has a restaurant and a swimming pool.

Two hotels overlook the lake: the old-fashioned, atmospheric Shoreham Hotel and Spa and the Hewitt-Wellington, which has what the locals regard as the best restaurant in town, although it should be noted that no one goes from New York City to Spring Lake just for the food.

The real draw is peace of mind, and the opportunity to breathe in the atmosphere—the generous sense of scale and space, the air of mid-summer languor, the solid, bourgeois approach to comfort—peculiar to the mid-Atlantic coast. There are times when the most profitable thing a person can do is sit on the porch and watch the grass grow. For this purpose, Spring Lake may count as a world capital.

SPRING LAKE ESSENTIALS

The **Greater Spring Lake Chamber of Commerce,** 1315 Third Ave. (P.O. Box 694), Spring Lake, NJ 07762 (☎ 908/449-0577) will send information on hotels, restaurants, shops, and sights.

GETTING THERE

Spring Lake is 60 miles south of New York City.

By Car　Take the New Jersey Tpk. to exit 11, then follow the Garden State Pkwy. to exit 98. Take Rte. 34 South to the traffic circle, go three-quarters of the way around the circle, and follow Rte. 524 East to Spring Lake.

By Train　NJ Transit (☎ 201/762-5100) offers rail service from Penn Station to Spring Lake along their North Jersey Coast Line. The Spring Lake station is a five-minute walk from the beach. A one-way ticket is $9.45; round-trip excursion tickets, for travel on weekends or nonrush hours, cost $14. The trip takes about two hours.

ACCOMMODATIONS

Spring Lake abounds in small, charming guest houses and larger oceanfront and lakefront hotels. Most establishments require a minimum two-night stay on weekends (some on weekdays as well) during the summer. Prices drop in the off season. The list that follows, with summer rates, is a small sampling.

The Breakers, 1507 Ocean Ave. (☎ 908/449-7700). $150 to $300 double, with a three-night minimum on weekends in July and August.

The Chateau, 500 Warren Ave. (☎ 908/974-2000). $107 to $210 double weekdays, $140 to $225 weekends.

Hewitt-Wellington, 200 Monmouth Ave. (☎ 908/974-1212). $165 to $280 double weekends, $160 to $250 weekdays. Continental breakfast buffet, afternoon tea, beach badges, and tennis court passes included. No children under 12 accepted.

Normandy Inn, 21 Tuttle Ave. (☎ 908/449-7172). $121 to $181 double; $250 or $286 suite.

Sea Crest by the Sea, 19 Tuttle Ave. (☎ 908/449-9031). $159 to $189 single or double; $259 suite.

Villa Park House, 417 Ocean Rd. (☎ 908/449-3642). $110 to $120 double.

DINING

The Sandpiper, 7 Atlantic Ave. (☎ 908/ 449-4700). Seafood and American grill. Open Monday through Thursday 11:30am to 2:30pm and 5 to 9:30pm; Friday and Saturday 11:30am to 2:30pm and 5 to 10pm; Sunday 11am to 2:30pm (for oceanside brunch) and 5 to 9pm. Dinner entrees $13.95 to $21.95. Bring your own wine or beer.

Whispers, at the Hewitt-Wellington Hotel, 200 Monmouth Ave. (☎ 908/449-3330). Eclectic cuisine. Dinner served Tuesday through Sunday from 5pm; closed January. Entrees $14.95 to $22.95; five-course tasting menu available. Bring your own wine or beer.

ATTRACTIONS

Spring Lake Historical Society's Museum, Municipal Building, second floor, Fifth and Warren aves. (☎ 908/449-0772). Historical photographs tracing the development of the town are on display. Open Tuesday 10am to noon and Sunday 2 to 4pm. Contributions accepted.

VICTORIANA AT THE SHORE: CAPE MAY

by Jon Pareles

THERE ARE NO PRIMARY COLORS IN Cape May, New Jersey. It's a town of mauves and chartreuses, ochres and pinks, the colors of hundreds of Victorian-era summer cottages that have made Cape May a national landmark. It's a seaside town, too, bordered by pale fine sand and green-gray waves.

Situated 160 miles from the Holland Tunnel at the southern tip of New Jersey, dangling into Delaware Bay just below the Mason-Dixon line, Cape May is outside the immediate orbit of New York City. It draws people from New Jersey and Pennsylvania and points south; Lewes, Delaware, is 70 minutes away by ferry. Cape May also stands apart from the rest of the Jersey Shore. It's a cozy, genteel haven. My wife and I have been visiting Cape May whenever we can set aside three or four days. This time, as we drove down the Garden State Parkway, we noticed that many of the cars had "firefighter" license plates. The annual New Jersey firefighters' convention was taking place that weekend in Wildwood, just north of Cape May. Historically speaking, those firefighters were arriving more than a century late.

Cape May, once a base for whalers, was a thriving resort by the 1850s. Carriages rolled across the broad beach front; steamships came up the coast; holiday makers filled big, L-shaped seaside hotels. In 1865, a railroad link to Philadelphia was completed. But arson fires repeatedly devastated the town; the largest, in 1878, destroyed 35 acres. The fires meant rebuilding, and as a result, much of the city dates from the 1860s through the 1890s. Yet by the 1920s, Cape May had been overshadowed by other seaside towns, from Atlantic City to Newport, Rhode Island. It became a quiet outpost, used for fishing and as a military base.

With little redevelopment, the 19th-century summer cottages remained. Eventually some locals began to see the whimsical old homes as a potential attraction. A preservation movement, begun in the 1960s, put Cape May's 600 Victorian buildings on the National Register of Historic Places in 1970 and secured landmark status for the district in 1976, though not before some beach motels had been established. Part of Washington Street was converted to a pedestrian shopping mall; dozens of cottages were turned into bed-and-breakfasts, more of them each year. Gradually, Cape May won back its tourists.

Now visitors are an unlikely coalition of beachgoers, Victoriana buffs, and bird-watchers, who prize Cape May's location on major coastal migration routes. The town also has some of the best restaurants in New Jersey.

Usually we stay at the Abigail Adams, a small, congenial bed-and-breakfast just one house away from the oceanside Beach Drive, where we're treated more like houseguests than tourists. In the summer season, the owner provides beach tags (required by the town for beach users) and passes for a parking lot a few blocks away; street parking is unmetered during the off season. The house is one of the Seven Sisters, a semicircle of seven identical houses designed by Stephen Decatur Button, whose imprint is all over Cape May. This time, however, we spent the weekend at a newly revived landmark: the Southern Mansion, an inn that has restored the George Allen Estate. Allen was a Philadelphia department store magnate who was instrumental in bringing the railroad to Cape May.

Until recently, the Southern Mansion was a haunted-looking three-story house occupying an overgrown city block. But new owners have poured millions of dollars into renovation. Built in 1863–64, the house is an American version of an Italian villa, with a 48-foot-long ballroom and 14 guest rooms. A 10-room annex, scheduled for completion before 1997, imitates the style of the original building. The mansion's exterior has been repainted its original shades of green, beige, and chocolate brown, and a meticulous renovation has put new slate on the roof and fresh gold leaf on the ballroom's giant mirrors.

Even the door hinges and window locks are highly decorated brass. When the new owners took over the estate, they found a trove of original fixtures and furniture in the basement. On the walls are photographs and memorabilia of Allen's daughter, Esther, who was married in the ballroom to one Ulysses Mercur.

Rooms with a View

We could glimpse a sliver of ocean over the rooftops from our third-floor room. It had comfortable Eastlake furniture—a couch, a rocking chair—and a tall, king-size four-poster bed, its mattress raised nearly three feet off the floor. For closets, a large armoire had been split in two on one wall of the bedroom, with, oddly, a sink installed between the halves; the toilet and a large shower were in a separate room. Unlike many bed-and-breakfasts, the rooms are equipped with a television (with cable) and telephone.

A stairway in the hall leads to a cupola with a panoramic view of both ocean and bay. We could have booked a private dinner for two there for $215 (including a bottle of wine and tax), brought from the Washington Inn across the street.

Cape May is still a fishing town, and we decided to visit one of its institutions, the Lobster House restaurant. Along Fisherman's Wharf, a working fishery has grown into a tourist complex: the restaurant, a raw bar, a souvenir shop, a fish market with a takeout counter, and a bar that serves drinks on a schooner. The Lobster House doesn't take reservations, though, and a few hundred firemen were ahead of us. A hostess said the wait would be 45 to 75 minutes; she was handing out beepers that would vibrate when a table was available.

Unwilling to wait, we called to reserve a table at the Lobster House's upscale rival, Axelsson's Blue Claw. Its own fish market was closed for the evening; it had a less glamorous marina view. There, we settled in for a leisurely dinner, including a luxurious pure-crab sautéed crab cake ($9.50) and a delicately tomato-scented sea bass ($24.95) cooked in parchment. As she took our orders, the waitress told us the firefighters would parade in Wildwood on Saturday. When we inquired about specifics, she got time and route information from a nearby table of firemen.

We drove back to town, past Jim's Bait and Tackle, where a shark seems to be tearing through the facade of the second floor. There's gratifyingly little night life in Cape May: a few bars have cover bands, while some shops on stay open until 10pm or later. Columbia Avenue, where gaslights cast flickering shadows on some of the best-preserved Victorians, was quiet except for the clip-clop of a couple taking a carriage tour. Minus the parked cars, it could have been the 19th century.

Along the beach, the better-known Jersey Shore lingers with a small video arcade that closes early and a convention hall where big bands sometimes play. The Beach Theater, a recently subdivided movie house with a classic neon sign, shows first-run movies for $6.50. There were plenty of available seats for the 10pm show of *Tin Cup*, the Kevin Costner golf movie. On the way out, we gave an extra glance to the Ocean Putt, a modest miniature golf course.

Fudge and Architecture

The next morning, we had breakfast in the ballroom: fresh fruit, cereal, and cinnamon French toast with sausages. We looked into the garage-size Firemen's Museum, with its gleaming 1928 fire truck; we passed the Sturdy Savings Bank, a new building with a rare Victorian-style drive-through window. And we walked into town, marveling anew at the eccentric architecture.

In some ways, Cape May's core is like Miami Beach's Art Deco district, backdated a few decades and moved north: block upon block of daft buildings, all within an easy stroll. Whatever restraint the Victorians may have exercised in their deportment and discourse, their summer cottages repressed nothing. Turrets and gables poke up asymmetrically, windows are scattered across facades, shingles lose their corners, and woodwork trim becomes lace, spider webs, vines, and arabesques.

The Abbey (Columbia and Gurney streets) is a Gothic-revival fancy with a 60-foot tower; a house at 130 Decatur Street has three peaked roofs, an arch like an eyebrow, and porthole-shaped windows on its turret. The Henry L. Hunt House, at 201 Congress Place, sticks out in various directions and styles, including a circular belvedere on the second floor that looks like a miniature merry-go-round. Other places have a reassuring symmetry, like the row of eight formerly identical houses on Stockton Place or the Mainstay (635 Columbia Avenue), another Button building that was once a gambling club. All over town, the colors—some researched, some applied by caprice or intuition—clamor for attention.

Victoriana fills many of Cape May's shops. We looked into Uniquely Yours at the aptly named Pink House (lace dresses, filigreed jewelry, hats) and the Whale's Tale (books, earrings, shells, soaps, toys, even Victorian-design rubber stamps) before things got too cloying. Like other seaside towns, Cape May caters to the sweet tooth. There are four candy makers on the three-block Washington Mall, and one, Fudge Kitchen, greets all passersby with samples. Purely for research purposes, we decided on a taste test.

We bought chocolate fudge at Laura's, Frahlinger's, Morrow's Nut House, and the Fudge Kitchen on the mall; then we walked to the beach, picking up another chunk at Petroff's. On a bench by the seaside, we watched long waves roll in while ants and yellowjackets joined us for the test. Fudge Kitchen was the clear winner, velvety and richly cocoa flavored. Laura's, slightly too buttery, was a second choice.

To the Lighthouse

As our blood glucose levels rose, we drove to the lighthouse at Cape May Point, a slim, conical tower 157$\frac{1}{2}$ feet high, which was built in 1859. Not long ago, it was repainted from white to a historically accurate tan, with a red top. It is still a working lighthouse, America's oldest, with an automatic beacon. But the town's Mid-Atlantic Center for the

Arts now administers it as a museum, and tourists can climb the 199 steps to the top.

The cast-iron staircase is perforated in a diamond pattern that creates magnificent moires from above and below. With a landing about every 30 steps, the climb wasn't difficult, and there was a cool breeze on the open-air (but securely caged) observation deck. We looked down on the marshy wildlife refuge next to the point's beach and saw a schooner in full sail gliding by a jetty. Offshore was a concrete bunker built under the beach during World War II; 50 years of erosion have raised it well above the waves. In another 40 years, the waves will be at the lighthouse door.

Near the lighthouse, we looked into the Cape May Point State Park office, picking up the found poetry of the *Checklist of the Birds of Cape May County:* "Brown Thrasher, American Pipit, Cedar Waxwing, Loggerhead Shrike." We looked at a display of nests—including one by an Eastern kingbird, which had woven in cigarette filters because nicotine repels insects—and we decided to return on Saturday for the weekly hawk-banding demonstration.

We drove to nearby Sunset Beach, which of course faces west. It has a rougher, more pebbly texture than the main beach, and among the pebbles are so-called Cape May diamonds, sea-polished bits of quartz. Offshore is another hunk of concrete: a failed experimental ship built after World War I that became beached while being towed. The concrete boat was inauspiciously called the *Atlantus;* like its namesake, it sank.

We planned dinner at one of our favorites, Frescos, where the Italian cooking makes up for noisy acoustics and slightly rushed service. Like many Cape May restaurants, it has no liquor license, so patrons bring their own wine; Collier's Liquors across the street has a good selection. A smoked-eggplant soup and a rigatoni arrabbiata, with mushrooms and fennel-infused sausage, were gloriously earthy and too generous to finish; grilled tuna arrived with a pesto sauce made of smoked almonds as well as basil. Dinner for two came to $60.

It was time for some exercise. Instead, we signed up for 18 holes at Ocean Putt ($3). I made a few of the par-2 holes by sheer luck, with a hole-in-one on the seventh (the big rabbit). Calculating angles and aiming carefully, I took four and five strokes per hole after that. A five-year-old boy just behind us was doing better. I wondered if it was possible to be awarded a handicap at miniature golf. But on the way back to the inn, the stars were out, and the waves crashed with serene indifference.

At Saturday's hawk-banding demonstration, we were in the minority without binoculars around our necks. Bill Clark from the Cape May Bird Observatory pulled male and female American kestrels, already banded, from tubes made of juice cans taped together. He pointed out distinctive markings, talked about how the kestrels hunt from the air (using ultraviolet vision to pick out fluorescent mouse droppings), and explained how the banding project has recovered about 1% of the 92,800 birds it has banded. As he spoke, the raptors attacked his hand, drawing blood.

While Mr. Clark displayed a merlin, or pigeon hawk, a buzz went through the crowd, and binoculars were aimed overhead. "A bald eagle," someone whispered, and the man from the observatory raised his own binoculars. "A juvenile bald eagle," he agreed as it swooped by.

A Flashy Parade

We took the 10-minute drive to Wildwood for the parade. Antique and new fire trucks rolled by, all flashing red lights, at least one with a Dalmatian in the cab. We began noting the logos on the doors, like the camel and palm tree from New Egypt, New Jersey, and the skunk from Cologne, New Jersey. And we wondered why all the high school marching bands were playing "Louie, Louie."

We briefly visited the Wildwood boardwalk, where a young Bruce Springsteen would have felt at home. It has a majestic Ferris wheel and an impressive-looking roller coaster, but we weren't in the mood, and turned back to Cape May. The beach was full, its water still warm enough in September for swimmers and surfers.

Cape May's restaurants are packed on Saturday nights, so we had made advance reservations at the Ebbitt Room of the Virginia Hotel. We still had to wait 20 minutes for a table, retreating to the veranda to avoid an arpeggio-happy lounge pianist. But dinner was gracious and full of innovative juxtapositions: snapper with flash-fried spinach, Champagne-shrimp sauce and wild rice, and sea bass with chanterelle risotto and "seabeans," a salty, crunchy vegetable cultivated, the waitress said, in tide pools in Vancouver, British Columbia. Dinner for two was $100.

We considered a moonlight carriage ride for two, but all the drivers were booked. So we rambled through town, with no particular place to go, enjoying the quiet streets.

On Sunday, we made the round of antiques shops, looking into all the nooks of the multidealer Rocking Horse. Back in town, we joined a group carriage tour. Betsy, the driver, offered tidbits of Cape May lore: that the Queen's Hotel (102 Ocean Street) used to be a bordello, how dunes were built to keep the ocean from flooding Beach Drive, and where Norman Rockwell spent summers (at 660 Hughes Street).

On foot, we looked in on the Congress Hall Hotel, a remnant of Cape May's 19th-century heyday that was last rebuilt in 1879; John Philip Sousa used to perform there, and President Benjamin Harrison made it his Summer White House in 1890–91. It's now under renovation, with fancy shops along its tall colonnade and the salvaged anchor of a Spanish warship on the lawn.

We stopped at Rick's Gourmet Cafe, which serves seven flavors of coffee along with muffins, croissants, Key lime pie, and tiramisu, and we contemplated the waves one last time. And then, reluctantly, we headed back toward the 20th century.

CAPE MAY ESSENTIALS

Information about Cape May, New Jersey, can be obtained from the **Greater Cape May Chamber of Commerce,** Railroad Station, Lafayette Street (☎ 609/884-5508), open weekdays 9am to 8pm, weekends 9am to 5pm.

GETTING THERE

By Car   From Manhattan, take the Garden State Pkwy. to the end; bear left and take the Cape May Canal Bridge, which leads onto Lafayette Street and into Cape May.

By Bus   New Jersey Transit (☎ 201/762-5100) operates a local bus to Cape May. The ride is five hours and costs $26.75 one way, $48.25 round trip (half-price for children 5 to 12; free for those under 4). Buses leave the Port Authority Bus Terminal, Eighth Ave. and 42nd St., Manhattan, daily at 12:45pm and 5pm (5:45pm on Saturday and Sunday).

ACCOMMODATIONS

Abigail Adams Bed and Breakfast by the Sea, 12 Jackson St. (☎ 609/884-1371). Open year-round. $125 for a room with an ocean view and shared bath to $175 for a room with an ocean view and a private bath in summer, $85 to $135 in winter. Rates are based on double occupancy and include breakfast. Two-night minimum on weekends, three-night minimum on holidays. Reservations necessary.

Southern Mansion at the George Allen Estate, 720 Washington St. (☎ 800/381-3888 or 609/884-7171). Open year-round. Rooms (all with private baths) $195 to $295 from June to September, with a three-night minimum; rates discounted in winter. Rates are based on double occupancy and include breakfast. Special packages also available. Children 10 and older welcome. Reservations suggested.

DINING

Axelsson's Blue Claw, 991 Ocean Dr. (☎ 609/884-5878). Open daily 5pm from the end of May through the end of October; then weekends from late October through late May.

The Ebbit Room of the Virginia Hotel, 25 Jackson St. (☎ 609/884-5700). Open daily 5:30 to 9:30pm (until 10pm on Friday and Saturday). Reservations recommended.

Frescos, 412 Bank St. (☎ 609/884-0366). Open early May to mid-October, daily 5 to 10pm.

The Lobster House, Fisherman's Wharf (☎ 609/884-8296). Open daily 11:30am to 3pm and 5 to 10pm (closed Sunday lunch). **Rick's Gourmet Cafe,** 315 Beach Dr. (☎ 609/884-3181). Open daily 7am to 10pm (until 6pm Wednesday). Closed from January 1 to mid-February.

ATTRACTIONS

Beach Theater, 711 Beach Dr. (☎ 609/884-4403). Call for current schedule. Tickets $7 adults, $4.75 seniors and children; $4.75 for all before 6pm.

Cape May Bird Observatory, Cape May Point (☎ 609/884-2736). An information center and workshop center operated by the New Jersey Audubon Society. Open daily 9am to 5pm. Free admission.

Cape May Firemen's Museum, Washington and Franklin sts. (☎ 609/884-9512). On display is a fire truck and memorabilia. Open all year, daily 8am to 6pm (if you arrive to find it closed, just go into the firehouse and someone will open it up for you). Free admission.

Cape May Lighthouse, Lighthouse Ave. (☎ 800/275-4278, 609/884-8656, or

609/884-5404). Early April to October 20, open weekdays 10am to 6pm, weekends 9am to 6pm; from Oct. 21 to November 30, open Friday through Sunday noon to 3pm; from December 1 to early April, closed for restoration. Admission $3.50 adult, free for one child accompanied by an adult, $1 for additional children.

Cape May Point State Park, Lighthouse Ave. (County Rte. 629), Cape May Point (☎ 609/884-2159). Nature trails, picnics, museum display. Open daily from dawn to dusk. Free admission.

Emlen Physick Estate, 1048 Washington St. (☎ 609/884-5404); also houses the **Mid-Atlantic Center for the Arts** (☎ 800/275-4278). A Victorian stick-style house museum offering daily guided tours from 10am to

5pm from mid-March through January 2; closed the rest of January and reopens for weekend visits in February. Admission $6 adults, $3 children 3 to 12.

CONFECTIONS

Fralinger's, 324 Washington St. (☎ 609/884-5695).
Fudge Kitchen, 513 Washington Mall and 728 Beach Dr. (☎ 800/233-8343).
Laura's Fudge Shop, 311 Washington Mall (☎ 609/884-1777).

Morrow's Nut House, 722 Boardwalk (☎ 609/884-4966) and 321 Washington Mall (☎ 609/884-3300).
Petroff's, 425 Beach Dr., (☎ 609/884-3075).

BEACHES

Sunset Beach, Sunset Blvd., Lower Township. No lifeguards are on duty and swimming is not recommended. No passes or beach tags are required.

Town Beaches, along Beach Dr. Beach tags are available for $4 per day; $9 per week or $15 for the season (from Memorial Day through Labor Day).

CARRIAGE RIDES

Cape May Carriage Company, Washington and Ocean sts. (☎ 609/884-4466). Operates all year except January, weather permitting. May through the end of September, daily 10am to 3pm and 6 to 10pm, October through December and mid-February to early May weekends only (same hours). A half-hour group ride accommodating up to eight people costs $8 for adults and $3 for children 2 to 11. A half-hour private ride for six people is $30 for two adults, $40 for four adults, $3 for each child.

MINIATURE GOLF

Ocean Putt Golf, 401 Beach Dr. (☎ 609/884-7808). Open, weather permitting, Memorial Day through Labor Day, daily 9am to 10pm; weekends only early April through late May and mid-September through mid-October. $2.50 per person during the day, $3 at night.

ANTIQUING AND OTHER SHOPPING

Rocking Horse Antiques, 405 W. Perry St., West Cape May (☎ 609/898-0737). Open daily 11am to 5pm.
Uniquely Yours, 33 Perry St. (☎ 609/898-0008). Women's apparel and gifts. Open mid-February through New Year's Day, weekdays 11am to 5pm, weekends 10am to 6pm; closed January 2 through mid-February.
Whale's Tale, 312 Washington Mall (☎ 609/884-4808). Jewelry, gifts, and toys. Open daily 10am to 9pm April through mid-October, daily 10am to 5pm thereafter.

ATLANTIC CITY FOR LOW ROLLERS

by Jon Pareles

W<small>E WERE LOW ROLLERS IN A HIGH-</small>
roller town. My wife and I learned that the moment we arrived at
Bally's Park Place to spend a weekend in Atlantic City.

Here was a city, I'd anticipated, for pop culture epiphanies. Its
streets are on the Monopoly board; Miss America is crowned there
every September. It's a place where American dreams of easy money
and perpetual pleasure are vigorously marketed, where there are shows
every night and the ocean is just a few steps away from the hoopla.
Beyond three evenings of entertainment—Donna Summer, the Beach
Boys, and a revue called "Hot Cha Cha"—our plans were indefinite:
stroll the boardwalk, laze on the beach, eat seafood, and gamble a
little. We lost our first gamble at the reception desk.

I thought I had reserved a nonsmokers' room through Accommodations Express (☎ 800/444-7666), a citywide reservations service.
Bally's Park Place, with 1,300 rooms, was the only casino hotel that
had a weekend room available three weeks in advance. At the desk, I
was shown that the reservation voucher actually said a nonsmoking
room was a "request"; by 5pm on a Friday, none were available.

Room 290 ($160 a night) had a king-size bed and an Olympic-
size bathroom, with a shower and a marble bathtub built for two. It
also had an aroma: two-thirds ashtray, one-third grease from a boardwalk restaurant, plus a touch of air-conditioner mold. There were
crumbs in the top dresser drawer. We figured we wouldn't linger there,
and anyway, it was time to go out on the town.

The way to the boardwalk, and just about anywhere else, led through the casino. On the hallway speakers, Donald Fagen sang, "What a beautiful world this could be." Past the bank machines, past the cash-advance machine, past the cash-advance counter—a liquid-asset meltdown waiting to happen—was the giant room, its upper reaches illuminated with neon fireworks announcing things like "Rapid 5 Way" and "Quartermania!"

Like most casinos, it was designed for disorientation, with no clear path to the exits, no daylight, no clocks. The smoke-filled room pulsated with a big, burbling, ever-changing C chord from the slot machines, all tuned to the same key and tootling at once—a Minimalist's dream—punctuated by the clatter of coins hitting metal and an occasional big jackpot siren. On the way through, I dropped quarters into machines; one paid back 50 cents.

The wide boardwalk relieved any claustrophobia. On one side, the Atlantic rolled in, green and luminous; on the other, casino hotel towers reared overhead, while pizza places and souvenir stands pressed up to the boardwalk. An elaborate old vaudeville theater, with most of its rococo facade still intact, was now a karaoke bar; someone was bellowing a Beatles song.

The true boardwalk attraction was the endless parade: muscular guys in fishnet tank tops, elderly couples gently supporting each other, Jersey girls in fluorescent bikinis and lone men ogling them, camera-toting tour groups, dealers in casino uniforms, sunburned families dressed in clashing T-shirts. Every so often, a couple would pass on wheels, pushed along in one of Atlantic City's trademarks: the rolling chair, a wickerwork pram big enough for two adults.

Inside Trump Plaza, a few blocks away, was a riot of reflective surfaces: mirrors, marble, crystal chandeliers. This, the decor suggested, is the palatial luxury that's on the other side of your winning bet. Lest we overlook just how opulent it was, there were reminders: A sign next to a flower arrangement announced that the blooms were "actual living specimens changed frequently for your viewing pleasure."

Like the other casino hotels, Trump Plaza strives to be a self-contained enclave, with dining options that climb the class ladder:

deli, all-you-can-eat buffet, Italian, steakhouse, Chinese. Living it up, we headed to the deluxe floor, where we found that one thing hasn't been changed by Donald Trump's first divorce. The ritziest place is still called Ivana's; it's a Continental restaurant in subdued shades of mauve and pink, with artificial orchids everywhere. We settled into a banquette and savored the cushioned quietude.

After the wine arrived, so did Sandye, carrying an old-fashioned-looking camera with a lollipop flash. For a second, we were a couple in a 1930s movie; we posed for photos. "Now cheek to cheek," Sandye instructed. Dinner was pricey but satisfying: fresh, filler-free crab medallions ($13.50), impeccably grilled salmon and vegetables ($28). Sandye returned from her darkroom with prints for our approval; our first Atlantic City souvenirs, if we wanted them, would be $70 for a full set, from 8x10s to wallet size.

Because we'd lingered over dinner, we ended up with seats near the back of the showroom for Donna Summer. By theater standards, though, we were still fairly close. After a comedian came "Miss Donna Summer," with a full-scale production: smoke, lights and, every few songs, another wig and glittering gown. Her voice was strong and sure, its gospel foundation coming through; her songs promised that we'd work through setbacks, find the love we sought, and then have a party. By the time she sang "Last Dance," people were on their feet, hands in the air, pounding on tables, all optimism renewed. "Be kind, have a good time," Miss Summer urged. Along with the rest of the audience, we poured into the casino.

Central casting had been at work, from the frowzy, downtrodden-looking working people at the quarter slot machines to a suave couple at the baccarat table: a young man in a black sport jacket with his hair slicked back and his arm around a blonde in a black spaghetti-strap dress. She wore a thin gold chain around one bicep.

We tried the slots somewhat more seriously this time. With $10 in quarters, we searched for a likely machine. Patriot Plus? Flaming Sevens? The main iconography seemed to be fruit, numbers, explosions or red, white, and blue symbols. The machines absorbed our money at a leisurely pace, giving back a quarter or two after we'd spent three. A woman asked my wife to guard her machine while she went to the restroom; when she returned, her next quarter bought a big jackpot. For us, good Samaritanism didn't pay off. Twenty minutes later, we'd lost the last quarter.

Outside on the boardwalk, the night skyline was a clash of corporate logos and egos. Bally's Park Place flashed pink lights, spelling out its ownership one 12-story-high letter at a time; the Taj Mahal monolith read Trump Taj Mahal Trump. A beggar strolled along, looking at the coins in his cup. "That ain't nothing!" he declared. "There's the money, right there!" he continued, gesturing toward Caesars.

At Peanut World, we looked at postcards, T-shirts, refrigerator magnets with names on them. (There was a Marla, but no Ivana.) On a bench outside, a man and a woman, both in security guard uniforms with badges, shared a smooch. We returned to our room, trying not to inhale.

Juice and Some Advice

The next morning brought a promising room-service breakfast of fresh-squeezed juice (a 12-ounce tumbler for $3.25) and muffins (two for $1.95). I looked at the Gaming Guide pamphlet, but it was too early to comprehend sentences like "Pass Line and Don't Pass Line Bets may be made only on the Come Out Roll and may not be bet after the point is established."

After breakfast, we begged the reception desk for a smoke-free room. To our surprise, we got one: Room 862 ($170 a night). No bathtub; two double beds rather than a king. Like the other room, it had no clock. But it was on a nonsmoking floor, and its view evoked Atlantic City's history before the casinos came. One of the city's most majestic hotels, the Marlborough-Blenheim, had stood on the current site of Bally's tower. But the older part of the complex, where our rooms were, was formerly the Hotel Dennis, a golden stone Beaux-Arts-style resort that was flourishing at the turn of the century. From Room 862, we looked along a line of mansard roofs toward the ocean. Our spirits improved.

Other casinos beckoned, each pushing a theme. Caesars worked the Roman angle with employees in togas and tunics. Claridge's had renovated a park by the boardwalk in exchange for building a people-mover overhead; the conveyor belt carried us into a morass of hokey nostalgia, with 1950s oldies on the speakers and varsity-letter Cs on the uniforms. Unfortunately, we were too early to see the daily jitterbug contest. The people mover, of course, was strictly one-way; to leave, we walked back through the park, a more pleasant route.

Taffy and Waves

Back on the boardwalk, the bracingly utilitarian slogan "Cut to fit the mouth" drew us into a saltwater taffy shop: James's, established in 1880. We left with half a pound, found a bench, and dug in to some of the best taffy either of us had ever tasted, newly made and robustly flavored. Waves splashed behind us, seagulls chortled, the sun beat down, the boardwalk parade ambled by; it was a definitive Jersey Shore moment. We returned to James's for some "chocolate-sealed" (dark chocolate–covered) taffy; it was even better.

Fortified by sugar, we entered the big one: the Trump Taj Mahal. The giant white complex was a grand Orientalist fantasy, with spires and crenellations, commingling cartoon visions of Arabia, Persia, and the Indian subcontinent. Employees wore permutations of purple harem wear, and as if to complete the picture a good number of the patrons were South Asians in veils and saris. They weren't there for the food; theme or no theme, there's no Indian restaurant in the Taj Mahal.

But there was an exhibition and sale of rock and movie memorabilia: a Beatles contract for a 1965 Atlanta concert (with an anti-segregation clause), personal replies to early fan mail from the Rolling Stones, a package of Supremes White Bread, and a set of rubber

Mr. Spock ears. As we were leaving, a veiled woman was examining a full-size Batmobile: multiculturalism, Atlantic City style.

The boardwalk was getting crowded; we decided to dine a few blocks inland. The Knife and Fork Inn, established in 1912, was where Susan Sarandon and Burt Lancaster had celebrated their luck in the film *Atlantic City*. A white quasi-Tudor building on the outside, with a heraldic pattern of crossed knives and forks, it had a dark, wood-paneled Romanesque dining room with vaulted ceilings. It was the Platonic ideal of a shore restaurant, with motherly service, vegetables à la carte, and hearty, straightforward seafood dishes, notably a bouillabaisse ($20) rich in fennel. A woman at the next table urged us to try the deep-dish blueberry pie, but we were sated.

We had wanted to see a Las Vegas–style revue, and "Hot Cha Cha," the Latin extravaganza at Merv Griffin's Resorts, filled the bill; it promised "more than 1,500 feet of ruffles." All those ruffles didn't hide the showgirls' legs or the showboys' chests, as they shimmied their way through a giddy gringo's-eye tour south of the border. Dancing cactuses? Neon pineapples? Definitely.

"Hot Cha Cha" was the kind of show where the blond American couple upstages the natives, and where Brazil was represented by Peter Allen's "I Go to Rio." Authenticity or political correctness wasn't even on a distant horizon, but gender bending was approved. During the Carmen Miranda number, two beefy men chosen from the audience reappeared in gargantuan drag, happily dancing with fruit headdresses.

Shows like "Hot Cha Cha" are where vaudeville went; the revue included a bolo-twirling act and a wily, rubber-faced, wordless comedian, Elan, who inveigled grown men into hopping over an imaginary jump rope. Perhaps all the audience participation in casino showrooms—the comedians always asking, "And where are you from?"—is a consolation prize; you may not win big, but you're a star anyway.

Exhilarated by the revue, we thought we'd try another casino. But on Saturday night, Resorts was packed; so was the Taj Mahal next door, with every slot machine in use and blackjack tables crowded two deep. Ditto for Bally's. We fled.

A Fair and Casinos

By Sunday, we had seen enough climate-controlled entertainment complexes, and decided to venture farther into the city. The fourth annual Kentucky Avenue Renaissance street fair was being held that weekend. "Renaissance," we discovered, as in urban renewal. A block away from the casinos, Atlantic City turns shabby; Atlantic Avenue is lined with pawnshops. But Kentucky Avenue was trying to reclaim some of its former luster.

On the way to the festival, we lingered outside Christ's Tabernacle, a Kentucky Avenue storefront where a tambourine-shaking gospel service was in full cry. It's the only regular live music on what was once Atlantic City's main street for black entertainment. From 1934 to 1985, Club Harlem had presented blues and rhythm-and-blues headliners, from Cab Calloway to Al Green. It was demolished in 1992 after its roof collapsed. Its red front doors are preserved, however, down the block at the Kentucky Avenue Museum. Sidney Trusty, once the drummer in Club Harlem's house band, was at the entrance collecting donations and urging visitors to sign the guest book.

The museum was like a scrapbook mounted on the walls: letters, photos, gold records, newspaper clippings, a hand-painted tie showing Mr. Trusty's drum kit, sports rankings from the Barmaids Association League. The jumble of memorabilia evoked a hardworking community, where entertainment, politics, and entrepreneurship were all entwined. Now Kentucky Avenue was looking forward to the big supermarket to be built on a vacant lot. Outside on the street fair stage, a group called Crystal Clear was singing a Marvin Gaye song, "Ah, mercy, mercy me, things ain't what they used to be."

We walked to Mississippi Avenue for a look at Atlantic City's own Little Italy, which is called Ducktown, and its renowned White House Sub Shop, a dinerlike place with a rippling aluminum interior and photographs of sandwich-loving celebrities through the years; was that Luciano Pavarotti or Dom DeLuise?

Back on the boardwalk, a sort of beauty pageant was in progress. Women in high heels and bikinis, with ribbons that read Miss Tropical Club, were doing a runway strut for a man with a video camera and various uninvited onlookers. "We used to be built like that," one gray-haired woman remarked to a friend. "Forty years ago."

Beach and Beach Boys

We still hadn't been to the beach. From our room, I called Bally's front desk to ask for a beach towel. Apparently the request was unprecedented; everybody used the pool. Leaving my wife to relax, I headed for the sand. The water looked clear; the shore, littered with cups and cans, was not. A jagged hunk of glass at the tide line finally turned me away. When I crossed the boardwalk again, a small knot of people had gathered near Bally's entrance, and there was music. A woman with deformed limbs was prone on a hospital gurney, playing "Amazing Grace" on an electric keyboard with her tongue, over and over.

Better entertainment beckoned: the Beach Boys at Trump's Castle, which is not on the beach but on Atlantic City's marina, a short drive away. Portofino, the castle's ornate Italian restaurant, had a striking view of the bay. Unfortunately, the restaurant had misplaced our reservation; we were seated behind pillars. But the food, particularly an asparagus and mushroom risotto ($16.75), made it worthwhile.

And the Beach Boys turned in a thoroughly professional show. Its four longtime members—Mike Love, Al Jardine, Carl Wilson, and Bruce Johnston—had their first names emblazoned on surfboards. A backup percussionist sang the old high notes for them; four dancers did cheerleader-like routines in red, white, and blue bikinis. The old songs still sounded like summer.

For this graying crowd, the Beach Boys didn't worry that they're not boys any more; Mr. Love introduced a song as "one of Abe Lincoln's favorites." A new song about the ravaged environment, with lines about a "trail of destruction and toxic waste," barely ruffled an audience that sang along with every hit. In Atlantic City, like Las Vegas, oldies acts are the rule and spontaneity is risky. When they're gambling, audiences apparently want their entertainment to be a sure thing.

Win Some, Lose Many

On our last night, we had to gamble. The big weekend crowds had left, and Bally's casino wasn't jam-packed anymore. My wife headed for the slot machines while I sought higher stakes. I bought $100 worth of red chips at the blackjack table, where the dealer immediately recognized me as a novice. He took pity, warning me when I miscounted, raising an eyebrow when I called for one card too many. I kept betting the $15 minimum, and somehow my stack of chips grew. At one point, I stubbornly insisted on drawing a card that both the dealer and the player next to me disapproved of, and I got lucky. "He saved the table," the dealer told my neighbor, who said, "Yeah, but it still ain't right."

Clearly, I was invincible.

But not for long. The stack of chips shrank, blipped upward, and disappeared. It had taken about 15 minutes. I placed some roulette bets, on groups of 12 numbers out of a possible 36; after one win, those chips disappeared even faster. So I caught up with my wife, who had come up with a system; play only machines that don't show a recent payoff. After midnight on Sunday, there were plenty to choose from.

She had held on to her stake until I came along. It dwindled; I stopped giving advice, and she built it up again. At one point, she was slightly ahead, and I suggested we win back our previous losses. We decided we liked Haywire, a machine that sometimes stuttered out triple payments; we searched the rows of slots for Haywires. We watched spinning bars, spinning cherries, spinning pots of gold, mesmerized. She walked away from an unyielding machine; I put a quarter in and got 20 back. But the coins were slowly draining away. With $2 left from the original stake, we joined innumerable other gamblers and quit while we were behind.

Driving out of Atlantic City, there's a 25-cent toll on the way to the expressway. I tossed a last quarter into the machine; there, at least, I knew better than to expect anything back.

ATLANTIC CITY ESSENTIALS

THE CASINOS

Bally's Park Place Casino Hotel and Tower, Boardwalk (☎ 609/340-2222 or 609/340-2709 for show information). Daily room rates vary seasonally, from a low of $85 to $175 double for January through March, up to $155 to $215 for June through September.

Offered indefinitely in the Park Cabaret Theater is "Legends in Concert," a musical revue featuring impersonators of such performers as Elvis Presley, Elton John, Tina Turner, and Madonna. For show information, call the number above or **Ticketmaster** at ☎ 800/736-1420.

Caesars Atlantic City, Boardwalk and Arkansas Ave. (☎ 609/348-4411 or 800/677-7469 for show information). Daily room rates vary seasonally, from a weekday low of $140 to $180 double in summer.

Claridge's Casino Hotel, Boardwalk at Park Place (☎ 609/340-3400 for reservations and show information). $110 to $145 double in low season, to $130 to $165 in July and August.

Merv Griffin's Resorts Casino Hotel, North Carolina Ave. and the Boardwalk (☎ 609/340-6830 for reservations or 800/336-6378 for show information). Daily rates vary seasonally, from a daily lows of $100 to $130 double in low season to $175 in July and August.

Trump's Castle, 1 Castle Blvd., near Brigantine Blvd. and Heron Ave. (☎ 609/441-2000). From $74 in low season, from $90 from April to June. Portofino Restaurant is open Thursday through Monday 6 to 10pm.

Trump Plaza, Boardwalk at Mississippi Ave. (☎ 609/441-6000 for reservations or 800/759-8786 for show information). The restaurants—Ivana's, Max's Steakhouse, Roberto's, and Fortune's—each serve dinner from 6 to 11pm on different days; call to see which ones are open on the days you are in town.

Trump Taj Mahal, Boardwalk, at Virginia Ave. (☎ 609/449-1000 for reservations and show information). $125 to $150 double in low season, $150 to $225 in summer.

DINING BEYOND THE CASINOS

Knife and Fork Inn, at Albany, Pacific, and Atlantic aves. (☎ 609/344-1133). Open Tuesday through Friday and Sunday 5:30 to 10pm, Saturday 5:30 to 10:30pm; closed Monday.

White House Sub Shop, Arctic and Mississippi aves. (☎ 609/345-1564). Open Monday through Saturday 10am to midnight, Sunday 11am to midnight.

ATTRACTIONS BEYOND THE CASINOS

James's Saltwater Taffy. There are three locations along the boardwalk: at New York Ave. (☎ 609/344-1519), open daily 9am to 11:30pm; at Pennsylvania Ave. (☎ 609/344-1519), open daily 9am to 11:30pm; and at Brighton Ave. (☎ 609/344-2408), open Sunday through Friday 9am to 11pm and Saturday 9am to midnight.

Kentucky Avenue Museum, 42 North Kentucky Ave., between Atlantic and Arctic aves. (☎ 609/348-8906). Open Saturday and Sunday 10am to 6pm; closed weekdays. Admission by contribution.

Pennsylvania

ELEGANCE IN THE POCONOS: SKYTOP LODGE

by Patricia Leigh Brown

THERE WAS TERROR IN OUR HEARTS when we walked into the pine-paneled lobby of Skytop Lodge, a grand 1920s Poconos resort brimming with people in corsages and other winsomely extinct species.

"Gentlemen wear coats after 6:30," read the sign posted outside the dining room. "Bermuda shorts, tailored slacks, buttoned collared sport shirts, and other modest sports attire may be worn until 6:30." No one in my family—weddings aside—has ever worn anything that might be construed as "attire." And all around Skytop that evening, there were grandmothers clutching tightly woven straw pocketbooks and children sipping Shirley Temples in ties and petticoats (this gleaned fleetingly before my 18-month-old overturned his high-chair tray and catapulted fresh berries, ice cream, and grilled cheese sandwiches all over the dining-room floor).

But a weekend at Skytop, a meticulously maintained fieldstone hotel that is set on 5,500 acres and looks like a grand French edifice or an oversize funeral home, depending on your mood, is an occasionally treacly but ultimately charming throwback to an era of manicured lawns and starched white table linens before the Poconos became ridden with the Claws 'n' Paws Wild Animal Park and the like.

From the long winding driveway, to the clipped lawns and rocker-lined verandah, it is a genteel, country clubbish place—blue-haired and almost Southern in feeling—where the drinks are mixed but the composition of the guests is not.

Built in 1928 on a plateau three miles north of the village of Canadensis in northeastern Pennsylvania, the 166-room resort still retains a 1920s atmosphere, including a coffee shop selling "patent medicines" and hiking sticks that have "Skytop" emblazoned in brass. Now a lone survivor in a region once rich with elegant resorts, Skytop was a private club, mostly for wealthy Philadelphians, until the 1960s. The landscape is formal, with two magnificent flower gardens and a manmade lake. The hotel has not one but two card rooms, the North Card Room and the South Card Room, and the floors have a reassuring creak.

The comfortable, overstuffed library is completely devoid of paperbacks. A letter from Robert Clothier, president emeritus of Rutgers University, sums up the feeling: "There has been created at Skytop an atmosphere and an environment in which beauty, peace, and confidence and good manners all have their natural place." Indeed, there is a sense that the dress code—a.k.a. "good manners"—is part of what draws people to Skytop year after year (Judge John J. Sirica supposedly used to escape Watergate here). Many of the people we met during our weekend stay, including vast numbers of families with grandparents, had been guests many times before. In addition to the 18-hole golf course, the swimming pools, the tennis courts, the lake, the trout stream, archery, croquet, putting green, jogging and hiking trails (and tobogganning, ice skating, and skiing in the wintertime), Skytop's guests may be searching for something more. "They may be," suggests Harris Frederick Smith, son of a founder, "trying to instill values in their children." Instilling values was not on our weekend agenda. All we wanted to have was a good time and escape the humidity. Even though "bathing attire" was not allowed anywhere but the pool area, we found Skytop to be a generally unstuffy and relaxed place to spend a family weekend, with a well-organized and good-humored staff.

Tennis, Gardens, Hikes

A flyer called *Skylites* fills you in on the daunting schedule of daily activities. On this particular weekend, there was a round-robin tennis clinic; a garden tour; a fitness hike; a wet workout in the pool; a van ride to the Goose Pond wilderness, a habitat of tree-covered swamps, shrubby bogs, open waters, and oak-pitch pine forests, and a 4pm tea and piano concert. There was also Camp in the Clouds, a fully staffed day camp for children ages 3 to 12. The Saturday night Elimination Dance and Grand March was described as an "ever popular" Skytop tradition.

Our room faced south toward a garden filled with zinnias, amaranthus, and dahlias. The room was comfortable and pretty, with green carpeting and pink and green chintz draperies. Thanks to corridors blessed with several sets of double doors, it was extremely quiet.

Our first morning, we headed for the lake. My husband, Roger, and elder son, Jacob, four and a half, embarked on a father-son rowboat expedition while I opted for a hike to the trout stream with 18-pound Gabriel on my back.

On our walk, we passed numerous joggers wearing headsets and people doing chin-ups on the fitness trail (as well as numerous houses with three-car garages). But most indicative of Skytop's zen were the trees. As if nature wasn't enough, they came inspirationally tagged with passages from the Psalms and Tennyson.

After gorging from some of the tallest blueberry bushes I'd ever seen, we came to the mouth of the trout stream where Ryan, a boy from New Jersey, was pulling in a nice brown trout using worms purchased at the Canadensis Gulf station. Although the three-quarter-mile trout stream itself is for fly-fishing only, the stream's mouth is fair game for bait fishermen (or so Ryan's father said). Gabriel watched enraptured. I had a severe case of trout envy.

Skipper and Co-Skipper

Back at the dock, we were treated to the sight of the father-son ship coming to shore, captains side by side, Dad's hand on one oar and son's hand on the other. The fishermen at the dock who were using bagels for bait weren't having much luck. "These fish aren't Jewish," sighed a lady from New Jersey.

Our token organized activity was "tractor-drawn hayride to a lakeside lunch picnic." Beforehand, we went downstairs to check out the "rec room": a vintage pine-paneled space containing a great indoor miniature golf course and a tacky souvenir shop selling bone china fawns, among other things. Skytop also has two outdoor playgrounds, a blessing.

At the appointed hour, a tractor laden with straw pulled up to the great circular driveway. Our teenage tractor mates were deeply ensconced in the book *Pocono Ghosts, Legends, and Lore*. As we passed the golf course, we paid silent homage to Marv and Marsha, two resident ghosts and former guests. Their ashes, according to the book, are strewn across the 15th fairway.

We had a wonderful summer picnic of hot dogs, hamburgers, and Rice Krispies treats, and later spent a blissful afternoon at the pool, or pools—including a baby pool that both children enjoyed. Skytop has old-fashioned locker rooms, with painted wire lockers and the musky smell of generations of feet. After a brief trip up to the tower, situated in the upper reaches of the mansard roof, we decided to investigate Camp in the Clouds, in the hopes of crashing the marshmallow roast, the day's finale.

Having survived parachute games, lifesaving skills, a drawing contest, pillow polo, and sponge tag, the three counselors still looked to be genuinely enjoying themselves. Outside, grave decisions were being made by the campfire concerning whether to have marshmallows burned or toasted, while inside several children were examining a red-bellied snake, a Skytop find. Then everybody played tag. Apparently, Skytop's gentility extends to Camp in the Clouds. "Corey!" one of the counselors said sharply. "We don't use that kind of language at camp!"

Dancing and Singing

After a so-so dinner—fresh ingredients, uninspiringly prepared—we went to the club room to watch *101 Dalmatians*. Then my husband and children went to bed. But it was difficult to sleep. The unmistakable strains of "Hokey Pokey" were wafting through the air.

It was time for the Elimination Dance and Grand March, led by not one but three social directors. The dance is a spectacle, somewhat akin to musical chairs, in which more than 200 people of all ages, dressed to the hilt, hold hands in twos and then weave inside and outside the hotel as they sing songs like "Zip-a-Dee-Doo-Dah" and "Battle Hymn of the Republic" at the top of their lungs.

I tried not to think dark thoughts about "family values" or

> **HOW TO PLAN YOUR OWN SKYTOP WEEKEND**
>
> **Skytop Lodge** is at 1 Skytop, Skytop, PA 18357-1099 (☎ **800/345-7759**). Daily rates (meals included) are $285 to $435 Monday through Thursday, $300 to $500 Friday through Sunday, plus 15% service charge. There's an additional $20 service charge for each child under 16 staying in parents' room (maximum 2 children); a separate children's room is half off adult rates midweek, $100 off on weekends and holidays. Golf and seniors packages available.

Disney's takeover of the universe as the crowd wound into increasingly elaborate human chains, clearly loving every minute of it. Like square dancing or the polka, it is exactly the kind of wholesome activity that has vanished from the landscape. It was clearly the highlight of the weekend for its participants. Glory Hallelujah! Bring on the punch and cookies!

Seeking relief, I went out to the south garden to join a stargazing session. I spotted what I thought was a shooting star, only to find out that it was actually a satellite, one of 4,000 orbiting the planet. Suddenly, that olde time yearning symbolized by the Grand March—life before T-shirts and sneakers, or, in my case, heavens uncluttered by man's imprint—seemed to make more sense. "Everyone smile!" yelled a stargazer, looking upward. "The C.I.A. is taking our picture!"

Before the 2¹/₂-hour drive back to New York City on Sunday morning, my family hiked to Indian Ladder Falls, one of several Skytop waterfalls, while I headed to the trout stream, accessible with a $14 Skytop permit. Beautiful little clearings of green were spaced at regular intervals along the stream. The trout were rising, but the clear, still water called for a fluid cast. Having fished hardly at all since becoming a mom, I had the distinction of losing three. But I perfected my knots (why is it no one talks about knots when waxing eloquent about fly-fishing?) and spent a perfect hour, having the water all to myself, on the stream.

I was thinking of fish. And of a time in the not-so-distant future when my sons, equipped with patience by then, will be able to share one of life's greatest joys with me.

BUCKS COUNTY, HISTORY'S COUNTRY HOME

by Lisa W. Foderaro

STRETCHED OUT LISTLESSLY ALONG the Delaware River in eastern Pennsylvania, its arcadian landscape dabbed with pre-Revolutionary houses, close but not too close to New York City, Bucks County has always held an attraction for those with an artistic bent.

At the turn of the century, a half-dozen landscape artists formed the New Hope Group and began exhibiting their works together nationally. The beauty of Bucks County was thus transported to the Corcoran Gallery in Washington, the Detroit Institute of Arts, and elsewhere. Year-round classes in *plein air* painting further established the reputation of New Hope as a leading art colony.

A few decades later, another infusion of artistic energy came from New York's literati, who made Bucks County their country playground in the 1930s and 40s. Moss Hart, the playwright, librettist, and director, bought a handyman's special on 87 acres in New Hope, following the lead of his longtime collaborator, George S. Kaufman. Then came Dorothy Parker, queen of the Algonquin Round Table, who plunked down $45,000 for a 14-room fixer-upper on more than 100 acres in Pipersville. And in 1940, Oscar Hammerstein II, the lyricist, settled his family on a 72-acre working farm in Doylestown, where there was surely more wind sweeping down the plain than in his native New York City. Perhaps it was no coincidence that three years later he penned the Broadway musical hit *Oklahoma!*

Today, Bucks County is still lovely to behold, its meadows and streams and old stone structures mostly unspoiled, particularly in the northern half. But in other respects, namely its commercial life, Bucks County has the feel of a tourist destination that has overripened.

Its creative edge has dulled, overtaken by the art galleries and modish shops and restaurants that have recently cropped up across the Delaware in Hunterdon County, New Jersey. New Hope itself, like Provincetown at the tip of Cape Cod, has become a honky-tonk mecca, with stores devoted entirely to wind chimes or T-shirts. Some of New Hope's finer antiques stores have moved across the river to Lambertville, New Jersey, in recent years. And in spite of some remaining gems, like the frowzy and esoteric Farley's Bookshop and the recently restored Mansion Inn, New Hope's esprit is better captured by a shop that shamelessly calls itself the Tourist Trap.

Fortunately, there's a lot more to Bucks County than New Hope. If you know where to look and what to avoid, you can piece together a weekend that takes advantage of the county's artistic past, enshrined in a handful of outstanding museums, as well as its rich history, which reaches back past the rompings of this century to the cheerless days of the Revolutionary War. One of the most potent images of the war, George Washington's troops crossing the Delaware, originated on these shores in 1776 when General Washington used McConkey's Ferry Inn as his headquarters during the maneuver. The tavern is now the cornerstone of Washington Crossing Historic Park.

A Country Inn

While many shops and restaurants have a worn-out Eisenhower-era feel, there are several inviting inns and bed-and-breakfasts. Few are as tasteful and fresh as Evermay-on-the-Delaware in Erwinna, a village in northern Bucks County. Dating from 1790, the three-story, 11-room inn, set on 25 acres, is a study in fastidiousness. On the ground floor, generous sprays of fresh flowers and real classical music (not Muzak) fill the double parlor, appointed with a camelback settee, grandfather clock, baby grand piano and other Victorian antiques. The only disappointment was a gas fireplace that threw off a lukewarm breath on a chilly day.

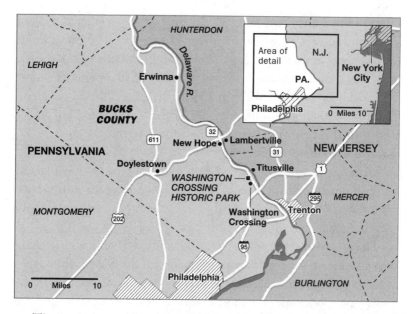

The innkeepers who restored Evermay 15 years ago, Ron Strouse and Fred Cresson, recently sold it. Doubling as chefs, they had drawn national praise for their six-course dinner on weekends. Thankfully, the new owners, William and Danielle Moffly, haven't changed a thing. They even enlisted the former innkeepers in the search for a new chef. He is Jeffrey Lauble, a graduate of the Culinary Institute of America and a former sous-chef at Evermay.

A recent dinner featured gingered butternut squash soup; wild mushrooms with ricotta and rosemary polenta; organic greens with grapefruit, pinenuts, and a mint vinaigrette; loin of venison in a hunter sauce; a cheese course of St. Andre, Montrachet goat cheese, and double Gloucester; and a warm pecan torte. The $52 prix fixe dinner, which begins with a glass of Champagne and an hors d'oeuvre, is served Friday, Saturday, and Sunday in the pale peach, candlelit dining room. Guests staying two nights are required to dine once at the inn. The restaurant is also open to the public.

All the inn's rooms are smartly furnished with antiques and include luxurious little touches like an extra layer of sheeting on top of the blankets and cordials of hazelnut liqueur set out in the evenings. Each room is named for a famous person in Bucks County history: The James A. Michener Room sports a weathered copy of *Texas* on the dresser, while the Oscar Hammerstein Room features framed sheet music from *South Pacific* and *Oklahoma!* Perhaps the most elegant guest room in the inn—and at $170 a night, the most expensive—is the Col. William Erwin Room on the second floor. There is no memento of old Colonel Erwin, a Revolutionary officer who owned much of the land around the inn, but the room has a baronial headboard and matching marble-topped bureau, as well as a Victorian settee and side chair, uneven wide-planked floorboards, and old-fashioned floral wallpaper. The decorative fireplace stuffed with dried flowers, while pretty, proved a huge frustration to a couple whose idea of nirvana is reading in bed in front of a blazing fire.

The inn, with seven columns and 17 shuttered windows marching across its cream-colored facade, fronts on the Delaware, although a little-trafficked road separates the property from the river. The third-floor guest rooms offer the most dramatic views of the water and the hills of Hunterdon County beyond. There are a few additional suites in a cottage and carriage house next to the main house.

The Michener Museum

A good starting point for exploring Bucks County is the James A. Michener Art Museum in Doylestown, the county seat. The outskirts have succumbed to unrestrained strip development, but downtown has some great architecture, a few inventive restaurants, particularly the Black Walnut at 80 West State Street, and an art cinema.

Bucks County may lack Hunterdon's thriving art galleries, but it can be proud of the Michener Museum, which opened in 1988 in a marvelously moody stone fortress built a century earlier as the county jail. The museum was named for the Pulitzer Prize–winning novelist, now 90 and living in Texas. A passionate art collector, Mr. Michener grew up in Bucks County and gave a $1 million endowment to the museum when it opened.

While the Michener Museum presents traveling shows of national and international artists, its spiritual core is the collection of 19th- and 20th-century works by such prominent local artists as the primitive painter Edward Hicks, known for his "Peaceable Kingdom" series, and two leading landscape painters from the turn of the century, Edward Redfield and Daniel Garber. The exhibition space of the museum is especially handsome, with high ceilings, skylights, and striking wood finishes. The museum's centerpiece is a serene, sun-filled room devoted to a 22-foot semicircular mural, *A Wooded Watershed,* which Garber painted in 1926 for the sesquicentennial celebration in Philadelphia. The mural, depicting an idealized scene of deer in a wood at the water's edge, had been lost for 60 years. But in 1992 it was discovered behind the stage curtain in an auditorium at Pennsylvania State University in Mont Alto.

In 1996, the museum opened a new wing, which includes a permanent exhibition space honoring nationally recognized artists in all media who lived in Bucks County. They include Hart, Parker, Hammerstein, the writer Pearl S. Buck, the most illustrious painters in the museum's collection, and others, including a long-gone gentleman by the name of Henry Chapman Mercer, who defies description in a single word. That's all right, however, because when you get to Bucks County and pick up any tourist brochure, you'll see his name—and the three landmark buildings he left as his legacy—everywhere.

Mercer was by all accounts a brilliant eccentric who was born in Doylestown and lived there at his death in 1930. He was an archeologist, architect, fiddler, tile maker, and collector who spoke six languages and apparently perused almost all of the 6,000 books in his library, as they bear his notations. After studying history at Harvard and law at the University of Pennsylvania and traveling the world, Mercer got down to business, creating handmade tiles and ceramic reliefs for installation in private and public buildings. He thus became a major figure in the Arts and Crafts movement, which was a creative rebellion against machine-made goods.

In 1908, with the help of a dozen men and one horse, Mercer began construction on his dream house, a bizarrely beautiful castle he designed himself of hand-mixed, hand-poured reinforced concrete, molding the material the way a sculptor molds clay. The five-story mansion, named Fonthill, has 44 oddly shaped rooms, 32 stairwells,

18 fireplaces, and 200 windows. Just about every square foot of the interior space, whether floor, wall, or ceiling, is covered with his colorful tiles. The effect is that of an inside-out gingerbread house.

The hearth in the library is surrounded by tiles telling the story of the discovery and exploration of the New World. Another fireplace in an upstairs bedroom is framed by tiles depicting Charles Dickens's *The Pickwick Papers*. And in many of the vaulted concrete ceilings are embedded colorful ceramic grape bunches, dragons, acorns, and fleurs-de-lys. Some of the ancient ceramics Mercer collected are also set in his walls, from Babylonian tiles used for invoices and letters from 2400 B.C. to dozens of Delft tiles dating from 1600.

As soon as he finished Fonthill in 1910, Mercer began work on a new tile production center, also on his property. The Moravian Pottery and Tile Works, housed in a Spanish mission-style building and also made of reinforced concrete, cranked out tiles that were used in thousands of buildings. The Tile Works, like Fonthill, is open for tours. Visitors can watch as workers create reproductions of Mercer's tiles much as they were made in his time, with local red clay, plaster molds, and large kilns. Hundreds of ceramic reliefs and tiles are sold in the gift shop, from a single decorative tile for $5 to a "fireplace narrative" of the legend of Bluebeard for $1,820.

Mercer's third legacy is the Mercer Museum, another castle in Doylestown, which is even bigger than Fonthill and—you guessed it—made from reinforced concrete. The museum, not far from Fonthill, houses Mercer's collection of more than 50,000 tools, modes of transport and everyday household items used in America from 1700 to 1850, before the industrial age. Much as tiles cover every inch of Fonthill, the artifacts literally coat the museum interior, with the larger pieces—from saw frames to animal yokes to stage coaches—lining the walls of a soaring central court and even hanging from the ceiling. Dozens of rooms off to the sides focus on specific trades or crafts: gunsmithing, fruit preservation, printing, hat making, animal husbandry, watchmaking, mining, and so on.

A stunning find, and one of the few items not made in America, is a vampire-killing kit from early-19th-century England. The attractive leather case, lined with green felt, displays a pistol with silver bullet, ivory crucifix, wooden stake, and garlic powder. A label inside reads: "This box contains the items considered necessary for the protection of persons who travel into little known countries of Eastern Europe, where the population is plagued with a particular manifestation of evil known as vampires."

Back from the Brink

While the Mercer Museum preserves a swath of social history by gathering together things from everyday life, another Bucks County site, Washington Crossing Historic Park, embraces the great-man theory of history, commemorating a momentous event from the nation's earliest days.

By December 1776, General Washington had suffered a string of defeats. The commander of the British forces, Sir William Howe, had driven the Continental Army from Long Island and New Jersey, forcing the American troops to retreat across the Delaware to Pennsylvania. Washington badly needed a victory to muster popular support for the cause of independence. His men were exhausted, freezing, and ill-equipped, and his soldiers' tours of duty were to expire at the end of the year. No new volunteers could be expected to join a losing campaign.

So Washington planned a daring assault on the Hessian garrison at Trenton, New Jersey. The garrison was nine miles south of McConkey's Ferry Inn, the Bucks County tavern on the Delaware that was his headquarters. On Christmas night, 2,400 soldiers crossed to the New Jersey shore in stinging snow and sleet, maneuvering their boats through a gantlet of ice floes. They successfully attacked the unsuspecting—and most likely hung over—garrison at dawn, winning the Battle of Trenton in two hours and reinvigorating the Colonists' commitment to the Revolution.

There are two Washington Crossing parks, the one in Bucks County, south of New Hope, and the other, Washington Crossing State Park, across the river in Titusville, New Jersey. Naturally, the Bucks County park focuses on the activities of 1776 on its side of the river. McConkey's Ferry Inn is the highlight. Washington is believed to have eaten Christmas dinner in the tavern hours before the crossing, and a copy of a letter he wrote, with "McConkey's Ferry" appearing beneath his name, lies on a dining-room table.

Walking through the same shadowy, low-slung rooms Washington did, you experience the rush that comes from suddenly feeling connected to a piece of history. Time is compressed, and a mythic figure is brought down to human scale.

Also part of the park are two of the original buildings from the Quaker village of Taylorsville, which grew up around the inn in the early 1800s. The Mahlon K. Taylor House, built in 1817, is fully restored with period furnishings, an example of a respectably comfortable household of the day. The Taylorsville Store, which opened in 1828, is now a general store called the Patriot selling mostly souvenirs, like Colonial costume coloring books and penny candy. (The village's name was changed from Taylorsville to Washington Crossing when the park was founded in 1917.)

Before going on a tour of the properties, however, visitors are asked to sit through a half-hour film about Washington's crossing. The 1967 documentary is narrated by a pipe-smoking Chet Huntley, the former news broadcaster for NBC, who owned a historic house in Bucks County and died in 1974. The film is laughably dated and strangely circular. In between reenacted scenes of fantastic hardship, such as soldiers walking through the snow with only rags wrapped around their feet, are repeated shots of schoolchildren in cat-eye glasses and Madras plaid shirts. They are shown pouring into the same auditorium where you are sitting, taking their seats and eagerly gazing toward the front of the room. Perhaps they are looking at what we get to see when the film finally ends.

The movie screen retracts, revealing a wonderful replica of the famous Emanuel Gottlieb Leutze painting, *Washington Crossing the Delaware,* which is in the Metropolitan Museum of Art. The original, from 1851, is 21 feet across and 12 feet high, and so is this copy, skillfully painted in 1970 by Robert Williams. Somehow, the film and this painting seem to say a lot about Bucks County. It is a place respectful of the arts, proud of its history and sometimes charmingly out of step.

WHERE TO GO, AND TO STOP: BUCKS COUNTY ESSENTIALS

GETTING THERE

To reach Bucks County from Manhattan, take the New Jersey Turnpike to I-78 West. To reach New Hope, which is central, continue on I-78 West to exit 29 and pick up Rte. 287 South. Continue on Rte. 287 to Rte. 202 South, which crosses the Lambertville Bridge, and take the New Hope exit, which leads onto Rte. 32 and into New Hope. To reach Erwinna, take Rte. 32 North. To reach Washington Crossing, take Rte. 32 South.

ACCOMMODATIONS AND DINING

The Black Walnut, 80 W. State St., Doylestown (☎ 215/348-0708). Open Tuesday through Thursday noon to 2:30pm and 5:30 to 9pm, Friday and Saturday noon to 2:30pm and 5:30 to 9:30pm, Sunday 5 to 8pm. Entrees $4.25 to $8.95 at lunch, $14.95 to $22.95 at dinner.
Evermay-on-the-Delaware, Rte. 32, Erwinna (☎ 610/294-9100). Rooms (all with private baths) $95 to $180 double. Continental breakfast included. There is a two-night minimum stay on weekends and a three-night minimum on holidays. There is one seating for dinner on Friday, Saturday, and Sunday at 7:30pm.
Mansion Inn, 9 S. Main St., New Hope (☎ 215/862-1231). Rooms (all with private bath) $160 to $245. Rates are based on double occupancy and include full breakfast. There is a two-night minimum stay on weekends and a three-night minimum on holidays.

SIGHTS AND SHOPPING

Farley's Bookshop, 44 S. Main St., New Hope (☎ 215/862-2452).
James A. Michener Art Museum, 138 S. Pine St., Doylestown (☎ 215/340-9800). On permanent display are the exhibitions "James A. Michener: A Living Legacy" and "A Visual Heritage of Bucks County." Open Tuesday through Friday 10am to 4:30pm, Saturday and Sunday 10am to 5pm; closed Monday. Admission $5 adults, $4.50 seniors, $1.50 students and children 12 to 16, free for children under 12.
Mercer Museum, 84 S. Pine St., Doylestown, and **Fonthill,** E. Court St. and Swamp Rd. (Rte. 313), Doylestown, both run by the Bucks County Historical Society (☎ 215/345-0210). The museum has an extensive display of items from everyday life in the 18th and 19th centuries; Fonthill is the "concrete castle" built in the early 1900s by Henry Mercer. Open Monday through Saturday 10am to 5pm (the Mercer remains open until 9pm on Tuesday), Sunday noon to 5pm. Admission to museum or Fonthill $5 adults, $4.50 seniors, $1.50 children 6 to 17, free for children under 6. A $9 combination ticket is also available.
Moravian Pottery and Tile Works, 130 Swamp Rd. (Rte. 313), Doylestown (☎ 215/345-6722). Installations and displays of current tile production, as well as workshops in making tile and mosaics. Open daily 10am to 4:45pm; 45-minute tours are offered every half-hour. Tour admission $3 adults, $2.50 seniors, $1.50 children.
Washington Crossing Historic Park, Rte. 32, Washington Crossing (☎ 215/493-4076).

Tours of three historic houses—Hibbs House, McConkey's Ferry Inn, and the Mahlon K. Taylor House—are offered Tuesday through Saturday 9am to 5pm and Sunday noon to 5pm; closed Monday. The grounds are open from 9am until dark Tuesday through Sunday. Admission to the grounds is free. For 45-minute guided tours of the houses, admission $4 adults, $3.50 seniors, $2 children 6 to 12.

Also inside the park is the **Patriot General Store,** on Rte. 532 (☎ 215/493-5411).

Open Monday through Saturday 10am to 5pm and Sunday 12:30 to 5pm.

Washington Crossing State Historic Park, Rte. 29, Titusville, NJ (☎ 609/737-0623). On the premises are the Johnson Ferry House, a visitor center with a display of Revolutionary War artifacts, and a nature center. Open daily 8am to 8pm Memorial Day through Labor Day, daily 8am to 4:30pm the rest of the year. Tours offered Wednesday through Sunday at regular intervals. Free admission; no charge for tours.

Down on the Farm in Mount Joy

by Ralph Blumenthal

 Somewhere a child wailed, troubling the unfamiliar night. Whose child was it, I wondered groggily from deep inside a soft cocoon of sleep. I stirred awake, heart pounding. Was it mine? Where was I? My watch said 20 minutes to five. There it went again, a piteous cry that suddenly became recognizable. Now I remembered. We were far from Manhattan's comforting lullaby of police sirens. We were on a farm in Pennsylvania. Our little daughter was safe in her bed. And that ghastly din was a rooster's crowing.

We had needed an antidote to civilization, a quick and cheap respite from famous-visitor gridlock and prewinter urban blues. Nothing so venturesome as a Club Med holiday. A weekend out of the city would do. But something different, something that would hold the interest of a fidgety kindergartener who stops to pet every dog she sees and thinks food comes from D'Agostino's. The answer was clear.

As it turns out, there are many farms within reasonable driving distance of the city that accept weekend guests. The list ranges from dude ranches run like resorts to working farms where visitors can pitch in with the chores. We sought the latter and found our barnyard nirvana quite by accident. The first half-dozen places I called, from friends' recommendations and listings in a book, *Farm, Ranch and Country Vacations in America* by Pat Dickerman (Adventure Guides), were filled. Clearly, we were on to something. But one farm in the Amish country of Pennsylvania helpfully recommended another nearby that only recently began taking guests and was not yet in the guidebooks.

The place, the Olde Country Log House Farm, about a mile outside Mount Joy, had chickens, sheep, and pigs, said the owner, Jim Brubaker, adding that his brother, Luke, next door, had chickens and dairy cows as well. Our host-to-be—who insisted right off on being called Jim—offered a room that could sleep the three of us (our elder daughter was not along) for $70 a night, including breakfast. It sounded fine, and we booked it. (There is a $10 surcharge for each child.)

Zeroing in on the Amish country was a wise choice, it emerged, because of the wealth of attractions. Family-style restaurants abound, as do farmers' markets, crafts and antiques stores, and shopping outlets. Then, of course, there's the burnished beauty of the Pennsylvania Dutch countryside, where life still moves to the slow clippety-clop of the horse and buggy. Another highlight, certainly from the viewpoint of one pint-size chocoholic, is the proximity of Hershey, with its Chocolate World manufacturing tour, zoo, and amusement park. (The amusement park is closed from late September through mid-May; other Hershey attractions stay open all year.)

The downside is the distance. With heavy traffic, snacks and bathroom stops, and a vicious rainstorm, the trip from mid-Manhattan took us four hours. Certainly there are closer farms to be found. But my doubts vanished once we turned into the bucolic farmyard of a red-shuttered, gray vinyl-sided farmhouse opposite animal stalls and four tall grain silos.

Our daughter Sophie didn't wait for us to unload the car. She had spotted some children carrying cats and ran to join them. The farmhouse was a happy surprise. I had pictured rustic, barnlike quarters. This was more *House and Garden* than Ma and Pa Kettle: a modern open kitchen adjoining a skylighted living room with gas fireplace, French doors opening onto a patio, ceiling beams hung with baskets of dried flowers and an interior wall striped with the exposed logs of the original homestead, believed to date from the 1700s.

Our blue-wallpapered upstairs room was no less fetching. A magnificent blue-and-white Amish quilt covered the bed and an electric candle with pinpoint bulb flickered cozily in the window. The bedside reading lamps were large and bright, an unexpected boon. The bathroom, equally pristine, was just outside our room; we were assured that

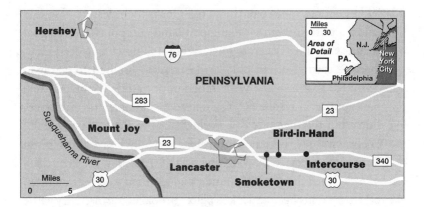

although there were two other bedrooms on the floor, we would be the only guests using it that weekend. When we got to look around later, we found that a fourth guest suite in another part of the house was larger and even lovelier, with its own bathroom, also for $70 a night, but it had been booked by a couple celebrating their anniversary.

We got a big welcome from Jim and his wife, Joanne (the gifted decorator, we learned), who introduced us to two visiting families from North Carolina and Maryland with whose children Sophie had instantly bonded. We were summarily waved to the breakfast table and, with the spontaneous intimacy of strangers at an inn, shared a feast of baked oatmeal with fruit topping, egg soufflé, bagels, and cinnamon-raisin bread with jam and honey butter. Jim needs only to work a bit on his coffee, which left us yearning for Starbucks back home.

Jim, who bears a passing resemblance to the craggy Paul Newman of *Nobody's Fool*, told us that he had traced the farm's ownership to 1867, and that his father had bought it in 1945, moving here from another Mount Joy farm. His farm spans 112 acres in two parcels, and his brother has another 75 acres, he said, inviting us on an exploratory tour.

Prying Sophie away from the cats, we went first to the chicken coop, where in the straw-lined chicken nests, Sophie was delighted to find an egg to collect. (Jim confessed later that he had left it there from the day before, his 30 chickens having "gone on strike," as he put it.) Next we moved to an outdoor pen where sheep, rams, and goats trotted toward us expectantly. Our host measured out a bucket of feed mix. "They eat grass and hay," he said. "This is their dessert." He told the children to feed them with an open hand and pointed out a goat with a curious foible: When it got scared, it fell down in a dead faint.

Then he started up an old Farmall tractor hitched to a wagon piled with bales of hay, and we climbed on for a ride to the pig shed over fields of harvested alfalfa. "You'll need deodorant," Jim cautioned. We didn't, but the pigs sure did. Packed flank to flank in pens of 25, the 1,200 swine gave off a powerful stench. And who wouldn't, given their prospects: They come weighing 40 to 50 pounds, are kept there four months until they're 250 pounds, and are then sold for slaughter. We rode toward his brother Luke's place, Brubaker Farms, dairy cattle suddenly seeming very alluring. "Look!" Sophie suddenly shouted, jumping off her hay bale. "A chipmunk!"

If I had never given much thought to how chickens were raised for food, a look at the operation in two huge sheds, each two city blocks long, showed me more that I wanted to know. The production cycle, in partnership with Tyson Foods, the Arkansas-based chicken empire, begins when Tyson delivers 52,000 day-old broiler hatchlings and the feed supply. The chickens, 26,000 in each shed, are fed and watered by automatic dispensers; farmhands need only walk through daily to remove any chickens that have died. Eight weeks later, Tyson returns to cart the grown chickens off to their fate. Then after the sheds are aired out for a week or two, Tyson delivers 52,000 new chicks. This must have been what Isaac Bashevis Singer had in mind when he become a vegetarian: "Not for my health," he explained, "but the health of the chickens."

The farm's 325 cows have a brighter future, at least as long as they give milk, which they do three times a day, at 4am, noon, and 8pm, when 20 at a time are led into the milking shed and hooked up to milking machines. While farmhands scurried through the shed, swabbing the teats with iodine solution and attaching the suction devices that drain the milk through plastic tubes, Jim hoisted Sophie underneath a waiting cow and showed her how to draw a spray of milk the old-fashioned way. For once, she was speechless.

The udders empty in five minutes, after which the suction devices drop off. This being the computer age on the farm as well, each cow wears a numbered electronic necklace that activates measurement of the animal's milk output at each milking. A good cow will give 80 to 100 pounds of milk a day; that's at least 10 gallons, the brothers explained. His cows are fed an appetite stimulant, said Luke Brubaker, who defends the use of federally approved chemical hormones to increase milk production, a practice that continues to split the industry. He and 150 other dairy farmers in his regional cooperative stringently supervise milk quality, he said, knowing that excess antibiotic traces or other impurities are punishable by the loss of the entire tanker load. "You could lose $10,000 by making a mistake," he said.

Jim said he had something special to show us, and led us past a sign reading "Cow Country—Watch Your Step" to a pen where a cow in the final stages of pregnancy stood shuddering, about to deliver a calf. Part of the umbilical sac had already emerged, and inside a hoof was visible. "He's having a baby?" Sophie asked, incredulous. It was time for a quick lesson in he and she.

Enthralled, we waited for the birth. And waited and waited and waited. "Could be a few hours yet," Jim guessed. We took a gamble and risked a quick trip back to his farmhouse for a break. We lost. When we returned within the hour, the cow had delivered. The newborn calf, a female still wrapped in its sac, lay unmoving by its mother, which also lay there blitzed. A cowhand climbed into the pen and gave the cow a shove. "Mommy's got to take care of it," she scolded. Roused, the cow began licking her calf clean as it made its first feeble attempts to unfold its legs and stand. The cowhand sprinkled the calf with nutrient-laced feed, which the mother then dutifully licked off. "It's the quickest way to get vitamins into her," the cowhand said.

One of the other visiting families arrived to see the new calf, and Jim showed us around the rest of his brother's farm. The other little girl insisted on seeing the pit where the cow manure was stored for fertilizer. "Well," said our guide, stalling, "it's not real pretty."

It was time for lunch and a drive around the area. Taking a recommendation from Jim, we stopped to eat at the Country Table on Route 283, an immaculately clean family-style restaurant stocked with religious tracts. Platters of roast beef, peppery cabbage slaw, corn, roast turkey, mashed potatoes, quiche, and fruit, along with salad and iced tea, came to $19.95, for all three of us.

On Route 340, we rode to Bird-in-Hand (probably named for a Colonial inn) and spent an hour roaming through the enclosed farmers' market, stocking up on jars of jam and apple and peach butter, sweet and hot pickled peppers, and bags of—what else?—Dutch pretzels. Then it was on to Intercourse, of which *The Intercourse News*, the local shopper, had this to say: "Much speculation exists concerning the name of this little country village." One theory ties it to an old race course and an entry road known as "Enter-Course." Another links the name to the joining of two main roads. Today it's the setting of Kitchen Kettle Village, a somewhat cutesy shopping complex with a one-pen petting zoo for children. We shared the parking lot with the delicate and graceful Amish buggies, the horses tied to hitching posts. We had finally got Sophie to stop pointing excitedly at the Amish, whom she kept calling "the British."

We skirted Lancaster, which seemed deserving of a more sustained tour on another visit; spot-checked the sprawling Rockvale Square and Tanger discount shopping outlets on Route 30 east of Lancaster; and circled back on Route 23 west of Lancaster, where we passed spectacular mansions and mock chateaux that might have been transplanted from East Hampton, Long Island.

Back at the Olde Country Log House Farm, the cats were waiting. Sophie scooped them up and disappeared.

For dinner on Saturday night (the farm provides only breakfast), we were torn between driving 45 minutes or so back to one of the Lucullan landmarks of Pennsylvania Dutch cuisine—Good 'n' Plenty in Smoketown or Plain and Fancy on Route 340 between Bird-in-Hand and Intercourse (each seating more than 600 people)—or finding something closer. We decided to take a drive through adjacent Mount Joy and almost immediately came upon an extraordinary oasis: a restored antique hotel and brewery carved into three restaurants. The thronged complex on North Market Street, in the center of town, was built around the old Central Hotel and Alois Bube's Brewery, one of the country's last intact pre-Prohibition breweries, registered as a national historic site.

Our timing was perfect. A last-minute cancellation had just opened up a table in the sought-after Catacombs, a dim and vaulted chamber

43 feet below the street. There we dined on vaguely medieval fare: skewered meats and fish, chicken and veal and salad, and a tankard of beer. The setting was extraordinary. But as with many such theatrical dining extravaganzas, the food came in second, and at $84 was hardly a deal.

Tearing Sophie away from the farm for the trip home was a lot easier than it might have been. We uttered a magic word. She said goodbye to a dried worm in the driveway and tumbled into the car. Forty minutes later, we were in Hershey's Chocolate World, a factory exhibition and gift shop, in a chocolate brown cart moving tantalizingly past mock rivers of flowing chocolate and cascades of chocolate bars and kisses. The tantrum came later.

FARM STAYS: ESSENTIALS

Here is information about the farm mentioned in the accompanying article and a sampling of other farms and ranches that offer visitor accommodations:

LANCASTER COUNTY, PA

Landis Farm, 2048 Gochlan Rd., Manheim (☎ 717/898-7028). Dairy farm that operates year-round. There is a single guest house that accommodates six people. Daily rates based on double occupancy. Room $70, $80 for four; $10 surcharge for each additional adult, $5 for each child. Breakfast available for an additional $5 for adults, $2.50 for children.

Olde Country Log House Farm, 1175 Flory Rd., Mount Joy (☎ 717/653-4477). Open year-round. Daily rates based on double occupancy and include breakfast. Rooms (some with private baths) $55 to $70 November through April, $60 to $75 May through November; $10 surcharge per child.

Old Fogie Farm, Stackstown Rd., Marietta (☎ 717/426-3992). Operates year-round. Daily rates based on double occupancy and include breakfast. Rooms (with private bath) $60 to $75; $10 surcharge per child. There are also family suites with kitchens available for $75 (not including breakfast).

Verdant View Room, 429 Strasburg Rd., Paradise (☎ 717/687-7353). The farm offers a "Winter Weekend Getaway" package through March; daily rates, based on double occupancy and including breakfast, are $60 per person for two nights; $10 supplement for each additional bed and $3 for each additional child's breakfast. For the same rate, there is also a three-room cottage with a kitchen that can accommodate up to 12 people. Daily buggy rides and seasonal sleigh and hay rides also available, including a two-hour tour of the area and a dinner with an Amish family. Buggy rides $8 per person; $12 each for the dinner ($8 for children). Part of a "Winter Getaways" program sponsored by the **Pennsylvania Dutch Convention and Visitors Bureau** (☎ 717/299-8901).

NEW YORK STATE

Hawthorne Valley Farm Main House, 327 Country Rd. 21C (off Taconic State Pkwy.), Harlemville (☎ 518/672-4790). A working dairy farm open most of the year except mid-June to mid-August (when it is open for summer camp for children 9 to 14). Open daily from Thanksgiving to the beginning of February, open weekends only from February through mid-June and mid-August through Thanksgiving. Accommodations are dormitory style. Daily rates $15 a bed, $7.50 for those under 12, free for those under 6. Private rooms $20 and $40, with bedding included. Guests provide their own food, sheets, and towels; kitchens are available. Cross-country skis and ice skates available for rental.

Hull-o-Farms Family Farm Vacations, Rte. 20, Durham (☎ 518/239-6950). Operates year-round. Two rental houses, of two bedrooms and three bedrooms. Daily rates (including all meals) $85 per adult, $50 for ages 10 to 14, $40 for ages 5 to 9, $25 for ages 2 to 4, free for those under 2. Two-day minimum stay on weekends.

Pinegrove Dude Ranch, Cherrytown Rd. (off Rte. 209), Kerhonkson (☎ 800/846-1571). Open year-round; weekends from mid-September to mid-June, then weekly from mid-June through mid-September. Two-night stay, including meals and all activities: $229 per adult ($114.50 for ages 4 to 16, free for those under 4) in winter; $260 per adult ($130 for children) in summer. Special packages are available, ranging from $405 per adult for four days in winter to $179 per adult for two nights during Mother's Day weekend (children are half-price for both).

WHERE TO EAT, SHOP, AND PLAY: LANCASTER COUNTY ESSENTIALS

GETTING THERE

To reach Lancaster County from Manhattan, take the Lincoln or Holland Tunnel to the New Jersey Turnpike; exit onto the Pennsylvania Turnpike (exit 6) and continue to Rte. 222 South (exit 21); continue on Rte. 222 South to Rte. 30 West and then onto Rte. 283 West.

RESTAURANTS

The Country Table Restaurant, 740 East Main St., Mount Joy (☎ 717/653-4745). Open Monday through Thursday 6am to 8pm, Friday and Saturday 6am to 9pm. Entrees $4 to $5 at lunch, $6 to $10 at dinner.

Good 'n' Plenty, Rte. 896, Smoketown (☎ 717/394-7111). Open Monday through Saturday 11:30am to 8pm. Full lunch or dinner $14.50; $6.50 for ages 4 to 10.

Plain and Fancy Farm Restaurant, Rte. 340, Bird-in-Hand (☎ 717/768-4400). Open Monday through Saturday 11:30am to 8pm, Sunday noon to 6pm. All you can eat $13.95; $5.95 for ages 4 to 11.

Alois's, Bottling Works, Catacombs, all part of Bube's Brewery, 102 N. Market St., Mount Joy (☎ 717/653-2056). Open Monday through Friday 5pm to 9pm, Saturday and Sunday 5pm to 9:45pm. Alois's: six-course meal $26. Bottling Works: entrees $3.95 to $15.95. Catacombs: entrees $16.95 to $23.95. Vintage photographs of the brewery are displayed in a museum called Cooper's Shed, open Monday through Friday 6 to 10pm and Saturday and Sunday 5 to 10pm.

AMUSEMENT PARK

Hershey Park, including Chocolate World, Christmas Candylane, Hershey Museum, and Zoo America, Hershey Park Dr., Hershey. All but Christmas Candylane are open year-round. Chocolate World, the visitor's center of Hershey Foods Corporation, offers a simulated factory tour on how chocolate is made. Free admission. Christmas Candylane, open mid-November to December 31, offers rides for adults and children, a train ride, and a theater with a Christmas show. Admission for the rides and attractions ranges from 75¢ to $3 for the rides or attractions. Admission to Hershey Museum $4.25 adults, $3.75 seniors, $2 children 3 to 15, free children under 2. Admission to Zoo America $5 adults, $4.50 seniors, $3.75 children 3 to 12. For hours, show times, and other information (☎ 800/437-7439).

SHOPPING OUTLETS

Rockvale Square Outlets, at Rtes. 30 and 896, Lancaster (☎ 717/293-9595). Open Monday through Saturday 9:30am to 9pm, Sunday noon to 6pm.

Tanger Factory Outlet Center, Rte. 30 East, Lancaster (☎ 717/392-7202). Open Monday through Saturday 9:30am to 9pm, Sunday 11am to 6pm.

THE BRANDYWINE VALLEY

by Lisa W. Foderaro

Iɴ ᴛʜᴇ ʙʀɪᴛᴛʟᴇ ʟɪɢʜᴛ ᴏғ ʟᴀᴛᴇ winter, the Brandywine Valley, stretching from southeastern Pennsylvania into northern Delaware, emerges in all its muted glory. From either side of narrow country roads, hay-colored fields rise and fall to the horizon. Naked tree branches appear pressed against a mottled gray sky, interrupted by an occasional gristmill or puff of chimney smoke.

This is the time of year when the Brandywine's enchantments don't hit you over the head but rather seep into your soul with their desolate beauty. It is the season most often depicted in a half-century of painting by Andrew Wyeth, who is Brandywine born and bred and, at 80, still an active resident and artist. "I prefer winter and fall, when you feel the bone structure in the landscape—the loneliness of it," he said years ago. "Something waits beneath it. The whole story doesn't show."

The giant among three generations of artists, Mr. Wyeth has his work permanently on view at the Brandywine River Museum in Chadds Ford, Pennsylvania, along with that of his father, sisters, and son. His paintings best convey the character of the countryside while also revealing truths in the everyday, whether the slant of light on a windowsill or a dead crow in a field.

If Mr. Wyeth is the Brandywine Valley's favorite son, the Du Ponts are its first family, and it is largely thanks to their generous legacy that the region also offers a rich cultural and educational diet. Longwood Gardens in Kennett Square, Pennsylvania, is internationally known for its 1,050 acres of cultivated plantings. For the winter traveler, there is a spectacular preview of spring in the dramatic conservatories: 3½ acres under glass that form a museum of international horticulture.

Winterthur, a sprawling mansion on the outskirts of Wilmington, Delaware, houses what is arguably the country's finest and largest collection of American decorative arts from 1640 to 1860.

Settled in the early 1600s by the Swedes, who were later joined by English and Welsh Quakers, the Brandywine Valley has a deep sense of its own history. The area, named for the Brandywine River (more creek than river), is dotted with covered bridges and Quaker meeting houses, gristmills and pre-Revolution stone houses. Brandywine Battlefield Park, where the Battle of Brandywine was fought in 1777, is one of several historic attractions.

Unfortunately, the valley has, like most places, become somewhat built-up over the years. (Mr. Wyeth himself admits that the area never looked quite as vast and uncluttered as it does on his canvases.) Fortunately, though, much of that development is confined to the few major routes that crisscross the area. The moment you turn off onto any of the smaller roads, you are blessedly thrust back in time. One of the most scenic drives through the countryside is along winding Route 100, beginning just outside Wilmington and continuing north for a dozen or so miles.

Sweetwater Farm

It would be hard to take in even a fraction of what the valley has to offer in a single day. Better to stay the weekend and savor the region at the unhurried pace of the Brandywine River itself. There are several good places to lodge (and eat) that are evocative of the area's history, perhaps none more so than Sweetwater Farm in Glen Mills, Pennsylvania.

A fieldstone mansion on 50 acres, Sweetwater has nine fireplaces, dark wood antiques, and a country breakfast that is unabashedly urbane. There are six guest rooms on the second floor of the 1815 main house, part of which dates from 1734 and was used as a hospital by the British during the American Revolution. Four guest rooms have working fireplaces, and all have four-poster, queen-size beds, and private baths. Three outbuildings housing five suites, three with working fireplaces, are situated on the property, where horses and goats can be seen grazing. A covered swimming pool hints at the pleasures of summer.

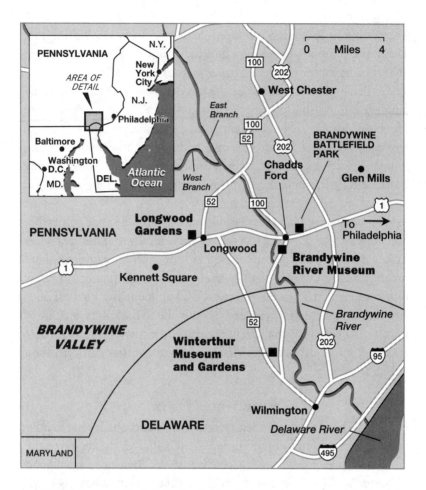

What is so refreshing about the inn to the veteran bed-and-breakfast-goer is its complete lack of cuteness: you won't find any ruffles or heart-shaped wreaths here. Indeed, there is a certain formality to its antiquated charm, fostered no doubt by 11-foot ceilings and amply proportioned rooms. The inn changed hands in 1995, and the new owners, Ric Hovsepian and Grace LeVine, have placed many family photographs around the common areas. That might have been irritating had Ms. LeVine not hailed from such an eye-catching family: She is the niece of Princess Grace Kelly.

The dignified demeanor of old wealth is further conjured by hefty moldings painted in Williamsburg colors, Oriental rugs, a few serious antiques, many good reproductions, and, of course, those ubiquitous fireplaces. They draw smoke so well and come with such an unending supply of dry wood that it is tempting to shirk sightseeing duties in favor of a good read by the hiss and crackle.

Mr. Hovsepian, a former caterer, does the cooking. Breakfast might be raisin bread French toast or scrambled eggs in a puff pastry with asparagus spears, and there is always fresh fruit.

The owners appear to be laid back about rules, which can be enforced with militaristic precision by some innkeepers. Breakfast is served from 9 to 10, but late sleepers won't go hungry if they slink downstairs at 10:30. And in spite of a noon checkout, it is not uncommon for guests to be encouraged to linger by the fire in the parlor through a cold and blustery Sunday afternoon.

Brandywine River Museum

Since much of the Brandywine Valley's identity is tied up with Andrew Wyeth (Wyeth Country is a familiar expression), it is only fitting that its one serious art museum is devoted largely to his and his family's paintings. Set in a renovated 19th-century gristmill on the bank of the Brandywine River in Chadds Ford, the museum is at once classic and modern: classic in its century-old brick facade with weathered herringboned shutters, modern in its curvilinear interior of white stucco and glass.

That duality finds parallels in Mr. Wyeth's work. Many consider him a traditionalist, in the sense that he has pursued realistic landscape and figurative painting in an age of abstraction, keeping alive the spirit of American painters like Winslow Homer and Thomas Eakins. The meticulous detail found in his rendering of fabric, grass, painted clapboard, hair—whatever—is indeed staggering. But to Mr. Wyeth, as well as to some art critics, his work is thoroughly modern, almost surreal in its immediacy. He has even said that he considers his paintings abstract because they transcend the physical elements to capture the spirit of a person or object.

The museum's first- and second-floor galleries contain the works of his father, N. C. Wyeth, a prominent artist and illustrator in his own day who was killed in Chadds Ford when a train struck his car at a railroad crossing. Andrew was 28. His father's tragic death had a profound effect on him and on his approach to landscape painting. Indeed, an all-encompassing melancholy seems to emanate from many of his canvases.

The galleries also display the works of Andrew Wyeth's two sisters, Henriette Wyeth Hurd and Carolyn Wyeth; his son, Jamie, and other artists who painted the Brandywine Valley, including Jasper Cropsey, William Trost Richards, and Howard Pyle.

The top floor is reserved for Andrew Wyeth's paintings. They depict the personalities and places in and around Cushing, Maine, where he and his wife, Betsy, spend the summer months, and Chadds Ford, where they spend the winter. A number of paintings were done in the 1990s, including one entitled *Ice Queen*, a luminous egg tempera painting of an old sleigh in a barn, the rich brown interior streaked by sunlight. "I've been blamed, from time to time, for the fact that my pictures are colorless, but the color I use is so much like the country I live in," reads a quote from Mr. Wyeth under another painting, *North Light*, a 1984 watercolor of his father's studio in the snow, done in shades of white. "Winter is that color here."

Longwood Gardens

The soaring glass conservatories at Longwood Gardens in nearby Kennett Square are, by contrast, an orgy of color, from lavender orchids and rosy camellias to the feathery yellow flowers covering the weeping branches of the acacia tree.

Entering the conservatories in the midst of winter is like stepping into another world. Outside, the air is cold and clear, but inside rooms like the East Conservatory and Palm House, the atmosphere is as sensuous as a Florida Key: humid, warm and fragrant. With most of Longwood's 11,000 different plants still hibernating, the conservatories are an irresistible opportunity to defy the calendar.

In 1906, Pierre S. Du Pont, then the chairman of Du Pont and General Motors, purchased the first 200 acres of what is today Longwood Gardens to save an arboretum from being cut for timber. During his life, he assembled and developed more than a thousand acres into one of the country's foremost gardens, leaving them upon his death in 1954 for the "sole use of the public for purposes of exhibition, instruction, education, and enjoyment."

The conservatories were established in the 1920s by Mr. Du Pont to grow flowers and fruits year round. Today, they are a stately network of 20 rooms and grand galleries. With tall arched windows, honeycomb glass ceilings, fountains, and winding brick walks, the conservatories are almost as arresting for their design as for the plants they contain, which are arranged thematically. There is, for instance, Fern Passage, with two alcoves of insect-eating plants, including one dear to every fourth-grader's heart: the Venus's-flytrap. The Silver Garden is host to plants found in the world's harshest environments, including the organ-pipe cactus, which is two stories high, covered with fine white needles, and as straight and narrow as, well, an organ pipe. The Banana Room instructs that bananas are technically herbs, not trees, despite the presence of a 20-foot plantain whose leaves easily measure 3 feet wide by 9 feet long.

From mid-January through mid-April, the conservatories honor spring, with profusions of tulips, hyacinths, daisies, and daffodils tucked among the permanent collection. The 75-year-old Orangery and the Exhibition Hall, which constitute about a quarter of the conservatory, were reopened in the fall of 1996 following a major renovation.

Winterthur

Visiting this unthinkably large Du Pont mansion is a bit like making a trek to the Metropolitan Museum of Art. You are overwhelmed by the realization that it would take years of return trips to begin to exhaust its contents. There are some 90,000 objects—furniture, textiles, ceramics, glass, paintings—in 75 rooms and display areas spread throughout nine floors.

So broad is the collection that, in addition to the one- and two-hour introductory tours, there are 25 special-interest tours available by request, focusing exclusively on, say, the Chinese export porcelain, or the Empire furniture. But don't be put off. Even an hourlong tour of a single floor offers a satisfying look at the treasures assembled in this century by Henry Francis Du Pont, a distant cousin of Pierre S. Du Pont. The tour guides deftly weave together strands from the Du Pont family's history with the forces in American and European history that led to the dominance of particular styles of decorative arts during certain periods.

The original 12-room Greek Revival house, built in 1838 and then passed through the hands of a succession of Du Ponts, received its first major addition in the late 1800s. The owners, Henry A. and Pauline Du Pont, also developed Winterthur into an elaborate, self-contained community, adding greenhouses, flower gardens, a dairy farm, a golf course, a sawmill, a post office, even a railroad station. But it was their son, Henry Francis, who, after inheriting the house in 1926, laid the groundwork for Winterthur, the museum. He added a nine-story wing to display his collection of furnishings made or used in America before 1860, transplanting architectural elements from other distinguished houses, like a fantastic free-floating spiral staircase from North Carolina. And he worked with a landscape architect to create naturalistic gardens that are almost as strong a draw today as the house.

Winterthur is set on 1,000 hilly acres, and a shuttle bus provides transportation from the visitor's center to the mansion, whose beige stucco facade with burgundy shutters is surrounded by towering tulip poplars. In addition to the period rooms, where antiques are viewed in domestic settings, three galleries in a building adjoining the mansion display still more decorative arts.

Mr. Du Pont opened the house as a museum in 1951 but continued to live on the property in a villa until his death in 1969. Of course, with homes in Manhattan, the Hamptons, and Florida, he wasn't there full-time.

Perhaps it's only natural that feelings of gratitude should mingle with envy, and even some serious reflection about the uses of money, as you wander through the wing that functioned as Mr. Du Pont's life-size dollhouse, or through the conservatories at Longwood Gardens. Both were built with a fortune founded on gunpowder. But the fact is that the residue from that gunpowder has made the Brandywine Valley a remarkably pleasant place to be.

BRANDYWINE VALLEY ESSENTIALS

GETTING THERE

To reach the region from the New York metropolitan area, take the New Jersey Turnpike South to exit 2 (Rte. 322); take Rte. 322 West over the Commodore Barry Bridge into Pennsylvania and continue on Rte. 322 West to Rte. 452; take Rte. 452 North about 4½ miles to Rte. 1 and continue along Rte. 1 to the various sites.

ACCOMMODATIONS

Sweetwater Farm, 50 Sweetwater Rd., Glen Mills (☎ 800/793-3892 or 610/459-4711). January through March, $155 to $165 double in main house, $150 to $250 cottage suite. April through December, $180 to $190 double in main house, $175 to $275 suite. Rates are based on double occupancy and include full breakfast. Children are welcome; an additional cot in the room is $25.

Guesthouses, Inc. (☎ 610/692-4575) is a bed-and-breakfast reservation service that represents about 75 private homes, small inns, and family-run hotels in the Brandywine Valley chosen for their historic or architectural significance. Room range from $100 to $200 a night, depending on the location and amenities. Rates are based on double occupancy. Guests pay no additional fee for the service.

DINING

Chadds Ford Inn, at rtes. 1 and 100 in Chadds Ford (☎ 610/388-7361). Traditional American fare in a charming stone house, which entered the hospitality business in 1736 when John Chad, an English Quaker, turned his father's home into a tavern. Andrew Wyeth prints adorn the walls, and a working fireplace warms the downstairs dining room. Open Monday through Friday 11:30am to 2pm and 5:30 and 10pm, Saturday 5:30 to 10:30pm, Sunday 11am to 2pm (for brunch) and 4 to 9pm. Entrees $5.95 to $12.50 for lunch, $10.95 to $24.95 for dinner.

Dilworthtown Inn, 1390 Old Wilmington Pike (¼ mile off Rte. 202), in West Chester (☎ 610/399-1390). Elegant Continental cuisine is served in a rambling house built in 1758, with 15 intimate dining rooms and authentic gaslight from chandeliers and sconces. Bring your reading glasses: There are more than 825 selections on the wine list. Open Monday through Saturday 5:30 to 9:30pm, Sunday 3 to 9:30pm. Entrees $14.75 to $24.75.

Griglia Toscana, 1412 N. Du Pont St. (off Rte. 52), in Wilmington, DE (☎ 302/654-8001). Contemporary Tuscan cooking in a soft, elegant dining room with cream-colored stucco walls and gilt-framed mirrors. The restaurant is in a shopping center, but you'll quickly forget that fact once you're inside. Open Monday through Friday 11:30am to 2pm and 5:30 to 10pm, Saturday and Sunday 5:30 to 10pm. Entrees $10 to $15 for lunch, $12 to $24 for dinner.

ATTRACTIONS

Brandywine Battlefield Park, Rte. 1, Chadds Ford (☎ 610/459-3342). Open Tuesday through Saturday 9am to 5pm and Sunday noon to 5pm. Admission $3.50 adults, $2.50 seniors, $1.50 children 6 to 12, free for children under 6.

Brandywine River Museum, Rte. 1, Chadds Ford (☎ 610/388-2700). Open daily 9:30am to 4:30pm. Admission $5 adults, $2.50 students, seniors, and children 6 to 12, free for children under 6.

Longwood Gardens, Rte. 1, Kennett Square (☎ 610/388-1000). November through March, the conservatories are open daily 10am to 5pm and the grounds are open daily 9am to 5pm. April to October, the conservatories are open daily 10am to 6pm and the grounds are open daily 9am to 6pm. Memorial Day through Labor Day, the conservatory and grounds are open for the Festival of Fountains on Tuesdays, Thursdays, and Saturdays until one hour after dusk (or about 10:30pm). Admission $12 ($8 on Tuesdays) adults, $6 teenagers 16 to 20, $2 children 6 to 15, free for children under 6.

Winterthur, Rte. 52, Winterthur, DE (☎ 800/448-3883). Museum and garden open Monday through Saturday 9am to 5pm and Sunday noon to 5pm. Admission $8 adults; $6 for groups, students, and seniors; $4 for children 5 to 11; free for children under 5. A guided tour is offered for an additional $5 fee.

Connecticut

THREE PATHS OF HISTORY

by William Grimes

SPRING IS THE SEASON OF NOBLE intentions. The old, shriveled winter creature you behold in the mirror cries out for renewal. So does that gray-tinged complexion. What better way to register the change of season than a self-improvement program that combines outdoor recreation with mental stimulation? Both in moderation, of course.

An ideal spring program is at hand in the dozens of small towns and cities across Connecticut, each with its own historical society, that offer walking tours. Some are guided by local historians, on a fixed schedule or as demand arises. Others are self-guided. That is, history-minded flaneurs can pick up a brochure and set forth, beholding the local wonders, free to think their own thoughts and form their own impressions.

A few towns, like Hartford and Litchfield, rent or sell audiocassette guides, allowing visitors to stroll or drive as they like. In a bid for glamour, the Huntington Historical Society offers a cassette guide to Southport narrated by Jason Robards.

Not all tours are created equal. Some focus on architecture, others on local worthies and eminent trees, while still others memorialize the brief, sometimes ephemeral brushes with greatness every town likes to claim.

Wethersfield had its moment. Until the late 18th century, it was known primarily for its red onions and for an infestation of witches in the 1640s that included a husband-and-wife team. In May 1781, however, destiny came knocking at the door of Joseph Webb, a merchant. Into his red clapboard house on Main Street walked George

Washington, accompanied by the Comte de Rochambeau. The two men, sitting at a table in what is now called the Council Room, laid plans for a decisive southward push by American and French forces.

Washington slept not one but four nights at the stark, rather barnlike clapboard structure, which was built in the 1750s and still stands steady as a rock, flanked by two other mid–18th-century houses. Together with the Buttolph-Williams House, the three make up the Webb-Deane-Stevens Museum, and they are the subject of a one-hour guided tour that is strong on the details of Colonial domestic life and architecture.

Visitors who note with surprise the rather flashy interior colors of the Webb house, which includes a stunning china cupboard in blue, mustard, and red with a scallop-shell dome, will learn that early American homes, lacking electricity, relied on bright interior paints to lighten rooms.

Visitors in the fall will take pleasure in the large and quite realistic plastic turkey on the dining room table of the Silas Deane house, and the surrounding pies and vegetable dishes that indicate a Thanksgiving feast. The meal changes seasonally. Because several of the Deanes fell victim to tuberculosis, an upstairs bedroom has been set up as a sickroom, with a handsome mahogany medicine chest on a nightstand. One of the chest's small drawers contains strands of copper wire, and by way of explanation, my guide delivered the kind of eye-opening 30-minute treatise that fully justified the modest cost of the tour. "The copper wires were stirred in vinegar, and the resulting chemical reaction created verdigris," she said. "When you mixed it with a liquid to disguise the taste and then drank it, it alleviated chest pains, although it did nothing for the tuberculosis. So if you ever see a little drawer like that with copper wires in it, that's what they were for."

With my store of knowledge enlarged by one eminently repeatable fact, I felt edified, yet not fatigued. This was as good as anything in *Bill and Ted's Excellent Adventure*.

Wethersfield is the ideal town for a half-day history tour. One of the most perfectly preserved Colonial towns in Connecticut, it has 150 buildings dating before 1850, and the Olde Towne Tourism District—yes, unfortunately, that's how it's spelled—has a detailed brochure with an annotated map that allows visitors to stroll, look, and absorb at their own pace.

For atmosphere, read *The Witch of Blackbird Pond* by Elizabeth Speare or *Harvest Home* and *The Other* by Thomas Tryon. All are set in Wethersfield. Then walk up and down Main Street, making sure to press as far north as Wethersfield Cove, the town's thriving harbor until a flood in 1692 swept away six warehouses and permanently altered the Connecticut River's course. Overnight, the port became an inlet.

On the way back, take a detour to see the Buttolph-Williams House (1720) on Broad Street. Imposing and stern, it figures prominently in *The Witch of Blackbird Pond.* Finish up with a visit to the Ancient Burying Ground, where, legend has it, the

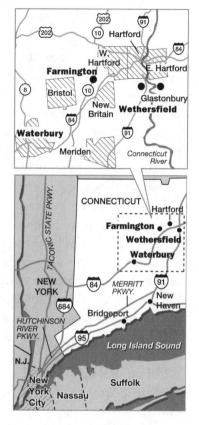

nine victims of the 1637 massacre that touched off the Pequot War are buried. The Wethersfield Historical Society offers tours and a printed guide to the cemetery.

The Industrial Revolution passed Wethersfield by. Instead of machine shops and mills, the 19th century left the gentle, benevolent legacy of Comstock, Ferre (pronounced Ferry), the oldest continually operating seed company in the United States. Stop in and buy a packet of seeds for the famous Wethersfield red onion, which was once shipped from the cove to ports up and down the East Coast, and all the way to the Orient.

The store's manager, Roger Willard, is rather restrained in his sales pitch for the local product. "There's nothing so great about it," he said, "except that it made Wethersfield famous."

A Town Near Hartford

Just a few miles west of Wethersfield is the once-mighty town of Farmington, so famous in the 19th century that when Mark Twain was introduced to Queen Victoria as a citizen of Hartford, he pointed out, helpfully, that Hartford was a town near Farmington.

Farmington is another half-day town with some good history to it, and, of course, a local historical society with a can-do attitude. Once the 12th-wealthiest town in the 13 colonies, Farmington has an abundance of 17th-century houses.

Visitors should contact the Farmington Historical Society to reserve a place on the Amistad Sights Walking Tour, a 12-stop proposition that traces Farmington's role in the events surrounding the first civil rights case to reach the Supreme Court.

In 1839, 53 adults and children from the Mende region of Sierra Leone, who had been captured and enslaved, were being transported from Havana to Puerto Rico aboard the ship *Amistad*. After a storm blew the ship out to sea and rations were depleted, the Africans, led by Sengbe Pieh, known as Joseph Cinque, rose up, killed the captain and the cook, seized control of the ship, and tried to head back to Africa.

Instead, the ship touched land at Montauk Point, Long Island, where the Coast Guard picked up the men and transported them to New Haven, where they were put on trial for mutiny and murder. The court ruled that because the Africans had never been slaves before their abduction, they could not be returned to Cuba or be held liable for their acts. The decision was appealed and went to the Supreme Court, where John Quincy Adams helped argue the case for the defense. The high court upheld the lower court's decision.

The *Amistad* case galvanized the Abolitionist movement. Farmington, an abolitionist hotbed and a stop on the underground railroad, played host to the Mende natives, who lived and worked in the town while money was raised to send them back to Africa.

Carol Leonard, a former head of the Farmington Historical Society, leads tours of the Amistad Sights trail, by request. A second local historian, Ernest R. Shaw, runs a little business called Heritage Trails Sightseeing Tours. Most of the time, he's busy taking small bands of tourists around Hartford on daily tours at $15 a pop, but his schedule also includes three Farmington tours.

On the "Ancient Evening Cemetery Tour," Mr. Shaw takes visitors through two graveyards, one dating from 1660. Informed sources say that there is sometimes a little surprise in one of the graveyards that elicits shrieks. On the Colonial Dinner Tour, which operates nightly, passengers leave from Hartford's main hotels for a bus tour of Farmington and dinner at an old stagecoach stop, built in 1789.

In a third tour, Mr. Shaw leads visitors along the locks and brownstone bridges of the old Farmington Canal. "Even Connecticut people are unaware there was an 80-mile canal, hand-dug, that ran from New Haven and ended up in Northampton, Massachusetts, on the Connecticut River," he said. It's a striking illustration of the truth that economics is not beanbag. "The idea was to put Hartford out of business," Mr. Shaw said.

Hartford had the last laugh. The canal opened in 1828 and went bankrupt 19 years later, a victim of the railroads.

The saga of the Farmington Canal serves as a reminder that history more often than not has a harsh tale to tell. In the struggle to survive and prosper, some Connecticut towns won; others lost, and lost painfully.

The Brass Capital

Waterbury, which won and lost in spectacular fashion, is a town that deserves its own Gibbon. Once known as the brass capital of the world, it employed tens of thousands of workers in vast factories that cast, rolled, stamped, and worked brass, the 19th-century equivalent of plastic, into a thousand articles of domestic and industrial use, including pins, buttons, kettles, architectural hardware, lighting devices, photographic equipment, and the famous Ingersoll dollar watches that sold in the millions. By 1890, the city was producing 60% of the nation's brass.

In the city's heyday, from 1850 to the end of World War I, the brass barons and the wealthy professionals of Waterbury built some dazzling houses and mansions in the Hillside District, which has 327 buildings listed with the National Register of Historic Places. The reigning style is Queen Anne; that is, an eclectic (some would say indiscriminate) conglomeration of turrets, towers, wraparound porches, peaks, and gables, with bright colors pointing up the gingerbread details.

New Yorkers will find some familiar names in Waterbury. Fulton Park was created by the firm of Frederick Law Olmsted, who designed Central Park with Calvert Vaux. Waterbury's brick, marble, and granite city hall is one of five buildings designed by Cass Gilbert, the architect who designed the Woolworth Building and the Custom House in Manhattan.

The Mattatuck Museum in downtown Waterbury is a lively little institution with an innovative program of history tours that allow visitors to get a fix on the social and architectural history of Hillside and the Gilbert district and also venture into the newer area of industrial history. It offers a bicycle or trolley tour that retraces Waterbury's manufacturing history. In addition to stopping off at industrial sites, the tour takes pains to provide a kind of illustrated social history. On Wood Street and Oak Street, the Scovill Company built two-story single-family row houses during World War I, each with a different facade to reflect a different national style, for their managers. The workers got barracks.

The tour is also valuable in lending specificity to arid terms like "industrial decline" and "retooling for the future." It is a poignant reminder of how difficult it is for a town to refashion its self-image. The signs of that struggle are evident everywhere in Waterbury, which has sagged badly since the brass industry moved overseas in the 1950s.

"I've been really impressed with the craftsmen here," said Marianne Vandenburgh, a former Ohioan who now owns the House on the Hill, a bed-and-breakfast establishment on Hillside, who carried out an extensive kitchen renovation. "I think it's because this is a town where people made things, and the tradition of working with your hands has been passed along from grandfather to father to grandson. That also may be a reason why it's hard for Waterbury to think of itself in a different way." Despite its troubles, Waterbury has beauty and charm. As a historical text, it makes rich reading, and its most compelling chapters may well be those of sad decline, which, as Gibbon knew, speaks more truthfully about the human condition than triumphant ascent.

ESSENTIALS

WETHERSFIELD

GETTING THERE

By Car From New York City, take I-287 North, then follow I-95 North to exit 48 (I-91 North) at New Haven. Proceed north to exit 26 for Wethersfield.

By Train Amtrak (☎ 800/872-7245) has service to Hartford; from there, you can reach Wethersfield, five miles south of Hartford, by taxi.

SEEING THE SIGHTS

Webb-Deane-Stevens Museum, Main St., Wethersfield (☎ 860/529-0612). The museum offers tours and programs throughout the year. May 1 to Oct 31, open daily (except Tuesday) 10am to 4pm; Nov 1 to April 30, open Saturday and Sunday 10am to 4pm. Tours depart on the hour from 10am to 3pm. Admission to four-house tour $7; three-house tour $6. Discounts for seniors, students with I.D., and AAA members; free for children under 6. Group tours may be arranged on specific themes, such as architecture or decorative arts. A self-guided walking tour, A Tour of the Old Village, is available from the museum.

Wethersfield Historical Society (☎ 860/529-7656). The society manages four sites open to the public: The **Old Academy Library,** 150 Main St. (Tuesday through Friday 10am to 4pm, Saturday 1 to 4pm; closed January and February); **Wethersfield Museum–Keeney Memorial,** 200 Main St. (open Tuesday through Saturday 10am to 4pm, Sunday 1pm to 4pm; admission $2, free for children); **Cove Warehouse,** Wethersfield Cove (at the north end of Main St.; call for hours; admission $1), with exhibits on the town's maritime history (open mid-May to mid-October; call for hours; admission $1); and the **Hurlbut-Dunham House,** 212 Main St., a brick Georgian house updated during the Victorian period (open mid-March through December; call for hours; admission $3).

ACCOMMODATIONS

Butternut Farm, 1654 Main St., Glastonbury (☎ 860/633-7197). Bed-and-breakfast in a Colonial farmhouse with antique furniture and a dynamic goose named Harry. Two rooms with private baths, plus a suite and an apartment with private baths. Rates $70 to $90, breakfast included. To reach the inn from New York, take I-91 or Rte. 2 to Glastonbury; from the center of town, drive south on Main St. 1.6 miles to the inn; enter from Whapley Rd. From Wethersfield, take Rte. 3, cross bridge, and follow Rte. 2 East to exit 8 (Glastonbury Center), which leads to Main St.

Chester Bulkley House, 184 Main St., Wethersfield (☎ 860/563-4236). Bed-and-breakfast in an 1830 Greek Revival house with five rooms, three with private bath, and a suite available on request. Rooms $70 with shared bath, $85 with private bath; $135 suite.

FARMINGTON

GETTING THERE

By Car   From New York City, take the Hutchinson River Pkwy. and Merritt Pkwy. to Rte. 8. Proceed north to I-84, exit 39 (Farmington); follow Rte. 4 into the center of town.

By Bus   Bonanza Buses (☎ 800/556-3815) run between the Port Authority Bus Terminal and Farmington. The fare is $24.95 for a same-day round-trip, $32 other round-trip.

INFORMATION

Information on the Farmington Valley may be obtained from the **Farmington Valley/ West Hartford Visitors Bureau,** 41 E. Main St., P.O. Box 1550, Old Avon Village, Avon, CT 06001 (☎ 800/468-6783, or 860/674-1035 in Connecticut).

SEEING THE SIGHTS

Hill-Stead Museum, 35 Mountain Rd., Farmington (☎ 860/677-4787, or 860/ 677-9064 for recorded information). This museum, in a 1901 house designed by Stanford White, has a famous Impressionist art collection that includes three Monets, a Degas, a Manet, and a Cassatt. May through October, open Tuesday through Sunday 10am to 5pm; November to April, open Tuesday through Sunday 11am to 4pm. The last tour begins one hour before closing. Admission $6 adults, $5 students and seniors, $3 children 6 to 12, free for children under 6 and museum members.

Stanley-Whitman House, 37 High St. (☎ 860/677-9222). A restored 1720 saltbox with period furnishings. May through October, open Wednesday through Sunday noon to 4pm; November through April, open Sunday noon to 4pm, and at other times by appointment. Admission $5 adults, $4 seniors, $2 children over 5, free for children

5 and under; $4 a person for groups of 10 or more. The house can arrange architectural and other walks for groups.

LOCAL TOUR GUIDES

Carol Leonard (☎ 860/678-4217) a former head of the Farmington Historical Society, offers group walking tours, by request, of *Amistad*-related sites, with groups of 8 to 20 preferred. The cost is $2 a person, with a $20 group minimum. Call her at the number above, or leave a message at the **Farmington Historical Society** (☎ 860/678-1645). **Heritage Trails Sightseeing Tours** (☎ 860/ 677-8867) offers a variety of tours guided by Ernest R. Shaw, a historian. The Farmington Canal Tour, which is offered in mid-May (May 10 and May 17 in 1997), costs $39.95 and includes lunch in a 1795 hotel that once catered to the canal traffic. The Ancient Evening Cemetery Tour, a tour of two ancient graveyards that is offered around Memorial Day and nightly in October, is $32, which includes dinner at a Colonial inn. The Colonial Dinner Tour of Farmington operates nightly and costs $30. Reservations are required for all tours.

Heritage Trails also sells two 90-minute self-drive audiocassette tours of Farmington and Hartford for $9.95 each, plus $2.50 per order if ordering by mail.

ACCOMMODATIONS

Barney House, 11 Mountain Spring Rd., Farmington (☎ 860/674-2796). Built in 1832, Barney House sits on spacious grounds that were formerly the estate of a founder of the Pony Express and Wells Fargo. The inn has seven rooms, all with private bath. Rates $79 single, $89 double, including continental breakfast.

WATERBURY

GETTING THERE

By Car From New York City, take the Hutchinson River Pkwy.and Merritt Pkwy.to Rte. 8 North to I-84 East, exit 21; or take the Hutchinson River Pkwy. to I-684 to I-84 West, exit 21 (Meadow St.).

By Train Waterbury is on the Waterbury branch of **Metro-North**'s New Haven Line (☎ 212/532-4900).

SEEING THE SIGHTS

Mattatuck Museum, 144W. Main St., Waterbury (☎ 203/753-0381). In addition to its permanent exhibitions on the town's history, the museum offers many historical tours. In addition to "Brass Beginnings," a 2¹/₂-hour tour of the city's industrial past, it offers one-hour walking tours of the Hillside District, the Cass Gilbert Historic District, the Waterbury Green, and Grand and Bank streets. Tickets for "Brass Beginnings" are $13; the one-hour tours cost $5.

For a one-hour self-guided tour of the Hillside District, consult the museum's brochure "Looking Up the Hillside." The museum also arranges group tours lasting from a half-day to two days on the region's architecture and history. It also sponsors "Our Towns," a series of lectures and walking tours. A full schedule is available on request.

ACCOMMODATIONS

House on the Hill, 92 Woodlawn Terrace, Waterbury (☎ 203/757-9901). Bed-and-breakfast at the top of the Hillside District, in a 1888 Queen Anne extravaganza. Four suites, each with private bath. Rates $100 to $150, including breakfast.

MORE HISTORICAL WALKS

Many towns and cities across Connecticut offer history tours. The state's 19 regional tourism councils have detailed information on local organizations and events. The councils' addresses and telephone numbers are listed in the booklet *Connecticut Vacation Guide,* which includes a brochure, "Connecticut Freedom Trail," that maps out an itinerary of 10 sites associated with the abolition of slavery. The vacation guide is available from the **Tourism Division,** Connecticut Department of Economic Development, 865 Brook St., Rocky Hill, CT 06067-3405 (☎ 800/282-6863, or 860/572-5318 for information on the Freedom Trail).

Local historical societies are also good sources of information. They are listed in the Directory of Historical Societies and Agencies in the United States and Canada.

The towns and organizations listed below offer unusually interesting or ambitious history tours:

Antiquarian and Landmarks Society, 66 Forest St., Hartford (☎ 860/247-8996), owns and operates 13 historic houses and properties across the state, nine of which are open to the public from mid-May to mid-October. The society also has a particularly good self-guided tour of Suffield, prepared with the Suffield Historical Society; it also offers a color brochure of the society's properties and walking tours of Suffield and Wethersfield.

Connecticut Trust for Historic Preservation, 940 Whitney Ave., Hamden (☎ 203/562-6312). Bicycle tours with detailed route descriptions are available in past issues of the trust's bimonthly newsletter. One tour is "Cycling to Historic Town Greens: Winsted to Colebrook to Winchester Center." Contact the trust for more information.

Fairfield Historical Society, 636 Old Post Rd., Fairfield (☎ 203/259-1598). Three self-guided tours are available at the society's headquarters: "Walking Through History: A Walking Tour of Black Rock and Southport Harbor" ($3.50); "Old Post Road and Town Center Walking Tour" (50¢); and "Cameron Clark: Colonial Revival" ($1), a driving tour of Colonial Revival homes designed by Clark. Two self-guided bicycle tours are available as well: "Tree Bike Tours Through Fairfield's Agricultural Past" ($3) and "Fairfield Bicycle Tour: Travel Back in Time" ($5). The society also offers walking tours of the Old Post Road historic district every other weekend from April to October ($3 for members, $5 for nonmembers). It also offers occasional tours of Southport, Black Rock, and the Tunxis Hill neighborhood.

Greater Middletown Preservation Trust publishes two detailed self-guided tours, "A Walking Tour of Early Middletown, 1650 to 1850," and "A Walking Tour of Main Street, Middletown." The tours may be obtained by sending a self-addressed, stamped envelope to the trust at 27 Washington St., Middletown, CT 06457.

Greater Hartford Architecture Conservancy (☎ 860/525-0279). The conservancy sells an audiocassette tour, "Hartford on Tour," for $6.99; credit card orders are taken by phone at the number above. The conservancy periodically offers walking tours and other events of interest to history buffs.

Litchfield Historical Society (☎ 860/567-4501). The society offers a guided group walking tour of historic Litchfield, as well as a self-guided brochure and audiotape tour.

Norwich Tourism Office (☎ 888/4-NORWICH or 860/886-4683). Norwich offers several self-guided tours of Washington and Broad Sts., Broadway and Union St., the Olde Burying Grounds, and the town's original settlement area, Norwichtown.

New Haven Preservation Trust (☎ 203/562-5919). The trust offers free guided tours of New Haven's 14 national historic districts and two local historic districts, as well as ethnic historic tours.

Salisbury Cannon Museum publishes an unusually detailed foldout brochure with a 25-stop tour called "A Capsule History and Historic Walking Tour of Salisbury Furnace at the Time of the American Revolution." It is available for $3 from the Salisbury Association, P.O. Box 553, Salisbury, CT 06068-0553.

APPLES AND ELEGANCE IN LITCHFIELD COUNTY

By Jon Pareles

THE PLAN WAS IMPECCABLE. ON A weekend in late October, my wife and I would spend a weekend in tony Litchfield County in Connecticut, where the country homes of the rich and powerful sit alongside apple orchards on tree-lined country roads. It's a place where overt ostentation is simply not done; the esthetic calls for old-money understatement and decorum. Litchfield County offers a storybook New England countryside of rolling hills and white frame houses, green-gray brooks and old stone walls, all of it preserved through assiduous zoning. For a weekend, we would live like the landed gentry, staying at the Boulders Inn, a country lodge on Lake Waramaug in New Preston.

According to plan, we'd make the 95-mile trip to the town of Litchfield. We would revisit its boulevard (Route 63 North) of stately white New England mansions and its fastidious green. Then we'd settle in at the Boulders. Perhaps we'd take one of the inn's canoes out for a paddle on the lake; perhaps we'd stroll the private trail up Pinnacle Mountain.

But the weather had other plans. On the Saturday we'd chosen, the skies opened up and flooded every exit route from Manhattan. By the time we left the interstates for Route 7 in New Milford, most of the afternoon was gone but the rain persisted. Indoor activities were called for.

Route 7 is the antiques corridor through New England, and we stopped desultorily at some places on the way; one, the Incurable

Collector, included a cookie jar museum with more than 2,000 examples, including more cute animals than a Disney retrospective. We dropped into New Milford's well-advertised weekend flea market, housed in a sprawling industrial shed. Expecting more antiques, we instead found Canal Street north, just the place for obsolete eight-track tapes, hubcaps, Garfield figurines, off-brand pharmaceuticals, used vacuum cleaners, and collector-priced baseball cards and comic books.

As we sloshed up Route 7, mini-malls gradually gave way to New England charm: a white-steepled church, a horse farm, a Colonial graveyard with skinny, listing tombstones. Roadside stands were piled with pumpkins that could fill a passenger seat. On Route 202, the antiques started getting fancier: Earl J. Slack had a set of 12 Hawkes goblets for $1,800, along with African masks, Chinese vases, and a hand-carved portable Buddhist altar from Siam. The elegantly punning Reid and Wright, a used and antiquarian bookseller, had two floors of neatly organized volumes, from century-old Baedekers to a gazeteer of British ghosts; in the parking lot, a Fotomat-size booth sold cappuccino. At Recherche Studio, there was a quintessential New England artifact: a sterling silver miniature oilcan, made by Tiffany. Its function was adding just a few drops of vermouth to that dry martini.

A Mill and Antiques

New Preston (population 1,217) is itself tucked into the Litchfield Hills next to the Aspetuck River, where an old mill house still stands. The center of town, about four blocks long, is a clutch of high-end antiques shops and a pharmacy that also sells wine and liquor, presumably to cure different kinds of ailments. We picked up county newspapers there. Doc's, a lakeside restaurant, had been recommended to us, but by the time we looked in we found out that it was booked solid from 6 to 9pm, even on this rainy night. It seemed we'd be cocooning at the Boulders.

We presented ourselves at the inn's reception desk and let the coddling begin. The inn was built in 1895, a wood frame clad in the giant stones that provide its name, on a broad lawn with the lake across the street. At first, it was a summer home; it has housed guests since the

1930s, when outlying cottages were added. More modern bungalows replaced them in the 1960s and 70s.

We had booked Gem North, half of a cottage up on the hillside with the best view. It has the inn's top price, $300 a night plus tax and a 15% service charge. (The rate includes breakfast and full dinner for two; without the dinner, the rate is $50 less.) A table was reserved for us that night, the woman at the desk said, and would we need an umbrella?

Handel on Cassette

Gem North was uncluttered but carefully equipped. It had a coffee maker and a refrigerator tucked away in an alcove, a Jacuzzi and a hair dryer in the bathroom, and a radio-clock-cassette player by the bed, with tapes of Handel. A window seat, and a deck, looked out on the lake, which was turning bluish silver in the drizzle, perfectly framed by the trees. Two chairs faced a modern fireplace that was already piled with split logs and crumpled newspapers awaiting a match. I lighted it, and felt my equanimity returning.

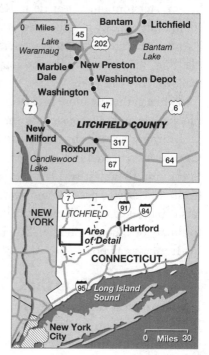

Dinner was served in the main house, in a sunporch facing the lake; during warmer weather, we could have dined outdoors on a patio with the same view. At the next table, a group was avidly discussing the bond market. But we turned our attention to the food, which rewarded it. Boulders follows New American cuisine strategies—seasonal ingredients, Europe-meets-Asia preparations, vertical constructions—with a meticulous flair. The mesclun salad came with cylinders of goat cheese wrapped in phyllo dough; salmon atop an herb and zucchini risotto all but melted with each bite. Desserts included an apple-ginger tart with a carmelized top, and a tower of mousse and orange-chocolate disks.

Replete, we looked around the main house, which has a homey parlor and a snug television room with an aquarium. A basement game room holds a pool table, a dartboard, and a pinball machine so old it rings bells and only scores in the thousands. We strolled back up to the cottage and rekindled the fire.

By the Fireplace

Nobody comes to Litchfield for nightlife, although we could have taken in a movie in nearby Bantam, where the theater plays the kinds of movies seen at the Film Forum and the Angelika in Manhattan. Instead, we eased back and perused the local papers. Stories in *The Litchfield County Times* mentioned residents like Henry Kissinger and Arthur Miller, Sam Waterston and Oscar de la Renta. They also detailed seething community issues: a peculiar gravel mine deal, a fast-food ban on Route 7, a town manager who smokes despite no-smoking rules in Town Hall, a ladybug infestation. The fire was cozy. "We should have brought marshmallows," my wife said.

While gathering more logs from the woodpile on the front porch, I looked up and saw constellations. The storm had finally cleared.

Morning brought bright sun and riotous colors. Golden and red leaves were reflected in Lake Waramaug and covered the path down to the inn. Breakfast was bounteous: a buffet of cereals, fruit salads (fresh and dried), pastries and juices, along with a choice of apple-raisin pancakes or omelets with home fries and bacon or sausage (ordinary or Cajun andouille). Sipping tea, we watched two men fishing from a small boat.

Into the Countryside

It was a perfect day to roam the area: clear, not too cool, with the leaves still on the trees thanks to the dry summer. We decided to visit some local attractions on a circuitous route that would take us through plenty of countryside. My rule of thumb was to follow as many roads as possible with "Hill" in their name, promising good vistas. Others had the same idea; sleek Saabs and BMWs shared the country roads with shiny Jeeps and finely preserved old pickup trucks. In the center of New Preston, a couple proudly toted a section of weathered white picket fence out of an antiques store.

The Silo, in New Milford, is a store and cooking school owned by the New York Pops's musical director, Skitch Henderson, and his wife, Ruth. Situated in an old farm up a narrow road, the Silo's store supplies things like trivets and wineglasses, cornichons and sun-dried tomato paste to local and weekending gourmets. Upstairs in its converted barn is a 25-seat classroom where chefs and cookbook authors give classes on most weekends. A large mirror over the demonstration kitchen's counter provides a better look at the chef's hands. Daniel Leader, author of *Bread Alone* (named after his bakery outside Woodstock, N.Y.), was browning onions for the focaccia he was going to make in a class on Italian breads. The aroma was tempting, but the outdoors beckoned.

Route 67, in Roxbury, was calmly scenic; it led past a bucolic stream, past winding driveways (presumably to opulent estates) and old houses bearing dates in the 1700s and 1800s, past streets with names like Clapboard Road and Sentry Hill Road.

Nearby, in the town of Washington, was the Institute for American Indian Studies, dedicated to prior county inhabitants like the Algonquians. A mother ushered her children through exhibits of arrowheads, baskets, and deerskin leather. Another room held heirlooms from local Indian families, including a pair of elaborately beaded moccasins that had been worn through from dancing. On the grounds, in a forest clearing, stood a reconstructed Indian village: a circle of thatched, hive-shaped homes covered in bark or reeds or twigs, as well as a longhouse and a dugout canoe. It was a ghost town, a silent reminder of a very different New England.

We drove into the center of Washington (chartered 1779, population 3,905), a town out of a Currier and Ives print with white Colonial buildings clinging to leaf-strewn hillsides. The Gunn Memorial Library wasn't exactly the usual small-town hub: It would soon be holding a forum on the United Nations featuring the historian Arthur

Schlesinger, Jr. In its own building, the library's historical museum, deserted except for a friendly curator, held a photo exhibition about the town's Flood of 1955. Invited to add reminiscences to the guest book, one visitor had written, "My family listened on a battery-powered radio as adventurous souls crossed the flooded center of town in a snorkel-equipped Jeep." Upstairs were rooms with Victorian furnishings, including two spectacular doll houses detailed down to miniature cane chairs and playing cards. A photograph with one showed the birthday party where a little girl, with all her friends in white pinafores, had received the house as a gift.

All Kinds of Apples

We asked the curator for directions to Averill Farm, an apple orchard. "They've got a beautiful old farm," she beamed. "They've been there since 1746." We drove in past rows of apple trees. Ida Red and Red Delicious apples hung down from laden branches, gleaming in the sun like ruby earrings. We could have picked our own, but only a few varieties were available on trees. The farm stand offered more variety: Romes and Empires, Holidays and Galas, Winesaps and Mutsus, Yellow Delicious and Rhode Island Greenings, along with Bosc pears and quinces.

The apples were red and green and yellow, dappled and shaded, spherical and ovoid. We asked the man weighing fruit what his favorite was, and he gave the question serious thought. "I like the Mutsu and the Macintosh," he said. "And the Spartan—go ahead, try one." It was like a crisper, richer Macintosh; we filled another five-pound bag for $2.75. On the way out, we passed the old stone farmhouse, beautifully kept after two centuries.

We circled back to Lake Waramaug and to the Hopkins Winery, a vest-pocket vineyard across the street from (and owned by) the Hopkins Inn. The grapes are processed yards away from their hillside arbors, in a converted barn; from a catwalk, we looked down on towering metal vats and big oak barrels while the heady smell of smashed grapes filled the air. The winery offers tastings of its red, white, sparkling, and apple wines.

At the inn across the street, overlooking another lobe of Lake Waramaug from high above, brook trout were swimming in a tank, awaiting their turn as dinner in the inn's German-style restaurant. But the sky was turning pink, so we headed back to the Boulders to watch sunset over the lake from our room.

The inn's Sunday dinner ($30 prix fixe for nonresidents) offered slightly fewer choices than the regular menu, but no less finesse in dishes like monkfish medallions in a lobster coriander broth. We lingered over hazelnut cheesecake and cups of tea, and felt all our senses gratified with the day. Back in the room, we gazed out on the blue-black lake and then into the fire, absorbing as much New England comfort as we could before the morning's trip back home.

LITCHFIELD COUNTY ESSENTIALS

A free guide to the county is available through the **Litchfield Hills Travel Council,** P.O. Box 968, Litchfield, CT 06759 (☎ 203/567-4506).

GETTING THERE

To reach the area by car from Manhattan, take the Henry Hudson Pkwy. to the Sawmill River Pkwy.; continue on the parkway to Rte. 684; continue on Rte. 684 to Rte. 84 East; continue on Rte. 84 East to exit 7 to pick up Rte. 7.

ACCOMMODATIONS

Boulders Inn, E. Shore Rd. (Rte. 45), New Preston (☎ 800/552-6853). Accommodations range from single rooms with fireplaces and views of Lake Waramaug to guest cottages. Weekend stays are $250 to $300 per night, including breakfast and dinner for two, plus a 15% service charge. Rates are based on double-occupancy and a minimum stay of two nights; children under 12 can be accommodated by special arrangement. Mid-week daily rates $150 to $250.

MUSEUMS

Gunn Memorial Museum, 3 Wykeham Rd. (at Rte. 47), Washington (☎ 203/868-7756). Open Thursday through Sunday noon to 4pm. Donations accepted.
Institute for American Indian Studies, 38 Curtis Rd. (off Rte. 199), Washington (☎ 860/868-0518). A reconstructed outdoor Algonkian Indian village, nature trail, and exhibitions. Open Monday through Saturday 10am to 5pm, Sunday noon to 5pm (closed Monday and Tuesday from January through March). Admission $4 adults, $3.50 seniors, $2 for children 6 to 16, free for children under 6.

APPLE PICKING

S. Averill Farm, 250 Calhoun St. (off Baldwin Hill Rd.), Washington (☎ 860/868-2777). Open daily 9am to 5pm during apple season.

ANTIQUING

Earl J. Slack, Rte. 202, Washington (☎ 860/868-7092). Open Saturday and Sunday 11am to 4pm.

The Incurable Collector, 267 Danbury Rd., New Milford (☎ 203/354-7662). Open Thursday through Tuesday 10am to 5pm (closed Wednesday).

Recherche Studio, Rte. 202, New Preston (☎ 203/868-0281). A collection of formal and country formal furniture, crystal, silver, and accessories. Open Friday through Sunday 10:30pm to 6pm, and by appointment.

Reid and Wright Antiquarian Book Center, 287 New Milford Turnpike, Rte. 202, New Preston (☎ 860/868-7706). Open Monday and Wednesday through Saturday 10am to 5pm and Sunday noon to 5pm.

WINE TASTING

Hopkins Winery, Hopkins Rd. (off Rte. 45), New Preston (☎ 860/868-7954). May through December, open Monday through Saturday 10am to 5pm, Sunday 11am to 5pm; January through May, open Friday through Sunday only. Free admission.

FOR GOURMETS

The Silo Cooking School, 44 Upland Rd. (off Rte. 202), New Milford (☎ 860/355-0300). In addition to cooking classes, the store sells kitchen-related items. Open daily 10am to 5pm.

Unwinding in the Connecticut River Valley

by William Grimes

ABOUT TWO HOURS NORTHEAST OF
the Bronx, New York City begins to loosen its iron grip, and the Middle
Atlantic gives way to New England. The transformation is obscured by
the numberless suburbs and exurbs that pull southern Connecticut into
the city's giant maw. But the influence gradually weakens, and then
dies, just about the time that the Connecticut River comes into view.

In days of yore, the stretch of river that runs from Middletown
south to Long Island Sound was home to 50 shipyards. Essex, near
the mouth of the river, supported nine shipyards, and in 1775 built
the first warship of the Revolutionary War, the *Oliver Cromwell*. The
neat clapboard houses in towns and villages along the river's banks
belonged to sea captains who made their living from the West Indies
trade, and took the clipper ships to China. In the 19th century, 6 tons
of elephant tusks found their way every month from Zanzibar to Deep
River, where they were turned into piano keys, a local industry that
gave its name to Ivoryton, near Essex.

Exhausted by its early labors, the river valley slipped into a dignified repose somewhere toward the end of the 19th century, and, to its
credit, has barely stirred since. Dotted with attractive small towns,
forests, and parks, it is ripe for browsing, rich in minor attractions
that afford maximum pleasure for minimum effort.

The area has history, but not too much. Chester, for example, a
picture-postcard town that Frank Capra might have found a little too
wholesome-looking, gave birth to Samuel Silliman, known to local

319

historians as the father of the modern inkwell. Nathan Hale taught school for a year in East Haddam. That's the kind of history we're talking about.

There are museums, but not too many, and not intellectually taxing ones. The region disdains to strive for a vulgar first. The Cockaponset State Forest is the state's second largest, after Pachaug Forest; likewise, the steam train that runs from Essex to Deep River is the state's second-biggest tourist attraction, after Mystic Seaport. The Connecticut River Valley is the touristic equivalent of the gentleman's C.

Inns and bed-and-breakfast establishments abound, some of them renowned, like the Griswold Inn in Essex, the Ivoryton Inn and the Bee and Thistle in Ivoryton, and the Old Lyme Inn in Old Lyme. One weekend, my wife and I set up base camp farther north, at the Riverwind Inn in Deep River. It was a fortunate choice. The town is less touristed than Essex, which, as luck would have it, was the site of a barbershop quartet convention the weekend of our getaway, not to mention the town's annual bluefish bake. Any American worried about the country's disintegrating moral fabric should stroll down Main Street in Essex and listen to a spontaneous rendition of "In the Shade of the Old Apple Tree" ringing out in four-part harmony.

New York can do strange, twisted things to the human soul. The owner of the inn greeted me with open hand and cheery countenance.

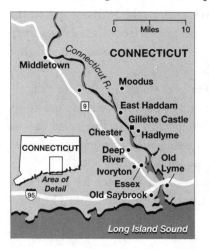

I was immediately suspicious. He began drawing me maps to aid me in my quest for leisure during the weekend, offered to telephone a restaurant to make sure I got a last-minute reservation, and, most unsettling, reached to grab one of my bags. I turned a cold eye upon him. What was the game here? Was he a Yankee skinflint seeking some novel gratuity?

By the end of the weekend, the truth emerged. He and his

wife are actually good-natured, conscientious innkeepers who try to anticipate the needs of their guests. Oh.

Riverwind is an early-19th-century farmhouse that the owners, Barbara Barlow and Bob Bucknall, restored and packed full of antiques, many of them pig-related, since Ms. Barlow says she cherishes fond memories of the hog farm in Smithfield, Va., where she grew up. On the wall of the bathroom of our suite, for example, hung a color print of pigs playing turn-of-the century lawn games. Along with pig-shaped homemade biscuits, the inn's breakfast includes warm slices of Smithfield ham.

The Goodspeed

The inn's location makes for quick and easy forays north and south. Just across the river in East Haddam sits the Goodspeed Opera House, a Victorian bandbox of a theater built by a local shipbuilder and banker in 1876. The ground floor originally housed retail shops. Restored in the 1960s, the Goodspeed stages three musicals every year. Some, like *Annie, Man of La Mancha,* and *The Most Happy Fella,* have gone on to wider fame and fortune in New York City.

Since my wife and I loathe musicals, it was gratifying to find out that the theater was between shows during our visit and therefore we would not have to wince our way through *Paint Your Wagon.* Its branch theater, in a converted knitting-needle factory in Chester, stages musical works in progress.

Gillette Castle

Those who do not enjoy musicals should cross the river, take in the view, then turn south on Route 151 and follow signs to Gillette Castle State Park. The castle is an architectural folly built in 1917 by William Gillette, who amassed millions writing plays like *Secret Service* and appearing onstage in the role of Sherlock Holmes. The house is ugly beyond description, a monstrosity of rough-hewn stone that suggests an ungifted child's papier-mâché classroom project on the Crusades.

It is so repellent that it commands a kind of respect. The interior, a riot of exaggerated textures and unbridled rustication, falls somewhere between a Bavarian hunting lodge and the house in *The Rocky Horror Picture Show*. Ceramic frog troubadours sit on the massive fireplace mantel. At one time, Gillette amused his guests with a miniature railroad that ran around the grounds. Today, only the stations remain. The view overlooking the river remains intact. This Gillette could not alter.

Timothy Dwight, the president of Yale University, gazed upon the river in 1810 and uncorked a purple ode to Connecticut, praising "the purity, salubrity, and sweetness of its waters, the frequency and elegance of its meanders, its absolute freedom from aquatic vegetables." The riverbanks did not escape his notice: "there covered with rich verdure, now fringed with bushes, now covered with lofty greens and now formed by the intruding hill, the rude bluff and the shaggy mountain." He liked what he saw and you will, too.

To sustain the mood, head southward on River Road to the water's edge, where a handful of Colonial houses are clustered near the Chester-Hadlyme Ferry, in operation since 1769. Pick up a map of Middlesex County and drive aimlessly through the Cockaponset State Forest, 15,000 acres of woodland with all sorts of intriguing, rutted roads unmarked on standard maps.

At Riverwind, the innkeepers claimed that the best-kept secret in the area was the Canfield–Meadow Woods Nature Preserve, a 300-acre area of ridges, valleys, and wetlands in Deep River and Essex, with marked trails and no bicycles. It takes a keen eye to spot entrances to the preserve, however. My navigational skills, sense of direction, and general ability to function as a competent adult were seriously called into question from the passenger seat as I searched vainly for a promising opening in the forest primeval.

Sundial Herb Garden

Just as idiosyncratic as Gillette Castle, but far more tasteful, is the Sundial Herb Garden in Higganum. There are actually three gardens: a knot garden of interlocking low hedges; a main garden, with a sundial in the center; and a topiary garden with a fountain in the center. Paths in the main garden lead to cleverly designed vantage points that permit the eye to scan the whole as the nose inhales dozens of exotic fragrances. A viewing guide leads visitors through the gardens.

Next to the gardens is an 18th-century barn with an herb shop and tearoom that serves an ambitious afternoon tea on Sundays from June to mid-October. Ragna Tischler Goddard, who owns the shop and created the garden over a period of 20 years, is an herbalist whose dedication and enthusiasm make her a saleswoman of almost supernatural powers. Only deep detestation of herbs and all they stand for would be proof against her densely annotated tour around the shop, during which, as if by magic, the merchandise piles up in one's arms. Fortunately, it's not a Jaguar dealership.

Essex Attractions

As the Connecticut River flows to Long Island Sound, it recovers some of its original sense of purpose. Pleasure craft and marinas come into view, and in Essex, something of the old maritime flavor comes back. The town still has a shipyard and a marine-engine works, although its best-known product is the E. E. Dickinson Company's witch hazel, distilled in Essex since 1857. In summer, the waterfront is crowded with yachts.

Essex has succumbed a bit to the culture of the twee curio shop and the monster-cookie outlet. But a walk down Main Street, down to the waterfront park, is still an inspiration, the kind of idealized small-town street that Americans normally experience only in Hollywood films. The street is lined with Federal-style and a few Colonial houses, and most of them blur the line between domestic architecture and domestic bliss. Tourists stop and gaze longingly, and you can almost read the thought bubble: "If only I lived there, I'd be happy."

The Griswold Inn, built in 1776, has an inviting taproom with a potbellied stove. The taproom began life as a schoolhouse, but the citizens of Essex, after weighing their priorities, rolled the thing on logs to its present location and gathered there to drink beer. The base of Main Street opens up on a park that includes the Connecticut River Museum, which has a full-scale working reproduction of the first submarine, David Bushnell's *American Turtle*. A one-man affair, it looks like an elongated brandy cask with propellers. In theory, the operator, cranking the propellers by hand, could direct the turtle and affix a mine to an enemy ship. This was attempted during the Revolution, without success.

The river and its towns read as a chronicle of small triumphs and quirky innovations, unfolding on something less than a heroic scale. It is the region that brought forth three new inkwells and a thousand piano keyboards. Its cranky Yankees built a little opera house, a stone castle, and now a geometric herb garden. All the little pieces fit together in a pleasing pattern. And the river holds it together. Not a great river, but a good, dependable one. Dickens looked up and down the Connecticut, reached into his rich adjectival store, and pronounced it "a fine stream." That seems about right.

CONNECTICUT RIVER VALLEY ESSENTIALS

For information on the Connecticut River Valley, call or write the **Connecticut River Valley and Shoreline Visitors Council,** 393 Main St., Middletown, CT 06457 (☎ 800/486-3346 or 860/347-0028). The commission has brochures on the 20 towns within its tourism district.

GETTING THERE

By Car   To reach Deep River and Chester from New York City, take I-95 to Rte. 81 (exit 63); go north to Rte. 148, then east. For Essex and Ivoryton, continue on I-95 to Rte. 9 (exit 70), and go north. Old Lyme is off exit 70, across the river from Old Saybrook.

By Train   Amtrak (☎ 800/872-7245) has six trains daily from Penn Station in Manhattan to Old Saybrook. The trip takes 2½ hours. The one-way fare is $27; 15% off for seniors and disabled travelers; half-fare for children under 16.

ACCOMMODATIONS AND DINING

BED-AND-BREAKFASTS

Riverwind Inn, 209 Main St., Deep River (☎ 860/526-2014). $95 to $165 single or double, full breakfast included.

INNS WITH RESTAURANTS

Bee and Thistle Inn, 100 Lyme St., Old Lyme (☎ 800/622-4946 or 860/434-1667). Doubles, all with private bath, $75 to $155; $5 less for single occupancy (except on weekends or in room no. 7, which is always $75). Cottage $210.

The restaurant serves nouvelle American cuisine. Open Monday and Wednesday through Saturday 8 to 10am, 11:30am to 2pm, and 6pm to closing; open Sunday 8 to 9:30am, 11am to 2pm (for brunch), and 6pm to closing; closed Tuesday.

Copper Beech Inn, 46 Main St., Ivoryton (☎ 860/767-0330). Rooms in the main house $105 to $155 single or double, including continental breakfast; rooms in the carriage house $125 to $175. Two-night minimum on weekends.

The restaurant serves country French cuisine. Open Tuesday through Thursday 5:30 to 8:30pm, Friday and Saturday 5:30 to 9pm, Sunday 1 to 7:30pm; closed Monday. Entrees $20 to $27.

Griswold Inn, 36 Main St., Essex (☎ 860/767-1812). $90 to $185 single or double, continental breakfast included.

The dining room serves traditional American cuisine. Open Monday through Saturday 11:45am to 3pm and 5:30 to 9pm (until 10pm Friday and Saturday); a $12.95 English buffet breakfast is served Sunday 11am to 2:30pm. Dinner entrees $16.95 to $23.95.

Inn at Chester, 318 W. Main St., Chester (☎ 860/526-9541). Rooms $105 with twin bed; $115 with double bed; $125 queen-size bed; $135 queen-size bed with canopy; $145

king-size bed with canopy; $215 suite. Rates include continental breakfast. Rates reduced from January 2 to March 15. Two-night minimum Thanksgiving and Christmas.

The Post and Beam Room serves New American cuisine. Open Monday through Saturday 5:30 to 9pm, Sunday 11:30 to 2:30pm (for brunch) and 4 to 7pm. Entrees $19 to $25.

Old Lyme Inn, 85 Lyme St., Old Lyme (☎ 860/434-2600). Rooms $99 to $158.

Restaurant serves classical American cuisine. Open Monday through Saturday noon to 2pm and 6 to 9pm, Sunday 11am to 3pm (for brunch) and 4 to 9pm. Entrees $19.95 to $27.95

RESTAURANTS

Du Village, 59 Main St., Chester (☎ 860/526-5301). Country French cuisine. Open Wednesday through Saturday 5:30 to 9pm, Sunday 5 to 8pm. Entrees $23 to $27.

Steve's Centerbrook Cafe, 78 Main St., Centerbrook (☎ 860/767-1277). Eclectic cuisine. Open Tuesday through Sunday 5:30 to 9pm; closed Monday. Entrees $11 to $17.

ATTRACTIONS

Connecticut River Museum, Steamboat Dock (at the foot of Main St.), Essex (☎ 860/767-8260). Open Tuesday through Sunday 10am to 5pm; closed Monday and major holidays. Admission $4 adults, $3 seniors, $2 children 6 to 12.

Florence Griswold Museum, 96 Lyme St., Old Lyme (☎ 860/434-5542). June through October, open Tuesday through Saturday 10am to 5pm, Sunday 1 to 5pm; November to May, open Wednesday through Sunday 1 to 5pm. Herb garden wraps around the Huntley-Brown House on the museum grounds. Admission $4 adults, $3 seniors, free for children 12 and under and members.

Gillette Castle State Park, East Haddam (☎ 860/526-2336). The park is open daily 8am to 7pm; admission is free. From Memorial Day to Columbus Day, the castle is open daily 10am to 5pm; from Columbus Day to late December, the castle is open weekends 10am to 4pm; the castle is closed from late December to Memorial Day. Admission to castle $4 adults, $2 children 6 to 11.

Sundial Herb Garden, Brault Hill Rd. (off Rte. 81), Higganum (☎ 860/345-4290). Gardens and shop open daily 10am to 5pm from the day after Thanksgiving until December 24; after December 24, open only on Saturday and Sunday 10am to 5pm. Reservations required for afternoon tea, which is served on Sundays only. On winter weekends, there are food demonstrations, tea tastings, and seminars on garden design and herbs. Group tours (including afternoon tea and garden visit) can be arranged by appointment on weekdays.

Valley Railroad, Essex (☎ 860/767-0103). Mid-June to September, open daily; September through October, open Wednesday through Sunday; late November to late December, open Friday through Sunday; early May through mid-June, open Wednesday through Sunday. Call for trip times. One-hour round trip $10 adults, $7.50 children 3 to 11; 2$^1/_2$-hour train out, riverboat back trip $15 adults, $7.50 children 3 to 11. Parlor car extra.

LOCAL THEATER

Goodspeed-at-Chester/The Norma Terris Theater, N. Main St., Chester. Season runs from June through November. Purchase tickets through the Goodspeed Opera House box office.

Goodspeed Opera House, Goodspeed Landing, East Haddam (☎ 860/873-8668). Season runs from April through December. Tickets $19 to $36.

DOWN-HOME
FOXWOODS CASINO

by Michael T. Kaufman

THERE I WAS STUDYING THE SEVEN
cards that had been dealt me in Pai Gow poker. No, I was not in some
sinister dive in Macao. I was in the cheery, one might even say wholesome, environs of the Foxwoods Resort and Casino in Ledyard, Connecticut, trying to project aplomb and savoir faire as my two $5 chips
lay at risk on the green felt table before me.

In fact, I had no idea what I was doing.

This was not particularly unusual. I have over the years spent time
in casinos on four continents as a dilettante and a patzer. I would on
those occasions imagine myself a cold-blooded James Bond type, betting the ranch without breaking a sweat. In real life, I turned out to be
a chickenhearted dabbler who has never been able to raise the stakes
to the point where losing brought significant pain, or winning, great
joy. I would spend my time at blackjack, a game familiar since childhood, or at the slot machines, where I could make a fool of myself in
private. In truth, gambling was a long way from my favorite sins.

So what was I doing with the Pai Gow hand?

Well, I was on an educational mission. I was using an expense
account advance to help me investigate and write about some of the
other activities offered at casinos. The idea was that with a bankroll of
$100, I would wander through the bustling Foxwoods casino trying
my luck here and there while looking to find my game.

The resort lies on a reservation in southeastern Connecticut, where,
with the help of a nun and Malaysian financiers, the tiny Mashantucket

Pequot tribe parlayed a claim of territorial sovereignty into, first, a successful bingo hall, and then the largest moneymaking casino in the Western Hemisphere, raking in profits of $600 million a year. A 600-room hotel seems to be booked every weekend into eternity. More rooms are being added.

There are arcades with shops selling Indian art and doohickeys from all over the United States. Every hour on the hour a light show takes place at a huge crystal statue of a dancing Indian. There are massive sculptures of Indians throughout the seven-acre resort, and a huge Indian museum has recently been built in the complex, which dominates its rural setting, surrounded by thick woods. It crossed my mind that all the Indian motifs might make some customers feel better about losing. After all, losses at Foxwoods are not going to some self-promoting plutocrat like Donald Trump or to a shadowy syndicate, but to Native Americans. So what if there are only a few hundred members of this tribe, or that each one stands to gain a couple of million dollars a year? You can still think of your gambling losses as something like reparations.

A Wary Warm-up

Fortified by the notion, I set off to see what I could do with my employer's $100. My first stop was at the $5 blackjack table, where I thought I would warm up with something familiar. I started with $20 in chips and after betting cautiously for about half an hour, I was up to $60. Ten minutes later, I was back down to $20. So much for warming up.

I moved over to acey-deucey. This is a game in which the dealer draws a card and places it between two others he has displayed face up. If the third card falls numerically between the two others, the players win; if not, the house wins. I bet $5. The dealer drew a 3 and a 10. The third card, an 8, fell within the spread, meaning that I won $5. Pretty terrific I thought. I played again and this time the two cards came up as 6 and 8, which meant that if the third card was anything but a 7, my fellow players and I would lose. My fellow players, all of them seemingly retired folk, oohed and aahed and contorted themselves in efforts to assure that a 7 turned up. In fact, a king turned up and we lost. Pretty boring, I thought. I played for about 15 minutes and lost $30.

I proceeded to the roulette wheel. Concentrated at first on betting whether the ball would end up on an odd or even number, virtually an even-money proposition. My intention was to warm up in this way and then attempt any of 10 other possible wagers, like betting on a particular number, where the payoff was 35 to 1; or betting on adjoining pairs (17 to 1), rows of three numbers (11 to 1), blocks of four numbers (8 to 1), or columns of 12 numbers (2 to 1).

After my timid overture, I felt suddenly inspired. It was March and in March there are three birthdays within my family. My daughter's is the 20th and mine is the 23rd, and amazingly those two numbers lie next to each other. Boldly I placed a $10 chip on the line between the two, which meant that if either came in, I would win $170. The croupier, dressed in a miniskirt with Indian designs, said no more bets and set the wheel spinning. The steel ball stopped on 15, which is the date in March of my wife's birthday.

Enter Reason

Disheartened, I went back to playing odd and even, nursing the dubious pleasure of small gains and small losses. Then a woman joined our glum band with a big stack of chips and the look of confident experience. "What numbers have been running?" she asked me, suggesting that what we were facing was not a matter of random chance or taunting fortune, but a situation in which discerning reason would bring benefit. I shrugged and stupidly told her that I had not noticed.

"No problem," she said pleasantly, and began placing chips all over the board. I counted 15 of the $10 chips. It seemed she knew what she was doing, but it was kind of hard to figure out, with all the hedges. I bet on the number 3 because that is how many children I have. My one number lost. One of her bets won but I could not tell from the size of

HOW TO PLAN YOUR OWN
FOXWOODS WEEKEND

Foxwoods Casino Resort Hotel, Rte. 2, Ledyard (☎ 800/369-9663). Daily room rates are based on double occupancy; rooms can accommodate up to four ($10 extra for a roll-away bed). December through March, $150 double; April through June, $190 double; July through August $225 double; September through December 1, $190 double. Daily rates for suites that can accommodate up to six people range from $140 off-peak to $300 peak.

Also on the premises is the **Two Trees Inn,** a New England–style inn. December through March, $115 double; April through June, $140 double; July through August, $175 double; September through November, $140 double.

her chip pile whether she had made a net gain or loss. She went ahead and scattered chips all over for the next spin. After about 10 spins, I was down a total of $60.

I thought it was time for a break, so I found my wife and we went to see if there were any tickets left to see Steve Lawrence and Eydie Gorme, who were singing at the theater adjoining the casino. Here we were lucky. One woman in front of us said the singers had been married for 40 years. Another said she remembered when they started out. The people in the audience seemed mostly older than the singers, who sang dozens of Gershwin songs. It was very pleasant. It cheered me up and I was ready to see what I could do with the $40 remaining from my advance.

I approached the craps table and watched the action. What was going on was even more confusing than what had been going on at roulette. There seemed to be 12 types of bets possible. You can bet with the shooter or against him. You can bet on particular numbers, or on particular combinations of numbers. Like the woman at roulette, many of the players were putting down bets all over the place. I considered joining them but in the end it seemed like too much responsibility.

Losing, Again

I moved on to chuck-a-luck, a game played with three dice. You can bet on any number from 1 to 6. If one of the dice shows your number, you win the amount you bet. If two dice show the number, you win twice the amount you bet. And if all three dice show the number, you win 10 times the amount wagered. You can also bet on the aggregate amount the dice show. I bet $10 on 4. The three dice came up 3, 2, 2. My nut was down to $30.

That's when I discovered Pai Gow poker.

In this game, the player is dealt seven cards, dividing them into a five-card hand and a two-card hand. To win, both hands must be higher than those held by the house. In the event that a player wins one hand but loses the other, the game is declared a push, in which no money changes hands. This seemed intriguing. I bet $10. In my seven cards were a pair of eights and garbage. What could I do? I offered the pair as my five-card hand and showed a king high for my two-card hand. I lost both to a pair of queens and a pair of twos. I played a second hand, and lost again. I liked this game and felt that if I kept going I was certain to get a push and maybe, who knew, even win. But I was down to my last $10 and since variety was what I was after, I looked for one more diversion.

I found it in pull tabs. This is a game, sold at many Indian reservations, in which for $2 a player can buy a ticket with five tabs. When these are pulled back, they reveal slot machine symbols, registering either nothing at all or payouts ranging from $2 to $50,000. I bought five. I pulled back the tabs. On the first four, there was zilch. I peeled back the tabs on the fifth card, certain that my dismal luck had to turn, confident that my educational evening was going to end on a high note.

Indeed, it did. I won $2. I bought my wife a cup of tea and we went off to watch the light show at the statue of the dancing Indian one more time.

EXPLORING MYSTIC SEAPORT AND ENVIRONS

by Ralph Blumenthal

WAITING FOR OUR DINNER TO COOK the old-fashioned way—in the hearth of a landmark Colonial inn in North Stonington, Connecticut—I leafed through the guest book, my eye caught by this recent entry: "Great, nothing has changed since 1635." Like, I wondered, the writer could know? Actually, the place, Randall's Ordinary, goes back to only about 1685, but why quibble? For a millennium-era family of Hypercard-carrying Manhattanites, it was plenty old and authentic enough to set the stage for a weekend tour of the historic Mystic area.

In addition to Mystic Seaport, the re-created 19th-century ship-building village, there is the town itself with its quaint drawbridge and, yes, Mystic Pizza, which inspired the movie (although the picture was actually shot in a converted lobster warehouse in Stonington); the Mystic Marinelife Aquarium; Stonington Borough, a sweet town of pastel-hued clapboard homes; Groton, with its naval submarine base; and gritty New London, with its museums and Whale Oil Row.

It was more by chance than by design that we alighted at the inn with the extraordinary name ("ordinary" being an old name for tavern) about 10 miles northeast of Mystic. Since every place I phoned in Mystic was booked for the weekend, I started calling farther afield, not realizing until later my genius in pairing our foray into history with a stay in 300-year-old lodgings now owned, no less, by an American Indian tribe: the Mashantucket Pequots, who operate the hugely successful Foxwoods gambling casino on their nearby reservation.

(Of course, our daughters would surely have considered it an even more brilliant juxtaposition to have put up at a Days Inn with pool.)

Time did indeed seem frozen at the 27-acre farmstead just off Interstate 95. Two oxen and a donkey grazed in the fields as we hauled our bags into the dim brown Colonial frame structure, which a settler named John Randall put up nearly a century before the American Revolution. Since expanded, it now houses the dining rooms and, upstairs, three guest rooms at $115 each on weekends. A dozen other rooms, including a deluxe suite, are in a transplanted 1819 barn, along with the inn's office and a lounge with a squawking African gray parrot. The Randall house is on the National Register of Historic Places, which explains, I figured, why the wrought-iron door latch to one of our rooms hung askew: Even the disrepair had to be landmarked.

Our two facing rooms, off a landing atop a flight of stairs, were alluring: wide-plank floors that listed and creaked authentically, four-poster beds with crocheted canopies, fireplaces, and—surprise!—bathrooms with whirlpool tubs. The old paned windows kept sliding shut: To hold them open for air, I had to prop them open with whatever was at hand. (When one window sprang shut, it fired an ice bucket lid into the yard below.) There were no television sets (there are in the barn rooms), but there was electricity, along with adequate reading lamps. A lumpy armchair in our room also seemed a candidate for the National Register; when I sat down there was a *sprong!* and a large coiled upholstery spring clonked to the floor.

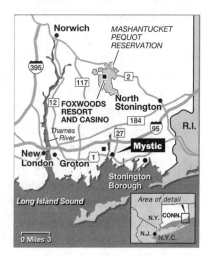

For our first outing, we headed for downtown Mystic, making a point (as I'd been advised) of parking a few blocks on the near side of the drawbridge to avoid traffic tie-ups. That allowed us the pleasure of walking into town across the Erector set span, inhaling the tangy breeze of the Mystic River where, far below, speedboats churned frothy wakes and sailboats carved the wavelets like curling soap chips.

There was a mandatory (for our family, anyway) stop at the thronged Mystic Drawbridge Ice Cream parlor dating from the 1800s and another at the well-stocked Army-Navy store a little farther down West Main Street, where every customer seemed to rate a personal greeting. Just beyond is Mystic Pizza, whose popularity has led to an expansion into the storefront next door. Police officers in shorts patrolled on bikes. I actually saw one driver talk his way out of a parking ticket. Now, that's incredible.

Along the river, we stopped to scout a nice-looking hotel for future reference: the Steamboat Inn, an old ship warehouse. It had some lovely rooms overlooking the water, starting at $195 a night with a two-night minimum stay on weekends.

Suddenly there were bells and a piercing whistle that made our younger daughter, Sophie, jump. Traffic gates came down, and the roadway split and reared up, counterbalanced by huge descending weights. Everything in town stopped, and we joined the crowd of gawkers. Then through the gap paraded a file of mast tips: the sailboats that line up for the drawbridge openings a quarter past every hour. In five minutes, the show was over. The weights rose, the roadway releveled, the gates swung up, and life resumed.

Mystic Seaport is a short drive away on Route 27, Greenmanville Avenue. Occupying 17 acres that once bristled with boatyards and marine commerce and then fell into decline in the 1880s, the seaport now bustles again with tall ships and dozens of galleries displaying old trades and crafts. We parked in one of the large lots across the road and entered by one of the two gates, paying $16 each (Sophie entered free) and stepping into an antique world of waving masts and clattering horse-drawn buggies. We clambered aboard one of the old ships, the *Charles W. Morgan*, an 1841 whaling bark that is the last remnant of the nation's wooden whaling fleet, and poked our heads into the old pharmacy, tavern, barrel shop, and general store. For lunch, we joined a lobsterfest near a mock lighthouse. Service was family style on rustic picnic tables under a large tent as a folk singer entertained with sea chanteys.

In the afternoon at the Village Green, children walked on stilts, rolled hoops, and tried out other old-fashioned games with the zest of discovering something new. A daily program offers demonstrations of sail handling, rope making, and fishing by net. There were also role players who invoked characters from 1876, musicians entertaining at the bandstand, and a stargazing show at a building called the planetarium.

Back in our rooms at Randall's Ordinary to rest before dinner, we could hear, through the floorboards, snatches of the menu being recited downstairs to early arrivals for the 7pm sitting. By the time we came down, I could almost recite it myself: Shaker herb soup, pork loin, duck breast, roast leg of lamb. . . .

With lip-smacking anticipation, we trooped to the hearth to inspect the selections of dark, sizzling meat. It was instructive to watch the cook in knee breeches maneuver the heavy iron skillets and pots over the open fire, which is where all meals at the inn are cooked from largely native ingredients and early American recipes. The ur-cuisine was introduced by the couple who opened the inn in 1987, Bill and Cindy Clark, antiques collectors who became adept at restoring old houses; they sold Randall's Ordinary to the Pequot Indians in February for $1.4 million.

But by the time we got back to our seats, the waiter had bad news: The kitchen had run out of all entrees but Nantucket scallops and capon. We had what was left, with peas and corn pudding. The scallops were delicious, the chicken so-so. "Maybe that's why they call it Randall's Ordinary," said my wife, Debbie, her churlish mood only partly mitigated by a dessert of pear and apple crisp. The bill, with a few drinks, came to $155—too much, we thought, authenticity notwithstanding.

We did better the next morning. Although the room came with a continental breakfast of large muffins and fruit salad, we couldn't resist splurging an extra $8 on Rhode Island johnnycakes, cornmeal pancakes served with fried apples and maple syrup; and maple toast, hearth-baked bread dipped in maple batter—as tasty as it sounds.

Thus fortified, we headed back toward Mystic to the Mystic Marinelife Aquarium, drawn by the promise of 3,500 sea creatures in 40 exhibits. Paying $10.50 each ($7 for Sophie), we emerged in a dim, labyrinthine underworld of fish tanks filled with kaleidoscopic marine life, sharks, and circling porpoises and dolphins. "Did you ever think how boring their life must be?" asked our teenager, the increasingly skeptical Anna.

I had always kind of lumped dolphins and porpoises together, but an exhibit highlighted the differences. (Porpoises are smaller, for one thing.) Here is another thing I learned: A blue whale's tongue is as large as a whole elephant. There was a poignant lesson, too, in the story of the helpful little wrasse that cleans parasites from the scales of other fish, and the perfidious false cleaner that mimics it only to take a bite out of the poor trusting host.

A booming announcement summoned us to the indoor marine theater where trained bottlenose dolphins and beluga whales leaped into the air and retrieved objects underwater. A dolphin's natural sonar, or echolocation, is so good that blindfolded it can distinguish between differently shaped toys in the water. Sophie liked it when the trainers tossed them fish so, as she reasoned, "they're not hungry after performing." Before leaving, we trekked the archipelago of small outdoor pools and islands with penguins and seals. The aquarium staff says that the dolphins will soon take a hiatus, leaving the high-leaping antics to the beluga whales.

Taking a restaurant recommendation from a friendly couple whose dog Sophie had stopped to pet, we headed for Stonington Borough, a few twisting miles east along the coast. This was indeed a gem of a town, with Water Street and adjacent lanes lined with attractive shops and pristine Colonial clapboards in a palette of luscious hues. Historical markers identified one house as the birthplace of Capt. Edmund Fanning, a late-18th-century trader and explorer; another as the birthplace of Capt. Nathaniel Palmer, a pioneer explorer of the Antarctic archipelago, described somewhat hyperbolically on the sign as having "discovered" Antarctica in 1820; a third as the home of Whistler's mother. Anna and I tried to outdo each other naming the colors in the fanciful terms of today's sports clothes catalogues. "Butter cream." "Cornflower." "Mint." "Melon." "Periwinkle." "Mocha." "Bone."

The restaurant we'd come for, the Skipper's Dock, was prettily situated on the water, but a chill wind and the fiercely setting sun drove us off the deck to the inside dining room, where we feasted on steamers and lobster, mussels, fish-and-chips, and corn and salad. With a few drinks and dessert, the bill for four came to a little more than $100.

On the way home, we stopped at the naval submarine base in Groton, where sinister German, Italian, and Japanese submarines flank the entrance to the museum. Inside are World War II battle flags, mementos and trophies of the silent service, and convincingly claustrophobic mock-ups of submarine attack centers with working periscopes.

The unquestioned highlight is the decommissioned nuclear submarine, *Nautilus*, which from its launching in 1955 broke all underwater speed and distance records, became the first vessel to cross the North Pole, and is now a national landmark open to visitors. Holding audiotape tour guides to our ears, we inspected the cramped bunks, well-equipped galley and ominous torpedo ports.

Our route back took us through New London, where we circled the pier and the historic downtown with its old burial ground, courthouse and railroad station, and 18th- and 19th-century buildings.

Deciding to indulge in one last lobster blowout, we took a detour back to Noank to find a popular restaurant called Abbott's Lobster in the Rough. After meandering, lost, in Noank, I eased the car over to ask directions when a man said: "Let me guess. You want Abbott's. Left on High. Left on Spring. Left on Pearl." Three juicy lobsters and $55 later, I was trying to translate the directions backward to find our way out when I spotted a large sign. NOW THAT WE'RE HERE, it said, HOW DO WE GET THERE? It told us.

MYSTIC ESSENTIALS

GETTING THERE

To reach Mystic Seaport by car from Manhattan, take I-95 to exit 90 and pick up Rte. 27; continue to the seaport.

ACCOMMODATIONS

Foxwoods Casino Resort Hotel, Rte. 2, Ledyard (☎ 800/369-9663). December through March, $150; April through June, $190; July and August, $225; September through December 1, $190. Rates are based on double occupancy. Rooms can accommodate up to four people; additional $10 for rollaway beds. Daily rates for suites that can accommodate up to six people range from $140 off-peak to $300 in peak season.

Also on the premises is the **Two Trees Inn,** a New England–style inn.daily rates are based on double occupancy. December through March, $115; April through June, $140; July and August, $175; September through November, $140.

Randall's Ordinary, Rte.2, North Stonington (☎ 860/599-4540). Weekends, $115 double room; weekdays, $75 single, $95 double. Sunday through Thursday, a double room for two with dinner is $130. A suite is available

for $195. The dining room is open daily 7 to 11am and noon to 3pm; dinner seatings are at 7pm Sunday through Friday, at 5 and 7:30pm Saturday. Children welcome.

Steamboat Inn, 73 Steamboat Wharf, Mystic (☎ 860/536-8300). Rooms $95 to $195 early December through early March; $125 to $225 from March until early May; $150 to $275 from May to early September; $135 to $250 from September to December. Daily room rates are based on double occupancy and include breakfast. Children welcome.

DINING

Also see Randall's Ordinary, under "Accommodations," above.

Abbott's Lobster in the Rough, 117 Pearl St., Noank (☎ 860/536-7719). Early May through Labor Day, open daily noon to 9pm; Labor Day to Columbus Day, open Friday through Sunday noon to 7pm; closed Columbus Day through April.

Mystic Pizza, W. Main St., Mystic (☎ 860/536-3700 or 860/536-3737. Open daily 10am to 11pm.

Skipper's Dock, 66 Water St., Stonington Borough (☎ 860/535-2000). Open January 31 through mid-September, daily 11:30am to 10pm.

ATTRACTIONS

Mystic Marinelife Aquarium, 55 Coogan Blvd., Mystic (☎ 860/572-5955). On display is "Robots in the Sea," an interactive exhibition that simulates the exploration of a shipwreck. Open Labor Day through July 1, daily 9am to 5pm; July 2 through Labor Day, daily 9am to 6pm. Admission $11, $10 seniors, $7 children 3 to 12. Special family activities are scheduled on weekends during the winter and daily through the summer.

Mystic Seaport, Rte.27 (exit 90 off I-95), Mystic (☎ 860/572-5315). Open August 25 to May 31, daily 9am to 5pm; June 1 through August 24, daily 9am to 6pm. Admission $16 adults, $15 seniors, $8 children 6 to 15, free for children under 5. In addition to the

exhibits, there are seasonal trips aboard rowboats, steamboats (mid-May through mid-October), and sailboats available; prices range from $3.50 for a steamboat ride ($2.50 for children) to $14 for an hour on a self-guided sailboat ($10.50 for Seaport members). Throughout the year, there are special activities free with seaport admission, including a Lobsterfest at the end of May, an antique marine engine exposition in August, and holiday events from November through December; specialized workshops in boatbuilding, navigation, and open-hearth cooking are offered for an additional fee.

Naval Submarine Base New London, Crystal Lake Rd. (exit 86 off I-95), Groton

(☎ 800/343-0079 or 860/449-3174). Although the base is not open to the public, you can visit the historic ship **Nautilus,** the first nuclear-powered submarine, and the **Submarine Force Museum,** both outside the front gate. You can also see four miniature submarines, including three pre–World War II varieties from Japan, Italy, and Germany, and a 1930s American explorer, used for exploring the ocean floor. Open November 1 to May 14, Wednesday through Monday 9am to 4pm (closed Tuesday); May 14 to Oct. 31, Wednesday through Monday 9am to 5pm, Tuesday 1 to 5pm. Free admission.

Whale Oil Row, New London. A row of historic Greek revival houses dating to the mid-1800s that are not open for tours, but can be viewed from the street. At no. 1 is the **Chamber of Commerce of Southeastern Connecticut** (☎ 860/443-8332), which offers a selection of tourist brochures and maps, some free; open Monday through Friday 8:30am to 5pm.

SHOPPING

Mystic Army-Navy Store, 37-39 W. Main St. at Steamboat Wharf, Mystic (☎ 888/536-1877 or 860/536-1877). Open November through April, Sunday through Thursday 10am to 7pm, Friday and Saturday 9am to 9pm; May through October, daily 9am to 9pm. **Mystic Army-Navy Store II** (☎ 860/572-5844) is located in the Olde Mistick Village Shopping Complex, near the aquarium.

ICE CREAM

Mystic Drawbridge Ice Cream, 2 W. Main St., Mystic (☎ 860/572-7978). Open May through December, daily 8am to midnight; closed the rest of the year.

Windjammer Cruises
from Mystic

by Michael T. Kaufman

It was time for a sea change.
Terra firma had grown too familiar. The little ad caught my eye.
"Windjammer cruises from Mystic, Connecticut," it said. "That's the
ticket," I said to myself, and added, "Shiver me timbers." I have no
idea what that means. Somehow it sounded right.

I called the number listed and communicated my interest to an
answering machine that greeted me by saying, "Ahoy, there." Pres-
ently a pamphlet arrived offering a variety of accommodations and
departure dates. There were five-day, three-day, and two-day voyages
to choose from. We signed on for a weekend sail.

Following instructions that came by mail, we drove up on a Friday
evening, arriving after dinner at the pier in downtown Mystic where
the *Clipper* was tied up. She was a 120-foot twin-masted vessel, and
even in the dark I liked the cut of her jib, or would have if her sails had
not been furled. (The company now uses the *Clipper's* sister ship, the
Mystic Whaler, for excursions.)

We were welcomed aboard by Craig Vandewater, the first mate,
who told us we would be heading out for Shelter Island in the morning. It turned out he was also a bassoonist with the Nassau Symphony
Orchestra. This happenstance is all the more amazing when you consider that the Oxford English Dictionary defines windjamming as
both sailing a vessel and playing a wind instrument. I had left my
O.E.D. behind and so did not learn this until I got home. I'm sorry I
did not have a chance to talk about it with Mr. Vandewater.

He showed us to our cabin, one of six that shared a head down a gangway toward the bow. The head had a toilet and a shower with hot and cold water. Our cabin, the cheapest of the private quarters, was neat, cozy, and functional. It was also very small, suitable only for two people who were quite fond of each other. There were two bunks, a sink, a skylight, and reading lamps. Since my wife was recovering from a broken arm, I did not protest when she took the lower berth, and I set about practicing getting into and out of the upper one, which jutted out just a foot below the ceiling.

Eventually I adapted a version of a high jumper's approach and got to the point where I could almost get into bed without bumping my head or scraping my shins. Then I practiced sleeping.

That proved taxing. The problem was that I was kept awake by my concern about what would happen when I awoke. Would I sit up, as was my custom, and thereby risk a concussion or a bloody nose? The prospect gave me a lot to worry about, but since worrying has been a hobby for a long time, I was quite happy.

My wife said I did sleep, and on Saturday morning, I rose to the sound of ship's bells, the smell of pancakes and bacon, and a glorious sunny Saturday morning. My wife and I met the 12 other passengers and our captain, John Eginton. Like Mr. Vandewater and three of the remaining four crewmen, he had a fine nautical beard. Inspired by it, I vowed not to shave for the length of the voyage.

By 9am, the *Clipper* set out under power down the Mystic River. Just ahead lay a drawbridge. The crew gave out cold pancakes, instructing us to throw them at the man who operated the bridge. "It's a tradition," the cook said. I had read enough to know that it is dangerous to ignore tradition at sea, so with the rest of the passengers, I scaled pancakes, missing badly. The man on the bridge threw his own pancakes and came closer.

Once we reached Long Island Sound, Captain Eginton gave orders to hoist the *Clipper's* 5,000 square feet of sail. The passengers joined in hauling for a minute or two to raise the two larger sails.

It was not quite 10am, and we were left to our own devices. I was eager for distractions. In a pattern that continued throughout the journey,

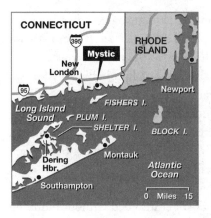

the other passengers were mostly paired off in what appeared to be married couples. They were all friendly enough, but conversations tended to resemble the banter at a table of a wedding reception where no one knew one another: "The ship is very beautiful, isn't she?" or "Did it take you long to get here?"

I chatted with the captain at the wheel, learning that on our course to Shelter Island we would be bucking tides and head winds. The routes, he said, were determined largely by weather conditions, with possible destinations including Block Island and Newport, Rhode Island, and on the longer sails Martha's Vineyard. I learned that the ship was nine years old and had been built in Rhode Island on the model of a Baltimore coastal schooner similar to the kind used by Yankee privateers in the Revolutionary War. The design had been adapted especially for passengers and was certified to take as many as 56 overnight passengers. There were two other kinds of cabins in addition to ours: one a little larger and two so-called owners' cabins, which have their own heads and showers. There is also something like steerage class available in the dining hall, where bunks flop down and can be curtained off to provide privacy.

After chatting, I began scanning the horizon. We passed New London, Connecticut, and I thought of Eugene O'Neill, who grew up there and wrote of "dat ol' davil, sea." We passed North Dumpling Island, where we saw a lighthouse and a recently built, scaled-down version of Stonehenge. Mr. Vandewater told me the island had been purchased by someone who had playfully seceded from the United States, issuing visas and setting up his own currency, the dumpling.

We passed some cormorants and enough expensive-looking pleasure craft to make me wonder about my standing in the economic pyramid. We passed Fishers Island and in the distance could see Plum

Island, where the Army reportedly raises and maintains all kinds of killer bacteria. I tried to hold my breath.

Then I lay down on a mattress on deck intent on reading. I read three pages and fell into a very pleasant sleep, awakening just in time for a lunch of crab salad. Like all the meals aboard, it was quite good and ample.

After lunch, I played Scrabble with my wife. We tried to use only nautical terms, but we failed. Later I read, scanned, and slept. In the face of a stiff wind, Captain Eginton tacked along a zigzag course for Shelter Island, arriving to tie up at Dering Harbor. There was just enough time for a brisk walk through the tiny commercial center before all of us, crew and passengers, gathered for a steak dinner in the lounge.

The conversation continued on deck, but the sun and sea and relaxation had taken their toll, so we turned in relatively early. I seemed to be getting the hang of things, and I slept much better.

As Sunday morning broke hazy, I felt myself being drawn into the increasingly familiar rhythms of life afloat: breakfast, hoisting sails, scanning, chatting, reading, napping, eating, and waiting to eat.

Now the wind was at our backs, and we were on a much more direct course than on the outward passage, in which we were forced to sail 50 miles to cover a point-to-point distance of about 28 miles.

There was one stretch of the Sound where giant tankers kept looming through the mist. As I listened to their pilots give their positions over the radio, I noticed that our captain and crew were not worried. This, I realized, was my moment. I knew just enough about vectors to calculate the chances of collision. There I was along the starboard rail, silently and happily worrying as I mentally plotted converging courses and watched one tanker after another pass us at distances of at least a mile.

And so it went, napping, eating, reading, chatting, hoisting, more waiting to eat, scanning, and anticipating collisions and disasters. But in fact, there were no tragedies or dramas. It made me wonder what would have happened to literature if Conrad, Melville, Stevenson, and O'Neill had known only such smooth sailing. No mutinies, no shipwrecks, no tempests, no failures of nerve, no crazed crewmen or breaching whales.

The *Clipper* returned to its berth on the Mystic River. It was late Sunday afternoon. We shook hands with our fellow passengers and the crew members, thanking them for safe adventure. We drove the 130 miles back to the city, and all along the way we could still feel the gentle pitching of the sea in our legs. After two days before the mast, home were the sailors, home from sea.

CRUISING ESSENTIALS

DAYLONG AND MULTIDAY CRUISES FROM MYSTIC

Mystic Whaler Cruises, 7 Holmes St. (exit 90 off I-95), Mystic (☎ 800/697-8420 or 860/536-4218), offers two-, three-, and five-night sails; overnight sails; half- and full-day sails; and three-hour dinner excursions aboard the *Mystic Whaler*. Per-person rates range from $210 to $335 for a two-day sail; $315 to $465 for a three-day sail; $525 to $695 for a five-day sail; $95 to $110 for a half- or full-day sail; $50 for a dinner cruise. Destinations include Sag Harbor, Greenport, and Dering Harbor, Long Island; Newport, Rhode Island; Shelter and Block Islands; Cuttyhunk and Martha's Vineyard.

Sterling Yacht Charters, 44 Water St. (exit 90 off I-95), Mystic (☎ 800/592-2485 or 860/572-1111), offers bare-boat and charters with a captain on motor and sailing yachts to such destinations as Block Island; Montauk, Long Island; Newport, Rhode Island; Essex, Connecticut; and Martha's Vineyard. Full- and half-day sails range from $350 to several thousand dollars, depending on the vessel; weekly rates are $2,500 for a bare-boat to $3,500 for one with crew.

Sylvina Beal Windjammer Cruises, 120 School St. (exit 89 off I-95), Mystic (☎ 800/333-6978). The schooner *Sylvina W. Beal,* in operation since 1911, offers overnight and three-day sails to Block Island and other destinations, such as Newport, Rhode Island, and Sag Harbor, Long Island. The season runs from Memorial Day through mid-September. Depending upon the season, per-person rates range from $195 to $295 for an overnight sail, and $275 to $355 for a three-day sail.

QUICK CRUISES FROM NEW YORK

Circle Line Cruises, Pier 83, Hudson River at 42nd St., Manhattan (☎ 212/563-3200). From March 6 through December 21, Circle Line offers a variety of cruises from Pier 83, including the three-hour, 35-mile cruise around Manhattan, past the Statue of Liberty, Ellis Island, the United Nations, and other landmarks. Daily sailings hourly from 9:30am to 3:30pm (except 12:30pm) and at 7pm, with additional cruise times on Saturdays and Sundays. Tickets $20 adults, $10 children under 12.

Circle Line also offers two-hour cruises, with weekend sailings geared to families ($15 to $17 for adults, $5 to $9 for children); dance and jazz cruises ($20 to $25); sunset cruises ($20 adults, $10 children); and lunch cruises ($21 per person).

The Pioneer, South Street Seaport, Pier 16 (on the East River; ☎ 212/748-8786), is a two-masted schooner from 1885 operated by the South Street Seaport Museum. Operates May through September, with daily afternoon and evening sails. Tickets $16 adults, $13 seniors, $12 students and children 12 and under.

Seaport Liberty Cruises (☎ 212/630-8888) offers a variety of sightseeing cruises from Pier 16 on the East River. One-hour cruises leave daily at noon, 1:30, 3, and 4:30pm. The fare is $12 adults, $10 for seniors, $6 for children under 12, free for children under 2. There are also live music cruises featuring jazz and blues on Wednesday and Thursdays at 7 and 9:30pm; ticket prices vary. Two-hour DJ cruises are offered Friday at 7 and 10pm and Saturday at 10pm; tickets $15. Reservations not necessary.

World Yacht, Pier 81, Hudson River at 41st St., Manhattan (☎ 212/630-8100), offers three-hour formal dinner cruises, with music, along the west side of Manhattan daily year-round; boarding begins at 6pm, with sailing from 7 to 10pm. Sunday through Friday, $62 per person; Saturday, $79 per person. A two-hour casual cruise with buffet and music sails on Monday and Tuesday from 7:30 to 9:30pm, with boarding at 6:30pm; $49.95 per person. Two-hour Sunday brunch cruises with music, from 12:30 to 2:30pm (with boarding at 11:30am) are $39 per person, $19 for children 12 and under.

ADVENTURES ALOFT: HOT-AIR BALLOONING

by Michael T. Kaufman

CABIN FEVER IS LAPSING. THE SEAson has changed, and what is needed to stir the blood is a new outlook on life, a change of perspective. One could run, ride horses, or fall dangerously in love, but all of this involves energy. Bungee jumping is appealingly passive but probably too drastic. What about hot-air ballooning? From winter quarters on the couch, it sounded like an ideal psychic pick-me-up.

The imagination took over. I could see myself wafting over a picturesque landscape like the great balloonists: the Montgolfier brothers, who first wafted before the French Revolution; Malcolm Forbes; Jules Verne's hero Phineas Fogg, and, of course, Babar, the elephant king. My wife was consulted. Fine, sure, she said, let's go.

As it turns out, there are quite a number of balloonists around New York who will take you up and, and what is much more important, bring you down. They charge about $200 for rides lasting one to two hours. Most will take as few as two people and as many as 10. Almost all the balloonists offer two departure times: early morning to watch the sunrise and late afternoon, when the winds are generally calmer.

After phone calls to a number of operators, a deal was struck with Matt Fenichel of Airvertising and Airventures of West Simsbury, Connecticut. He was chosen because he has been flying for more than 19 years, because the area in which he operates was relatively unknown to us and mildly intriguing, but mostly because of his low-key but unmistakable take-charge tone.

"You realize that if the weather is at all questionable, we don't go; we reschedule," he explained on the phone. "If it's blowing more than 8 miles an hour at ground level, we stay put, and it won't do you any good to beg." We booked for a Saturday-afternoon flight with the following morning as a fallback. We reserved a hotel room in the Farmington Valley area, 90 miles from New York City, and as our scheduled liftoff neared, we anxiously followed the weather reports.

As things turned out, the appointed day was snowy, rainy, and windy. I wondered if things were balmy in Simsbury. My wife wondered if I was balmy in the British sense. At about that point, Mr. Fenichel called to say the weather was awful up there, too, and that we should come up the following week. I did not beg.

A week later, all systems proved to be go. The two-hour drive from Manhattan was pleasant. We checked into the Avon Old Farms Hotel, a neo-olden-times establishment nearby. We called Mr. Fenichel, who told us to meet him in the parking lot behind the Gemini restaurant in the area. There he and the six members of his crew unpacked and unfurled a blue balloon they had towed in a trailer. Since we were the only passengers, a relatively small balloon was being readied, but it still measured 87 feet from top to bottom. We joined the crew members in pulling it open as Mr. Fenichel blew air into the bag with a gas-generated fan. The basket was attached. We climbed in. Mr. Fenichel turned up the gas on the propane burner just above our heads, and we had liftoff.

The sensation is not at all like flying. Nor is it like taking an elevator ride. Rising in a slow, steady ascent above rooftops and then treetops, being driven forward by a weak breeze, we felt more a part of nature than its conquerors. All of us who have been on planes know that what keeps us up there is Bernoulli's principle, which holds that air currents across curved surfaces like those of the wings produce a drop in pressure. But how many of us really believe that?

By contrast, the technology that takes and keeps a balloon aloft is homey, basic, and much more immediately credible. You don't need to be a rocket scientist to know that hot air rises. It is something that can

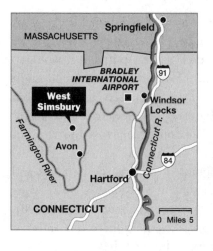

be fully grasped by anyone who has ever heard a teapot whistle or seen a legislature in session.

"It's really very simple," Mr. Fenichel explained. "I turn up the flame, and we go up a bit. I turn the flame down, and we hover awhile. When the air in the balloon cools a bit, we start to descend and I turn up the gas again." As he spoke, his hand on the gas valve, we had risen to about 800 feet, heading slowly over the Farmington River.

It was a comfortable height offering distant views of Hartford to the west and Springfield, Massachusetts, to the north. Immediately below us, new suburban developments gave way to old tobacco farms and a wilderness of forest, ponds, and marshes near the fast-moving river. At one point, six deer could be seen, and Mr. Fenichel allowed the balloon to settle down a bit for a closer view. The deer were unaware of our presence until the pilot turned up the burner so that we could rise above looming trees. They heard the rather loud noise and bolted.

It was not scary, not even when our basket brushed the uppermost branches of tall trees. "Don't worry about that," Mr. Fenichel said. "Sometimes we do that to slow down." In this case we were doing it to take a look at buds and birds. During the ride, I grew very attached to the basket and thought how wonderful and comforting that it was made of wicker, not plastic or aluminum, but the stuff of rocking chairs and baby carriages. "It's a funny thing, but nobody has ever found anything that's as light and strong and flexible," our pilot explained.

The wind, not very strong, shifted direction, and we did the same. "Up here Mother Nature is in full command," our pilot said. "I can control our altitude, but she controls our direction." As we passed over roads, cars would stop, and people would get out to look and wave and shout to us. Mostly they shouted, "Where are you coming down?" We shouted back truthfully, "We don't know." As we drifted in this manner, it occurred to me that ballooning, while pleasant enough for anyone, could be therapeutic for control freaks and anxiety sufferers. First you don't know if you are going to rise, and when you do you have no idea where you are going to end up.

We saw more deer, more houses, more cars, and more people happily waving to us. We saw planes heading to and from Bradley International Airport in Windsor Locks, somewhere over the ridge ahead of us. We could only hope they saw us. I kept looking for the van in which Mr. Fenichel's crew was presumably tracking us, to meet us on landing. Mr. Fenichel tried to reach them by radio but failed. Aha, I thought, things are getting interesting. Neither my wife nor Mr. Fenichel seemed much concerned. Aha, I thought, perhaps I am more of a control freak than I knew.

Not wishing to alarm anyone, I just asked how long we had been aloft.

"About an hour and a half," the pilot said, and then, clearly reading my mind, added, "We have enough gas here for about two hours more, but we'll come down when we find the next suitable spot." On our trajectory all I could see were trees, but then a sudden gust shifted our flight. "Oh, look," I said hopefully, "a nice snow-covered field." "I'm afraid that's a pond with thin ice," the pilot said. Once again I thought how good it was to have him along.

Within minutes, a real field not far from a road loomed into view, and Mr. Fenichel, after guiding the balloon over a stand of trees, brought it down in a landing that was no more jarring than a jump of two feet.

And as we climbed out of the basket, we were welcomed by the cheers of the chasers, who had successfully tracked us to the spot. They were joined by five farm youngsters who very happily joined in deflating the balloon, rolling it up, and stowing it and the basket in the trailer behind the van. Twenty minutes later, we were headed back to the parking lot behind the restaurant for the last part of the flight, the Champagne ritual.

Mr. Fenichel explained that this in fact dated back to the 18th-century balloonists, who landed in farmers' fields as we had just done. Often they would be met not by happy youngsters, but by farmers who attacked the balloons with pitchforks, thinking they were infernal devices of diabolical design. The balloonists took to carrying wine with them to soothe and placate farmers, and a tradition was born.

We drank the wine and had some fine cranberry cake provided by our tracking team. We toasted them and our adventure and said goodbye. We had a fine meal at the hotel restaurant and a good night's rest, and the next morning we drove back toward the city through a landscape over which we had hovered. It had been a good weekend, and we were content, not unlike Babar and his wife, Celeste.

HOT-AIR BALLOONING ESSENTIALS

Here is information about two balloon trips in the New York metropolitan region. Schedules and rates are subject to change, so confirm times and prices when you call to reserve.

Airvertising and Airventures, West Simsbury, CT (☎ 860/651-4441). Different packages and charter rides available year-round. Rates start at $200 per person for a 1- to 1 1/2-hour group ride to $245 for a private ride. The company also offers weekend excursions ($600) and weeklong trips ($2,000).

Berkshire Balloons, P.O. Box 706, Southington, CT (☎ 203/250-8441). Dawn and dusk flights east of Waterbury, followed by a Champagne toast, are offered year-round at $200 per person for a one-hour flight. Overnight packages, including a bed-and-breakfast stay, are $515 for two people.

Other Destinations
Within Easy Reach of
New York City

HOOKED: EIGHT ANGLERS REVEAL THEIR SECRET FISHING HOLES

❧

I<small>T'S BEEN SAID THAT</small> NEW YORK IS
a cynical town. But fishermen know otherwise.

Look around the waters' edges this summer—any day, any hour—
and you will see them, bleary-eyed optimists in spite of themselves.
They are in Queens or Brooklyn, say, fishing for porgies on the Cross
Bay Boulevard Bridge, or for blues on the 69th Street pier in Bay
Ridge, or for stripers on the beach at Breezy Point. They are crabbing,
not about the traffic on the Belt Parkway.

For fishermen, this is the season when the waters of the city beckon
with promise and the whole city becomes a gigantic pier. Members of
this single-minded fraternity know that the glory of New York lies in
its diversity: its fluke, bluefish, flounder, blue crabs, sticklebacks, bull-
head catfish, snappers and even its sea robins, the once-notorious "trash
fish" that has recently been elevated to the culinary firmament.

There are 324 marine species to be found within a radius of 10
miles or so of the Empire State Building. So many fish. So little time.

And so, armed with gadgets, be it a simple fly rod or the video
depth finders beloved by Stealth Fishermen, those for whom the fish
is the thing take to the waters. If you love to fish, it really doesn't
matter whether you're headed for a party boat in Sheepshead Bay in
Brooklyn or to the Connetquot on Long Island, a dream of a stream,
fly-fishing only, where the accompaniment might be the splash of a
muskrat's tail. The humidity lifts, the smog and traffic fade. Life is
pared down to its blissful essence: you and the fish.

Eight *New York Times* anglers divulge their favorite regional fishing haunts, from Catskill and Connecticut rivers to New Jersey inlets and the Atlantic Ocean. Read it carefully. Don't pass it on.

—PATRICIA LEIGH BROWN

Two Fly-Fishing Favorites

Dreaming is the best part of fly-fishing. You don't have to catch anything, you just have to believe that the fish are there. And when you occasionally hook one, you can dream about it for a hundred nights, especially if it gets away.

When I dream about fishing, I am usually on the Brodhead River, a tributary of the Paradise, in the tiny town of Henryville, Pennsylvania., just northwest of the Delaware Water Gap, in the Poconos. An inn there, Henryville House, was once a fishing shrine that drew the likes of Theodore Roosevelt, Calvin Coolidge, Annie Oakley, and Buffalo Bill. Today, the inn and its adjoining motel units have fallen out of use by fishermen. But the well-stocked stream still flows nearby, offering every kind of fishing water from fast-flowing riffles to deep slow-moving runs, and every sort of hatch from delicate early-morning Baetis to evening spinner falls.

I dream particularly of an evening some 20 years ago when just after sunset I was absentmindedly roll-casting a tiny caddis imitation known as a Henryville Special, an artificial fly that was named after the place I was fishing, obviously enough, but that I've found to be effective throughout the Northeast. To my surprise, I heard a heavy splash somewhere off in the dark and found myself on to what 15 minutes later turned out to be a 19½-inch brown trout, the biggest fish I've ever captured. The best part of the experience was feeling him slowly regain his strength as I held him in the current just before releasing him.

The stream is owned by the Henryville Conservation Club, so it is accessible only to club members and their guests. When I choose to go fishing on a whim, then, I head up to Roscoe, New York, in the Catskills, at the confluence of the Beaverkill River and Willowemoc Creek, two of the most famous streams in Eastern fly-fishing lore. So much has been written about the Beaverkill that when you fish there you are likely to suffer from a form of Harold Bloom's anxiety of influence, what with your sense that so many great fishermen have waded there before you. The water is big; each pool is storied; the best stretches are no-kill, which means you have to return whatever you catch. My favorite water is still the big old Cairn's Pool, a little below the highway bridge, which challenges your ability to cast for distance.

On my happiest day of fishing there I crossed the stream to the opposite side and perched myself on the shore next to the channel that runs there. I spotted a huge trout lazing on the bottom, and tried unsuccessfully to interest it in a dozen different flies. No luck. It would come up to the surface, eye whatever I was offering and turn away with what I took to be a look of disdain. But the game was still breathtakingly exciting. After all, you really don't have to catch a thing when you go fishing.

—CHRISTOPHER LEHMANN-HAUPT

Farm Pond Fishing

Farm ponds, the original local watering holes, literally dot the rural countryside and can be the source of good ultralight-tackle fishing. Most contain pan fish: bluegills, crappie, perch, or, if they are deep and muddy, catfish. Occasionally something bigger. I discovered the pond near our country house in upstate New York about 20 years ago. It was full of small perch very eager to take my lures. I'd play them for a bit and let them go.

I grew to love the pond. It was far enough off the road to give one the feeling of isolation. Very often my arrival would startle a group of ducks or a lone magnificent heron. There was a giant turtle living there and abundant signs that deer, raccoons, and other animals were using it as well. It became a very pleasant place to take my two daughters and get a fishing fix, too.

Suddenly, one summer, the catch changed. Mixed in with the perch were largemouth bass. Immediately, my place for solitude and communion became a place of monopoly and greed. If there were small

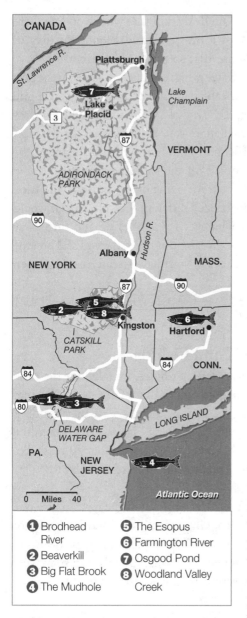

CANADA

St. Lawrence R.

Plattsburgh

Lake
Champlain

Lake
Placid

7

3

87

VERMONT

ADIRONDACK
PARK

90

Albany

Hudson R.

NEW YORK

MASS.

87

90

2   5
8

Kingston

6

Hartford

CATSKILL
PARK

CONN.

84

84

84

1

3

80

LONG ISLAND

DELAWARE
WATER GAP

PA.

NEW
JERSEY

4

Atlantic Ocean

0   Miles   40

❶ Brodhead
    River
❷ Beaverkill
❸ Big Flat Brook
❹ The Mudhole

❺ The Esopus
❻ Farmington River
❼ Osgood Pond
❽ Woodland Valley
    Creek

bass, there would be big ones. I'd have my own private lunker hole.

A few years went by; the bass drove out the perch but weren't getting much bigger. I even resorted to transferring some of my catch to another pond, hoping that the reduction in population would fatten up the survivors.

Finally, one afternoon, I spotted it. Twelve inches or more and weighing well over a pound. The one I was waiting for. My trips to the pond increased but that largemouth wouldn't bite.

Then, in September of that fateful year, my older daughter came home from college for the weekend. Late Saturday morning, the entire family went down to the pond to do some fishing for old times' sake. It was a warm day and there wasn't much action. After a while, my wife and I decided to go home to prepare lunch. We were halfway up the hill when we heard our daughter scream. We arrived back at the pond just in time to see her pull it out of the water. She had caught my fish, the big one.

Because of our high regard for all living things and to give another sportsman a chance at it, we released it. The fish was never seen again. But it will be back, I'm sure of it.

—Joseph J. Vecchione

Casting for Trout at Woodland Creek

Woodland Valley Creek is the perfect mountain stream. From its source, somewhere up on Slide Mountain, down to its terminus, at Phoenicia, where it flows into its larger and more illustrious cousin, the Esopus, Woodland Creek flows gently and dreamily through some of the prettiest country in the Catskills.

Because it seldom grows wider than 30 feet, a mediocre fly caster like me can reach a rising fish on the opposite bank (where the good risers invariably are). I can negotiate its manageable currents in hip boots; no need for chest waders here. I can pitch a dry fly onto the manageable currents and be assured of at least three or four seconds of dragless float. There is even room overhead for a backcast in most spots.

Lurking under some of its granite shelves and compact boulders are big brown trout, fish that are 18 inches or longer. These are wary and challenging fish, made so by having withstood season after season of harassment by anglers, mergansers, minks, and other predators.

In addition, there are younger and more easily caught stocked browns, as well as a good population of small stream-bred rainbow trout. These fish spend their youth in this tributary, and because of their eagerness to rise to a fly, offer fine sport. Upon reaching a length of eight inches or so, they migrate downstream to the Esopus, and, ultimately, the Ashokan Reservoir, where they mature and sometimes reach lengths in excess of 20 inches. In the spring, these big rainbows migrate back upstream to the hospitable waters of Woodland Creek to spawn—and tantalize anglers. Also, during early season runoff, you might even encounter tiny, exquisite brook trout in the creek's smaller headwaters.

Within a mile upstream of its confluence with the Esopus, there are two Department of Environmental Conservation public-access points with small parking areas off Woodland Valley Road. These are among the most fishable and easily approached spots on the stream. For a little more than two miles upstream of the second access area, there is a lovely stretch of water that is posted as "Fly Fishing Only." Above this stretch, access to the stream is limited because of posted land.

The Woodland Valley campsite and trailhead are slightly more than 4½ miles upstream of the creek's terminus. In the summer months, this section of the stream is narrow and shallow, a mere trickle compared with its lower stretches. Come spring, the section will swell back to fishable porportions with winter runoff. Upstream of the campsite, on to the end of Woodland Valley Road, access to the stream is again limited because of posted land.

Tight lines.

—MICHAEL VALENTI

In Search of Pike and Big Bass at Osgood Pond

There were huge pike down in the weeds of Osgood Pond near Paul Smiths, New York, in the Adirondacks above Saranac Lake. We knew because some days we got them to bite on our lollygagging flatfish lures or flashing spoons and spinners. Mostly, though, we lost them—the fish and the lures—ending up with a rowboat full of weeds and nothing else. The caretaker of our bungalow colony once caught a four-foot pike with teeth like a shark's and kept the head pickled in a glass jar. He used to come back with his boat full of weeds, so I learned that if you want to catch a big fish, you have to be prepared for a boat full of weeds. Calvin Coolidge went pike fishing there, too, in the 1920s, out of White Pine Camp on the far end of the lake. On one trip in 1926 he had barely thrown his line in when he hooked a three-pound pike.

I was fishing with my dad there once and he hooked a big pike. I put down my own rod to net it but I beaned it by mistake with the net and the pike went crazy, gnashing around and tangling my dad's line around mine. There was nothing to do but cut my line free. In the confusion, I cut my dad's line instead, so the big one got away.

There were big bass there, too. I liked to wait until dusk when they came in to feed and then set the boat maybe 50 feet off shore and cast into the shallows with a Jitterbug or Hula Popper in black or pseudo-frog. I liked to listen to the burble and gurgle as I reeled in, waiting for the heart-stopping crash and tug that meant I had a bass on the line. It happened less often than I expected but more often than I was entitled to.

—RALPH BLUMENTHAL

Fly-Fishing Connecticut's Farmington River

I decided this summer to use my fishing rod as a way to explore the region, so it is not unusual to find myself occasionally drifting into the Orvis fishing store near Grand Central Terminal.

The store offers something akin to a running Baedeker's of rivers and streams in the New York area, a tote board that lists water temperatures at each venue and whether fishing conditions there are considered "normal" or "excellent." For a novice fly-fisherman like myself, "normal" holds a hint of disappointment. But week after week, the Farmington River in northwestern Connecticut kept coming up "excellent." One weekend, I decided to give the Farmington a try. What I found was most excellent indeed.

Some 2½ hours after leaving New York City, the Farmington appeared as I began to drive through a fragrant, cool forest, past houses with the distinctive feel of New England. The river, already busy with fishermen, was picturesque, particularly near the tiny village of Riverton.

What makes the Farmington an enjoyable outing is that the river in many ways is kind to those just learning to fly-fish. The river is cold and can be deep in spots, so waders are needed. But in most areas, the wading is easy. It is also wide, so that you can cast without fear of snagging more bushes than fish.

In addition, the Farmington is stocked with trout several times a summer. And these fish can be confidence builders, because unlike their wild cousins elsewhere, they are not the brightest of the bunch when it comes to avoiding being caught.

—BARRY MEIER

The Catskills' Venerable Esopus

The Esopus is a hoary name in American trout fishing, a wide stream in the Catskill Mountains that drains into the Ashokan Reservoir, part of New York City's water system. Its rocky, continuously interesting course and its wild trout have won fame among masterhand fly-fishermen. But for me, the Esopus is where I learned the importance of not catching fish.

Pretty much a novice when I discovered it, I found the swiftly flowing water a mystery. There are few deep pools in which trout usually lurk. Someone once surveyed the river and determined there were 47 fish every 10 yards. I seriously doubt it! In a half-dozen visits, I almost always left fishless.

Casting blindly into turgid riffles, I told myself it was only right that I wasn't catching fish. Fishing wasn't supposed to be easy. I had to pay dues, learning to read the river bottom and to acquire intimate knowledge about the life cycle of stoneflies.

In the meantime, the Esopus sufficed as a nice place to spend time. Wading bare-legged into its icy water on a 90° day was always refreshing. In the fall, the soft, humpy peaks of the Catskills were splashed with color. In all seasons, an afternoon of slowly walking upriver, trying a desultory cast or two, provided an interlude of blessed solitude in an overstimulated life.

One day beneath Five Arch Bridge, a trout snatched my fly the moment it hit the water, and it was so unexpected I froze. Instinctively, I stabbed the rod tip up and brought in the fish. It was a thrill, to be sure. But by then I had learned that catching fish is just one pleasure of the sport, and not even the most important.

—TRIP GABRIEL

Big Game Fishing the "Mudhole"

It is out there. It really is out there.

You probably won't believe me, but if you get in a boat—not necessarily a big boat, but a good sea boat—you will find the beginning of it about 20 miles southeast of New York Harbor, and only 13 miles off the New Jersey coast.

When the Verrazano-Narrows Bridge starts to disappear on the horizon off your stern, it happens. All at once the dirty opaque water of the New York Bight suddenly ends, sometimes in a sharply defined wall, and the water turns a clear aquamarine. Move on farther and it turns as blue and clear as the Caribbean.

And here is some of the best big game fishing in the world.

You are in what fishermen call the Mudhole, named for its soft bottom. It's a trench, sometimes as deep as 250 feet, that is the old bed of the Hudson River, extending almost 100 miles out to the Hudson Canyon, a huge rent in the continental shelf.

In the summer, eddies of water from the Gulf Stream break off and sometimes spin in sight of land. Fish of all types traveling north in the warm stream are funneled into the Mudhole, and they stay, feeding on the abundant bait fish.

I have seen schools of skipjack tuna in the thousands here, running so fast that you can't catch them even with your boat at full throttle. I have caught yellowfin tuna up to 200 pounds and have hand-fed a bluefin tuna the size of a Volkswagen. I have seen dozens of hammerhead sharks prowl in our bait slicks, had a great white shark over 20 feet long circle us at anchor, and watched white and blue marlin attack our trolling lures.

I've caught dozens of mahimahi, a tropical game fish more familiar to Hawaiians, been surrounded by frolicking whales and porpoises, and studied green turtles and rare giant leatherback turtles as they sunned themselves.

All the while, if you look really hard, on a clear day you can just see the very top of the World Trade Towers peeking over the horizon. Shhhhh!!!

—Keith Meyers

Angling at Big Flat Brook

Everyone who fly fishes for trout ought to have a home stream. Big Flat Brook in the mountains of Sussex County, in New Jersey's northwestern corner, fills the bill for me.

It is not my favorite stream hereabouts (I'll keep that a secret), but it has the virtue of being the closest: a little more than an hour from my home in northeastern New Jersey, which in turn is a half-hour ride from midtown Manhattan. Offering a full array of deep pools, swift runs, and riffles in a beautiful setting, Flat Brook is seldom discouragingly crowded.

This is not a wild fishery or a catch-and-release fishery. The limit during most of the season is six fish, and while regulars increasingly return fish to the stream, many other people keep them. The hatchery rainbows, browns, and brookies that replace them are somewhat dull in coloring and less palatable than they might be, and sometimes less of a challenge.

But generally the fishing experience itself is fine, offering a good mixture of success and difficulty. Under some conditions I have happily taken the limit, sometimes keeping a few fish for the table and sometimes releasing all. One glorious Memorial Day memory is of nice-size rainbows darting all over a deep, clear pool, pursuing—and catching—March Brown nymphs, fished on a dead drift. (I had the pool to myself; all the holiday visitors had left.)

But my most recent memory is of a day in May when a pod of trout up to 18 inches or so, driven to extremes of caution by low, clear water, refused every offering. It is the only time I have ever been skunked on Flat Brook. But maybe, just maybe, I've figured out how to approach them the next time.

—WILLIAM K. STEVENS

WHERE TO CAST A LINE: FLY-FISHING ESSENTIALS

Here is a sampling of county, state, and federal parks in the New York metropolitan region where fresh- and saltwater fishing is permitted. State fishing licenses are required for freshwater fishing and can be obtained at county clerk offices and many sporting goods stores.

Some parks also require daily fishing or parking permits, which are issued at the sites themselves. For more information, call the individual site.

NEW YORK

A New York State **fishing license** costs $14 ($35 for nonresidents); children under 16 do not need a license. For information, call ☎ 518/457-3521.

Free permits, issued by the **New York City Department of Environmental Protection** (☎ 914/985-2275, 914/657-2663, or 607/363-7000), are needed for fishing in any of the city's 19 reservoirs and three controlled lakes around the state; a state fishing license is also required.

The **Center for Environmental Health** (☎ 800/458-1158) at the New York State Department of Health in Albany issues a health advisory on hazardous chemicals found in fish in various waters in the state.

QUEENS

Fort Tilden/Breezy Point, Gateway National Park, Flatbush Ave. at Marine Park Bridge, Rockaway (☎ 718/318-4300 or 718/338-3799). Twenty-four-hour saltwater fishing is allowed daily. A $25 season parking permit is needed for fishing; a driver's license, car registration, a fishing rod more than seven feet long, and a reel are required to obtain a permit. The permit can be obtained at Fort Tilden, Floyd Bennett Field, or Breezy Point.

LONG ISLAND

Caleb Smith State Park, Jericho Tpk., Smithtown (☎ 516/265-1054). Season runs April 1 through October 15. Daily permits for fly-fishing are available, at $15, for eight river and five pond sites. There are two daily sessions, from 7 to 11am and 11:30am to 3:30pm; Friday through Sunday, there is a third session, 4pm to sunset. New York state fishing license required. Reservations can be made up to two weeks in advance.

Captree State Park and **Robert Moses State Park,** Babylon (☎ 516/669-0449). Surf-fishing daily from dawn to dusk. No permit or state license necessary. Parking $4 at Captree and $5 at Robert Moses.

Caumsett State Park, W. Neck Rd., Huntington (☎ 516/423-1770). Season runs April 1 through December 31. One-day parking permits, at $4, are issued Monday through Friday 8am to 1pm, for same-day saltwater fishing from 8am to 4:30pm.

Connetquot River State Park Preserve, Rte. 27, Oakdale (☎ 516/581-1005). Season runs February 1 through October 15. Beginning April 1, daily permits for 32 fly-fishing sites are available at $15, for any of three daily sessions: 7 to 11am, noon to 4pm and 5pm to sunset. Prior to April 1, there are two daily sessions from 8am to noon and noon to 4pm, during which caught fish have to be returned to the water. Closed Monday during fishing season; closed Monday and Tuesday prior to April 1 and after October 15. New York state fishing license required. Reservations are required. Parking $4.

Jones Beach State Park, Meadowbrook Pkwy., Wantaugh (☎ 516/785-1600). Season runs April 1 through December 31. Saltwater fishing daily, from dawn to dusk. No state license required. One-day parking fee $5 daily from Memorial Day through Labor Day; weekends only from May 3 through Memorial Day and Labor Day through October.

WESTCHESTER COUNTY

Some Westchester County parks are open only to residents; we've only included those open to all below. New York State fishing licenses are required for fishing in most Westchester County parks.

Croton Gorge, Rte. 129, Cortlandt (☎ 914/271-3293). Daily 8am to dusk. New York State license required. Parking fee required weekends only from Memorial Day through mid-September: $3.50 for Westchester residents with a county park pass, $7 for nonresidents.

Croton Point Park, Croton Point Ave. (off Rte. 9), Croton-on-Hudson (☎ 914/271-3293). Daily 8am to dusk. No license needed. Daily parking fee required from Memorial Day through mid-September; $3.50 for Westchester residents with a county park pass, $7 for nonresidents.

Franklin Delano Roosevelt State Park, Taconic State Pkwy. at Rte. 202, Yorktown (☎ 914/245-4434). Daily, dawn to dusk. Boat rentals $4 an hour, from 8am to 5pm, or $20 a day; plus a $25 deposit. New York state license required. Daily parking fee, May 10 through September 1, $4; weekends only,

September 6 through October 13. Seasonal fishing permits for boat owners are $15.

George's Island Park, Dutch St. (off Rte. 9A), Montrose (☎ 914/737-7530). Daily 6am to dusk. No license needed. Parking fee $3.50 for Westchester residents with a county park pass, $7 for nonresidents.

Rockefeller State Park Preserve, Rte. 117, Pocantico Hills, Mount Pleasant (☎ 914/631-1470). Shore fishing mid-June through the end of November with lures or worms only allowed daily 7am to dusk. New York state fishing license. Parking $4 a day. No permit required.

Twin Lakes, California Rd., Eastchester (☎ 914/242-6300). Daily 8am to sunset. New York State license required. Daily parking fee, $3.50 for Westchester residents with a county park pass, $7 for nonresidents.

Ward Pound Ridge Reservation, rtes. 35 and 121 south, Cross River (☎ 914/763-3493). Daily 8am to dusk. New York state license required. Parking fees, daily, May through the end of October, then weekends only: $3.50 for Westchester residents with a county park pass, $7 for nonresidents.

NEW JERSEY

In New Jersey, **fishing licenses** for residents are $16.50, $7.75 for children 14 and 15 and seniors 65 to 69; no license is required for children 14 and under. There are also special licenses for seniors 70 and older (no charge, but they must display identification) and for families ($27.50 for both parents and $2.25 per child 14 to 18). A trout stamp for residents is $7.75. A nonresident license is $25.25 for one year or $16.50 for 7 days. A trout stamp for nonresidents is $15.50. For information, call ☎ 609/292-2965 or 908/735-8240.

Gateway National Recreation Area, Sandy Hook Unit, off State Hwy. 36, Sandy Hook

(☎ 908/872-0115). Saltwater fishing daily at designated beach and bay areas, or from sunset to sunrise along the entire beach and bay for any time except Memorial Day through Labor Day, when fishing is not permitted on lifeguarded beaches. No permit or state license is necessary for day fishing. A $25 permit, good for the year, is required for night fishing and can be picked up at the National Park Rangers station. Beach parking from Memorial Day through Labor Day is $4 on weekdays, $5 on weekends and holidays; free parking at other times.

High Point State Park, Rte. 23, Sussex (☎ 201/875-4800). April through October.

Three lakes, with two open for fishing, dawn to dusk, and the third, open 8am to 8pm; from November through April, daily 8am to 4:30pm. New Jersey state fishing license required. Memorial Day through Labor Day, parking $5 weekdays, $7 weekends and holidays.

Hopatcong State Park, Lakeside Blvd., Landing (☎ 201/398-7010). Lake Hopat-cong open Memorial Day through Labor Day, daily 8am to 8pm; otherwise, sunrise to sunset. New Jersey state fishing license required.

Memorial Day through Labor Day, parking $5 weekdays, $7 weekends and holidays.

Liberty State Park, off exit 14B of the New Jersey Tpke., Jersey City (☎ 201/915-3400 or 201/915-3403). Hudson River fishing year-round daily 6am to 10pm. No license required.

Worthington State Forest, off Rte. 80 (Old Mine Rd.), Columbia (☎ 908/841-9575). Delaware River fishing daily from dawn to dusk. New Jersey state fishing license required.

CONNECTICUT

In Connecticut, seasonal fishing licenses for freshwater fishing are $15 for residents, $25 for nonresidents; a three-day license for a nonresident is $8. All licenses are available through town clerks. For information, call ☎ 860/424-3105.

Bigelow Hollow State Park, Rte. 171, Union (☎ 860/928-9200). From April through February, freshwater fishing daily, 24 hours; closed March. Connecticut state fishing license required. Parking from Memorial Day through Labor Day, weekends and holidays $5 for Connecticut residents, $8 for nonresidents; free parking on weekdays (except holidays).

Burr Pond State Park, 385 Burr Mountain Road, at Winstead Road, Torrington (☎ 860/482-1817). Year-round freshwater fishing daily, 8am to sunset; the park is closed to fishing for a short time during the spring to allow for the stocking of trout. Connecticut state fishing license required. Parking weekdays $4 for Connecticut residents, $5 for nonresidents; weekends $5 for residents, $8 for nonresidents.

Hammanasett Beach State Park, Hammanasett Connector, exit 62 off I-95, Madison (☎ 860/245-2785). From mid-May through Labor Day, saltwater fishing from

Meigs Point Jetty daily, 24 hours; free permits, issued after 5pm, are necessary for night fishing. From Labor Day through mid-May, fishing is allowed 9am to sunset. No state license or permit required for day fishing. Parking from Memorial Day through Labor Day, $5 weekdays and $7 weekends and holidays for Connecticut residents; $8 weekdays and $12 on weekends for nonresidents. Parking from mid-April through Memorial Day and Labor Day to end of September, weekend is $5 for Connecticut residents and $8 for nonresidents; free parking on weekdays.

Lake Waramaug State Park, Lake Waramaug Rd., New Preston (☎ 860/868-2592). Year-round freshwater fishing daily 8am to sunset; no boat launch available. State fishing license required. Parking from Memorial Day through Labor Day, weekend and holiday $5 for Connecticut residents, $8 nonresidents; free parking year-round on weekends.

Macedonia Brook State Park, Macedonia Brook Rd., Kent (☎ 860/927-3238). From mid-April through December, freshwater fishing in a state-stocked brook, daily, 8am to sunset. Connecticut state fishing license required. Free parking.

Mashamoquet Brook State Park, Rte. 44, Pomfret (☎ 860/928-6121). From mid-April through March, freshwater fishing daily 8am to sunset. the park is closed to fishing from March through mid-April while the water is stocked with fish. Connecticut state fishing license required. Parking from Memorial Day through Labor Day, weekends and holidays $5 for Connecticut residents, $8 for nonresidents; free parking year-round on weekdays.

Quaddick State Park, Quaddick State Farm Rd. (off Rte. 44), Thompson (☎ 860/928-9200). Freshwater fishing daily, dawn to sunset. State fishing license required. From Memorial Day through Labor Day, weekend and holiday parking: $8 for nonresidents; $5 for residents; weekdays, except holidays, are free at all times.

Newport, Old Money's Oceanside Retreat

by Robin Pogrebin

Needless to say, the hotel neglected to mention the foghorn.

What foghorn is that, you may ask.

Oh, just the tone resembling a test of the emergency broadcasting system that pierced the otherwise peaceful sea air every 10 seconds during my first attempt to sleep through the night on Narragansett Bay. (I seriously contemplated setting out in my pajamas to find the fog patrol and destroy the horn, but it occurred to me that I might then have a shipwreck on my conscience.)

Aside from that minor hitch, my husband and I had a truly idyllic weekend in Newport, Rhode Island. While the downtown harbor bustled with tourists filling up on fried clams at restaurants along the water and dodging in and out of shops along Thames Street, the City-by-the-Sea on the tip of Aquidneck Island also offered quaint narrow side streets, mansions of old-money grandeur, and seaside silence.

Newport, founded in 1639, became a thriving seaport, with captains bringing pineapples—now the island's symbol of hospitality—home from trips to the West Indies as well as sugar and molasses to make Newport rum. These days, Newport is perhaps best known as the country's yachting capital, although the city lost the America's Cup to Australia in 1983. White sails whip across the bay in regattas throughout the summer.

Having arrived on a Saturday after an easy 3$^{1}/_{2}$-hour drive from New York City, we had hoped to spend both nights at the Castle Hill

Inn and Resort. Unfortunately, the hotel had only Sunday night available. As a result, our first home base was Oceancliff I and II, a two-building condominium resort on Ridge Road that did not come close to approximating Castle Hill's old-world charm. Nevertheless, after upgrading from what felt like a basement room on the ground level to an airy second-floor duplex, we were very comfortable and, in fact, would recommend the place to those traveling as a family.

The first floor of our room had a living room, bedroom, bathroom, kitchen area, and outdoor deck overlooking the water. On the second floor, reached by a spiral staircase, was a large master bedroom and a bathroom with a Jacuzzi-style tub.

Oceancliff shares its site with the Oceancliff Historic Inn, a former villa, built in 1896.

After checking in, my husband and I headed back to the harbor to find a restaurant for lunch and decided on Christie's of Newport. While the food was unremarkable, Christie's had just the feeling we were looking for: outdoor tables overlooking the water, hearty lobster rolls served with french fries, and an upbeat crowd.

Later, I felt compelled to sample the requisite "you're in a New England town, how could you not have some fudge" fudge. Every afternoon at four except on Mondays and Tuesdays, the big wooden paddles come out at Country Kettle Fudge on Thames Street, where the staff beats fudge by hand in copper kettles. The shop features fudge in about 20 different flavors, including such unusual varieties as pistachio, chocolate chip, and cheesecake. (My preference was the triple chocolate, and I went back for more the next day.)

A Restful Afternoon

We spent the rest of Saturday afternoon relaxing at the hotel (I napped; it was possible to do so at that hour) and then made the 10-minute drive back into town for dinner. With stores open late and restaurants in full swing, the harbor was abuzz with sidewalk traffic, including people trolling for antiques in stores along Franklin and Spring streets or stopping in for beer and chowder at pubs along Bowen's Wharf or Bannister's Wharf.

For dinner, we chose a place called Scales and Shells, and I can hardly imagine Newport offers better. Conveniently situated on Thames Street, the restaurant beckons with a crisp, teal blue–trimmed exterior, wide windows, and black-and-cream-checked tablecloths. Inside, crowds cluster at the raw bar to suck on Neddicks oysters, Cherrystone clams, or lobster claws and sip cold glasses of white wine while they wait for their tables.

The wait can be considerable; the main restaurant does not take reservations. Having learned this in advance, we had secured a table in the restaurant's upstairs area, called UpScales, which accepts reservations and offers a somewhat more limited menu.

Among the specialties of the husband-and-wife chef team, Debra and Andy Ackerman, are sizzling servings of lobster fra diavolo over linguine in huge sauté pans and marinated toro tuna (she cooks upstairs, he downstairs). My husband started with clams (Sicilian littlenecks steamed in white wine, garlic, and thyme) and finished with clams (linguine alle vongole). I had the fried artichokes as an appetizer, followed by butterflied shrimp from the restaurant's mesquite grill, accompanied by an ear of corn that was blackened from the grill, with the kernels sweet as candy. For dessert, we shared a homemade apple tart and a chocolate raspberry gelato. The bill came to $75, including tip.

Then we returned—stuffed—to our hotel, to bed and to . . . the foghorn. It sounded throughout the night, which, from what I could tell, was hardly even cloudy.

Strolling and Shopping

The next morning, we started with breakfast at the Coffee Corner, a place on Broadway and Friendship streets, a short distance from the harbor, that had been recommended for its French toast. We had the pancakes, which were only so-so; I suspect it is better to try one of the more central breakfast spots recommended by Richard Saul Wurman in his *Newport Guide*, among them Annie's, Muriel's, and Poor Richard's.

Driving back into town (where parking is hard to find on weekends), we walked around a bit. The shopping inclined can stop in at everything from the Gap and Rockport to the Nutcracker Suite Christmas Shop, which sells strikingly original ornaments all year round and an impressive variety of painted nutcrackers, displayed on the staircase.

For lack of time, we never made it to the historic district known as the Point.

After our stroll, my husband went to play squash at the Newport Squash Club while I toured the Elms mansion, built in 1901 as a summer residence for the Pennsylvania coal magnate Edward J. Berwind. Modeled after the Château d'Asineres near Paris, it evoked another world, rich with pillars of purple breccia marble, doors of Santo Domingo mahogany, and chandeliers of Baccarat crystal.

The Elms's sprawling grounds, especially the meticulously maintained formal gardens, offer tranquil strolling away from the bustle of the city. This is the elegance that inspired drawing-room chroniclers like Edith Wharton and Henry James, and seeing Newport's opulence firsthand, it is easy to see why.

The Newport Preservation Society owns eight remarkable mansions (once incongruously called "cottages") in Newport, which was long a destination of robber barons, yachtsmen, and society figures who made it one of the world's most elite summer resorts. Rosecliff, for example, built in 1902, was the filming site for *The Great Gatsby*. The Vanderbilts summered in Newport, as did John F. and Jacqueline Kennedy, who were married at the Auchincloss family's Hammersmith Farm, known for a time as the Summer White House. It is now open for tours.

After picking up my husband, we drove over to Ocean Drive for the much touted brunch at Castle Hill, which lasts from 11:30am to 3pm and offers everything from baked oysters to eggs Benedict. Seating for the brunch is first come, first serve, although guests of the hotel are given priority. As we were not yet guests (check-in time is

2pm), we had to take what was available, which was a table indoors rather than on the deck.

The room we ate in—the Sunset Room—was lovely, with wrap-around windows overlooking the water and tablecloths and upholstered high-backed chairs. But the wooden tables outside topped with Bass and Guinness beer umbrellas were clearly the place to be, with direct views of the expansive green lawn sloping down to the water and live music from a bass and piano duo.

In the late afternoon, we got in line with the rest of the world to tour the mansion to beat all mansions: the Breakers. Built in 1895 as the summer home of Cornelius Vanderbilt, it has 70 rooms, 27 fire-places, and a breathtaking view of the Atlantic Ocean. We marveled at the music room, which was built in France, disassembled, shipped to Newport, and reassembled at the Breakers by French artisans; the billiard room, with its ceiling and floor mosaics; and the formal din-ing room, with 12 rose alabaster columns with gilded capitals.

The tour even took us through the kitchen and pantry to admire such details as the mortar in which herbs were crushed, the pantry where fresh flowers were cut every morning, and the 200 place settings of Vanderbilt china trimmed in 22-karat gold. Walking through the 114,000-square-foot mansion under 40-foot ceilings, one cannot help wondering what it would be like to repose at this palace every summer.

Entering Castle Hill

Time to check in at Castle Hill, truly a gem of a hotel, perched on the site of a former watch house on a secluded peninsula. While expen-sive (our room was $200 for the night), it is not particularly extrava-gant. A large bouquet of fresh flowers decorated the lobby and sitting room, with their dark wood walls, Victorian furniture, and lush Per-sian carpets. The inn has four intimate dining rooms and a bar.

The hotel proper has only 10 guest rooms, but it has other accom-modations: six cliffside guest rooms in what it calls the Harbor House, 18 private beachfront cottages with kitchens, and a chalet with five bedrooms. Our room was cozy and inviting, with a four-poster bed, windows overlooking the lawn and bay, yellow wallpaper, a small, drop-leaf desk stocked with bound volumes of *Reader's Digest* condensed books, and a spacious bathroom with powder blue bath rugs. Thornton Wilder was one of the inn's frequent visitors.

As we pulled into the parking lot on Sunday evening, however, the scene was far from placid. Rather, we found ourselves in the thick of what is evidently a tradition in Newport: Sunday sunset cocktails at Castle Hill. The porch, bar, and lawn were overflowing with people in their 20s and 30s holding plastic cups of icy daiquiris: men, showered after a day at the beach, in crisp collar shirts; women beginning to shiver in short dresses and sandals as the setting sun took the day's warmth with it.

Although Sunday cocktails at Castle Hill is clearly not about eating, there was a casual barbecue set out on the lawn, and my husband and I enjoyed a picnic of burgers and grilled chicken sandwiches, while the social constellations shifted and whirled behind us, and sailboats went gliding by on the bay.

With just about an hour of light left in the sky, we set out to walk as much of the famous Cliff Walk as we could before nightfall. According to the map, the path, with mansions on one side and sea on the other, starts in town at Memorial Boulevard and concludes four miles away, at the beginning of Bellevue Avenue. We began at the Bellevue Avenue end and completed the walk just after dark.

On the Cliffs at Dusk

The path, which is rocky at first and later becomes paved, was beautiful at that hour: The fading light gave the jagged coastline a gentle blue-gray hue as the waves crashed 60 feet below.

As lights came on in the majestic homes along the water, we could get a better glimpse of the life going on within the elegant bay windows: Land's End, a house built in 1870 with a yellow exterior and black trim, which belonged to Edith Wharton; Rough Point (1891), the secluded hideaway of Doris Duke; the Chinese Tea House (1914), and Alva Belmont's Oriental pavilion, where she held several of her "Votes for Women" rallies.

Upon finishing the walk, we took a cab back to our car, and—unwilling to call it a weekend just yet—drove into town for dessert: warm crème brûlée, apple tart, and a glass of port at Pronto on Thames Street.

Back at Castle Hill, we snuggled into bed looking forward to the morning's free corn johnnycakes, a Newport tradition, to be eaten with butter, not syrup. Too tired to read, we turned out the light and would have fallen asleep quickly had it not been for . . . the foghorn, back for a repeat performance.

Faced with the second fitful night of sleep in a row, I might have entertained ever more violent fantasies of ferreting out the fog patrol and hurling the offending horn into the sea once and for all.

But after another full day of falling in love with the place, I found that the honks were beginning to sound almost soothing, like Newport's own nautical lullaby.

NEWPORT ESSENTIALS

Further information about lodgings, attractions, sailing expeditions, and Newport's annual jazz and folk festivals is available from the **Newport County Convention and Visitor's Bureau,** 23 America's Cup Ave., Newport (☎ 800/326-6030).

GETTING THERE

By Car   From Manhattan, take I-95 North to the exit for Rte. 138 East, near Wyoming, RI, then follow the signs to the Jamestown and Newport bridges.

By Bus   Bonanza Bus Lines (☎ 800/ 556-3815) runs four buses daily from the Port Authority, at Eighth Ave. and 42nd St., Manhattan, to Newport; the six-hour ride costs $37 one way or $65 round trip (half-price for children under 12).

By Train   Amtrak (☎ 800/872-7245) has daily train service from Penn Station, at Seventh Ave. and 34th St. in Manhattan, to West Kingston, RI, which is about a half-hour drive from Newport (a cab from the train station costs about $40). The off-peak fare is $37 one way on weekdays ($74 round trip) or $46 one-way ($92 round trip) on weekends and at peak times (half-price for children 2 to 15). For the same rates, Amtrak also offers daily service from Penn Station to Providence, RI, where public buses run regularly to Newport ($3).

ACCOMMODATIONS

Castle Hill Inn and Resort, Ocean Dr. (☎ 888/560-5300 or 401/849-3800). Rooms range from $155 to $325 in the high season (May through October), and from $95 to $225 in the low season (November through April); $25 for each additional person. Rates are based on double occupancy; two- or three-night minimums may apply on weekends. **Oceancliff I and II,** Ridge Rd. (☎ 401/ 846-6667). From May 25 through September 6, rates range from $215 to $245; $75 to $160 at other times.

DINING

Annie's, 176 Bellevue Ave. (☎ 401/849-6731). Open daily 7am to 4:30pm; in summer, daily 7am to 10pm. Entrees $8 to $12.

Christie's of Newport, 351 Thames St. (☎ 401/847-5400). Open Monday through Wednesday 11:30am to 9pm, Thursday through Sunday 11:30am to 9:30pm. Entrees $18 to $20.

Coffee Corner, 283 Broadway (☎ 401/849-2902). Open daily 7am to 2pm. Entrees $4 to $6.

Muriel's, at Touro and Spring sts. (☎ 401/849-7780). Open Monday through Saturday 8am to 3pm, Sunday 9am to 3pm. Entrees $6 to $10.

Poor Richard's, 254 Thames St. (☎ 401/846-8768). Open daily 7am to 4:30pm. Entrees $8 to $15.

Pronto, 464 Thames St. (☎ 401/847-5251). Open daily 5pm to 10pm. Entrees $11 to $24.

Scales and Shells, 527 Thames St. (☎ 401/846-3474; 401/848-9378 for Upscales, the upstairs dining room). Open Sunday through Thursday 5pm to 9pm, Friday through Saturday 5pm to 10pm. Entrees $12 to $20.

ESTATE VISITS

Newport Preservation Society, 424 Bellevue Ave. (☎ 401/847-1000), manages eight estates. Tour prices depend on how many estates you visit; for example, visitors can see all eight for $35.50 for adults, or any two for $13. Prices for individual tours of the estates range from $6.50 to $10. Call for current tour schedule.

The Breakers, Ochre Point Ave., at Ruggles Ave. (☎ 401/847-6544).

Chinese Teahouse, Bellevue Ave. (☎ 401/849-2287).

Elms, Bellevue Ave. (☎ 401/847-0478).

Hammersmith Farm, Ocean Dr. (☎ 401/846-7346).

Land's End, Ledge Rd. Private.

Newport Squash Club, 8 Freebody St. (☎ 401/846-1011).

Rosecliff, Bellevue Ave. (☎ 401/847-5793).

Rough Point, Bellevue Ave. Not yet open to the public.

SHOPPING

Country Kettle Fudge, 359 Thames St. (☎ 401/849-2228). Open daily 11am to 6pm.

Nutcracker Suite Christmas Shop, 22 Mill St. (☎ 401/846-7385). Open Monday through Saturday 10am to 5pm, Sunday 11am to 5pm.

EVENTS

Annual Classic Yacht Regatta, Labor Day weekend. Race on Saturday from 10am to 4:30pm at the Museum of Yachting, Fort Adams State Park, on Ocean Dr. (☎ 401/847-1018). In addition to the sailing races, there is a parade on Sunday at 2pm, exhibitions, and a slide show. Admission $3, $6 for families, $2.50 for seniors.

Annual Newport International Boat Show (☎ 800/582-7846). Held over three days in September from 10am to 6pm, along the water from the Newport Yachting Center on America's Cup Avenue to the Newport Harbor Hotel and Marina. Admission $12 on weekdays, $15 on weekends.

Bicycling from Boston to the Bronx

by Bruce Weber

I SING THE BODY EXHAUSTED.
Dehydrated and jelly-legged, sunburned and sweat-grimy, I'd been bicycling the road from Boston since dawn and had spent a big part of the warm afternoon on unexpectedly vertical terrain in northeastern Connecticut. New York City, my final destination, seemed as distant as China. And for an hour, ever since Union, Connecticut (the gateway to Nipmuck State Forest, an extremely popular place among black flies), I'd been saying two words in my head, over and over, repeating them like a mantra: Stafford Springs, Stafford Springs, Stafford Springs.

In college, there'd been a guy who lived on my hall whose hometown was Stafford Springs, Connecticut. I didn't know him at all, don't know what happened to him, but 20 years later, huffing and puffing through the pretty hills of nowhere, I conjured him up, remembered him as an affluent sort. And putting that memory together with the bold print with which the town was emblazoned on my wrinkled Connecticut road map, I concluded: There will be a motel in Stafford Springs. There will be an excellent restaurant there.

The sad punch line, of course, is that Stafford Springs is not a particularly affluent place; it's pleasant enough, but actually a little run-down. And more to the point, the closest motel is almost 20 miles away, in Enfield, at the exit off Interstate 91. Now, if you are in a car and tired of driving, 20 more miles to go is an irritation. On a bike, it is evil itself, the essence of unfairness.

So. As if on cue, a beautiful afternoon had suddenly grayed over. It was nearly five, maybe 2½ hours before dark. I drank two bottles of grape Gatorade (a relatively new flavor, really good, I think) and, having no choice (I wasn't carrying a sleeping bag), pedaled on.

People tend to ask why I like to ride a bicycle over stretches more frequently traversed by planes, trains, and automobiles. I usually say I like the idea of the bicycle as an implement of travel rather than of simple recreation.

The old saw about traveling by bicycle is that it's seeing the world at congenial speed; at 10 miles an hour, exposed to the elements, you're connected with the road and the scenery in a way you can never be in an automobile. All that's true. On a bicycle you can count roadside mailboxes and judge the quality of the hand-painted ducks and hunting dogs on them. Animals—skittering chipmunks, barking dogs, grazing horses, the occasional fox or deer peering curiously from the woods at roadside—become compatriots. I talk to them: "Hi, pal"; "Shut up, you ugly mutt!" Once, on a whim, I delivered Marc Antony's funeral oration at a herd of stupefied cows. (You feel worse about roadkills, flattened raccoons and opossums, than you do in a car.)

But beyond that, leaving the house on a bicycle, I've always liked the idea of ending up somewhere else, traveling toward a place rather than circling back to where I began. And I've never been much of an advance route planner, preferring the love-hate relationship one develops along the way, in myriad foldings and unfoldings, with that cold bearer of both good news and bad, the road map.

There's something random and idiosyncratic about a trip like this, a series of solitary experiences tied together with a ribbon of road; even if they're mundane, they're singular and personal. And it's titillating; it feels a little unsafe. You can have an adventure and then, when it's over, you can actually measure your achievement in miles.

And part of the point of a long bike trip is to wear yourself out. It's the thing you banish from your mind as you begin but take the hugest pride in at the end of the day. The muscles that ache in weird places (your hands hurt from gripping the handlebars and absorbing the rattle of the road); the creakiness in your knees and ankles from hours of rotating in their joints; the odd strain in your backside; the thirst

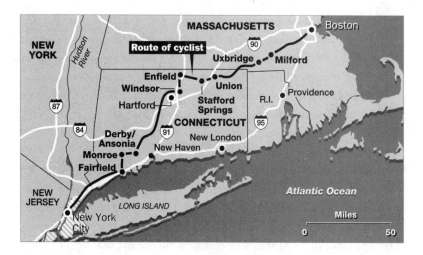

that goes on all day and lasts for hours into the night, and the sense of utter depletion you can feel, it seems, in your cells: This sounds torturous, I know, but I experience it as reward.

A day on a bike has purchasing power. You buy yourself a ravenous appetite and the freedom to indulge it. You buy a well-deserved, untroubled, and renewing sleep. And because getting to a distant place on your own power is both a physically difficult task and a conceptually simple one, you buy yourself an unambiguous test. You reach your destination or you don't. Hard work toward a definite goal; it's easy to concentrate. How many things are like this in life?

Awkward Start? Good

I'd taken my bike up on the train from Manhattan the previous day and started back from downtown Boston at chill dawn. Trying to slip through the door of the Omni Parker House Hotel, I accidentally caught one saddlebag on the jamb, and the bike nearly clattered to the sidewalk. It was an awkward start, but I wouldn't say inauspicious. The start of a journey should be awkward, because the pleasure—and the achievement—lies in finding a rhythm.

I rode through the Commons, then over Storrow Drive to the esplanade along the Charles. At Massachusetts Avenue, I crossed the river to the north bank and followed it west. There were runners out, student types, and a couple of crews were already on the water. Wearing tights and a windbreaker, I was cold anyway, and uncomfortable on the bike seat. I felt like an unwelcome stranger, like a Yankee in Fenway Park. I had a discomforting moment of doubt: It's a long way home.

I turned south in the woodsy suburb of Weston. It was about seven by then, and the sun had begun to burn away the early mist, dappling the road. Traffic was heading against me; it was Friday, a workday in the city.

South of Natick, where I stopped for breakfast with Glenn and Nina, some conveniently situated old friends, I found Route 16, an amiable state road with modest grades and modest traffic. It points southwest, almost right at New York City, and that was helpful. Though traveling by bike is by design a scenic meander, you need a straight shot now and then for the sake of psychic momentum. I put a couple of towns behind me, Sherborn and Holliston, and began to see the map of Massachusetts in my head from the vantage of someone who'd covered some distance on it. In Milford, Massachusetts, I passed a bike shop and stopped to pick up some spare inner tubes, which I'd foolishly left without. And there, from a salesman, I got the first warning of the hills to come.

"Any way of getting around them?" I asked.

"Nope," he said, with an unkind trace of relish, I thought.

It was midmorning and I stripped to shorts and short sleeves. I rode through Hopedale, Menden, Uxbridge, quaintly stolid and unremarkable towns of the sort that pepper the nation, though in a dirt parking lot in Uxbridge, behind a convenience store, there was a slightly bizarre sight: a two-seater airplane, upside down, lying on its roof with its landing gear sticking up like the legs of a dead insect.

Just north of the tristate junction of Massachusetts, Connecticut, and Rhode Island, the road bent west and grew rural. The land began to roll a bit; houses grew farther apart. Roadside delivery boxes declared that neighbors were getting different newspapers: *The Worcester Telegram and Gazette* and *The Norwich Bulletin*. Between Douglas and Webster, there's a body of water fantastically called—no kidding, look on the map—Lake Chaubunagungamaug. And to an outsider who just happened to be passing through, a smug New Yorker used to living at the center of the universe, it felt like a place between places, wonderfully nowhere.

Route 16 gave way to Route 197, which dipped into Connecticut, and at a crossroads I decided, for reasons as impetuous as thought through, to go west now and south later. The idea was to go around Hartford to the north, and the next day head down toward New York through Litchfield County; I'd been there and vaguely remembered it as lovely. Of course, it didn't quite happen this way, mainly because Route 197 turned out to be what the bike store salesman was talking about. An undistinguished squiggle on the map and in fact a beautiful rural byway traversing deep woods, the road has a number of hateful qualities, particularly if you're on a bicycle, pretty tired, nearly 40 years old, and not in the shape you once were. Who knew Connecticut had a mountain range in it?

In the couple of hours that I spent trudging (as in walking and shooing away clouds of bugs) up the hills of 197 and gliding down, two things happened. It occurred to me that Litchfield County has similar terrain, so I began revamping my plan. And I started to think: Stafford Springs. Stafford Springs.

Rules of the Road

Two good rules for the bike traveler. Get your miles in early, before the sun gets high and before a lot of cars hit the road. And whenever possible ride near water: River roads and beach roads are not only scenic; they're also flat.

At dawn on Saturday, I left Enfield and plunged south, along the Connecticut River. I was feeling good. There were miles behind me; I'd got through a tough day. It was a dewy and damp morning, but sunny, and the rhythm of the ride was warming. The state road, 159, passed through Windsor Locks, then over the interstate highway, snuggling against the river and through the town of Windsor, its wide quiet streets and large well-scrubbed houses yielding a picture of sturdy New England. It was a pretty stretch, 10 miles or so, a ride you'd take for pleasure if you lived near there and the kind of place you'd take bike trips to discover.

I turned west, away from the river, alas, to circumvent Hartford. I ate breakfast at a homey-looking cafe in Bloomfield—unfortunately, the waffles were disappointing—and turned south again, passing through West Hartford, an affluent suburb. Meaning to angle to the southwest, I missed a turn—the road was straight and easy and I had that feeling you get that traveling south you're somehow going downhill—and by the time I discovered my mistake I was in the blue-collar neighborhoods of New Britain, a city with a despondent, recession-weary feel. But I was enjoying myself, pumping hard, and the road kept dropping to the south and I followed it. By late morning, I was in Meriden, and at a McDonald's I grabbed rest and sustenance: a chocolate milkshake for energy, a Coke for thirst, and then, because I got goose-pimply as my sweat dried, a cup of coffee.

As it turned out, the afternoon was, once again, tougher. Eventually I would make it to Fairfield, on Route 1, along the Sound, but the day before had, in fact, taken a toll. From Meriden, zigzagging my way to the southwest on a number of pesky hills, grueling not so much in grade but in number, I needed frequent stops, at one point lying in the sun by a roadside picnic table and actually dozing until a dog licked my nose and woke me up.

The guy who owned the dog wanted to trade bicycling stories; half my age, he pulled up his pant legs and showed me his calves, which reminded me of cannonballs, and he said he'd ridden to Toronto and back that morning, or something like that.

"Yo!" he said. "Where'd you come from? Boston? What time'd you leave?" It was maybe three in the afternoon; this was near Ansonia, Connecticut, maybe 75 miles from New York.

"You'll make it," he said, meaning that night.

I thanked him for the chat as I mounted and rode slowly off.

"Yo!" he said. "No problem."

From there it was slow and steady to Derby, where I made another wrong turn; instead of turning south along the Housatonic River, I turned north. I hadn't gone far before I realized my mistake, but I kept going anyway. Weary as I was, it was a great stretch of road. There was a slightly encouraging breeze, the pavement was brand-new, the vista along the river—hills rose steeply from the opposite bank—was inspiring, and I was zipping along comfortably at speeds I hadn't hit all day. There were college crews racing on the river, and keeping up with them, coming toward me on the road, were several long-haired teenage boys on Rollerblades.

"Go Yale!" they were shouting.

I paid for this interlude, of course. The road followed the river for five or seven miles, then crossed it, over a dam, and began to climb on the opposite side; at a crossroads, I consulted the map and learned, heartbreakingly, that I wanted Route 111, which pivoted directly into the slope.

It turned out to be the heftiest climb of the whole journey, an unrelenting mile. I didn't need this, nor did I need the friendly guy who lived halfway up and who was mowing his lawn as I passed.

"Hey!" he said, with a proud smile. "Killer hill, huh?"

Pain and Persistence

In Fairfield Sunday morning, I woke ready for the final sprint along Long Island Sound to the city, but getting out of the motel bed and planting my feet on the floor, I felt a razorish pain near the heel of my left foot. I couldn't rotate the ankle at all, and could barely hobble into the bathroom. Was my Achilles tendon torn? I had no recollection of a trauma; I hadn't twisted my ankle or inadvertently kicked anything. What can you do to yourself in your sleep? The sun was just up. I was 55 miles from home. Gingerly, I arranged myself on the bike.

Route 1, of course, gets a fair amount of traffic, but not at 6am on a Sunday. I covered some ground, but within an hour, the whole ankle was swollen; it had stopped feeling like a torn tendon and started feeling like a sprain. I made it about halfway to the city, to Cos Cob, Connecticut, and, sitting on the side of the road on a patch of grass in front of a tennis court, I thought about calling an ambulance.

I didn't. Playing with pain, as it were, I continued riding and made it to the New York line, then negotiated the suburban trail on Route 1 through Mamaroneck and Rye, the meaner streets of New Rochelle, and finally the rugged Eastchester section of the Bronx. At high noon, as I checked a map on Boston Road, a cop stopped and directed me to the Gun Hill Road subway. I took the subway to Manhattan; so shoot me. I got home in time to see the Knicks whip Charlotte, my swollen ankle propped on a coffee table.

Two days later, I walked, easily enough, to the doctor. The ankle was still swollen but it didn't hurt. The explanation was simple: I'd overextended myself.

"You ever do 50 push-ups after not doing any for six months?" the doctor said. "It doesn't hurt right away, but when you wake up in the morning. . . ." He said it was likely that I hurt one ankle and not the other because I probably held my feet in slightly different positions on my bike pedals.

I know how this all sounds. You are thinking: Jerk! No wonder you got hurt. What kind of a stupid thing are you doing bicycling back to Manhattan from Boston in a weekend? And the best way I know to answer this is to go back to my moment of dejection in Stafford Springs.

The woman who gave me the sad news about the closest motel also said I would have to climb an enormous hill to get out of town. And she was right. I had to walk up most of it, mounting the bike again only as I neared the crest, but soon the road mercifully leveled for good.

It was just then that the sun came out again, directly in front of me because I was traveling west, and the sensation of moving toward the light was palpable and energizing.

I reached Enfield sooner than I'd expected. I napped (read: collapsed) in the motel, then went across the road to a Chinese restaurant in the strip mall there. Drinking beer and eating spareribs, I was so tired that I realized when I'd finished that for 20 minutes or so I'd been reading and rereading the paper place mat. According to the chart there, I was born in the year of the snake. The incredibly mundane conclusion of my weary mind was this: If I hadn't made it past Stafford Springs, I'd never know that.

Afterward, lying in bed, some other things I realized that day occurred to me. For one, things that seem torturous and tormenting don't stay that way; anguish isn't permanent. For another, I was going to make it home. Drifting off to sleep I thought, "Now I'm getting somewhere."

LEARNING TO SNOWBOARD AT VERMONT'S STRATTON MOUNTAIN

by Neil Strauss

THE FIRST TECHNICAL TERM ADDED to a beginner's vocabulary when learning to snowboard is "face plant." These words describe what happens when the downhill edge of a moving snowboard touches the mountain, sending the rider flying with a violent jerk face first into the snow. From the chairlift at Stratton Mountain in Vermont, snowboarders and skiers have a bird's-eye view of faces being planted all over the slopes. For beginners, face plants are a common occurrence; for the intermediate snowboarder, face plants are a constant fear, and for anyone who has spent a long day on the mountain, face plants are what happen over dinner in a hot bowl of soup.

On a wintry Friday, some friends and I drove to Stratton with the purpose of learning how to snowboard. Although this is not the closest mountain to Manhattan (it's a more than four-hour drive), Stratton, which calls itself the birthplace of snowboarding, has distinct advantages over closer mountains. Hunter, just 2¹/₂ hours from New York City, tends to get overcrowded, with toddlers on leashes and large groups of teenagers and families knocking one another over. Mount Snow, just south of Stratton in Vermont, offers more of a singles scene. As saturated with trails as it is with expensive ski wear, the medium-size mountain is a better place to ride once you have passed the face-plant phase of snowboarding. And though Killington, also in Vermont, is the biggest resort in the area, with the self-given nickname the Beast of the East, most of the trails are not snowboard-friendly.

Stratton is a well-groomed, picturesque mountain, almost entirely devoid of the ultrasteep, mogul-filled, or bone-breaking slopes that attract hotshots. Even a tyro can ride to the top of the mountain and find a variety of long, gentle, winding trails to take. The mountain's specialty is intermediate trails: nice declines, long and wide, that evenly fluctuate from steep to not so steep. It's perfect for the beginning snowboarder. There is also an area of the mountain set aside for snowboarders only, full of snow mounds that serve as jumps and a hollowed-out half-pipe dug lengthwise into the surface of the snow for those who are good enough for flips, spins, and other stunts.

Though skiers and snowboarders often complain of pricey lift tickets and equipment rentals, the real robbery takes place before the trip even starts. It happens when shopping for ski apparel. If you talk to the commission-oriented sales staff at most sports stores and gravitate toward the products labeled as specially made for snowboarders, it can easily cost $1,000 to buy the clothing you need to be warm, dry, and safe: a Burton Duo-Lite parka with advanced snow-sealing enclosures ($220); Smith Classic goggles with Fog-X ($60); direct-grip Gore-Tex gloves ($100); snow pants with removable kneepads ($180); a wool sweater ($100 to $200); long underwear with moisture-wicking fabric and other clothes for layering ($100 to $200); forward-lean socks and silk-blend sock liners ($25), and a Mossimo hat ($25). A waterproof outfit put together by scavenging department stores, vintage shops, and friends' closets can look just as good and function just as well on the slopes, minus only the brand names.

Though there are some quaint old inns and hotels 20 minutes from Stratton in the town of Manchester, we chose to stay closer to the slopes, at the mountain's own condos. For those who reserve early and are willing to pay a little extra, a condo can be rented so close to the mountain that you can literally ski to the chairlifts. Ours was a comfortable but generic-looking affair with two bedrooms, a nice-size kitchen, a living room, and a stone fireplace. Though $300 a night was steep, it included lift tickets for the four of us (normally $49 a weekend per person) and

free passes to the Stratton Sports Club, where those who haven't had enough exercise can swim and play tennis and those who are exhausted can relax in the sauna or get a massage.

Having become something of an expert in beginner hills, I can say that Stratton's was among the best. It was long and evenly sloped, which is an advantage over, say, Mount Snow's, which is so small that you hardly have time to learn anything on the way down. Stratton's is also shielded by trees from the rest of the trail, so that beginners aren't knocked over by experts.

Though snowboarding magazines offer hundreds of photographs of riders flying through the air as if jet-propelled, they never capture one of snowboarding's equally striking images: the tangle of bodies on the ground invariably found at the exit of the beginner hill chairlift. Exiting a chairlift on a snowboard can be harder than traversing a mountain because only one of your feet is strapped into the board when you're not heading downhill, making maneuvering on the tiny exit ramp a difficult balancing act.

The Ski and Snowboard School is at the base of the bunny hill, which is where my friends and I signed up for $25 group lessons after renting boots and an all-purpose snowboard called a freestyle board for $31 a person. Though snowboarding has been around since 1969, when a Utah surfer named Dimitrije Milovich tried to find a way to entertain himself in the winter, it began entering the popular consciousness in the mid-1980s. Now, at Stratton, almost every teenager and about one-third of everybody else had snowboards strapped to their feet.

More so than in skiing, owning your own equipment for snowboarding can make a big difference. At the rental counter, none of us were given boots snug enough to prevent our feet from lifting out of the heel of the boot (a no-no in snowboarding); the Burton-brand boards, though new, were already worn away on the base and edge, and the bindings could not be set for our particular riding stances, as we didn't know what they were yet.

As we split off into different lesson groups, some of us found the experience frustrating, others rewarding. It all depended on the size of the group and whether the instructor was someone who really wanted to teach or a vacationing college student just working at the mountain so he could spend the winter skiing and partying. In my 12-member group, with two instructors who were members of the party category, most of the time was spent sitting in the snow waiting for each member of the group to tumble, one by one, down 25-yard sections of the hill. I did, however, receive a few essential tips on how to scrape down the hill on the heel and toe edges of the board and how to execute a falling-leaf pattern (gliding down the hill alternating from the front to the back of the board without ever completing a more difficult full turn).

Most of the staff spoke the language of surfers—"dude," "rad," "wipe out"—so incessantly that the students began picking it up. Though some beginners take lessons all weekend, we decided not to sign up for the next course and learn from our mistakes instead.

As anyone who has switched from skiing to boarding will tell you, learning to snowboard is not all that difficult. It's easy to adjust to the fact that you can slide down the mountain facing any direction, and that your feet are strapped fast to the board and won't come out even after a severe fall. The challenge is in learning a new type of balance and coordination, different from skiing, surfing, and skateboarding, in which your legs and feet are in constant communication with the slope of the mountain.

After a few frustrating, bruising runs down the bunny trail, we decided to throw caution to the wind and take the poetically named

American Express lift midway up the mountain. It proved to be the brightest idea we had all day. From the beginning to the end of each run down the mountain, we all became better snowboarders. Just having more time to fall, to get frustrated, to navigate through forking trails made all the difference. And snowboarders sharing the chairlift with us were happy to offer advice, suggest trails, and even help us down the hill. We were always quick to apologize to our new friends for bowling them over when clumsily exiting the chairlift.

By the end of the day, we were taking the lifts to the top of the mountain and learning to turn from the heel edge of the board to the toe edge. As in skiing, you don't just point your feet down the mountain and go. You carve from side to side (or from the toe side of the board to the heel side) for control and speed-reducing friction.

For a nourishment break, it's best to avoid the main base lodge, home to an overpriced junk food cafeteria and a lost-and-found desk where people can be seen filling out stolen-property forms for snowboards that disappeared during their meal. (Tip: Invest $2 in the ski and snowboard checking hut.) Instead, snatch some free orange juice from one of the tents offering ski equipment demonstrations at the base of the hill and head to the resort's entrance, where there sits, well groomed as artificial snow, an artificial town square with ski wear shops, restaurants, and cafes. The best of these was Mulligans, a pub and restaurant no less overpriced, but with a light pecan-crusted salmon for those in need of a protein boost and smoky, sumptuous baby back ribs for meat eaters who don't mind a few stains on their expensive ski clothes.

In the late afternoon and evening, Manchester is the destination of choice. In its own promotional brochures, the town sometimes calls itself Historic Manchester Center. The first impression we had in driving through Historic Manchester Center was, "Wow, there are a lot of outlet stores!" Ralph Lauren, Calvin Klein, Giorgio Armani, Tommy Hilfiger, Movado, and dozens more promise bargains at their company outlets, though the prices don't seem to be any cheaper than at Bloomingdale's. Instead, we spent our time at the Museum of Fly-Fishing, which is not just an eye-opening initiation into a very active subculture but also a way to see the tackle of Presidents Jimmy Carter and Ronald Reagan.

For dinner, we made reservations at the Black Swan, a 20-year-old restaurant operated by the Whisenhunt husband-and-wife team: Richard, the chef, and Kathy, the hostess. The restaurant is in a 160-year-old farmhouse that has been divided into several tiny dining rooms. The main courses we sampled—the filet mignon with bearnaise sauce, the rack of lamb with garlic mashed potatoes—were delicious, and the array of choices on the dessert tray were as beautiful to look at as they were to eat.

We ended the night early at the Equinox Hotel, a tastefully garish Colonial-era hotel with a sprawling lobby that took an hour to explore and a cozy tavern where a band, though ailing from the flu, was playing high-spirited folk and pop standards. The hotel also had a school of falconry and, for those intrigued by their visit to the Museum of Fly-Fishing, a pond for practicing the sport.

On Sunday morning, muscles we didn't even know we had used ached—from the ankle to the neck—and bruises had begun to emerge on our shins and backsides. Some of us refueled with eggs and pancakes, others with Advil.

We began the morning as voyeurs, gliding down to the mountain's snowboard park. The area is basically an intermediate slope with four snowy ramps for snowboarders to jump from and, at the bottom, an icy half-pipe with riders cruising up the rounded edges and launching themselves into the air. Punk songs by NOFX and Bad Religion blared from a nearby boom box, giving the area the feeling of a skateboard park. Watching the riders fly over the snow clutching the edges of their boards five or six times in a single run down the half-pipe answered the question that had long been burning in our minds: Just why is it that snowboards seem cooler than skis?

We spent the day all over the mountain, finding favorite trails (Upper Drifter, Old Smoothie, Suntanner) and taking chairlifts like Snow Bowl and North American, which started in the middle of the mountain and had shorter lines than the lifts at the bottom. The gondolas, the only lift that goes directly to the top of the mountain, were closed while workers chipped away at the ice on the support poles.

Though the trails are generally well marked, about 60% of the runs from the top of the mountain are marked with black diamonds, for experts only. Though not as difficult as the black diamonds on other mountains, we ran into a bit of a predicament when we followed some skiers through a clearing and found ourselves on a double black diamond trail called Upper Spruce. As I was doing my best to keep from losing control on the steep slope, I suddenly saw one of my friends whiz past at lightning speed. It would have been impressive if he wasn't heading down headfirst on his back. He slid a good 50 yards before he was able to stop himself, and in the process just may have invented a new sport. We also learned a thing or two about moguls on the run. Lesson No. 1 was not to lean back, or the moguls become something akin to the jumps in the snowboard park.

Perhaps the greatest feeling of the day was catching the last lift up the mountain at 4:30pm, and winding down the trails all alone, actually able to snowboard with some coordination and a minimum of face plants after two days. We decided to celebrate by eating at the one restaurant that every guidebook and ski instructor had recommended: the Birkenhaus, an Austrian-style inn and restaurant near the mountain.

Because it was Sunday night, and weekend warriors were already beginning their long drive home, it was almost empty. The best thing about the meal was the bread: we left our Wiener schnitzel, our salads, our potato pancakes, and our chicken half-eaten. Perhaps resorts do come to life only on holidays and Fridays and Saturdays. On Sundays, they probably give their chefs the night off.

STRATTON AND MANCHESTER ESSENTIALS

Stratton, on Stratton Mountain Rd. in Stratton Mountain, VT (☎ 802/297-2200), has 90 trails, 12 lifts, and a snowboard park open to skiers and snowboarders from November to April, daily 8:30am to 4pm. Daily lift tickets are $44 weekdays, $49 on weekends and holidays ($32 every day for seniors and children). Daily snowboard and boot rental is $31. Introductory lesson with equipment and lift ticket is $59 ($25 per person for a group lesson).

GETTING THERE

By Car From New York City, take I-95 North to I-91 North in New Haven, CT; stay on I-91 from New Haven to Vermont exit 2 at Brattleboro, VT. Follow the signs to Rte. 30. Drive approximately 40 miles north on Rte. 30 to the Village of Bondville, and turn left at the Stratton Access Road, located in the center of Bondville; it is 4 miles to the resort.

An Alternate Route: Take I-87 North to I-787 North at Albany, NY; from there, take I-787 to the exit for Rte. 7 East (the sign will say "To Bennington, VT"). Follow Rte. 7 East, which turns into Rte. 9 at the Vermont border, to Bennington. In Bennington, follow U.S. Rte. 7 North to exit 4 at Manchester, VT; turn right at the bottom of the exit ramp on Rte. 11 East/30 South. After approximately 5 miles, the routes will divide; stay right following Rte. 30 South approximately 7 miles into the Village of Bondville; continue following the directions above.

By Bus   Greyhound (☎ 800/231-2222) travels to Manchester, VT, three times daily from the Port Authority Bus Terminal in Manhattan; the trip takes approximately 5 hours. Fares are $100 round-trip for adults, $90.60 for seniors, $50 for children 2 to 11.

By Train   Amtrak (☎ 800/872-7245 for information and reservations) travels to Brattleboro, VT, daily from Penn Station in Manhattan, departing at 11:20am and arriving 4:45pm. From Brattleboro, Stratton can be reached by either car or bus. Depending on availability, one-way fares range $44 to $48 for adults (seniors are eligible for a 15% discount), $22 to $24 for children 2 to 15.

ACCOMMODATIONS

For mountainside accommodations on **Stratton Mountain,** call ☎ 800/787-2886.
The Equinox, Main St. (Historic Rte. 7A), Manchester Village, VT (☎ 800/362-4747).
Open year-round. 183 rooms and suites (some wheelchair accessible). $169 to $299 double.

DINING

The Birkenhaus, Middle Ridge Rd., Stratton Mountain, VT (☎ 802/297-2000). Open seasonally in summer and winter, daily 7:30 to 9am and 6 to 9pm. Dinner appetizers $6.50 to $10.50, entrees $16.50 to $23.50.
The Black Swan, Main St. (Historic Rte. 7A), Manchester Village, VT (☎ 802/362-3807). Open year-round, Thursday through Monday 5:30 to 9pm. Dinner appetizers $4 to $7, entrees $11.75 to $23.50.
Mulligans, in the Village Square, Stratton, VT (☎ 802/297-9293). Open year-round, except May. In winter, open weekdays 11am to 10pm, Friday 11am to midnight, Saturday 11am to 11pm. Dinner appetizers $3.75 to $7.95, entrees $10.95 to $19.95.

ATTRACTIONS BEYOND THE SLOPES

American Museum of Fly-Fishing, Main St. (Historic Rte. 7A) and Seminary Ave., Manchester Village, VT (☎ 802/362-3300).
November through March, open weekdays 10am to 4pm; April to October, open daily 10am to 4pm. Admission $3.

MORE SNOWBOARDING ESSENTIALS:
OTHER AREA RESORTS THAT WELCOME SNOWBOARDERS

It is now possible to snowboard, rent snowboard equipment, and take snowboarding lessons at most major American ski resorts. Aside from having to wear leashes connecting their boards to their boots, snowboarders are usually free to do anything that skiers do. Like Stratton, many resorts now have snowboard parks, which are runs for snowboarders only. These usually include snow structures designed for performing by snowboarders. Common structures include half-pipes (giant tubes cut in half), table tops (flat areas of snow), and rails (logs).

IN NEW YORK STATE

Hunter Mountain, Hunter, NY (☎ 518/263-4223; 800/775-4641 for mountainside accommodations). 53 trails and 13 lifts, plus one snowboard park with one half-pipe. Open from November to April, daily 9am to 4pm. Daily lift tickets are $34 weekdays and $42 weekends; $22 weekdays, $28 weekends for children and seniors. Daily snowboard and boot rental $28; $18 for children and seniors. Introductory lesson with equipment and lift ticket is $45; $25 per person for group lesson.

Whiteface Mountain Ski Area, Rte. 86, Wilmington, NY (☎ 800/462-6236; 800/447-5224 for mountainside accommodations). 66 trails; 10 lifts. Open November to April, daily 8:30am to 4pm. Daily lift tickets are $34 weekdays; $39 weekends; $15 weekdays and $20 weekends for children; and $20 weekdays and weekends for seniors. Daily snowboard and boot rental $30. Introductory lesson with equipment and lift ticket is $40. $20 per person for a group lesson. Snowboard park planned for this season.

IN VERMONT

Killington Resort, Killington Rd., Killington, VT (☎ 802/422-6200; 800/621-6867 for mountainside accommodations). 212 trails; 32 lifts. Open October to June, weekdays 9am to 4pm, weekends 8am to 4pm. Daily lift tickets are $48 weekdays and weekends; $29 for children and seniors. Daily snowboard and boot rental $32; $20 for juniors. Introductory lesson with equipment and lift ticket is $48. $25 per person for group lesson. Two snowboard parks; three half-pipes.

Mount Snow, Rte. 100, West Dover, VT (☎ 802/464-3333; 800/245-7669 for mountainside

accommodations). 130 trails, 24 lifts. Open November to May, weekdays 9am to 4pm, weekends 8am to 4pm. Daily lift tickets are $45 weekdays and $47 weekends; $26 weekdays and $28 weekends for children. Daily snowboard and boot rental $32. Introductory lesson with equipment and lift ticket is $50. $26 per person for a group lesson. Two alpine parks, open to both snowboarders and skiers.

Okemo Mountain Resort, 77 Okemo Ridge Rd., Ludlow, VT (☎ 802/228-4041; 800/786-5366 for mountainside accommodations). 88 trails; 13 lifts. Open November to April, weekdays 9am to 4pm, weekends 8am to 4pm. Daily lift tickets are $44 weekdays and $48 weekends; $28 weekdays and $30 weekends for children and seniors. Daily snowboard and boot rental $30. Introductory lesson with equipment and lift ticket is $50; $40 for children and seniors. $25 per person for group lesson. One snowboard park.

Stowe Mountain Resort, 5781 Mountain Rd., Stowe, VT (☎ 802/253-3500; 800/253-4754 for mountainside accommodations). 47 trails; 11 lifts. Open November to April, weekdays 8am to 4pm, weekends 7:30am to 4pm; skiing to 10pm Thursday through Saturday. Daily lift tickets $48 ($50 holidays); $28 for children and seniors ($30 holidays). Daily snowboard and boot rental $20; $13 for children. Introductory lesson with equipment and lift ticket is $70. $25 per person for group lesson. Four snowboard parks.

Sugarbush Resort, Sugarbush Access Rd., Warren, VT (☎ 802/583-2381; 800/537-8427 for mountainside accommodations). 112 trails; 18 lifts. Open November through May, weekdays 9am to 4pm, weekends 8:30am to 4pm. Daily lift tickets $47; $28 for children and seniors. Daily snowboard and boot rental $28. Introductory lesson with equipment and lift ticket is $44. $24 per person for group lesson. One snowboard park.

INDEX